WELL-BEING IN ORGANIZATIONS

A Reader for Students and Practitioners

Edited by

Cary L. Cooper
and
Ivan T. Robertson

*University of Manchester
Institute of Science & Technology, UK*

JOHN WILEY & SONS, LTD
Chichester · New York · Weinheim · Brisbane · Singapore · Toronto

Copyright © 2001 by John Wiley & Sons, Ltd,
Baffins Lane, Chichester,
West Sussex PO19 1UD, England

National   01243 779777
International (+44) 1243 779777
e-mail (for orders and customer service enquiries): cs-books@wiley.co.uk
Visit our Home Page on http://www.wiley.co.uk
or http://www.wiley.com

Other Wiley Editorial Offices

John Wiley & Sons, Inc., 605 Third Avenue,
New York, NY 10158-0012, USA

Wiley-VCH Verlag GmbH, Pappelallee 3,
D-69469 Weinheim, Germany

John Wiley & Sons Australia Ltd, 33 Park Road, Milton,
Queensland 4064, Australia

John Wiley & Sons (Asia) Pte Ltd, 2 Clementi Loop #02-01,
Jin Xing Distripark, Singapore 129809

John Wiley & Sons (Canada) Ltd, 22 Worcester Road,
Rexdale, Ontario M9W 1L1, Canada

Library of Congress Cataloguing-in-Publication Data

Well-being in organizations : a reader for students and practitioners / edited by Cary L.
Cooper and Ivan T. Robertson.
    p. cm. — (Key issues in industrial & organizational psychology)
    Includes bibliographical references and index.
    ISBN 0-471-49558-1
    1. Job stress. 2. Work environment. 3. Work—Psychological aspects. I. Cooper, Cary
L. II. Robertson, Ivan, 1946- III. Series.

    HF5548.85 .W395 2001
    658.3' 14—dc21
                                                            2001017583

British Library Cataloguing in Publication Data
A catalogue record for this book is available from the British Library

ISBN 0-471-49558-1

Typeset in 10/12pt Plantin by Dorwyn Ltd, Rowlands Castle, Hants
Printed and bound in Great Britain by Antony Rowe Ltd, Chippenham, Wilts
This book is printed on acid-free paper responsibly manufactured from sustainable forestry,
in which at least two trees are planted for each one used for paper production.

WELL-BEING
IN ORGANIZATIONS

CONTENTS

ABOUT THE SERIES

Each book in this exciting series draws together the most authoritative and important recent developments on a topic of central importance to industrial and organizational psychology. Selected from volumes of the International Review of Industrial and Organizational Psychology, these collections provide students and practitioners with the ideal tool for:

- Essays, dissertations and new projects
- Quickly updating an area of knowledge for the busy professional
- Source material for lecture courses and seminars
- Beginning research students
- Keeping the consultancy library relevant

Key Issues in Industrial and Organizational Psychology
Edited by Cary L. Cooper and Ivan T. Robertson

Current books published in this series are—

Organizational Psychology and Development
A Reader for Students and Practitioners
Edited by Cary L. Cooper and Ivan Robertson

Personnel Psychology and Human Resource Management
A Reader for Students and Practitioners
Edited by Ivan Robertson and Cary L. Cooper

Well-Being in Organizations
A Reader for Students and Practitioners
Edited by Cary L. Cooper and Ivan Robertson

ABOUT THE EDITORS

Cary L. Cooper
Ivan T. Robertson

Manchester School of Management, University of Manchester Institute of Science and Technology, PO Box 88, Manchester M60 1QD, UK.

Cary L. Cooper received his BS and MBA degrees from the University of California, Los Angeles, his PhD from the University of Leeds, UK, and holds honorary doctorates from Heriot-Watt University and Wolverhampton University. He is currently BUPA Professor of Organizational Psychology and Deputy Vice Chancellor of UMIST. Professor Cooper was Founding and current President of the *British Academy of Management* and is a Fellow of the British Psychological Society, Royal Society of Arts, Royal Society of Medicine and Royal Society of Health. He is also Founding Editor of the *Journal of Organizational Behavior* and co-editor of *Stress Medicine*, serves on the editorial board of a number of other scholarly journals, and is the author of over 90 books and 400 journal articles.

Ivan Robertson is Professor of Work and Organizational Psychology in the Manchester School of Management, UMIST, and Pro-Vice-Chancellor of UMIST. He is a Fellow of the British Academy of Management, and the British Psychological Society, and is a Chartered Psychologist. Professor Robertson's career includes several years experience working as an applied psychologist on a wide range of projects for a variety of different organizations. With Professor Cooper he founded Robertson Cooper Ltd (www.robertsoncooper.com), a business psychology firm which offers consultancy advice and products to clients. Professor Robertson's research and teaching interests focus on individual differences and organizational factors related to human performance. His other publications include 25 books and over 150 scientific articles and conference papers.

CONTRIBUTORS

Ronald Burke   *Schulich School of Business, Faculty of Administrative Studies, York University, 4700 Keele Street, North York, Ontario M3J 1P3, Canada*

Cary L. Cooper   *Manchester School of Management, UMIST, PO Box 88, Manchester M60 1QD, UK*

Dov Eden   *Faculty of Management, The Leon Recanati Graduate School of Business Administration, Tel-Aviv University, Ramat Aviv, 69 978 Tel-Aviv, Israel*

Michael M. Harris   *School of Business Administration, University of Missouri, St Louis, MO 63121–4499, USA*

Gary R. Henderson   *Graduate School of Management, University of California, Irvine, California 92717, USA*

Helge Hoel   *Manchester School of Management, UMIST, PO Box 88, Manchester M60 1QD, UK*

Nerina L. Jimmieson   *Department of Psychology, University of Queensland, Brisbane, Qld 4072, Australia*

Janice Langan-Fox   *School of Behavioural Science, The University of Melbourne, Parkville, Victoria 3052, Australia*

Elchanen I. Meir   *Department of Psychology, Tel-Aviv University, Ramat Aviv, 69 978 Tel-Aviv, Israel*

Debra L. Nelson   *Department of Management, College of Business Administration, Oklahoma State University, Stillwater, Oklahoma 74078, USA*

Michael P. O'Driscoll   *Department of Psychology, The University of Waikato, Private Bag 3105, Hamilton, New Zealand*

Jone L. Pearce — *Graduate School of Management, University of California, Irvine, California 92717, USA*

Charlotte Rayner — *Strategy of HRM Division, Staffordshire University Business School, Leek Road, Stoke on Trent ST4 2DF, UK*

Anne Spurgeon — *Institute of Occupational Health, University of Birmingham, Edgbaston, Birmingham B15 2TT, UK*

Deborah J. Terry — *Department of Psychology, University of Queensland, Brisbane, Qld 4072, Australia*

Michael L. Trusty — *Anheuser-Busch Companies, 1 Busch Place, St Louis, MO 63118, USA*

Aharon Tziner — *School of Business Administration, Bar-Ilan University, Box 45, Ramat Gan 52900, Israel*

INTRODUCTION

The last twenty years has seen enormous changes in the workplace in the developed and developing world. Jobs are no longer for life, hours of work are longer, major restructuring in organizations are a regular occurrence, new technology is hastening the pace of change and demanding an immediacy of response (e.g. emails, WAP phones, etc) and the two-earner family is now the average family, creating problems of balance between work and home. These changes have created key issues for organizations about developing and maintaining well-being in the workplace.

This volume will explore the research in a range of topics to do with employee and organizational well-being. This is provided by some of the leading scholars internationally in their field, from the US, England, Australia, Canada, Israel and New Zealand. It is broken down into three sections: health-related issues in organizations, gender in organizations and individual/organizational adjustment. In the first section, we explore some critical issues of concern to both academics and industry, not only in terms of their health implications but also their impact on productivity and performance. The issues examine the following topics: employee control and health, workplace bullying, working time and health/performance, the interface between job and off-job roles, and acts of betrayal and their implications on organizations.

The second section highlights two themes under the general rubric of 'gender in organizations', that is, the health and stress implications of women's careers and the changing nature of men's role at work. As more and more women work, and pursue careers not just jobs, the nature and balance of gender relations becomes a critical industrial and organizational psychological issue.

Section three examines how individuals and organizations adjust to the increasing pressures of work. The literature is reviewed in the areas of work adjustment, respite and other breaks from the stress of work and the programs in the workplace to help employees cope with drugs and alcohol. What employees and employers can do to help create a better climate at work is essential not only for the well-being of employees but also for the productivity and bottom line performance of the organization.

Each of these topics is thoroughly reviewed, drawing on material from the leading review volumes of the International Review of Industrial and Organizational Psychology. We hope that this compendium of quality reviews will help to improve research and practice in I/O psychology. In the end, we must attempt to move organizations in the direction of understanding the simple truth of John Ruskin's comments about work in 1851: 'In order that people may be happy in their work, these three things are needed: they must be fit for it; they must not do too much of it; and they must have a sense of success in it.'

Part I

HEALTH-RELATED ISSUES IN ORGANIZATIONS

Chapter 1

WORK CONTROL AND EMPLOYEE WELL-BEING: A DECADE REVIEW

Deborah J. Terry
The University of Queensland

and

Nerina L. Jimmieson
The Queensland University of Technology

It is widely recognized that control is a construct that has central importance to our understanding of psychological functioning and adjustment (Skinner, 1996). Indeed, White (1959) saw humans as being intrinsically motivated to control their environment. Moreover, several decades of research—employing both correlational and experimental methodologies—have revealed that a sense of control relates positively to a range of different indicators of well-being (see Miller, 1979; Skinner, 1996; Thompson, 1981). One of the difficulties with the construct of control is that it can be conceptualized at different levels of abstraction (i.e., both personal and societal; C.S. Smith, Tisak, Hahn & Schmieder, 1997) and, despite the fact that there is general agreement that psychologists are most concerned with psychological or personal control (Skinner, 1996; C.S. Smith et al., 1997), a myriad of different constructs has been used to refer to aspects of personal control (see Skinner, 1996). However, as Skinner noted, prototypical definitions of control focus on the link between agents and outcomes; in other words, on the extent to which people are able to influence the outcomes that they experience in their environment.

In common with many areas of psychology, the construct of control has played a central role in industrial and organizational psychology. As Ganster and Fusilier (1989) pointed out in their review of the literature on control in the workplace for the *International Review of Industrial and Organizational Psychology*, much theorizing in this context has been predicated on the basis that jobs that impose limitations on personal control are associated with unfavorable work outcomes. In their review, Ganster and Fusilier (1989; see

Work Control and Employee Well-being: A Decade Review by Deborah J. Terry and Nerina L. Jimmieson taken from IRIOP 1999 v14, Edited by Cary L. Cooper and Ivan T. Robertson: © 1999 John Wiley & Sons, Ltd

also Ganster, 1989) presented a comprehensive coverage of the theoretical perspectives in industrial and organizational psychology that have at least, in part, been based on the construct of work control. In addition to research that has focused directly on this construct, Ganster reviewed literature on employee participation in decision-making (e.g., Locke & Schweiger, 1979), job design (e.g., Hackman & Oldham, 1976), and machine-pacing (e.g., Johansson, Aronsson, & Lindstrom, 1978), which are all aspects of the work environment that are assumed to have their impact on work outcomes through their influence on the extent to which employees have control over their work environment. The review was extremely timely, to the extent that it located the construct of work control in the broader literature on industrial and organizational psychology, at the same time as providing a valuable review of the extant literature on the effects of direct measures of employee control.

The present review contrasts with the review conducted by Ganster and Fusilier (1989) in that it is focused entirely on research that, either subjectively or objectively, assessed the construct of work control. As noted above, at the time that Ganster and Fusilier conducted their review, it was timely to conduct a review that reflected the breadth of literature that could be identified as, at least indirectly, revolving around the control construct. A decade later, the challenge is different—the breadth of the domain has been identified, now it is necessary to examine, in depth, the extent of support for the assumption that jobs that impose limitations on personal control are associated with unfavorable work outcomes. To do this in an effective manner, it seemed appropriate to base the discussion on research that has employed direct measures of employee control. Although recent factor analytic work by B.K. Evans and Fischer (1992) suggests that such notions as employee participation and job autonomy are related to a higher-order work control dimension, the unique effects of job characteristics that should impact on outcomes through control (such as job autonomy) are often difficult to ascertain because several task dimensions are manipulated simultaneously (Ganster & Fusilier, 1989). Moreover, there have been several recent reviews of the published literature on the effects of participation (e.g., Cotton, 1995; Sagie, 1995; Wagner, 1994) and job autonomy (Wall & Martin, 1994).

The present review begins with a discussion of the conceptual model that has formed the basis for the majority of the research on the construct of work control—that is, Karasek's (1979; see also Karasek & Theorell, 1990; Theorell & Karasek, 1996) demands–control model. This is followed with: (1) a summary of the results of the early tests of the theory (reviewed in depth by Ganster & Fusilier, 1989; see also Ganster, 1988, 1989; Parkes, 1989); (2) a detailed review of the empirical research pertaining to the demands–control model published since 1989 (papers published in 1988 or 1989 that were not reviewed by Ganster & Fusilier, 1989, are also included in this review); (3) a discussion of the two main responses to the lack of convincing support for the demands–control model—these responses have focused, respectively, on methodological and theoretical issues; and (4) a summary of the other types of effects that direct measures of work control have been found to have on employee adjustment. The chapter concludes with a discussion of possible future directions for research on work control. The central tenet of this final discussion is that the concept of work control should remain an important focus for concern in research on employee well-being, but researchers need to focus more on the mechanisms that underpin the effects of work control, at the same time as addressing the methodological problems that have characterized previous research in the area.

CONCEPTUAL BACKGROUND

The job demands–job decision latitude model (Karasek, 1979; Karasek & Theorell, 1990; Theorell & Karasek, 1996)—also referred to as the job demands–job control or demands–control model (as it is in the present review)—has provided the underlying theoretical basis for the majority of studies examining the effects of work control. This model specifies two constructs that can vary independently in the work environment, namely, job demands and job decision latitude. Job demands refer to the psychological stressors existing in the work environment, whereas job decision latitude is defined as the extent to which employees have the potential to control their tasks and conduct throughout the working day. The central tenet of the demands–control model is that job decision latitude mitigates the negative effects of job demands on employee adjustment.

More specifically, Karasek (1979; Karasek & Theorell, 1990; Theorell & Karasek, 1996) refers to jobs characterized by a combination of high job demands and low job decision latitude as 'high strain jobs', whereas low job demands and high job decision latitude result in 'low strain jobs'. A key feature of Karasek's demands–control model is that it proposes that there is a synergistic relationship between job demands and job decision latitude (or control), such that the combined effects of high job demands and low job decision latitude engender a level of strain that exceeds the additive effect of either aspect of the work environment. Thus, the negative effects of high job demands should be most marked for employees whose jobs have little potential for control or, in Karasek's terms, job decision latitude. To the extent that a demanding job is likely to be stressful, the demands–control model is analogous to the stress-buffering hypothesis which proposes that a range of different resources protects individuals from the negative effects of life stressors (see S. Cohen & Edwards, 1989; S. Cohen & Wills, 1985, for reviews). The demands–control model is also in accord with Miller's (1979) minimax hypothesis, which proposes that a belief in situational control reduces negative responses to stressful situations because it provides the individual with the knowledge that they can minimize the maximum aversiveness of a stressful event—in other words, the potential for situational control can be used to avoid the experiences of unbearable adversity.

The demands–control model, however, goes beyond the general stress-buffering hypothesis in that it is proposed that a demanding job may actually engender high levels of employee adjustment when the job is also characterized by high levels of control. Karasek (1979) refers to this combination of work characteristics as an 'active job' which enables the employee to develop new behavior patterns both on and off the job. In other words, job demands, when accompanied by high levels of work control, act as a source of job challenge, rather than as a source of employee strain. 'Passive jobs' are those characterized by low levels of both job demands and job decision latitude—such positions are considered to result in a decline in overall work activities performance and, ultimately, may engender a sense of learned helplessness. Although Karasek envisaged some positive implications of an active job, it should be noted that neither passive or active jobs were seen as having marked effects on well-being.

In the context of understanding work stress, Karasek's job demands–control model is potentially important because it directs attention towards the organizational-level factors that may need to be addressed in order to help mitigate the effects of work stress. There are many individual-level interventions (e.g., employee assistance programs) available for employees who are exhibiting the negative consequences associated with work stress (see Bunce, 1997). Although often successful, individual-level interventions are limited to the extent that they implicitly, at least, attribute primary responsibility for the management of work stress to employees rather than focusing on organizational-level strategies to reduce job demands in the workplace. As noted by Ganster (1989), the identification of organizational-level variables that moderate the effects of stress could have useful practical implications. If such characteristics can be identified, more positive work environments could be created without necessarily reducing workplace demands and expectations (see also Ganster 1988, 1989; Karasek, 1979; Parkes, 1991; Payne, 1979).

EARLY TESTS OF THE DEMANDS–CONTROL MODEL

Utilizing a range of different occupations in the United States of America (USA) and Sweden, Karasek (1979) was the first to report empirical tests of the demands–control model. In the USA sample, job demands were operationalized with a seven-item measure of quantitative workload, whereas job decision latitude was assessed with eight items that targeted perceptions of both decision authority and skill discretion. In the Swedish data, job demands were measured with two items (i.e., the extent to which the job was both hectic and psychologically demanding), and job decision latitude was a combined measure of intellectual stimulation and expert ratings of skill level required to perform the job. Results revealed some preliminary evidence for the proposed interactive effect of job demands and job decision latitude on employee adjustment. The negative effects of job demands were reduced under conditions of high job decision latitude when predicting exhaustion, job dissatisfaction, and life dissatisfaction among male employees in the USA, and depression among the Swedish sample of male employees.

However, Ganster and Fusilier (1989) cautioned against reaching strong conclusions concerning the extent to which job demands and job decision latitude interact to predict levels of employee adjustment from Karasek's (1979) early research findings. Ganster and Fusilier highlighted several factors that complicate the interpretation of these findings. Specifically, they noted that standard procedures for detecting interaction effects among continuously measured independent variables (i.e., moderated multiple regression analyses in which a multiplicative term is used to test the significance of the proposed demand–control interaction, once the component main effects are controlled) were not utilized (as recommended by Aiken & West, 1991; J. Cohen & P. Cohen, 1983). Instead, Karasek tested the interactive hypothesis by examining mean differences, via analysis of variance (ANOVA) procedures, among the four job quadrants formed by identifying employees experiencing low and high levels of job demands and job decision latitude, respectively. In addition, Ganster and Fusilier questioned the adequacy of the job decision latitude construct as an index of work control by pointing out that the items used by Karasek (1979) to measure job decision latitude in the US sample (this measure has most often been used in subsequent tests of the demands–control model) reflected both decision authority (e.g., freedom over work methods) and skill discretion (e.g., required to learn new things). Moreover, close inspection of the skill discretion items revealed that Karasek confounded the measurement of work control with conceptually different constructs; that is, skill utilization and job complexity. Thus, Ganster and Fusilier concluded that, although the findings reported by Karasek may be interpreted as support for the stress-buffering role of job decision latitude, the same inferences cannot be made for work control.

Ganster and Fusilier (1989) went on to review another methodological approach adopted by Karasek and his colleagues (e.g., Alfredsson, Karasek & Theorell, 1982; Alfredsson, Spetz & Theorell, 1985; Karasek, Russell & Theorell, 1982; LaCroix & Haynes, 1987; Theorell, Alfredsson, Knox et al., 1984; Theorell, Hjemdahl, Ericsson et al., 1985). Utilizing data obtained from a series of national health surveys from the USA and Sweden, levels of job demands and job decision latitude were assigned in these studies on the basis of an individual's occupational classification (i.e., participants' job decision latitude scores were imputed or inferred from the average score on the relevant variable obtained from employee occupying the same job classification). In the early occupational-level studies, cardiovascular disease and associated risk factors served as the primary outcomes of interest. Ganster and Fusilier concluded that the studies employing aggregated measures of demands and control (i.e., the imputation method) provided modest support for the proposal that the combination of high job demands and low job decision latitude is associated with elevated risks of myocardial morbidity and mortality. However, Ganster and Fusilier (1989; see also Ganster, 1989) argued that research conducted at the occupational-level of analysis is difficult to interpret. They pointed out that occupational classifications based on a broad range of different occupational groups are likely to be confounded with a host of other variables (e.g., socio-economic status, variability in job characteristics within occupations, and individual health behaviors). In addition, it was noted that occupation-level studies of work control overlook the importance of individual perceptions of job demands and job decision latitude within homogeneous occupational groups.

In response to these methodological considerations, a second research approach emerged in which employees' perceptions of work stress and work control were obtained from homogeneous occupational groups. These studies also departed from Karasek's (1979) original methodology by discarding the job decision latitude construct in preference for more focused measures of work control. In this respect, researchers utilized measurement scales that placed a stronger emphasis on Karasek's dimension of decision authority (rather than skill discretion) by asking general questions relating to how much influence employees had over various aspects of their work tasks. In addition, hierarchical multiple regression analyses were used to test the significance of Work Stress × Work Control interactions. Despite these methodological improvements, the individual-level studies reviewed by Ganster and Fusilier (1989) did not find convincing support for the hypothesis that work stress and work control interact to predict employee adjustment. Such research was conducted across a variety of different occupational groups, such as secondary school teachers (e.g., Payne & Fletcher, 1983), clerical workers (Spector, 1987), and healthcare professionals (e.g., McLaney & Hurrell, 1988; Tetrick & LaRocco, 1987).

In summarizing the extant research findings, Ganster and Fusilier (1989) noted that the 'exploration of control as a potential "antidote" to stressful work demands is rich with possibility' (p. 272) and encouraged organizational scholars to continue this line of research. In particular, they highlighted a number of goals for future research, including the need for field experimentation, the importance of distinguishing between various facets of work control, the examination of the indirect effects of work control (i.e., do employees use control to alter their perception of work demands), and the use of objective indicators of the work environment as measures of demands and control.

RECENT TESTS OF THE DEMANDS–CONTROL MODEL

During the past decade, many tests of the demands–control model have continued the trend of discarding the job decision latitude construct in preference for more focused measures of work control, although a number of studies have continued to rely on Karasek's (1979) original methodology. As in the past, it has been common for research of this type to be based on data obtained from participants at one point in time using measures obtained from a single source (i.e., the participant). In other words, the cross-sectional, mono-method design is still frequently employed. The results of the recent cross-sectional tests of the demands–control model are reviewed first, followed by studies that have used more conservative designs—these include: (1) longitudinal studies; (2) studies that have obtained objective measures of demands and/or control; (3) studies that have focused on cardiovascular outcomes; and (4) experimental studies.

Cross-sectional Research

Across a wide variety of different occupational settings, recent cross-sectional, self-report tests of the demands–control model have failed to find convincing support for the hypothesis that work stress and work control interact to predict employee adjustment. Based on a sample of 274 prison officers, Morrison, Dunne, Fitzgerald, and Cloghan (1992) found only weak support for the demands–control model. on one of seven dependent variables (job satisfaction), there was evidence that the relationship between perceived job demands and job satisfaction was buffered if employees perceived low constraints in the work environment (a construct similar to work control adopted by Payne, 1979). In a cross-sectional study of a relatively small sample of manufacturing employees. Perrewe and Anthony (1990) found no evidence that perceptions of work control (assessed using a 16-item scale that formed the basis for a subsequent 22-item scale of this variable, see Dwyer & Ganster, 1991) interacted with a range of different measures of demands, including work overload, variance in workload, or underutilization of skills. Similarly, in a sample of female social workers, Melamed, Kushnir, and Meir (1991) found no evidence that the effects of a broadly-based measure of work demands were moderated by perceived work control (assessed using a 6-item measure designed as a direct operationalization of the control construct). Using Karasek's (1979) original measures of demands and control, Landsbergis (1988) also found no evidence—when the appropriate moderated regression analyses were conducted—for the demands–control model in a sample of health workers. Using a variety of self-report measures of demands and control, comparable results have been reported in samples of clerical workers (e.g., Carayon, 1993a; Sauter, 1989), driving instructors (e.g., Parkes, 1991, Study 1), and retail employees (e.g., Jimmieson & Terry, 1993). In the past decade, a number of other cross-sectional studies have been conducted on heterogeneous samples of workers (see below)—these studies have also failed to find consistent support for the demands–control model.

Longitudinal Research

Cross-sectional research that relies on self-report measures (i.e., where all the measures are obtained contemporaneously from the single source) is likely to inflate the observed correlations between predictors and outcomes because of common method variance, which is contributed to by response consistency effects that emanate from the influence of both stable dispositional factors (such as negative affectivity) and unstable occasion factors (such as mood; see Spector, 1992; Spector & Brannick, 1995; Zapf, Dormann, & Frese, 1996). Such confounding effects are likely to make the evidence of main effects of demands and control (see below) difficult to interpret; moreover, as noted by Wall, Jackson, Mullarkey, and Parker (1996), common method variance may obscure the presence of demand by control interactions—this is due to correlated errors that serve to reduce the magnitude of true interaction effects (see M.G. Evans, 1985).

Contrary to the possibility that cross-sectional studies may obscure demands–control effects, recent longitudinal studies have provided only minimal support for the interactive hypothesis of Karasek's (1979) demands–control model. In one of the first longitudinal studies in the area, Bromet, Dew, Parkinson, and Schulberg (1988) found support for the interactive hypothesis in the prediction of the occurrence of alcohol-related problems, but not for two affective measures of psychological well-being. Using measures of demands and discretion similar in focus to the measures developed by Karasek (1979), Bromet et al. found that self-reported alcohol problems were the highest under conditions of high work demands and low discretion. In contrast, Carayon (1993a) found no evidence of interactive effects involving quantitative workload and work control (essentially a measure of job decision latitude) on a variety of different employee adjustment measures (e.g., anxiety, depression, daily life stress, and physical health). However, Carayon's results should be interpreted with caution. Essentially, the research was cross-sectional in design, given that the focal analyses (i.e., those testing the interactive effects of demands and control) were conducted only on data obtained contemporaneously (either at Time 1 or Time 2).

Using measures derived from Karasek (1979), longitudinal studies conducted by Parkes and her colleagues have also found no support for the critical two-way interaction (Demands × Control) in the prediction of either anxiety and social dysfunction (e.g., Parkes, 1991, Study 2), or scores on a self-report measure of psychosomatic health complaints (Parkes, Mendham,

& Von Rabenau, 1994, Study 2). Daniels and Guppy (1994) reported similar results in a sample of accountants—there were no significant interactions involving measures of work stress and either job autonomy or participation in decision-making. The latter studies are important (Daniels & Guppy, 1994; Parkes, 1991; Parkes et al., 1994, Study 2), to the extent that each of the studies controlled for baseline levels of adjustment (as did Bromet et al., 1988). Because of their instability, the effects of occasion factors can be reduced by assessing the predictors and the outcomes at different points in time; however, to fully control for the potential biasing effects of both occasion factors and dispositional factors, the effects of prior adjustment should be controlled in the prediction of subsequent adjustment (Zapf et al., 1996).

Use of Objective Measures of Work Characteristics

Another way of controlling common method variance is to avoid same-source measurement; that is, to obtain measures of either the independent or dependent variables from an external source. Interestingly, perhaps the most convincing support for Karasek's demands–control model comes from research that has utilized objective indicators of the work environment (Dwyer & Ganster, 1991; Fox, Dwyer, & Ganster, 1993; Parkes, 1991, Study 1). This research has also made use of objective outcome measures, as has an extensive body of research that is characterized by its focus on cardiovascular outcomes—the latter research is discussed below.

In a study of a sample of 115 manufacturing employees, Dwyer and Ganster (1991) examined the extent to which objective work stress indicators and a measure of perceived work stress interacted with perceptions of work control to predict self-reported job and work satisfaction and a variety of employee withdrawal behaviors. On the basis of job analysis, Dwyer and Ganster coded each job for a variety of physical (e.g., exposure to chemical hazards) and psychological (e.g., production responsibility) job demands. Perceptions of work control were assessed with a generic 22-item scale that tapped a range of different job control dimensions, whereas the withdrawal data (voluntary absenteeism, tardiness, and days off due to illness) were compiled from computerized records.

Results revealed that the combination of high psychological demands (objectively assessed) and low employee perceptions of work control was associated with high incidences of tardiness and sick leave; thus, work control appeared to buffer the negative effects of high levels of demand on withdrawal behaviors. In addition, the subjective measure of work stress interacted with the work control measure to predict levels of voluntary absenteeism and task satisfaction. Closer inspection of the latter two interactions revealed that, as predicted by the demands–control model, perceived work demands were associated with poor adjustment under conditions of low subjective control.

Interestingly, under conditions of high subjective work control, subjective work stress was, in fact, negatively related to voluntary absenteeism and positively related to task satisfaction. This pattern of results provides support for the 'active job' component of Karasek's (1979) demands–control model, namely, that under conditions of high control, high levels of demand are associated positively with employee adjustment.

Parkes (1991, Study 1) also found some support for the demands–control model in relation to withdrawal behaviors. In a study of driving instructors, she analyzed the effects of self-reported demands and discretion (assessed using Karasek's, 1979, measures) on subsequent absenteeism. The absenteeism measure reflected the number of absences (mostly due to minor illness) of less than one week that occurred during the 2-year period following the assessment of demands and control—this information was obtained from personnel records. In support of the demands–control model, Parkes found a weak Demands × Discretion interaction on absenteeism ($p < 0.06$) that reflected the fact that participants low in demands and high in discretion had lower levels of subsequent absenteeism than the other participants.

Fox et al. (1993) also found some support for the demands–control model in a sample of 136 nursing staff from whom a number of objective indicators of work stress (e.g., number of patients under care, percentage of patient contact time, and number of patient deaths witnessed) and employee well-being and performance (e.g., systolic blood pressure, diastolic blood pressure, salivary cortisol levels, and ratings of job performance) were obtained, in addition to a subjective assessment of work control (using Dwyer & Ganster's, 1991, 22-item measure of this variable). Salivary cortisol levels (at home) were higher for those nurses who had higher patient contact times and low perceptions of work control. There was, however, more consistent support for Karasek's demands–control model when employee perceptions of work stress were taken into account. In this respect, subjective quantitative workload and subjective work control interacted to predict systolic blood pressure (at both work and home), diastolic blood pressure (at home), salivary cortisol levels (at work), and job satisfaction. A subjective measure of the frequency of stressful work events was also found to interact with subjective work control to predict levels of job satisfaction. In each case, the data suggested a buffering role for work control—work stress was related to poor adjustment for those who perceived low levels of work control, but not for those who considered that they had some control over their work environment.

Research on Cardiovascular Outcomes

In the past decade, a specific focus of research testing the demands–control model has continued to be its predictive utility in relation to physical health outcomes—in particular, indicators of cardiovascular disease. This body of research has been reviewed recently by Schnall, Landsbergis, and Baker (1994), Kristensen (1995), and Theorell and Karasek (1996); thus, it is not reviewed in depth here.

In the recent cardiovascular studies, there has been a continuing reliance on operationalizations of the construct of control as aggregated occupation scores (e.g., Alterman, Shekelle, Vernon, & Burau, 1994; Georges, Wear, & Mueller, 1992; Hammar, Alfredsson, & Theorell, 1994; Moller, Kristensen, & Hollnagel, 1991; Piper, LaCroix, & Karasek, 1989; Reed, LaCroix, Karasek, Miller, & MacLean, 1989; Theorell, deFaire, Johnson, Hall, Perski, & Stewart, 1991); however, the individual-level assessment of control based on Karasek's (1979) measure of this variable has also been common (e.g., Albright, Winkleby, Ragland, Fisher, & Syme, 1992; Georges, Wear, & Mueller, 1992; Green & Johnson, 1990; Light, Turner, & Hinderli, 1992; Schnall, Schwartz, Landsbergis, Warren, & Pickering, 1992; Van Egeren, 1992). A variety of cardiovascular criteria have been considered—these have included diagnosis of coronary heart disease, cardiovascular mortality, myocardial infarction, recurrence of myocardial infarction, and the incidence of risk factors for coronary heart disease (e.g., elevated blood pressure, elevated serum cholesterol, as well as smoking behavior and distribution of body fat).

Taken together, research using cardiovascular disease outcomes as criteria has found only very limited support for the demands–control model. Although the research has linked the two components of the model to a variety of CHD-relevant outcomes (for reviews, see Kristensen, 1995; Schnall, Landsbergis, & Baker, 1994; Theorell & Karasek, 1996; see also the discussion below on the main effects of work control), most of it has been limited by its failure to test for the critical demands–control interaction using moderated regression analyses (see Aiken & West, 1991; J. Cohen & P. Cohen, 1983). Typically, support for the demands–control model has been detected by comparing high strain participants (scoring below the median on discretion and above the mean on demands) with those falling in the other cells formed by dichotomizing scores on the two independent variables. Other methods have included the correlation of quotient scores (demands divided by latitude) with the cardiovascular criteria (e.g., Green & Johnson, 1990; Theorell, deFaire, Johnson et al., 1991; Theorell, Perski, Orth-Gomer, Hamsten, & deFaire 1991), and the comparison of cardiovascular cases with matched controls on demands and control (or derived quotient scores). However, as Schnall, Landsbergis, and Baker (1994) noted, these methods do not allow detection of true interactive effects between demands and control. If such effects have been directly tested, they have been generally found to be nonsignificant (Chapman, Mandryk, Frommer, Edye, & Ferguson, 1990; Reed et al., 1989; Schaubroeck & Merrit, 1997; cf. Johnson & Hall, 1988).

Experimental Research

There have only been a small number of experimental studies that have tested the interactive relationship between work stress and work control in the prediction of employee adjustment. In their review, Ganster and Fusilier (1989) outlined the findings of a laboratory-based study conducted by Perrewe and Ganster (1989), in which levels of work stress and work control were manipulated among a sample of undergraduate students performing a letter-sorting activity. This study provided no evidence to support the hypothesis that objective levels of work control would moderate the effects of objective work stress on levels of anxiety, satisfaction, and several physiological indicators of arousal. However, partial support for Karasek's (1979) demands–control model was found, in that perceptions of behavioral control over the experimental activity (as measured by a post-task manipulation check) weakened the relationship between subjective ratings of work stress and a self-report measure of anxiety.

Subsequent laboratory research has attempted to replicate the pattern of findings reported by Perrewe and Ganster (1989). Given that time pressure is commonly used as an indicator of demand in stress research (e.g., Bandura, Cioffi, C.B. Taylor, & Brouillard, 1988; see also French & Caplan, 1972, for a discussion of this issue), Jimmieson and Terry (in press) followed Perrewe and Ganster's lead and manipulated work stress by varying high and moderate levels of quantitative workload. They, however, attempted to strengthen the experimental design utilized by Perrewe and Ganster by increasing the dimensions of work control manipulated in the experiment.

Consistent with Perrewe and Ganster (1989), Jimmieson and Terry (1998) found no evidence to suggest that objective levels of work stress and work control interacted to predict task satisfaction, post-task mood (after control of initial mood), and subjective task performance. Similarly, at the subjective level of analysis, this study found no support for Karasek's (1979) demands–control model. Since Perrewe and Ganster's (1989) finding that subjective work control buffered the negative effects of subjective work stress on levels of self-reported anxiety was not replicated, Jimmieson and Terry conducted further analyses on the six subscales of the mood questionnaire. These analyses revealed a Subjective Work Stress × Subjective Work Control interaction on the measures of (low) confusion and (low) fatigue. As proposed in Karasek's demands–control model, the negative effects of subjective work stress were most evident for participants who perceived that they possessed low levels of work control over the experimental activity.

Jimmieson and Terry (1997) provided a further test of the demands–control model using a more complex experimental task. As noted by Ganster and Fusilier (1989), sorting letters under time pressure for a period of 20 minutes is unlikely to be of sufficient duration to elicit detrimental effects on levels of adjustment. Furthermore, the simplistic nature of a letter-sorting activity is likely to limit the usefulness of work control in this context. In this respect, Campbell and Gingrich (1986) argued that employee participation during the goal-setting process for complex tasks provides individuals with a better understanding of the task requirements, thus facilitating higher levels of task performance. In contrast, the basic cognitive processing required for the performance of simple tasks may mean that any efforts to increase cognitive processing through employee participation will be ineffective.

In accord with theoretical definitions of task complexity that highlight the need for individuals to make multiple decisions that must take into account poorly defined or possibly antagonistic contingencies (see Campbell, 1988, 1991; Frese, 1989; Kohn & Schooler, 1978, 1979; Wood, 1986), an in-basket activity should include sufficient task components for task-specific information to play an interactive role in determining levels of adjustment. However, Jimmieson and Terry (1997) found only minimal support for an interactive relationship between the objective manipulations of work stress and work control on a variety of measures of adjustment (similar to those used by Jimmieson and Terry, 1998, as well as qualitative and quantitative measures of performance). At the subjective level of analysis, however, there were significant Work Stress × Work Control interactions on the measures of positive mood, subjective task performance, and task satisfaction. The negative effects of subjective work stress were most evident for participants who perceived that they possessed low levels of behavioral control over the experimental activity.

Summary

Although large national health surveys have found some evidence linking demands and control to a range of different indicators of cardiovascular disease, several methodological limitations (including occupational confounds, and failure to employ the appropriate analytic techniques for detecting interactions) have restricted the interpretability of these findings. Other research testing the demands–control model has addressed many of these criticisms; however, it has generally been unsuccessful in establishing empirical support for the proposition that work control buffers the negative effects of work stress on employee adjustment. Failure to support the demands–control model has also been evident in recent research that has employed more sophisticated longitudinal research designs. Utilizing objective indicators of stress and/or strain, research conducted by Dwyer and his colleagues (Dwyer & Ganster, 1991; Fox et al., 1993; see also Parkes, 1991, Study 1) has, however, revealed some support for the model, as has recent experimental research (at least at the subjective level of analysis).

One conclusion that can be drawn from recent tests of the demands–control model is that, with the exception of the cardiovascular research, studies that have not relied entirely on self-report measures have found stronger support for the demands–control model than have other types of research (i.e., cross-sectional and longitudinal, self-report studies). It is possible that the support for the demands–control model found by Dwyer and her colleagues (Dwyer & Ganster, 1991; Fox et al., 1993; see also Parkes, 1991, Study 1) may be attributable to the fact that the interactive effects were not attenuated due to the presence of common method variance (see Evans, 1985). However, recent longitudinal studies have not found consistent support for the demands–control model; thus, it is difficult to sustain this argument, given that the effects of common method variance are also controlled in this type of design (as long as initial adjustment is controlled in the analyses predicting subsequent adjustment).

An alternative explanation for the supportive results obtained by Dwyer and her colleagues (Dwyer & Ganster, 1991; Fox et al., 1993, see also Parkes, 1991, Study 1) is that the demands–control effect is specific to particular outcomes, a possibility that is discussed in more depth below. Dwyer and Ganster (1991) and Parkes (1991, Study 1) focused on withdrawal behaviors, which are outcomes that have not received much attention on the literature, whereas Fox et al., focused on cortisol level, which is also a relatively unusual outcome variable. However, it should be noted that, in addition to cortisol level, Fox et al., used a number of measures of blood pressure as outcome variables. Such measures have commonly been employed in the cardiovascular research—the discrepancy between the results obtained by Fox et al., and the typical results emerging from the cardiovascular research (i.e., only weak support for the demands–control model) may be related to differences in the assessment of work control (cf. Schaubroeck & Merritt, 1997), an issue that is also discussed below.

The second conclusion that can be reached on the basis of the review of the previous decade of tests of the demands–control model is that, in the context of specific work-related tasks, the perception that high levels of task control are available does appear to mitigate the negative effects of high levels of demands—at least at the subjective level, and particularly in relation to more complex tasks (Jimmieson & Terry, 1997; cf. Jimmieson & Terry, 1998; Perrewe & Ganster, 1987). The results of recent experimental tests of the demands–control model need to be interpreted with caution, given that they were obtained in a laboratory setting using simulated work activities. Nevertheless, they suggest that future research on work control might benefit from a more focused approach. This point is discussed below as part of a broader discussion of the methodological issues that researchers have recently addressed in an effort to account for the lack of more convincing support for the demands–control model.

METHODOLOGICAL DEVELOPMENTS

In response to the lack of stronger support for the demands–control model, a number of researchers have focused on methodological problems that may account for the weak findings. The potential role of common method variance has been discussed in relation to the results of recent research employing longitudinal designs and designs that have incorporated objective measures. Other methodological issues that have been addressed include: (1) the nature of the sample; (2) the assessment of demands and control and, to a lesser extent; (3) the possibility that interactive effects between demands and control are specific to certain outcomes.

Nature of the Sample

The lack of stronger support for the demands–control model in research conducted at the individual level of analysis has been attributed to restricted variance in the work demands and work control variables (see Carayon, 1993a; Karasek, 1979; Payne, 1979; Payne & Fletcher, 1983). Specifically, single occupational groups may not have sufficient variation in job characteristics to detect interactive effects between the two variables. More recently, several large-scale studies have surveyed employees across multiple organizations using perceptual measures of demands and control.

Warr (1990) sampled 1686 managerial, supervisory, and manual workers in his test of Karasek's (1979) demands–control model, and found no significant interactions between perceptions of quantitative workload and job decision latitude in the prediction of anxiety, depression, and satisfaction. Similarly, Kushnir and Melamed (1991) found no evidence of an interactive relationship between work overload (frequency of overtime and perceptions of overload) and work control (assessed with a 6-item scale that focused on the perceived freedom to make work-related decisions) and a variety of different indicators of employee adjustment (e.g., anxiety, irritability, satisfaction, and psychosomatic health) in a sample of 798 managerial and non-managerial employees working in 21 different manufacturing plants. Although Landsbergis, Schnall, Deitz, Friedman, and Pickering (1992) found some support for the model in relation to job satisfaction, job demands and job decision latitude (assessed using Karasek's measures) failed to interact to predict levels of anxiety in 297 employees recruited from eight New York City worksites. More recently, Fletcher and Jones (1993) found no evidence that high levels of self-reported work demands and work control (assessed using Karasek's measures of these variables) interacted to predict job satisfaction, life satisfaction, anxiety, depression, or blood pressure in a sample of over 2000 men and women working in a variety of different occupations; neither did Stansfeld, North, White, and Marmot (1995) in a study of the effects of psychological work demands and perceptions of work control (assessed using measures similar to Karasek's original measures) on psychiatric ill-health and life dissatisfaction among some 10 000 English civil servants (see also Chapman et al., 1990; Kauppinen-Toropainen, Kandolin, & Mutanen, 1983; Marshall, Barnett, Baruch, & Pleck, 1991, for similar results). In a heterogeneous study of 1200 Chinese workers, Xie (1996) did, however, find that the effects of high levels of job demands on anxiety, depression, job satisfaction, and life satisfaction were most evident for those workers who perceived low levels of decision latitude (demands and decision latitude were assessed using Karasek's measures).

Taken together, the results of recent tests of the demands–control model in heterogeneous samples do not suggest that the lack of previous support for the model is a function of a restriction in the range of scores on the measures of demands and control in homogeneous samples. Instead, the results point to the possibility that the stronger support for the demands–control model that was obtained in the early occupation-level research (see Johnson & Hall, 1988) may be due to the confounding effects of sociodemographic and work variables that covary with occupational level (Fletcher, 1991; Ganster, 1989; Ganster & Fusilier, 1989; Payne & Fletcher, 1983).

In light of the fact that the extent of support for the demands–control model does not appear to be a function of the nature of the sample, it may be preferable for researchers to employ relatively homogeneous samples in which pilot work suggests that there is a sufficient range in levels of both demands and control (see Ganster & Fusilier, 1989, for a demonstration that single and multiple occupation samples have similar coefficients of variation on the majority of measures of demands; see also Spector, 1987, for evidence of the full range of demand and control scores in a sample of clerical workers). As noted by Xie (1996), large multi-occupational studies have their drawbacks. Foremost, it is difficult to control for the range of sociodemographic variables that may distinguish employees of different occupations. Furthermore, a large-scale, multi-occupational study, by necessity, requires the use of measures of demands and control that are relevant across the range of occupations under consideration. By relying on such measures, researchers are not able to focus on the particular demands and facets of control that might be most relevant to a particular employee group, which may lessen the likelihood of detecting demand by control interactions. This point is relevant to the next section, which focuses on the possibility that measurement issues may explain the lack of stronger support for the demands–control model in previous research.

Assessment of Work Control

In their review, Ganster and Fusilier (1989) criticized the use of the job decision latitude construct as a measure of work control (see also Ganster,

1988, 1989; Kasl, 1989). The items used by Karasek (1979) to measure job decision latitude reflect both decision authority (i.e., freedom to make work-related decisions) and skill discretion (i.e., the breadth of skills used in the work context and the opportunity to learn new things). Closer inspection of the skill discretion items, in particular, reveals that Karasek confounded the measurement of work control with conceptually different constructs, including skill utilization, job complexity, and job variety (see also Carayon, 1993a; Kasl, 1989; Kushnir & Melamed, 1991). As noted by Wall et al. (1996), it is not necessarily the case that skill discretion reflects job control—a highly skilled job may, in fact, have little potential for control, a pattern of results that was evident in their distinction between the work characteristics of skilled and unskilled jobs (Wall, Jackson, & Mullarkey, 1995).

In support of the view that Karasek's (1979) measure of job decision latitude comprises two distinct components that may not be tapping the same underlying dimension, C.S. Smith et al. (1997) found that, across multiple, independent samples, the job decision latitude scale loaded on two separate factors reflecting, respectively, decision authority and skill discretion (see also Barnett & Brennan, 1995; Carayon, 1993a). In a subsequent set of analyses that considered Karasek's decision latitude items in addition to items developed by Ganster to assess perceived work control (see Dwyer & Ganster, 1991; C.S. Smith et al., 1997), Ganster's general control items (he also developed some items to assess predictability at work) and the decision authority items did not yield separate factors but the skill discretion items did. Moreover, the correlation between the general control items and the decision authority subscale was higher than the correlation between the two decision latitude subscales (decision authority and skill discretion). Thus, as noted previously, it is unclear whether any of the results reported in support of the demands–control model in studies that have utilized Karasek's measure of work control (i.e., job decision latitude) can be attributed specifically to the control construct, although the findings reported by C.S. Smith et al. do provide some evidence for the concurrent validity of the decision authority subscale as a measure of work control.

Further evidence attesting to the problematic nature of the job decision latitude construct comes from a recent study conducted by Wall et al. (1996; see also Wall, Jackson, & Mullarkey 1995). Wall et al. (1996) proposed that a specific control measure would moderate the relationship between work demands and employee adjustment, but that such an effect would not be evident in relation to the traditional measure of job decision latitude. The specific control measure was a 10-item measure that required employees to indicate the extent to which they could exert control over the timing and methods of their daily work tasks. Results revealed that this operationalization of the work control construct interacted with a measure of cognitive job demands to predict levels of anxiety, depression, and job satisfaction in a large sample of manufacturing employees, such that demands were associated negatively with well-being when control was low but not when it was high. Indeed, when control was perceived to be high, there was some evidence that demands related positively to well-being which is consistent with Karasek's (1979) view that, under the right work conditions, high levels of demands may be a source of challenge, and hence relate positively to employee adjustment. As expected, the job decision latitude measure failed to interact with demands in the prediction of any of the outcome measures.

On the basis of Wall et al.'s (1996) results, it is tempting to conclude that problems with the assessment of control can explain the lack of convincing findings for the demands–control model. However, it should be noted that other researchers have developed and used focused measures of work control. Kushnir and Melamed (1991) used a six-item measure of perceived freedom to make decisions over a range of different work domains, whereas Carayon (1993a) employed five items that assessed perceptions of control over a range of aspects of work. As noted previously, neither of these studies found any support for the demands–control model. Moreover, Kushnir and Melamed conducted their study on a large, heterogeneous sample of employees; thus, Wall et al.'s findings cannot easily be attributed to their use of a focused control measure combined with a heterogeneous sample.

It is possible that Wall et al.'s (1996) findings in support of the demands–control model relate not only to the use of a focused measure of control but also to the manner in which demands were assessed. Wall et al. noted that Karasek's (1979) items assessing work demands reflect affective responses in that the employee is required to indicate perceptions of work stress; for instance, by indicating the extent to which they have experienced 'excessive work'. They argued that the fact that both the independent (demands) and dependent variables (measure of adjustment) assess affective responses means that common method variance is likely to inflate the correlations between the variables (see also Brief, Burke, George, Robinson, & Webster, 1988; Parkes, 1990), and make it difficult to detect true interactive effects. However, as noted previously, this argument cannot easily be sustained because, although there is some support for the demands–control model in studies that have utilized objective measures of work demands (i.e., Dwyer & Ganster, 1991; Fox et al., 1993), longitudinal designs (that also control for common method variance) have not found convincing support for the model. Moreover, most of the support for the demands–control model reported by Fox et al. (1993) and Dwyer and Ganster (1991) was actually found in relation to their subjective, not objective, measures of demands.

Although Wall et al. (1996) found support for the demands–control model using a focused measure of work control and a descriptive measure of work demands, the results need to be replicated, given that the weight of the comparable research evidence is contrary to the model (e.g., Carayon, 1993a; Kushnir & Melamed, 1991). Indeed, as Wall et al. (1996) noted, there is a possibility that their support for the model could be in accord with a general pattern of results that is not supportive of the model, with the occasional report of a supportive finding. Nevertheless, Wall et al. raised some interesting and relevant methodological points that need to be addressed in future research. However, it may also be necessary to take into account recent theoretical developments in the conceptualization of the demands–control model (see below). Such developments are important, in that they may help to clarify the conditions that are most likely to yield evidence for the stress-buffering role of work control.

Specificity in Demands–Control Effects

Parkes (1991) suggested that the effects of high strain jobs (high demands, low control) may be specific to a particular type of affective response. In relation to this point, she pointed out that previous research has not been able to test adequately for specificity of demands–control effects because of the fact that measures of affective state (e.g. burnout, anxiety, depression, satisfaction) are typically moderately intercorrelated. To test for such effects, it is necessary to analyze residualized (rather than raw) outcome scores, in which the effects of the other affective outcomes are controlled (Parkes, 1991). Using such a technique, Broadbent (1985) and Hesketh and Shouksmith (1986) found significant (negative) main effects of work discretion on residualized anxiety but not residualized depression scores. In a similar vein, Parkes (1991) found that the effects of demands and control (moderated by locus of control) predicted residualized anxiety but not social dysfunction scores (also residualized). Future researchers need to follow Parkes's (1991) recommendations in order to determine if demands–control effects are specific to anxiety-related affective responses. In tests of the demands–control model, there is a tendency for researchers to use a number of correlated affective outcomes, which means that the specificity of possible demands–control effects can be examined only if residualized outcome scores are used in the analyses.

The above review of recent tests of the demands–control model suggests that the effects of a high strain (high demands/low control) position may be specific to nonaffective outcomes, in particular absenteeism (Dwyer & Ganster, 1991; Parkes, Study 1, 1991) and health-related outcomes (Fox et al., 1993). This suggestion clearly needs to be verified; nevertheless, it does point to the possibility that Karasek's (1979) focus on illness outcomes should be maintained in future research. Although previous cardiovascular research has failed to yield consistent support for the demands–control model, the methodological problems relating to sampling and to the assessment of the critical predictor variables mean that results of this research are very difficult to interpret.

Summary

In sum, researchers over the past decade have addressed a number of methodological problems that may account for the lack of stronger support for the demands–control model. Taken together, the research indicates little support for the view that evidence for the model would be stronger if heterogeneous samples were studied. There is, however, some support for the view that Karasek's (1979) original measures should be discarded in favor of more focused measures of work control (Wall et al., 1996). Nevertheless, the lack of consistent support for the demands–control model in studies that have employed focused measures of control points to the possibility that other factors need to be taken into account. The possibility that demands–control effects are outcome-specific is one potentially fruitful direction for future research. Other directions for future research relate to theoretical rather than methodological concerns with previous research. The theoretical issues that have been addressed in recent research are discussed below.

THEORETICAL DEVELOPMENTS

A number of researchers testing the utility of the demands–decision latitude model have focused their attention on theoretical issues that may account for the lack of stronger support for the model. In this respect, researchers have focused on: (1) the multidimensional nature of the work control construct; and (2) the possibility that there are additional organizational and dispositional characteristics that may interact with high job strain (i.e., high work stress and low work control) to predict employee adjustment.

A Multidimensional Approach to Work Control

As previously noted, recent tests of the demands–control model have increasingly employed more focused measures of work control in order to avoid a confounding of work control with other job characteristics (i.e., skill utilization and job complexity). It is important to note, however, that most researchers have typically relied on unidimensional work control measures. In his comprehensive review of the work control literature, Ganster (1988; see also Steptoe, 1989) similarly noted that researchers have tended to view work control as a unidimensional construct, and have, as a consequence, relied on global measures of work control. Work control is, however, a multidimensional construct, to the extent that employees can perceive a sense of personal control over multiple facets of their occupational environment, and that the perception of high levels of control over one facet does not necessarily mean that control will be perceived in relation to other facets.

In an early discussion of the notion of control in the work context, Gardell (1977) made a distinction between instrumental and conceptual forms of personal control. According to Gardell, instrumental control reflects employees' control over their job tasks, whereas conceptual control reflects employees' opportunities to engage in conceptual thought processes that contribute to organizational policies and procedures (see Carayon, 1993b, who found empirical support for this conceptual distinction). Ganster (1988, 1989) developed a more complex work control taxonomy that illustrates the potential multidimensional nature of the work control construct (see also Breaugh's, 1985, discussion of different aspects of work autonomy). Specifically, Ganster proposed that employees may have the opportunity to choose among a variety of different work tasks to complete (i.e., task control), and have the option to choose among available methods for the completion of those work tasks (i.e., method control). Employees may also be able to determine the pace at which they complete work tasks (i.e., pacing control), have varying levels of control over the scheduling of their working hours (i.e., scheduling control), and they may have different opportunities to be involved in wider organizational decision-making processes (i.e., decision control). In addition, Ganster made a distinction between control over the work activities of other employees (e.g., supervision), control over the timing and quantity of interpersonal interaction (e.g., customer contact), and control over the physical aspects of one's working environment (e.g., privacy, noise, lighting, and temperature).

Literature examining the job content implications of advanced manufacturing technology (AMT) has also acknowledged that the notion of personal control may be multidimensional in the work setting. In this respect, Wall, Corbett, Clegg, P.R. Jackson, and Martin (1990) made a distinction between two types of work control: timing and method control. Timing control refers to the ability of employees to determine the scheduling of their job-related activities—the potential for scheduling control contrasts with the situation in which the employee is required to respond to the pace of automated technology systems. Method control reflects the extent to which employees are free from technological prescriptions when deciding how to complete a given work task. Wall and his colleagues employed confirmatory factor analytic procedures to show that measures of method and task control can be empirically distinguished (e.g., P.R. Jackson, Wall, Martin, & Davids, 1993; Wall, Jackson, & Mullarkey 1995). Additional support for the distinction between the measures was provided by the fact that, although the measures had some correlates in common, they each had a number of unique correlates.

Tannenbaum and his colleagues (Tannenbaum, 1962, 1968; & Cooke, 1979; Tannenbaum, Kavcic, Rosner, Vianello, & Weiser, 1974) reported strong empirical evidence that perceptions of work control increase as a function of hierarchical level. Drawing on this early work, Staw noted that the salience of different types of work control may change across different hierarchical levels in the organization (see also Moch, Cammann, & Cooke, 1983). From a related viewpoint, Frese (1989) observed that the salience of work control domains may vary as a function of their proximity to an employee's daily work activities, which relates to the distinction that Hammer and Stern (1980) drew between work control that impinges on a person's own work roles and work control that is gained through more general participation in wider organizational decision-making processes (see also Gardell, 1977; Hammer & Stern, 1980).

It has also been suggested that the traditional job decision latitude construct can be decomposed into more specific work control dimensions. Indeed, Karasek (1979) encouraged future researchers to distinguish among several different aspects of his job decision latitude construct. Söderfeldt, Söderfeldt, Muntaner et al. (1996) argued that, in relation to health care workers, both decision authority and skill discretion should be considered in more depth in order to provide a more focused definition of work control. They contrasted at least four aspects of decision authority, such as closeness of supervision, decisional power within a situation (e.g., control over resources), non-decisional power over a situation (e.g., the setting of informal rules), and ideological control (e.g., control over the operative goals of the organization). Skill discretion concerns not only a choice of skills, but control over the fulfilment of work goals. Söderfeldt et al. also included the notion of administrative control in their taxonomy, and highlighted the need for future research to establish whether these forms of work control have differential effects in determining reactions to stressful working conditions.

Ganster (1988, 1989) argued that the failure of researchers to adopt a multidimensional view of work control might have accounted for the weak and inconsistent findings of the extant tests of Karasek's demands–control model. A multidimensional model of work control is likely to be important not only for statistical purposes (i.e., the presence of relatively independent subscales will impact adversely on the internal consistency of the composite scale and, hence, weaken its predictive utility), but also because global control measures may not reflect the extent to which the employee has control over the aspects of the work environment that are most relevant to the types of work stress being experienced (Ganster, 1989; Sargent & Terry, in press).

To date, only a small number of researchers have attempted to distinguish among different domains of work control when testing Karasek's (1979) demands–control model. In an early study, McLaney and Hurrell (1988) utilized four distinct measures of work control that assessed the extent to which a sample of nurses perceived that they could influence the variety of their work tasks (task control), contribute to organizational decision-making processes (decision control), alter the physical environment in which they worked (environmental control), and access the resources needed to complete their job duties (resource control, cf. Söderfeldt et al., 1996). Although these measures of work control were found to exert positive main effects on levels of job satisfaction (the effects of decision control were substantially weaker), none of the 32 Work Stress × Work Control interactions were significant.

Using the same work control typology, Hurrell and Lindström (1992) found that having control over work tasks was negatively related to the frequency of symptom reporting (e.g., headache, heart symptoms, sleep problems, and stomach trouble) among 231 early-career male managerial staff in Finland and 396 mid-career male managers in the USA. Perceptions of job control over work resources were also related to psychosomatic health complaints in the USA sample of mid-career managers. This study, however, did not report any tests of the demands–control model (Karasek, 1979), but it did provide further empirical support for a multidimensional concept-ualization of the notion of work control.

Jimmieson and Terry (1993) examined the extent to which specific domains of work control differentially interacted with levels of task stress (work overload and skill underutilization) and role stress (role conflict and role ambiguity) to predict employee adjustment in a sample of 116 retail employees. Jimmieson and Terry made a distinction between task control (i.e., the extent to which employees could influence the variety, scheduling, and pacing of their work tasks) and decision control (i.e., the extent to which employees had the opportunity to contribute to decision-making processes in the wider organizational environment). There was some evidence to suggest that employees who experienced a combination of high role ambiguity and low task control reported higher levels of depersonalization in their interactions with customers. There was, however, no support for the demands–control model (Karasek, 1979) when levels of decision control were taken into account.

In a recent study that distinguished among different facets of work control, Sargent and Terry (in press) proposed that task-relevant sources of control (such as work pacing, task organization, and scheduling control) would be more likely than peripheral sources of work control (such as mobility, resource allocation, and organizational decision control) to moderate the effects of work demands. This proposal was predicted on the basis of S. Cohen and Wills's (1985; see also S. Cohen & Edwards, 1989) stress-matching hypoth-esis. According to S. Cohen and Wills, there should be an adequate match between the demands of the situation and the type of buffer under consider-ation if stress-buffering effects are to be detected. Cohen and Wills's stress-matching hypothesis has received some support in relation to the effects of social support (Terry, Nielsen, & Perchard, 1993), although the hypothesis has yet to be systematically tested. The notion that task-relevant sources of work control are more likely to buffer the negative effects of work stress is also consistent with Jimmieson and Terry's (1993) findings and with Frese's

(1989; see also Hammer & Stern, 1980) action sequence proposal, which hypothesizes that the control domains most central to an employees' work activities are likely to have immediate and strong effects on employee adjustment, whereas those control dimensions that are less proximal to daily work activities are likely to have less impact on adjustment.

In a sample of administrative staff employed in a tertiary institution, Sargent and Terry (in press) found some support for the expectation that the stress-buffering effects of work control would be specific to task-related aspects of control. Three facets of work control (i.e., task, scheduling, and decision control) were considered, as were a number of sources of work stress (work overload, underutilization of skills, role conflict, and role ambiguity). As predicted, each of the significant buffering effects involved task control–task control buffered the negative relationship between role ambiguity and job satisfaction (in both cross-sectional and longitudinal analyses) and between work overload and (low) depressive symptomatology (again, in both cross-sectional and longitudinal analyses). Moreover, when a composite measure of work control was used (responses to each item summed, irrespective of focus of control) only very weak support for the demands–control model was obtained, even though the reliability of the combined scale was adequate. Task control is likely to be particularly relevant to a person with ambiguous role demands—such stress should be responsive to the extent to which an employee has the capacity to control how, and in what sequence, task requests are handled. The fact that task control buffered the negative relationship between work overload and low depressive symptoms at both Times 1 and 2 is also interpretable in light of the stress-matching hypothesis, given that a person who has too much to do is likely to be able to handle this stress if the job has some flexibility in terms of its allocation of time and energy to tasks.

Focusing specifically on the distinction between timing and method control, Mullarkey, Jackson, Wall, Wilson, and Grey-Taylor (1997; see also Wall et al., 1990) hypothesized that these two forms of work control would buffer the negative effects of two work stressors specific to AMT work environments (i.e., technological uncertainty and technological abstractness). Using the measures described by P.R. Jackson et al. (1993) and Wall, Jackson, and Mullarkey (1995), it was found that technological demands were related negatively to employee anxiety for those employees who characterized their job as high in timing control, whereas there was a positive relationship between demands and anxiety for those who perceived low levels of timing control—similar but weaker results were evident for technological abstractness. There was, however, no evidence to suggest that method control interacted with either of the indicators of work stress to predict employee adjustment.

Although the positive relationship that Mullarkey et al. (1997) observed between demands and strain under low timing control is consistent with the demands–control model, the strong negative relationship between demands and strain under high control is not entirely consistent with the model. In particular, the high strain observed for low demands, high control positions is inconsistent with Karasek's view of these positions as not having any adverse effects on well-being; however, Karasek did note that 'passive' positions (low demands, low control) may result in a decline in work performance and a sense of helplessness. Mullarkey et al. interpreted their findings in light of the machine-pacing literature that suggests that high timing control may lead to tedious periods of worker inactivity. The operation of slow moving machinery (i.e., high timing control) that makes few technological demands (i.e., low uncertainty and abstractness) is likely to result in a relatively low-challenge job, and a variety of associated negative reactions (e.g., frustration, boredom, and dissatisfaction). In relation to the lack of interactive effects involving method control, it was suggested that the items designed to tap this type of work control were relatively general in nature and, therefore, did not assess an appropriate moderator of the very specific technological demands assessed in the study.

At a broader level, Sutton and Kahn's (1986) stress antidote model distinguished among the extent to which employees can predict the occurrence, duration, and timing of work-related events (predictability) how much they understand how and why things occur in the organization (understanding), and the extent to which employees have the potential to influence events or processes at work (control). Sutton and Kahn proposed that each of these three variables would weaken the negative effects of work stress on employee adjustment. Ganster and Fusilier (1989) located one study that had attempted to test this model (e.g., Tetrick & LaRocco, 1987). Tetrick and LaRocco found that both understanding and control of work-related events moderated the negative effects of role stress on levels of job satisfaction in a sample of healthcare professionals.

Jimmieson and Terry (1993) have since provided a further test of the stress antidote model in a sample of retail employees. They developed scales to measure prediction, understanding, and control, but failed to find empirical support for the distinction among the three variables. Factor analytic procedures revealed that the measures of control (i.e., task control and decision control) could be empirically distinguished from the measures of prediction and understanding. However, the items developed to measure prediction and understanding could not be empirically distinguished. It was suggested that understanding organizational events may be reflected, in part, by the extent to which employees can predict the occurrence, duration, and timing of work-related events. There was support for the stress-buffering effects of the combined measure of prediction and understanding, in that the negative effects of role conflict on feelings of depersonalization and job satisfaction were more marked for employees who rated their job as being low in prediction and understanding. Although offering some support for the stress-antidote model, there is a need for the development of psychometrically sound measures of prediction and understanding. In this respect, the predictability subscale of Dwyer and Ganster's 22-item work control scale (see C.S. Smith et al., 1997) may provide a useful starting point for more systematic research in this area; however, the empirical distinctiveness of the predictability subscale is open to question (Dwyer & Ganster, 1991; Fox et al., 1993; cf. C.S. Smith et al., 1997).

In sum, recent research suggests that the lack of stronger evidence for the demands–control model may be due to a focus on global measures of control. By assessing a single construct of work control, researchers may have masked the fact that some types of control have the potential to buffer the negative effects of job demands, whereas others do not. Sargent and Terry's (in press) research supports the view that focused measures of work control are more likely to show buffering effects if they assess task control rather than more peripheral aspects of work control (also see Jimmieson & Terry, 1993). However, Mullarkey et al.'s (1997) finding that the highest levels of strain among manufacturing workers were experienced under conditions of high timing control and low demands points to the possibility that high levels of control are not always desired (see Bazerman, 1982), a point that is discussed in more detail below. Recent research on dimensions of control also points to the importance of incorporating a range of different control-related variables into stress-buffering models, rather than focusing specifically on the notion of control.

Conjunctive Moderator Effects

In light of the weak and inconsistent support for Karasek's (1979) demands–control model, other theoretical developments in relation to this model have focused on the possibility that there are additional organizational and dispositional characteristics that may moderate the effects of high strain (i.e., high work stress and low work control) on employee adjustment. As noted by R.E. Smith, Smoll, and Ptacek (1990; see also S. Cohen & Edwards, 1989; Parkes, Mendham, & von Rabenau, 1994), conjunctive moderator effects occur when the effect of a variable is observed only under a particular combination of scores on the two moderator variables. Thus, in the context of the demands–control model, a conjunctive moderator effect would be evident when job demands impacted adversely on adjustment only under conditions of low control and high or low levels of a third variable. In the context of the demands–control model, another way to conceptualize the role of third variables is as secondary conditioning or moderating variables—that is, as variables that further moderate the impact of the primary moderating influence (i.e., work control).

Social support

The variable that has received the most research attention as a possible secondary moderating variable in relation to the job demands–control model is the notion of social support. In 1979, Payne (see also Fletcher, 1991; Payne & Fletcher, 1983) proposed that job strain is a function of three major job characteristics; that is, demands (including the overload component of demands, in addition to other sources of work stress), constraints (e.g., work control and autonomy), and supports (e.g., natural, physical, intellectual, technical, and social resources). He suggested that by adding various supports to the organizational system, such as interpersonal support, less adaptive energy is needed to cope with high job demands under conditions of low control. More recently, Karasek and Theorell (1990) have reconceptualized the demands–control model to include work-related social support. The demands–control–support model predicts that job strain (i.e., high job demands and low job decision latitude) will be most marked when employees have low levels of social support at work. In other words, employee strain should be highest under high work stress combined with low levels of both work control and social support (see Johnson, 1986). This proposal is in line with the stress-buffering model of social support, which proposes that social support protects the individual against the adverse effects of stress (e.g., by helping the person redefine the problem, providing a solution to it; Finney, Mitchell, Cronkite, & Moos, 1984; see also Parkes, Mendham, & von Rabenau, 1994).

Although Payne and Fletcher (1983; see also Melamed, Kushnir, & Meir, 1991) found only weak support for their demands–supports–constraints model, a growing body of research has found stronger support for the joint moderating roles of work control and social support in the stress–strain relationship. In a secondary analysis of national survey data in Sweden, Johnson and Hall (1988) found that low levels of social support accentuated the negative impact of high job demands and low job decision latitude on cardiovascular health indicators; however, unexpectedly, the highest cardiac risk was evident when active work conditions (high demands and high control) were associated with low support (see also Kristensen, 1995; Theorell & Karasek, 1996, for reviews). Landsbergis et al. (1992) similarly found that a lack of social support lessened job satisfaction for those jobs characterized by high job demands and high job decision latitude (i.e., an active job), a pattern of results that they suggested was indicative of the beneficial impact of a cooperative rather than a competitive work environment.

There is also evidence for the demands–control–support model in the prediction of affective work outcomes. Karasek and Theorell (1990) presented some suggestive evidence in this respect. In a more detailed analysis of the joint effects of support, demands, and discretion (demands and discretion were assessed along the lines suggested by Karasek, 1979), Parkes et al. (1994) found that, in both cross-sectional and longitudinal studies, elevated psychosomatic health scores were associated with high strain jobs (i.e., high job demands and low job decision latitude) under conditions of low, but not high, levels of social support at work. In a more recent longitudinal study, Sargent and Terry (in press) similarly found that high levels of supervisor support mitigated the negative effects of high strain jobs on job satisfaction and depersonalization. High levels of non-work support and co-worker support also mitigated the negative effects of high strain jobs on supervisor ratings of work performance.

In sum, there is consistent evidence—across a small number of studies—that the negative effects of a high strain position (high demands and low control) are most marked when levels of social support are low. Future research needs to examine, in more depth, the secondary moderating roles of different types and sources of support. Such research should also examine the mechanisms that underpin the effects of social support—for instance, in relation to colleague support, group norms rather than interpersonal mechanisms may account for the differing effects of high and low work strain as a function of level of support.

Organizational level

In the search for conjunctive moderator variables, other researchers have sought to identify the presence of objective organizational characteristics that may influence the presence of demand by control interactions in the prediction of employee adjustment. In this respect, research attention has focused on a variety of occupational status variables. For instance, Hurrell and Lindström (1992) found that the main effects of job demands and job decision latitude on health status changed as a function of an employee's career stage. Fletcher and Jones (1993) found evidence to suggest that levels of job demands and job decision latitude were higher for white-collar employees than for workers involved in manual labour. Research of this nature points to the possibility that the moderating role of work control in the stress–strain relationship may not occur at all levels of the organization.

Preliminary evidence to suggest that the stress-buffering properties of work control on employee adjustment may vary as a function of hierarchical level was provided by Westman (1992), who found that work control buffered the negative effects of role conflict on psychological health for clerical employees, but not for the managerial employees of a large financial organization. In a consideration of possible explanations for the finding that work control is less important at higher levels of the organization, Westman suggested that organizations may provide employees at the managerial level with other resources such as power, prestige, and higher levels of income that may help to buffer the negative effects of work stress. Because low-status employees tend to lack access to these external coping resources, work control opportunities may be a particularly salient method for dealing with the demands of the job.

In contrast, Xie (1996) proposed that the demands–control model would be less useful in explaining employee adjustment among blue-collar workers than among white-collar employees (see also Fletcher & Jones, 1993). Based on an analysis of the social environment in contemporary China, Xie pointed to the possibility that blue-collar workers are not socialized to seek high levels of personal control at work. In this respect, there is often little opportunity for blue-collar workers to exert personal control over issues directly related to their jobs, whereas more substantive control over operational issues tends to be confined to the managerial employees of an organization (Von Glinow & Teagarden, 1988). Thus, Xie expected that the stress-buffering effects of work control on employee adjustment would be stronger in a sample of managers, professionals, and public servants ($n = 647$) than in a sample of blue-collar employees ($n = 440$) obtained from a variety of Chinese organizations.

In support of his proposal, Xie (1996) found that anxiety, depression, and psychosomatic health complaints were highest among white-collar employees under conditions of job strain (i.e., high job demands and low job decision latitude—assessed using Karasek's 1979, measures). In addition, highest rates of job and life satisfaction occurred for white-collar employees when their jobs were active (i.e., high job demands and high job decision latitude). For blue-collar workers, however, job decision latitude did not buffer the negative effects of job demands (or the two-way interaction was substantially weaker), and in the case of psychosomatic health problems, job decision latitude exacerbated rather than buffered the negative effects of high job demands. Although Chinese cultural norms that discourage complaints about personal sufferings may account for this stress-exacerbating role (see Xie, 1995). More generally, the stress-exacerbating role of job latitude points to the possibility that not all employees desire jobs that are characterized by high work control.

Taken together, the evidence suggesting that the stress-buffering role of work control may vary as a function of organizational level should be interpreted with caution, given that Westman (1992) and Xie (1996) obtained conflicting results; moreover, other researchers have found no evidence for the moderating role of organizational level in relation to the demands–control model (Fletcher & Jones, 1993; Warr, 1990—in both the latter studies, gender also failed to emerge as a secondary moderator variable). The lack of evidence for the secondary moderating role of organizational level is consistent with the general lack of support for the moderating effect of organizational level on the relationship between role stress and employee adjustment (e.g., Fisher & Gitelson, 1983; Pearce, 1981). Thus, it would appear that organizational level does not act as a reliable secondary moderator in relation to the demands–control model and, even if such effects are detected, they can only be explained in very speculative terms. As Xie (1996) noted, a number of factors are likely to distinguish blue- and white-collar workers, or non-managerial and managerial workers. In his work, Xie controlled for a number of the demographic variables that may vary as a function of organizational level. However, there are other contextual work factors that are also likely to be relevant in this regard. Given the equivocal results obtained in relation to organizational level and the difficulty of explaining such effects, researchers should focus on specific contextual work variables rather than pursuing research on the possible moderating effects of organizational level. Recently, research has considered the secondary moderating role that access to work-related information—a contextual work factor—may play. This research is discussed in the next section.

Informational control

Focusing on characteristics of the work environment other than organizational level (and related variables), Jimmieson and Terry (1997, 1998, in press) have, in a series of studies, examined the moderating role of informational control. Drawing on the broader psychological literature, a distinction can be made between behavioral and informational forms of personal control. The majority of early experimental studies conducted in the personal control litera-ture was concerned with manipulations of behavioral control over aversive stimuli. Averill (1973) defined behavioral control as the 'availability of a re-sponse which may directly influence or modify the objective characteristics of a threatening event' (pp. 286–287). Miller (1979) and Thompson (1981) provided similar definitions of behavioral control, in that they focused on the extent to which an individual perceives that he or she has the ability to modify an aversive event. Consistent with these definitions, experimental studies have manipulated behavioral control by providing individuals with the option to avoid exposure to a noxious stimulus, reduce some instances of a noxious stimulus, terminate a noxious stimulus prematurely, schedule rest periods from a series of noxious stimuli, limit the intensity of a noxious stimulus, or self-administer a noxious stimulus. Similarly, work control research has focused on the notion of behavioral control as the major construct of interest—typically work control is operationalized as the extent to which em-ployees perceive that they have the ability to directly manipulate various as-pects of the occupational environment.

A number of theorists have pointed out that there exists a type of personal control that does not rely for its beneficial effects on the ability of the individual to make an external response (Averill, 1973; R. Katz & Wykes, 1985; Thompson, 1981). As defined by Thompson (1981), cognitive control is the belief that one has a cognitive strategy available to influence the outcome of an aversive event. The types of cognitive strategies that can be used in an effort to satisfy an individual's need for personal control vary considerably (see Rothbaum, Weisz, & Snyder, 1982). Jimmieson and Terry (1997, 1998) focused on the role that informational control may play in the stress–strain relationship. Informational control, unlike other forms of cognitive control, can be objectively manipulated and, therefore, potentially provides organizations with a strategy for improving employee well-being. Thompson (1981) defined informational control as a communication—that is, information gain—that is delivered to an individual prior to an aversive situation. Similarly, Fiske and S.E. Taylor (1991) referred to informational control as a sense of personal control that is achieved when an individual obtains information about a noxious event. Informational control can be conceptualized as a form of cognitive control, because it typically decreases levels of appraised threat associated with an aversive event (Averill, 1973). Furthermore, informational control is a type of personal control that is not reliant for its beneficial effects on the ability of the individual to make an external response (R. Katz & Wykes, 1985).

For several decades, informational control has played an important role in a range of different theoretical models that has been developed to understand human behavior under conditions of stress (see R. Katz & Wykes, 1985, for a review). For instance, the safety signal hypothesis argues that information reduces the amount of time individuals spend in fearful anticipation of the stressful event (Seligman, 1968, 1975). Similarly, the information-seeking perspective argues that information lowers the conflict and, therefore, the arousal associated with unpredictability (Berlyne, 1960). Janis (1958) proposed that informational control stimulates the individual to mentally rehearse the impending stressful event, develop accurate expectations about the characteristics of the impending stressful event, and ultimately, cope better than those individuals who do not have high levels of informational control (see also Lykken, 1962; Perkins, 1968).

It is possible that the effects of behavioral control are contingent on the extent to which individuals perceive that they have access to high levels of informational control. In the goal-setting literature, Earley (1985) found that participants who were provided with choice when performing a class scheduling activity indicated higher levels of assigned and personal goal acceptance when choice was accompanied by high levels of information concerning the experimental activity. Participants also demonstrated better task performance when provided with high levels of both choice and information. These results were replicated in a subsequent field study in which levels of choice and information were manipulated in a sample of 40 animal caregivers whose major responsibility was the cleaning of animal cages.

Given that there is some empirical support for the view that the positive effects of behavioral control are more evident when accompanied by high levels of informational control (e.g., Earley, 1985), Jimmieson and Terry (1998) proposed that the stress-buffering effects of behavioral control may also be more marked at high, rather than low, levels of informational control. In relation to a letter-sorting activity, Jimmieson and Terry manipulated task information, in addition to the manipulations of work stress and behavioral control. A high level of task information was operationalized by providing participants with a communication concerning the step-by-step procedures involved in performing a letter-sorting activity, and temporal information concerning the arrival of additional letters (e.g., introduction by the experimenter on three occasions at regular 5-minute intervals). Contrary to predictions, there was no evidence to suggest that the stress-buffering effects of behavioral control were most marked for participants allocated to the high task information condition. These results may have been due to the relatively simplistic nature of a letter-sorting activity. It is likely that participants possessed the fundamental knowledge, skills, and abilities necessary to perform the letter-sorting activity, thus making the task-specific information provided to participants ineffectual (Daft & Macintosh, 1981; Wood, 1986; see also Chesney & Locke, 1991; Kernan, Bruning, & Miller-Guhde, 1994).

In response, Jimmieson and Terry (in press, Experiment 1) conducted further experimental research to examine the main and interactive effects of stress, behavioral control, and informational control in the context of a complex task—that is, an in-basket activity. High informational control was operationalized by providing participants with procedural information: (1) information concerning the features of a typical in-basket activity; (2) an example in-basket item and a possible response to the in-basket item; (3) information about how much time was available for the activity; and (4) the number of in-basket items to be addressed during the specified time period. There was a consistent pattern of results in support of the stress-buffering role of task information. Specifically, the negative effects of work stress on quantitative performance were stronger for participants who were not provided with procedural information than for participants allocated to the high procedural information condition. When levels of subjective task performance and task satisfaction were considered, procedural information buffered the negative effects of work stress on these outcome variables only under conditions of low behavioral control. In other words, the positive effects of task information (i.e., as a stress buffer) on levels of adjustment were more evident for participants allocated to the low behavioral control condition. Jimmieson and Terry (in press, Experiment 2) partially replicated this pattern of findings in a subsequent laboratory study that extended the experimental design by also manipulating low and high levels of task complexity. In this study, procedural information buffered the negative effects of work stress only under conditions of low behavioral control for participants performing the complex version of the in-basket activity.

In an attempt to interpret this pattern of findings, reference can be made to at least two sequential models of personal control. Based on the early work of Wortman and Brehm (1975), Greenberger and Strasser (1986) argued that employees, rather than entering a state of learned helplessness, respond to a reduction in work control by engaging in a variety of indirect strategies aimed at restoring a sense of personal control at work. In a comprehensive overview of potential response patterns to less than desired levels of control at work, Greenberger and Strasser (1986) suggested that employees may engage in a variety of information-seeking behaviors that serve to restore a sense of prediction and understanding concerning the work environment (see also Greenberger, Porter, Miceli, & Strasser, 1991). Thus, the provision of informational control may play an important role in determining adjustment among employees whose jobs do not provide opportunities for more direct forms of work control (see also Ganster, 1988, 1989. The salience of informational control under conditions of low behavioral control is a process similar to Bell and Staw's (1989) sequential work control model. They argued that outcome control over promotion, remuneration, and other benefits is the most desirable form of personal control in the work context, but when this control strategy is not possible, employees will direct their work control efforts towards job-related behaviors (e.g., determining work schedules). When neither of these work control strategies is possible, employees will strive to gain a sense of prediction and understanding concerning the work environment (see also Staw, 1977, 1986). Given that there are likely to be limited opportunities for behavioral control in many organizations (see Greenberger & Strasser, 1986), the search for other job characteristics that may compensate for low behavioral control, particularly those characterized by high job demands, is an interesting proposal that has received limited research attention in the area of occupational stress and health.

In addition to task-related information, D. Katz and Kahn (1978) highlighted the importance of more contextual forms of information concerning how one's role relates to other organizational functions, and contributes to the overall performance and long-term goals of the organization. Spreitzer's (1995a,b, 1996) definition of job-related information is also consistent with the notion of contextual information. Spreitzer focused on the extent to which employees perceive that they have an understanding of senior management's strategic outlook for the organization (i.e., the vision, mission, and subsequent objectives and goals for the organization). As noted by Sutton and Kahn (1986; see also Jimmieson & Terry, 1993), this type of job-related information provides employees with a sense of prediction and understanding concerning the wider organizational environment.

Jimmieson and Terry (1997) manipulated low and high levels of work stress, behavioral control, and contextual information in a study of 192 psychology students performing an in-basket activity. High levels of contextual information were manipulated by providing participants with information that typically accompanies an in-basket activity (e.g., company profile, mission statement, organizational structure, and quarterly newsletter). This information was intended to provide participants with an understanding of broader organizational issues, such as the importance of their job to the overall performance of the organization and its strategic goals. The manipulation of contextual information had only minimal effects on the outcome measures, a pattern of results that was consistent with Earley's (1986) finding that information about broad organizational outcomes was less important than task-specific information in providing employees with the resources needed for effective job performance. In non-experimental situations, however, contextual information may play a significant role in determining employees' affective responses to the work environment. For instance, D. Katz and Kahn (1978) hypothesized that contextual information is likely to be an important variable in the development of long-term indicators of employee adjustment, such as organizational commitment.

Taken together, the research conducted by Jimmieson and Terry (1997, 1998, in press) points towards a more complex pattern than the proposed conjunctive moderating role of informational control, in that the results suggest that informational control may compensate for the negative impact of low behavioral control. Clearly, the results need to be replicated in the field; nevertheless, they accord with sequential models of work control (Greenberger & Strasser, 1986; Bell & Staw, 1989) and, thus, suggest a possible direction for future research in the area.

Dispositional variables

In addition to examining the effects of secondary moderator variables that relate to the work environment, attention has been directed towards the role that dispositional variables may play in their respect. One obvious variable to take into account in relation to the demands–control model is locus of control, or people's generalized beliefs about the extent to which they have control over their lives. There is evidence that generalized control beliefs are a dispositional predictor of perceptions of work control (Spector, 1992; see also Parkes, 1989). Moreover, it can be argued, on the basis of person–environment theory (French, Caplan, & Van Harrison, 1982; see also Parkes, 1991), that the positive effects of high levels of work control should be most marked for employees with an internal locus of control, whereas externals should respond most favorably to low levels of environmental control. In other words, as Parkes (1991) noted, the effects of control in the work environment should be dependent on the extent to which the degree of available control is dispositionally congruent.

In a review of the early work linking work control and dispositional control beliefs, Jackson (1989) concluded that firm conclusions could not be drawn on the basis of the small number of extant studies. However, there was some support for the congruency hypothesis obtained in a field study conducted by Marino and White (1985): Higher levels of job specificity (assumed to reflect low job autonomy) were positively associated with lower job stress for internals, whereas the opposite was true for the externals. More recently, Parkes (1991) reasoned that, on the basis of the demands–control model, locus of control should emerge as a secondary moderating variable (i.e., that there should be evidence of a demand by control by locus of control interaction). Assuming a congruency model, the impact of high control should be positive for internals but negative for externals.

In a cross-sectional study of civil servants and a longitudinal study of student nurses, Parkes (1991) found that demands and discretion interacted—in the form predicted by Karasek (1979)—for externals but not internals. Inspection of the cell means formed by the crossing of the demands and control scores (assessed using scales derived from Karasek's, 1979, measures) revealed that, under conditions of low demands, externals responded more negatively to high discretion than internals. This pattern of results was consistent with the congruency prediction, but the fact that the impact of high demands and high control was similar for internals and externals was contrary to the congruency prediction, suggesting instead that when demands are high, situational factors override the impact of dispositional variables. Parkes's results provide some support for the view that the effects of different levels of environmental control are dependent on the match between the control and the person's control beliefs. The results, however, need to be replicated, given that Daniels and Guppy (1994), in a longitudinal study of 244 accountants, found that perceptions of high levels of job autonomy buffered the negative effects of stress only for internals (not externals, as found by Parkes, 1991).

In addition to dispositional control beliefs, the Type A behavior pattern (associated with a hard-driving, competitive, and time-pressured disposition; see Friedman & Rosenman, 1974) has been proposed as a possible secondary moderator variable in relation to the demands–control model. In line with the view that Type A individuals have a need to control their environment, Kushnir and Melamed (1991) proposed that Type As would be more distressed by conditions of low work control that Type Bs (individuals who do not display the Type A behavior pattern), and that they would find passive jobs (low demand and low control) particularly distressing. Data collected from a large heterogeneous sample of Israeli workers failed to reveal any perceived control (assessed using a focused 6-item measure) by Type A interactions; however, there were relatively weak workload by control by Type A interactions on job satisfaction and irritability. Inspection of these interactions revealed only weak support (on irritability) for the prediction that Type As would find low demand, low control positions more distressing than Type Bs.

A final dispositional variable that has been looked at in relation to the demands–control model is negative affectivity. According to the stress reactivity hypothesis, individuals with a tendency to experience negative distress will react more negatively to environmental stress than individuals low in negative affect. On the basis of this prediction, O'Brien, Terry, and Jimmieson

(1998) proposed that the effects of a high strain work environment (high strain, low control) would impact most negatively on individuals high in negative affectivity. Using the in-basket task developed by Jimmieson and Terry (1997, 1998; in press), O'Brien, Terry, and Jimmieson found, as expected, that demands and control (experimentally manipulated) inter-acted—in accord with Karasek's (1979) predictions—for participants high in negative affectivity but not for those low in negative affect. This result was evident on a post-experiment measure of task satisfaction, but not on measures of performance (both subjective and objective) or post-task mood (after the effects of pre-task mood were controlled).

In summary, only a few studies have examined the secondary moderating effects of dispositional variables in the context of the demands–control model. In relation to generalized control beliefs, Parkes (1991) found, in two different studies, some support for the view that externals prefer low control situations (but only when demands were low), whereas Daniels and Guppy (1994) found that high levels of autonomy helped buffer the negative effects of job demands only for internals. Taken together, these results provide some supp-ort for a congruency model of control; however, the inconsistent pattern of results indicates the need for future research of this type. In relation to Type A behavior and negative affectivity, recent studies have reported some results suggestive of secondary moderating effects; however, these results will need to be replicated before they can be interpreted with any confidence.

Summary

Increasingly, researchers have considered the role of conjunctive or secondary moderating variables in tests of the demands–control model. Such variables are intuitively appealing because their presence could easily explain the lack of stronger evidence for the model. In this respect, there is evidence—across a small number of studies—that the negative effects of a high strain position (high demands and low control) are most marked when levels of social sup-port are low. However, tests of the secondary moderating role of organiza-tional level have failed to yield convincing results—indeed, even if stress-buffering effects of work control were found to be dependent on organiza-tional level it would be very difficult to account, with any confidence, for such effects. In contrast, recent laboratory research has revealed that high levels of informational control may help to compensate for low levels of behavioral control. Such results need to be replicated in the field; however, they are important in that they suggest that the provision of information may serve to buffer high levels of demands in occupations that are inherently low in control. The secondary moderating roles of dispositional variables are unclear

—more research needs to consider whether the stress-buffering effects of work control depend on the match between the potential for situational control and the person's generalized control beliefs, and whether they depend on broader dispositional tendencies.

OTHER EFFECTS OF WORK CONTROL

Main Effects

Although previous research has provided only equivocal evidence for interactive effects of work control, this body of research has demonstrated consistent evidence of significant main effects of work control. Such effects are in line with the view that people have a fundamental motivation to achieve a sense of control over their environment (White, 1959; see also Frese, 1989; Ganster, 1989; Ganster & Fusilier, 1989), which may, at least in part, emanate from the negative consequences of low control for a person's self-image (e.g., reactance theory, Brehm, 1996, & learned helplessness theory, Seligman, 1975; see Thompson, 1981).

Using both Karasek's (1979) measure of decision latitude and more focused measures of work control, research conducted over the past decade has linked high levels of work control to low levels of anxiety (e.g., Carayon, 1993a; Kushnir & Melamed, 1991; Landsbergis et al., 1992; Mullarkey et al., 1997; Payne & Fletcher, 1983; Spector, 1987; Stansfeld et al., 1995; Wall et al., 1996), depression (e.g., Carayon, 1993a; Fletcher & F. Jones, 1993; Mullarkey et al., 1997; Stansfeld et al., 1995; Wall et al., 1996), psychological distress (e.g., Barnett & Brennan, 1995; Marshall et al., 1991), frustration (e.g., Spector, 1987), irritability (e.g., Kushnir & Melamed, 1991), burnout (e.g., Melamed et al., 1991), psychosomatic health complaints (e.g., Carayon, 1993a; Fox et al., 1993; Hurrell & Lindström, 1992; Kushnir & Melamed, 1991), and lifestyle factors, such as alcohol consumption (e.g., Bromet et al., 1988). Positive main effects of work control have also been reported on measures of task satisfaction (e.g., Dwyer & Ganster, 1991), job satisfaction (e.g., Fletcher & F. Jones, 1993; Fox et al., 1993; Greenberger et al., 1989; Kushnir & Melamed, 1991; McLaney & Hurrell, 1988; Melamed et al., 1991; Mullarkey et al., 1997; Parkes et al., 1994; Sargent & Terry, in press; Sauter, 1989; Tetrick & LaRocco, 1987; Wall et al., 1996; Warr, 1990), life satisfaction (e.g., Fletcher & F. Jones, 1993; Stansfeld et al., 1995), and job performance (e.g., Greenberger et al., 1989).

Because of the general reliance on cross-sectional designs, the main effects of work control are difficult to interpret. Although negative affectivity is most often considered to be a nuisance variable in relation to the effects of perceived stress, negative affectivity—as well as more transient mood effects—

could also inflate that strength of the relationship between perceptions of work control and well-being. Because of a tendency to focus on the negative aspects of themselves and their environment, individuals high in negative affectivity are likely not only to report high levels of subjective distress, but may also perceive low levels of work control.

In general, longitudinal studies have found weaker support for main effects of work control than cross-sectional studies. For example, in two longitudinal studies, Parkes (1991) and Parkes et al. (1994) (cf. Bromet et al., 1988) found non-significant main effects of discretion on subsequent adjustment (after control of initial adjustment), whereas the main effects of discretion were significant in the accompanying cross-sectional studies. Similarly, Sargent and Terry (in press) found a significant main effect of task control on a contemporaneous measure of affective well-being, but the comparable effect was non-significant in the analysis of the subsequent adjustment scores (after control of initial well-being). In studies that have employed objective outcome measures and focused measures of work control, the main effects of work control have also been nonsignificant (Dwyer & Ganster, 1991; Fox et al., 1993; Schaubroeck & Merritt, 1997; cf. Greenberger et al., 1989). Interestingly, both Dwyer and Ganster and Fox et al. found that the main effect of control was significant in the prediction of self-report measures of job satisfaction (assessed at the same time as control). Thus, there is evidence suggesting that the main effects of work control may be due to the confounding influence of common method endemic in mono-method, cross-sectional research.

Nevertheless, it should be noted that significant main effects of job decision latitude have consistently been reported on a range of cardiovascular outcomes (Chapman et al., 1990; Georges, Wear, & Mueller, 1992; Karasek & Theorell, 1990; Pieper, LaCroix, & Karasek, 1989). The discrepancy between the results of these latter studies and others that have focused on objective outcome measures (see above) may be due to the assessment of control—the supportive data have been obtained using Karasek's (1979) measure of job decision latitude, whereas the non-supportive data have been obtained using focused measures of control. Thus, the significant main effects of control on cardiovascular outcomes may be due not to the control component of measures of job decision latitude, but to the component that assesses skill discretion. Indeed, skill underutilization has emerged as a reliable predictor of poor employee adjustment in work stress research (e.g., Jimmieson & Terry, 1993; Sargent & Terry, in press).

In sum, although there have been a large number of reports of significant main effects of work control on a range of different outcome measures, much of the research has been cross-sectional in design. Thus, not only is the direction of causality difficult to determine, significant relationships between perceptions of control and contemporaneous self-report outcome measures may reflect the confounding influence of common method variance. The results of longitudinal studies suggest that this may be the case, as do a number of recent studies employing objective outcome measures. Future research needs to examine the extent to which the significant main effects of control on cardiovascular outcomes may reflect the impact of perceptions of skill utilization, rather than work control. More attention also needs to be paid to the possible indirect effects of work control, given that the lack of evidence of direct effects in longitudinal research may reflect the fact that work control impacts on subsequent adjustment through mediating mechanisms. Such mechanisms are discussed below.

Indirect Effects

In their review, Ganster and Fusilier (1989) noted that work control may not only exert direct or interactive effects on levels of employee adjustment. They suggested that one direction for future research was to explore the extent to which employees utilize work control to alter their job demands, thereby reducing levels of strain. Frese (1989) also suggested that work control may act as a stress-reduction mechanism that allows employees to adjust job demands and other job characteristics to their desired level. Similarly, Sutton and Kahn (1986) highlighted the possibility that perceptions of prediction, understanding, and control at work provide employees with the opportunity to reduce both the objective and subjective experience of job demands (see also Parkes, 1989).

To provide evidence of a mediating model, it is necessary to demonstrate that the observed effects of work control are no longer significant when the effects of work stress are statistically controlled (Baron & Kenny, 1986). In support of the indirect effects of work control, Jimmieson and Terry (1993) found that the positive effects of decision control (and two theoretically related control variables; that is, prediction and understanding) were mediated, through their relationships with perceptions of work stress, on subsequent psychological well-being, depersonalization, and job satisfaction (although initial levels of adjustment were not controlled).

Carayon (1993b) posited a different causal sequence to the extent that he hypothesized that work stressors would influence levels of employee adjustment through their effect on work control. Drawing on the job design model proposed by Rosenfield (1989)—which defines control as the central element through which other variables influence mental health—Carayon (1993b) argued that the negative effects of work stress (i.e., workload, speed of work, and cognitive load) on stress outcomes (i.e., psychological complaints and mood disturbances) would occur through their effects on two operationalizations of the work control construct; namely, instrumental control (i.e., control that impacts on daily work activities, such as work pacing) and conceptual control (i.e., control that provides opportunities to participate in wider organizational decision-making). Path analysis revealed partial support for the model in that job demands were related to instrumental control for a sample of office workers. However, job demands exerted a main effect on employee adjustment, irrespective of levels of work control, and work control was not a significant predictor of any of the stress outcomes.

Although relatively few studies have examined indirect effects of work control (or alternative causal pathways; see Carayon, 1993b), the evidence provides some evidence that the effects of work control are mediated through perceptions of work stress (Jimmieson & Terry, 1993). This type of model not only accords with theoretical models of work control (Frese, 1989; Parkes, 1989; Sutton & Kahn, 1986), it also accords with the broader theoretical models of stress and coping, in which subjective evaluations of the potentially stressful context are regarded as critical mediating processes in the relationship between more stable situational (for instance, work control) and person variables and stress outcomes (e.g., Lazarus & Folkman, 1984; Lazarus, 1991; see also Terry, 1994; Terry, Callan, & Sartori, 1996; Terry, Tonge, & Callan, 1995). Despite the theoretical support for indirect effects of work control, future research needs to replicate Jimmieson and Terry's (1993) results. Such research should employ longitudinal research, in an endeavour to establish the temporal relations among work control, demands, and adjustment. Researchers also need to explore the possible mediating role of both subjective evaluations of work demands and more objective assessments of the demands of the work environment.

Curvilinear Effects

Warr (1987) has raised another potential relationship between work control and employee adjustment. He argues that a number of job characteristics, including work control, may exhibit a curvilinear association with measures of employee adjustment. His vitamin model of stress and health predicts that a moderate level of work control will have the most beneficial impact on psychological well-being, whereas decrements in psychological well-being will be found at either extremely low or high levels of work control (see also Bazerman, 1982; Rodin, Reenert, & Solomon, 1980). In this respect, it is argued that extremely high levels of work control will lead to a range of undesirable physiological, psychological, and behavioral consequences due, for instance, to a concern for self-presentation that may be particularly marked when people perceive that they will not be able to perform a task or set of tasks over which they have complete control (see Burger, 1989, for a review; see also Steptoe, 1989).

On methodological rather than substantive grounds, Fletcher and Jones (1993) pointed out that a significant interaction may be a spurious consequence of a curvilinear relationship between the outcome variables and either of the predictor variables (see Lubinski & Humphreys, 1990). It is necessary, therefore, to statistically control for the squared value of the work stress and work control variables (over and above their linear effect) before introducing the two-way interaction term between these variables into the hierarchical regression equation (see also J. Cohen & P. Cohen, 1983).

Warr (1991) provided a test of the vitamin model in a sample of 1686 English workers, and found evidence of a non-linear relationship between job decision latitude and levels of job satisfaction—the increase in satisfaction as a function of decision latitude levelled off at high levels of decision latitude; thus, there was not strong support for the curvilinear hypothesis. Warr found no evidence of demands–control interactions, even when the possible non-linearity in the relations between either of the variables and the outcome under consideration was taken into account. Fletcher and Jones (1993) also provided tests of the demands–control model and the vitamin model. In separate analyses of data obtained from male ($n = 1289$) and female ($n = 985$) employees recruited from a medical facility, there was evidence of a two-way interaction between job demands and job decision latitude for males in the prediction of job and life satisfaction (but not for two measures of psychological well-being). However, additional analyses revealed that, after controlling for the main effects of job demands and job decision latitude and their associated quadratic terms (squared values of the two variables), the two interactions were no longer significant. This pattern of findings can be taken as some evidence of non-linearity in the prediction of job and life satisfaction in the male sample but, overall, Fletcher and Jones concluded that there was only weak support for Warr's (1987) proposition that the effects of work stress and work control on employee adjustment are curvilinear in nature. However, Fletcher and Jones's study does highlight the need for future tests of the demands–control model to adopt this statistical approach in order to identify the presence of spurious interactions due to the non-linear effects of either work demands or work control.

Summary

In summary, recent research has considered some further roles, in addition to the stress buffering role, that work control may have on employee adjustment. With the exception of efforts to test for curvilinear effects of work control, this research focus has been incidental rather than intentional. For this reason, when reviewing previous research on work control, only scant attention has been paid to the possible direct and indirect effects of work control. The present review indicates that there have been numerous reports of significant main effects of work control; however, for the most part, these have been reported in cross-sectional, self-report studies, which suggest that they may be a reflection of the confounding effects of common method variance. Despite Ganster and Fusilier's (1989) call for more research attention on indirect effects of work control, little research of this type has been conducted, although there is some suggestive evidence that perceptions of work stress may play a mediating role in the control–adjustment relationship. In relation to possible curvilinear effects of work control, there is little evidence that moderate levels of control are most beneficial for employee well-being. It should, however, be noted that the studies that have tested for curvilinear effects of work control have been based on relatively heterogeneous samples of employees—it is likely that the adverse effects of high levels of work control will be dependent on both personal dispositions (i.e., desire for control; see Greenberger et al., 1989) and the extent to which the job demands make salient the self-presentational concerns associated with high control.

CONCLUSIONS AND FUTURE DIRECTIONS

The present paper has reviewed the past decade of research testing Karasek's (1979) demands–control model. Building on Ganster and Fusilier's (1989) timely discussion of the construct of work control and how it relates to a range of different areas of interest in industrial and organizational psychology, the aim of the present review was to focus on direct operationalizations of the work control construct. As shown in the review, this construct continues to be a popular area for research, much of which has been designed explicitly to test Karasek's assumption that, when accompanied by high levels of work control, work demands do not impact negatively on employee adjustment.

Taken together, the past decade of research has continued to yield only sporadic support for the demands–control model. It could be concluded that this pattern of results should be interpreted as a general lack of support for the model, and that efforts to identify possible buffers of the negative effects of work demands should be based on alternative theoretical models. However, such a recommendation may be premature. As revealed in this review, recent methodological and theoretical developments have yielded more promising support for the demands–control model. In particular, a number of specific conclusions can be drawn:

1. The evidence suggests that some aspects of work control may be more important than others—in this respect, task-relevant aspects of control appear to act as stress buffers, particularly when the source of stress is task-related.
2. Although research employing multidimensional measures of control has found significant demand–control interactions on affective outcomes, recent studies using composite control measures suggest that stress-buffering effects may be most evident on absenteeism and health-related outcomes. Such results suggest that the lack of more

convincing support for the demands–control model in relation to cardiovascular outcomes may be due to the methodological problems with this latter body of research.

3. Recent research supports, in particular, the conjunctive moderating role of social support. Across a relatively small number of studies there is consistent evidence that stress-buffering effects of control are most evident when accompanied by high levels of social support.

4. Under conditions of low control, recent experimental research points to the possible compensatory role of informational control.

5. Although commonly reported in the literature, the main effects of work control may be a spurious outcome of common method variance; however, there is some preliminary evidence to suggest that indirect effects of work control should be examined in future research.

A more general conclusion that is clearly supported by the present review is that Karasek's (1979) concept of decision latitude needs to be refined, both conceptually and methodologically, to focus on the specific construct of work control. Future progress in the understanding of the interplay among work stress, work demands, and employee adjustment will be hampered if researchers continue to rely on a construct that is, operationally, confounded with other salient features of the work environment.

If the second decade of research on work control has sharpened researchers' theoretical and operational treatment of the construct of work control, then the challenge for the next decade of research is to identify the mechanisms that underpin the effects of work control. More specifically, the next decade of research should seek not only to verify the importance of task-relevant dimensions of control, the health and absenteeism-related effects of high demands and low control, and the secondary moderating role of social support, but to identify the mechanisms that underpin these effects. In particular, future research needs to examine the mediating role of: (1) both subjective and objective indicators of work stress; (2) coping responses adopted in the work context; and (3) specific health-related processes (e.g., lifestyle factors, as well as autonomic immunological, and endocrine responses; see Steptoe, 1989). In relation to the possible secondary moderating role of social support, research needs to examine the basis for the effects of a supportive work environment—for instance, the availability of work support may have its beneficial effects at an interpersonal level (e.g., by assisting workers to adopt effective coping responses, e.g., Terry, Rawle, & Callan, 1995), or through group-related mechanisms that render the work unit a cooperative rather than a competitive environment. In addition to examining the mechanisms underlying the effects of work control, researchers need to distinguish among different types of control, and to examine possible compensatory roles of cognitive forms of control. In a related vein, more focused research needs to address the possibility that in some work contexts, or for some people, work control is not desirable—the possible negative effect of high levels of work control remains a relatively unexplored area of research.

The third decade of research on work control will make a significant contribution to the work control literature only if the methodological limitations of previous research continue to be addressed. It is imperative that researchers use focused measures of work control, rather than relying on Karasek's (1979) multifactorial measure of job decision latitude. The reliance on cross-sectional, self-report research also needs to be replaced with the use of long-itudinal, multimethod designs. In the context of the demands–control model, the effects of common method variance not only make any main effects of the predictor variables difficult to interpret, they may also obscure the presence of true interactive effects. Longitudinal research (with the appropriate control of initial adjustment) ensures that both transient and more stable sources of common method variance are controlled. Decontaminating the data for the confounding effects of same-source measurement also controls for these sources of common method variance, at the same time as allowing researchers to assess both the non-affective consequences of low work control and the relative importance of subjective and objective characteristics of the work environment. Future research should also avoid the use of large hetero-geneous samples—the difficulties involved in interpreting any effects of work control in such samples, combined with the necessity of relying on general measures of work control, make the use of relatively homogeneous work groups more desirable.

In closing, our general conclusion is not much different from Ganster and Fusilier's (1989) conclusion a decade ago: The research conducted during the past decade points to the potential insights that the notion of work control can offer to an understanding of employee responses to work demands. Nevertheless, both conceptually and operationally, researchers need to take a more sophisticated look at this construct. The question as to whether control serves as an effective stress buffer in the work context does not have a simple answer, particularly if the tool that is used to answer the question does not directly reflect the construct that it is designed to assess, or if it is based on an ill-defined conceptualization of the construct. Moreover, any model that is based on the view that work control can help to buffer the negative effects of work stress needs to take into account the other characteristics of the work environ-ment, the characteristics of the employee, and the extent to which there is a match between the type of available control and the source of the stress. Such a model also needs to be able to specify the processes that account for any stress-buffering effects of work control. Thus, the question as to whether work control can act as an antidote to the negative effects of work stress remains viable, but future attempts to answer it need to be more focused and based on a more complex view of the construct of work control than they have been in the past.

REFERENCES

Aiken, L.S. & West, S.G. (1991). *Multiple Regression: Testing and Interpreting Interactions*. Newbury Park, CA: Sage.

Albright, C.L., Winkleby, M.A., Ragland, D.R., Fisher, J. & Syme, S.L. (1992). Job strain and prevalence of hypertension in a biracial population of urban bus drivers. *American Journal of Public Health*, **82**, 984–989.

Alfredsson, L., Karasek, R.A. & Theorell, T.G. (1982). Myocardial infarction risk and psychosocial work environment: An analysis of the male Swedish working force. *Social Science and Medicine*, **16**, 463–467.

Alfredsson, L., Spetz, C.L. & Theorell, T.G. (1985). Type of occupation and near-future hospitalization for myocardial infarction and some other diagnoses. *International Journal of Epidemiology*, **14**, 378–388.

Alterman, T., Shekelle, R.B., Vernon, S.W. & Burau, K.D. (1994). Decision latitude, psychological demand, job strain, and coronary heart disease in the Western Electric study. *American Journal of Epidemiology*, **139**, 620–627.

Averill, J.R. (1973). Personal control over aversive stimuli and its relationship to stress. *Psychological Bulletin*, **18**, 286–303.

Bandura, A., Cioffi, D., Taylor, C.B. & Brouillard, M.E. (1988). Perceived self-efficacy in coping with cognitive stressors and opioid activation. *Journal of Personality and Social Psychology*, **55**, 479–488.

Barnett, R.C. & Brennan, R.T. (1995). The relationship between job experiences and psychological distress: A structural equation approach. *Journal of Organizational Behavior*, **16**, 259–276.

Baron, R.M. & Kenny, D.A. (1986). The moderator–mediator variable distinction in social psychological research: Conceptual, strategic, and statistical considerations. *Journal of Personality and Social Psychology*, **51**, 1173–1182.

Bazerman, M.H. (1982). Impact of personal control on performance: Is added control always beneficial? *Journal of Applied Psychology*, **67**, 472–479.

Bell, N.E. & Staw, B.M. (1989). People as sculptors versus sculpture: The roles of personality and personal control in organizations. In M.B. Arthur, D.T. Hall, & B.S. Lawrence (Eds), *Handbook of Career Theory* (pp. 232–251). Cambridge: Cambridge University Press.

Berlyne, D.E. (1960). *Conflict, Arousal, and Curiosity*. New York: McGraw-Hill.

Breaugh, J.A. (1985). The measurement of work autonomy. *Human Relations*, **38**, 551–570.

Brehm, J.W. (1996). *A Theory of Psychological Reactance*. New York: Academic Press.

Brief, A.P., Burke, M.J., George, J.M., Robinson, B.S. & Webster, J. (1988). Should negative affectivity remain an unmeasured variable in the study of job stress? *Journal of Applied Psychology*, **73**, 193–199.

Broadbent, D.E. (1985). The clinical impact of job design. *British Journal of Clinical Psychology*, **24**, 33–44.

Bromet, E.J., Dew, M.A., Parkinson, D.K. & Schulberg, H.C. (1988). Predictive effects of occupational and marital stress on the mental health of a male workforce. *Journal of Organizational Behavior*, **9**, 1–13.

Bunce, D. (1997). What factors are associated with the outcome of individual-focused worksite stress management interventions? *Journal of Occupational and Organizational Psychology*, **70**, 1–17.

Burger, J.M. (1989). Negative reactions to increases in perceived personal control. *Journal of Personality and Social Psychology*, **56**, 246–256.

Campbell, D.J. (1988). Task complexity: A review and analysis. *Academy of Management Review*, **13**, 40–52.

Campbell, D.J. (1991). Goal levels, complex tasks, and strategy development: A review and analysis. *Human Performance*, **4**, 1–31.

Campbell, D.J. & Gingrich, K.F. (1986). The interactive effects of task complexity and participation on task performance: A field experiment. *Organizational Behavior and Human Decision Processes*, **38**, 162–180.

Carayon, P. (1993a). A longitudinal test of Karasek's Job Strain model among office workers. *Work and Stress*, **7**, 299–314.

Carayon, P. (1993b). Job design and job stress in office workers. *Ergonomics*, **36**, 463–477.

Chapman, A., Mandryk, J.A., Frommer, M.S., Edye, B.V. & Ferguson, D.A. (1990). Chronic perceived work stress and blood pressure among Australian government employees. *Scandinavian Journal of Work, Environment, and Health*, **16**, 258–269.

Chesney, A.A. & Locke, E.A. (1991). Relationships among goal difficulty, business strategies, and performance on a complex management simulation task. *Academy of Management Journal*, **34**, 400–424.

Cohen, J. & Cohen, P. (1983). *Applied Multiple Regression for the Behavioral Sciences*. New York: Erlbaum.

Cohen, S. & Edwards, J.R. (1989). Personality characteristics as moderators of the relationship between stress and disorder. In R.W.J. Neufeld (Ed.), *Advances in the Investigation of Psychological Stress* (pp. 235–283). New York: Wiley.

Cohen, S. & Wills, T.A. (1985). Stress, social support, and the buffering hypothesis. *Psychological Bulletin*, **98**, 310–357.

Cotton, J.L. (1995). Participation's effect on performance and satisfaction: A reconsideration of Wagner. *Academy of Management Review*, **20**, 276–278.

Daft, R.L. & Macintosh, N.B. (1981). A tentative exploration into the amount and equivocality of information processing in organizational work units. *Administrative Science Quarterly*, **26**, 207–224.

Daniels, K. & Guppy, A. (1994). Occupational stress, social support, job control, and psychological well-being. *Human Relations*, **47**, 1523–1544.

Dwyer, D.J. & Ganster, D.C. (1991). The effects of job demands and control on employee attendance and satisfaction. *Journal of Organizational Behavior*, **12**, 595–608.

Earley, P.C. (1985). Influence of information, choice, and task complexity upon goal acceptance, performance, and personal goals. *Journal of Applied Psychology*, **70**, 481–491.

Earley, P.C. (1986). Supervisors and shop stewards as sources of contextual information in goal setting: A comparison of the United States with England. *Journal of Applied Psychology*, **71**, 111–117.

Edwards, J.R. & Cooper, C.L. (1990). The person–environment fit approach to stress: Recurring problems and some suggested solutions. *Journal of Organizational Behavior*, **11**, 293–307.

Evans, B.K. & Fischer, D.G. (1992). A hierarchical model of participatory decision-making, job autonomy, and perceived control. *Human Relations*, **45**, 1169–1189.

Evans, M.G. (1985). A Monte Carlo study of the effects of correlated method variance in moderated multiple regression analysis. *Organizational Behavior and Human Decision Processes*, **36**, 305–323.

Finney, J.W., Mitchell, R.C., Cronkite, R.C. & Moos, R.H. (1984). Methodological issues in estimating main and interactive effects: Examples for the coping/social support and stress field. *Journal of Health and Social Behavior*, **19**, 23–24.

Fisher, C.D. & Gitelson, R. (1983). A meta-analysis of the correlates of role conflict and ambiguity. *Journal of Applied Psychology*, **68**, 320–333.

Fiske, S.T. & Taylor, S.E. (1991). *Social Cognition*. New York: McGraw-Hill.

Fletcher, B.C. (1991). *Work, Stress, Disease, and Life Expectancy*. Chichester, UK: Wiley.

Fletcher, B.C. & Jones, F. (1993). A refutation of Karasek's demand–discretion model of occupational stress with a range of dependent measures. *Journal of Organizational Behavior*, **14**, 319–330.

Fox, M.L., Dwyer, D.J. & Ganster, D.C. (1993). Effects of stressful job demands and control on physiological and attitudinal outcomes in a hospital setting. *Academy of Management Journal*, **36**, 289–318.

French, J.R.P. & Caplan, R.D. (1972). Organizational stress and individual strain. In A.J. Marrow (Ed.), *The Failure of Success* (pp. 30–68). New York: Amacon.

French, Jr J.R.P., Caplan, R.D. & Van Harrison, R. (1982). *The Mechanisms of Job Stress and Strain*. New York: Wiley.

Frese, M. (1989). Theoretical models of control and health. In S.L. Sauter, J.J. Hurrell & C.L. Cooper (Eds), *Job Control and Worker Health* (pp. 107–128). Chichester, UK: Wiley.

Friedman, M. & Rosenman, R. (1974). *Type A Behaviour and Your Heart*. New York: Knopf.

Ganster, D.C. (1988). Improving measures of work control in occupational stress research. In J.J. Hurrell, L.R. Murphy, S.L. Sauter, & C.L. Cooper (Eds), *Occupational Stress: Issues and Developments in Research* (pp. 88–99). New York: Taylor & Francis.

Ganster, D.C. (1989). Worker control and well-being: A review of research in the workplace. In S.L. Sauter, J.J. Hurrell & C.L. Cooper (Eds), *Job Control and Worker Health* (pp. 3–24). Chichester, UK: Wiley.

Ganster, D.C. & Fusilier, M.R. (1989). Control in the workplace. In C.L. Cooper & I.T. Robertson (Eds), *International Review of Industrial and Organizational Psychology* (Vol. 4, pp. 235–280). Chichester, UK: Wiley.

Gardell, B. (1977). Autonomy and participation at work. *Human Relations*, **30**, 515–533.

Georges, E., Wear, M.L. & Mueller, W.H. (1992). Body fat distribution and job stress in Mexican-American men of Hispanic Health and Nutrition Examination Survey. *American Journal of Human Biology*, **80**, 1368–1371.

Green, K.L. & Johnson, J.V. (1990). The effects of psychosocial work organization on patterns of cigarette smoking among male chemical plant employees. *American Journal of Public Health*, **80**, 1368–1371.

Greenberger, D.B., Porter, G., Miceli, M.P. & Strasser, S. (1991). Responses to inadequate personal control in organizations. *Journal of Social Issues*, **47**, 111–128.

Greenberger, D.B. & Strasser, S. (1986). Development and application of a model of personal control in organizations. *Academy of Management Review*, **11**, 164–177.

Greenberger, D.B. & Strasser, S. (1991). The role of situational and dispositional factors in the enhancement of personal control in organizations. In L.L. Cummings & B.M. Staw (Eds), *Research in Organizational Behavior* (pp. 111–145). Greenwich, CT: JAI Press.

Greenberger, D.B., Strasser, S., Cummings, L.L. & Dunham, R.B. (1989). The impact of personal control on performance and satisfaction. *Organizational Behavior and Human Decision Processes*, **43**, 29–51.

Hackman, J.R. & Oldham, G.R. (1976). Motivation through the design of work: Test of a theory. *Organizational Behavior and Human Performance*, **16**, 250–279.

Hammar, N., Alfredsson, L. & Theorell, T.G. (1994). Job characteristics and incidence of myocardial infarction. *International Journal of Epidemiology*, **23**, 277–284.

Hammer, T.H. & Stern, R.N. (1980). Employee ownership: Implications for the organizational distribution of power. *Academy of Management Journal*, **23**, 78–100.

Hesketh, B. & Shouksmith, G. (1986). Job and non-job activities, job satisfaction, and mental health among veterinarians. *Journal of Occupational Behavior*, **7**, 325–339.

Hurrell, J.J. & Lindström, K. (1992). Comparison of job demands, control, and psychosomatic complaints at different career stages of managers in Finland and the United States. *Scandinavian Journal of Work, Environment, and Health*, **18**, 11–13.

Hurrell, J.J. & McLaney, M.A. (1989). Control, job demands, and job satisfaction. In S.L. Sauter, J.J. Hurrell, & C.L. Cooper (Eds), *Job Control and Worker Health* (pp. 97–103). Chichester, UK: Wiley.

Jackson, S.E. (1989). Does job control control job stress? In S.L. Sauter, J.J. Hurrell, & C.L. Cooper (Eds), *Job Control and Worker Health* (pp. 25–53). Chichester, UK: Wiley.

Jackson, P.R., Wall, T.D., Martin, R. & Davids, K. (1993). New measures of job control, cognitive demand, and production responsibility. *Journal of Applied Psychology*, **78**, 753–762.

Janis, I.L. (1958). *Psychological Stress*. New York: Wiley.

Jimmieson, N.L. & Terry, D.J. (1993). The effects of prediction, understanding, and control: A test of the stress antidote model. *Anxiety, Stress, and Coping*, **6**, 179–199.

Jimmieson, N.L. & Terry, D.J. (1997). Responses to an in-basket activity: The role of work stress, behavioral control, and informational control. *Journal of Occupational Health Psychology*, **2**, 72–83.

Jimmieson, N.L. & Terry, D.J. (1998). An experimental study of the effects of work stress, work control, and task information on adjustment. *Applied Psychology: An International Review*, **47**, 343–369.

Jimmieson, N.L. & Terry, D.J. (in press). The moderating role of task characteristics in determining responses to a stressful work simulation. *Journal of Organizational Behavior*.

Johansson, G., Aronsson, G. & Lindstrom, B.O. (1978). Social psychological and neuroendocrine reactions in highly mechanized work. *Ergonomics*, **21**, 583–589.

Johnson, J.V. (1986). The impact of workplace social support, job demands, and work control upon cardiovascular disease in Sweden. In *Division of Environmental and Organizational Psychology Research Report* (Vol. 1). Stockholm: University of Stockholm.

Johnson, J.V. & Hall, E.M. (1988). Job strain, work place social support, and cardiovascular disease: A cross-sectional study of a random sample of the Swedish working population. *American Journal of Public Health*, **78**, 1336–1342.

Karasek, R.A. (1979). Job demands, job decision latitude, and mental strain: Implications for job redesign. *Administrative Science Quarterly*, **24**, 285–308.

Karasek, R.A. Russell, R. & Theorell, T.G. (1982). Physiology of stress and regeneration in job related cardiovascular illness. *Journal of Human Stress*, **3**, 29–42.

Karasek, R.A. & Theorell, T.G. (1990). *Healthy Work: Stress, Productivity, and the Reconstruction of Working Life*. New York: Basic Books.

Kasl, S.V. (1989). An epidemiological perspective on the role of control in health. In S.L. Sauter, J.J. Hurrell & C.L. Cooper (Eds), *Job Control and Worker Health* (pp. 161–190). Chichester, UK: Wiley.

Katz, D. & Kahn, R.L. (1978). *The Social Psychology of Organizations*. New York: Wiley.

Katz, R. & Wykes, T. (1985). The psychological difference between temporally predictable and unpredictable stressful events: Evidence for information control theories. *Journal of Personality and Social Psychology*, **48**, 781–790.

Kauppinen-Toropainen, K., Kandolin, I. & Mutanen, P. (1983). Job dissatisfaction and work-related exhaustion in male and female work. *Journal of Occupational Behavior*, **4**, 193–207.

Kernan, M.C., Bruning, N.S. & Miller-Guhde, L. (1994). Individual and group performance: Effects of task complexity and information. *Human Performance*, 7, 273–289.

Kohn, M.L. & Schooler, C. (1978). The reciprocal effects of the substantive complexity of work and intellectual flexibility: A longitudinal assessment. *American Journal of Sociology*, 84, 24–52.

Kohn, M.L. & Schooler, C. (1979). The reciprocal effects of the substantive complexity of work and intellectual flexibility: A longitudinal assessment. In M.W. Riley (Ed.), *Aging from Birth to Death: Interdisciplinary Perspectives* (pp. 47–75). Boulder, CO: Westview Press.

Kristensen, T.S. (1995). The demand–control–support model: Methodological challenges for future research. *Stress Medicine*, 11, 17–26.

Kushnir, T. & Melamed, S. (1991). Work-load, perceived control, and psychological distress in Type A/B industrial workers. *Journal of Organizational Behavior*, 12, 155–168.

LaCroix, A.Z. & Haynes, S.G. (1987). Gender differences in the stressfulness of workplace roles: A focus on work and health. In R.C. Barnett, G.K. Baruch, & L. Biener (Eds), *Gender and Stress* (pp. 96–121). New York: Free Press.

Landsbergis, P.A. (1988). Occupational stress among health care workers: A test of the job demands–control model. *Journal of Organizational Behavior*, 9, 217–239.

Landsbergis, P.A., Schnall, P.L., Deitz, D., Friedman, R. & Pickering, T. (1992). The patterning of psychological attributes and distress by 'job strain' and social support in a sample of working men. *Journal of Behavioral Medicine*, 15, 379–405.

Lazarus, R.S. (1991). Psychological stress in the workplaces. *Journal of Social Behavior and Personality*, 6(7), 1–13.

Lazarus, R.S. & Folkman, S. (1984). *Stress Appraisal, and Coping*, New York: Springer-Verlag.

Light, K.C., Turner, J.R. & Hinderli, A.L. (1992). Job strain and ambulatory work blood pressure in healthy young men and women. *Hypertension*, 20, 214–218.

Locke, E.A. & Schweiger, D.M. (1979). Participation in decision-making: One more look. In B. Staw (Ed.), *Research in Organizational Behavior* (pp. 265–339). Greenwich, CT: JAI Press.

Lubinski, D. & Humphreys, L.G. (1990). Assessing spurious 'moderator effects': Illustrated substantively with the hypothesized ('synergistic') relation between spatial and mathematical ability. *Psychological Bulletin*, 107, 385–393.

Lykken, D.T. (1962). Perception in the rat: Autonomic response to shock as a function of length of warning interval. *Science*, 137, 665–666.

Marino, K.E. & White, S.E. (1985). Departmental structure, locus of control, and job stress: The effect of a moderator. *Journal of Applied Psychology*, 45, 168–175.

Marshall, N.L., Barnett, R.C., Baruch, G.K. & Pleck, J.H. (1991). More than a job: Women and stress in caregiving occupations. In H. Lapata & J. Levy (Eds), *Current Research on Occupations and Professions* (pp. 61–81). Greenwich, CT: JAI Press.

McLaney, M.A. & Hurrell, J.J. (1988). Control, stress, and job satisfaction in Canadian nurses. *Work and Stress*, 2, 217–224.

Melamed, S., Kushnir, T. & Meir, E.I. (1991). Attenuating the impact of job demands: Additive and interactive effects of perceived control and social support. *Journal of Vocational Behavior*, 39, 40–53.

Miller, S.M. (1979). Controllability and human stress: Method, evidence, and theory. *Behavior Research and Therapy*, 17, 287–304.

Moch, M., Cammann, C. & Cooke, R.A. (1983). Organizational structure: Measuring the distribution of influence. In S.E. Seashore, E.E. Lawler, P.H. Mirvis, & C.

Cammann (Eds), *Assessing Organizational Change: A Guide to Methods, Measures, and Practices* (pp. 177–201). New York: Wiley.

Moller, L., Kristensen, T.S. & Hollnagel, H. (1991). Social class and cardiovascular risk factors in Danish men. *Scandinavian Journal of Social Medicine*, **19**, 116–126.

Morrison, D.L., Dunne, M.P., Fitzgerald, R. & Cloghan, D. (1992). Job design and levels of physical and mental strain among Australian prison officers. *Work and Stress*, **6**, 13–31.

Mullarkey, S., Jackson, P.R., Wall, T.D., Wilson, J.R. & Grey-Taylor, S.M. (1997). The impact of technology characteristics and job control on worker mental health. *Journal of Organizational Behavior*, **18**, 471–489.

O'Brien, A., Terry, D.J. & Jimmieson, N.L. (1998). Negative affectivity and responses to work stress: An experimental study. Manuscript submitted for publication.

Parkes, K.R. (1989). Personal control in an occupational context. In A. Steptoe & A. Appels (Eds), *Stress, Personal Control, and Health* (pp. 21–47). Chichester, UK: Wiley.

Parkes, K.R. (1990). Coping, negative affect and the work environment: Additive and interactive predictors of mental health. *Journal of Applied Psychology*, **75**, 399–409.

Parkes, K.R. (1991). Locus of control as moderator: An explanation for additive versus interactive findings in the demand–discretion model of work stress? *British Journal of Psychology*, **82**, 291–312.

Parkes, K.R., Mendham, C.A. & von Rabenau, C. (1994). Social support and the demand–discretion model of job stress: Tests of additive and interactive effects in two samples. *Journal of Vocational Behavior*, **44**, 91–113.

Payne, R.L. (1979). Demands, supports, constraints, and psychological health. In C.J. Mackay & T. Cox (Eds), *Response to Stress: Occupational Aspects* (pp. 85–105). London: International Publishing Corporation.

Payne, R.L. & Fletcher, B.C. (1983). Job demands, supports, and constraints as predictors of psychological strain among schoolteachers. *Journal of Vocational Behavior*, **22**, 136–147.

Pearce, J.L. (1981). Bringing some clarity to role ambiguity research. *Academy of Management Review*, **6**, 665–674.

Perkins, C.C. Jr (1968). An analysis of the concept of reinforcement. *Psychological Review*, **75**, 155–172.

Perrewe, P.L. & Anthony, W.P. (1990). Stress in a steel pipe mill: The impact of job demands, personal control, and employee age on somatic complaints. *Journal of Social Behavior and Personality*, **5**, 77–90.

Perrewe, P.L. & Ganster, D.C. (1989). The impact of job demands and behavioral control on experienced job stress. *Journal of Organizational Behavior*, **10**, 213–229.

Pieper, C.F., LaCroix, A.Z. & Karasek, R.A. (1989). The relation of psychosocial dimensions of work with coronary heart disease risk factors: A meta analysis of five United States data bases. *American Journal of Epidemiology*, **129**, 483–494.

Reed, D.M., LaCroix, A.Z., Karasek, R.A., Miller, D.W. & MacLean, C.A. (1989). Occupational strain and the incidence of coronary heart disease. *American Journal of Epidemiology*, **129**, 495–502.

Rodin, J., Reenert, K. & Solomon, S.K. (1980). Intrinsic motivation for control: Fact or fiction? In A. Baum, J.E. Singer & S. Valins (Eds), *Advances in Environmental Psychology*, **2**, Hillsdale, NJ: Erlbaum.

Rosenfield, S. (1989). The effects of women's employment: Personal control and sex differences in mental health. *Journal of Health and Social Behavior*, **30**, 77–91.

Rothbaum, F., Weisz, J.R. & Snyder, S.S. (1982). Changing the world and changing the self: A two-process model of perceived control. *Journal of Personality and Social Psychology*, **42**, 5–37.

Sagie, A. (1995). Employee participation and work outcomes: An end to the dispute? *Academy of Management Review*, **20**, 278–280.

Sargent, L.D. & Terry, D.J. (in press). The effects of work control and job demands on employee adjustment and work performance. *Journal of Occupational and Organizational Psychology*.

Sargent, L.D. & Terry, D.J. (1998). The moderating role of social support in Karasek's job strain model. Manuscript submitted for publication.

Sauter, S.L. (1989). Moderating effects of job control on health complaints in office work. In S.L. Sauter, J.J. Hurrell & C.L. Cooper (Eds), *Job Control and Worker Health* (pp. 91–103). Chichester, UK: Wiley.

Schaubroeck, J. & Merritt, D.E. (1997). Divergent effects of job control on coping with work stressors: The key role of self-efficacy. *Academy of Management Journal*, **40**, 738–754.

Schnall, P.L., Landsbergis, P.A. & Baker, D.B. (1994). Job strain and cardiovascular disease. *Annual Review of Public Health*, **15**, 381–411.

Schnall, P.L., Schwartz, J.E., Landsbergis, P.A., Warren, K. & Pickering, T. (1992). The relationship between job strain, alcohol, and ambulatory blood pressure. *Hypertension*, **19**, 488–494.

Schwartz, J.E., Pieper, C.F. & Karasek, R.A. (1988). A procedure for linking psychosocial job characteristics data to health surveys. *American Journal of Public Health*, **78**, 904–909.

Seligman, M.E.P. (1968). Chronic fear produced by unpredictable electric shock. *Journal of Comparative Physiological Psychology*, **66**, 402–411.

Seligman, M.E.P. (1975). *Helplessness: On Depression, Development, and Death*. New York: Freeman.

Skinner, E.A. (1996). A guide to constructs of control. *Journal of Personality and Social Psychology*, **71**, 549–570.

Smith, C.S., Tisak, J., Hahn, S.E. & Schmieder, R.A. (1997). The measurement of job control. *Journal of Organizational Behavior*, **18**, 225–237.

Smith, R.E., Smoll, F.L. & Ptacek, J.T. (1990). Conjunctive moderator variables in vulnerability and resiliency research: Life stress, social support and coping skills, and adolescent sports injuries. *Journal of Personality and Social Psychology*, **58**, 360–369.

Söderfeldt, B., Söderfeldt, M., Muntaner, C., O'Campo, P., Warg, L. & Ohlson, C. (1996). Psychosocial work environment in human service organizations: A conceptual analysis and development of the demand–control model. *Social Science Medicine*, **42**, 1217–1226.

Spector, P.E. (1987). Interactive effects of perceived control and job stressors on affective reactions and health outcomes for clerical workers. *Work and Stress*, **1**, 155–162.

Spector, P.E. (1992). A consideration of the validity and means of self-report measures of job conditions. In C.L. Cooper & I.T. Robertson (Eds), *International Review of Industrial and Organizational Psychology* (Vol. 7, pp. 123–151). Chichester, UK: Wiley.

Spector, P.E. & Brannick, M.T. (1995). The nature and effects of method variance in organizational research. In C.L. Cooper & I.T. Robertson (Eds), *International Review of Industrial and Organizational Psychology* (Vol. 10, pp. 249–274). Chichester, UK: Wiley.

Spreitzer, G.M. (1995a). Psychological empowerment in the workplace: Dimensions, measurement, and validation. *Academy of Management Journal*, **38**, 1442–1465.

Spreitzer, G.M. (1995b). An empirical test of a comprehensive model of interpersonal empowerment in the workplace. *American Journal of Community Psychology*, **23**, 601–629.

Spreitzer, G.M. (1996). Social structural characteristics of psychological empowerment. *Academy of Management Journal*, **39**, 483–504.

Stansfeld, S.A., North, F.M., White, I. & Marmot, M.G. (1995). Work characteristics and psychiatric disorder in civil servants in London. *Journal of Epidemiology and Community Health*, **49**, 48–53.

Staw, B.M. (1977). Motivation in organizations: Toward synthesis and redirection. In B.M. Staw & G.R. Salancik (Eds), *New Directions in Organizational Behavior* (pp. 55–95). Chicago, IL: St Clair Press.

Staw, B.M. (1986). Beyond the control graph: Steps toward a model of perceived control in organizations. In R.N. Stern & S. McCarthy (Eds), *The Organizational Practice of Democracy* (pp. 305–321). Chichester, UK: Wiley.

Steptoe, A. (1989). Psychophysiological mechanisms relating control, coping and health. In S.L. Sauter, J.J. Hurrell, & C.L. Cooper (Eds), *Job Control and Worker Health* (pp. 191–203). Chichester, UK: Wiley.

Sutton, R.I. & Kahn, R.L. (1986). Prediction, understanding, and control as antidotes to organizational stress. In J. Lorsch (Ed.), *Handbook of Organizational Behavior* (pp. 272–285). Englewood Cliffs, NJ: Prentice-Hall.

Tannenbaum, A.S. (1962). Control in organizations: Individual adjustment and organizational performances. *Administrative Science Quarterly*, **1**, 236–257.

Tannenbaum, A.S. (1968). *Control in Organizations*. New York: McGraw-Hill.

Tannenbaum, A.S. & Cooke, R.A. (1979). Organizational control: A review of studies employing the control graph method. In C.J. Lammers & D.C. Hickson (Eds), *Organizations Alike and Unlike* (pp. 183–210). London: Routledge & Kegan Paul.

Tannenbaum, A.S., Kavcic, B., Rosner, M., Vianello, M. & Weiser, G. (1974). *Hierarchy in Organizations*. San Francisco, CA: Jossey-Bass.

Terry, D.J. (1994). The determinants of coping: The role of stable and situational factors. *Journal of Personality and Social Psychology*, **66**, 895–910.

Terry, D.J., Callan, V.J. & Sartori, G. (1996). A test of a stress-coping model of adjustment to a large-scale organizational change. *Stress Medicine*, **2**, 105–120.

Terry, D.J., Nielsen, J. & Perchard,L. (1993). Effects of work stress on psychological well-being and job satisfaction: The stress buffering role of social support. *Australian Journal of Psychology*, **45**, 168–175.

Terry, D.J., Rawle, & Callan, V.J. (1995). The effects of social support on adjustment: The mediating role of coping. *Personal Relationships*, **3**, 97–124.

Terry, D.J., Tonge, L. & Callan, V.J. (1995). Employee adjustment to stress: The role of coping resources, situational factors, and coping responses. *Anxiety, Stress, and Coping*, **8**, 1–24.

Tetrick, L.E. & LaRocco, J.M. (1987). Understanding, prediction, and control as moderators of the relationships between perceived stress, satisfaction, and psychological well-being. *Journal of Applied Psychology*, **72**, 538–543.

Theorell, T.G., Alfredsson, L., Knox, S., Perski, A., Svensson, J. & Wallers, D. (1984). On the interplay between socio-economic factors, personality, and work environment in the pathogenesis of cardiovascular disease. *Scandinavian Journal of Work, Environment, and Health*, **10**, 373–380.

Theorell, T.G., deFaire, U., Johnson, J., Hall, E.M., Perski, A. & Stewart (1991). Job strain and ambulatory blood pressure profiles. *Scandinavian Journal of Work Environmental Health*, **17**, 380–385.

Theorell, T.G., Hjemdahl, P., Ericsson, F., Kallner, A., Knox, S., Perski, A., Svensson, J., Tidgren, B. & Wallers, D. (1985). Psychosocial and physiological factors in relation to blood pressure at rest: A study of Swedish men in their upper twenties. *Journal of Hypertension*, **3**, 591–600.

Theorell, T.G. & Karasek, R.A. (1996). Current issues relating psychosocial job strain and cardiovascular disease research. *Journal of Occupational Health Psychology*, **1**, 9–26.

Theorell, T.G., Perski, A., Orth-Gomer, K., Hamsten, A. & deFaire, U. (1991). The effects of the strain of returning to work on the risk of cardiac death after a first myocardial infarction before age 45. *International Journal of Cardiology*, **30**, 61–67.

Thompson, S.C. (1981). Will it hurt less if I can control it? A complex answer to a simple question. *Psychological Bulletin*, **90**, 89–101.

Van Egeren, L.F. (1992). The relationship between job strain and blood pressure at work, at home, and during sleep. *Psychosomatic Medicine*, **54**, 337–343.

Von Glinow, M.A. & Teagarden, M.B. (1988). The transfer of human resource management technology in Sino-US cooperative ventures: Problems and solutions. *Human Resource Management*, **27**, 201–229.

Wagner, J.A. (1994). Participation's effects on performance and satisfaction: A reconsideration of research evidence. *Academy of Management Review*, **19**, 312–330.

Wall, T.D., Corbett, J.M., Clegg, C.W., Jackson, P.R. & Martin, R. (1990). Advanced manufacturing technology and work design: Towards a theoretical framework. *Journal of Organizational Behavior*, **11**, 201–219.

Wall, T.D., Jackson, P.R. & Mullarkey, S. (1995). Further evidence on some new measures of job control, cognitive demand, and production responsibility. *Journal of Organizational Behavior*, **16**, 431–455.

Wall, T.D., Jackson, P.R., Mullarkey, S. & Parker, S.K. (1996). The demands–control model of job strain: A more specific test. *Journal of Occupational and Organizational Psychology*, **69**, 153–166.

Wall, T.D. & Martin, R. (1994). Job and work design. In C.L. Cooper & I.T. Robertson (Eds), *Key Reviews in Managerial Psychology* (pp. 158–188). Chichester, UK: Wiley.

Warr, P.B. (1987). *Work, Unemployment, and Mental Health*. Oxford: Oxford University Press.

Warr, P.B. (1990). Decision latitude, job demands, and employee well-being. *Work and Stress*, **4**, 285–294.

Warr, P.B. (1990). Decision latitude, job demands, and employee well-being. *Work and Stress*, **4**, 285–294.

Westman, M. (1992). Moderating effect of decision latitude on stress–strain relationship: Does organizational level matter? *Journal of Organizational Behavior*, **13**, 713–722.

White, R.W. (1959). Motivation reconsidered: The concept of competence. *Psychological Review*, **66**, 297–333.

Wood, R.E. (1986). Task complexity: Definition of the construct. *Organizational Behavior and Human Decision Processes*, **37**, 60–82.

Wortman, C. & Brehm, J.C. (1975). Responses to uncontrollable outcomes: An integration of reactance theory and the learned helplessness model. In L. Berkowitz (Ed.), *Advances in Experimental Social Psychology* (pp. 278–336). New York: Academic Press.

Xie, J.L. (1995). Research on Chinese organizational behavior and human resource management: Conceptual and methodological considerations. In S.B. Prasad (Ed.),

Advances in International Comparative Management (pp. 15–42). Greenwich, CT: JAI Press.

Xie, J.L. (1996). Karasek's model in the people's Republic of China: Effects of job demands, control, and individual differences. *Academy of Management Journal, 39,* 1594–1618.

Zapf, D., Dormann, C. & Frese, M. (1996). Longitudinal studies in organizational stress research: A review of the literature with reference to methodological issues. *Journal of Occupational Health Psychology,* 1, 145–169.

Chapter 2

Workplace Bullying

Helge Hoel
University of Manchester Institute of Science and Technology

Charlotte Rayner
Staffordshire University Business School

and

Cary L. Cooper
University of Manchester Institute of Science and Technology

INTRODUCTION

Bullying or harassment in the workplace has become a major occupational stressor, creating enormous legal and financial problems for organizations (Earnshaw & Cooper, 1996). Many of the early research projects in this field were carried out in the Scandinavian countries (e.g., Leymann, 1987; Einarsen & Raknes, 1991), but this field of research has grown very fast over the last 5–10 years. The terminology for this phenomenon has been widespread, with different countries attributing different labels: in the US and Canada they have referred to it variously as workplace harassment (Brodsky, 1976); employee abuse (Bassman, 1992), emotional abuse (Keashly, 1998), mistreatment at work (Price Spratlen, 1995) and petty tyranny (Ashforth, 1994); in Germany, Austria and Scandinavia as mobbing; and in the UK and Ireland as bullying (Rayner & Cooper, 1997).

Definition

In order to define 'bullying' given the diverse descriptive labels, it is important to explore the characteristics that make it up. From the research into bullying in a primary or secondary school context, several parameters have emerged that would be useful in exploring workplace bullying: the type, frequency and duration of acts which targets experience, the reaction of the

Workplace Bullying by Helge Hoel, Charlotte Rayner and Cary L. Cooper taken from IRIOP 1999 v14, Edited by Cary L. Cooper and Ivan T. Robertson: © 1999 John Wiley & Sons, Ltd

target including their perceived power in relation to the perpetrator and, finally, the intent of the perpetrator (Besag, 1989; Stephenson & Smith, 1989; Smith, 1997).

Frequency and duration

The frequency and duration of the acts which the bullied experience are important elements of definition which separate the topic (as far as this is possible) from workplace violence. In workplace bullying, someone is subjected to negative behaviours from another individual or a group of people consistently for a period of time (e.g. Leymann, 1996; Einarsen, Raknes, Mathiesen & Hellesøy, 1994). Workplace violence (see Cox & Leather, 1994; Mantell, 1994; LaBar, 1994) on the other hand, includes single items of trauma such as a raid on a bank as well as multiple incidents of harassment from different individuals, for example as experienced by taxi or bus drivers.

Given that bullying at work is thought of as a concept involving persistency, the duration of the behaviours is important with many definitions centring around six months. There are some significant differences in operationalization: Leymann looks for the bullying to have gone on for *at least* six months (e.g. Leymann, 1992b); the Norwegian Bergen group look for behaviours *within* the last six months (e.g., Einarsen & Skogstad, 1996); and the Finnish group led by Björkqvist considers persistent behaviour within the last *year* (Björkqvist, Österman & Hjelt-Bäck, 1994). Frequency presents more of a problem, with weekly acts being highlighted by Leymann and his colleagues. His definition is thus quite precise; exposure to acts weekly for at least six months constitutes bullying (Leymann, 1996). Einarsen has derived measurement scales from the work of Olweus (1993) in the school context, where they have judged people to be bullied if their reported frequency is at least 'now and then' or 'weekly'. While this does provide a comparator for incidence in schools, the vagueness of 'now and then' is of concern. On the other hand, anecdotal data relating to bullying (e.g. Adams, 1992; Bassman, 1992; Randall, 1997) indicate that it is possible to bully someone without exhibiting weekly behaviour. This is particularly salient where a 'group of people' are being bullied and/or observing others being bullied as a 'secondary' experience.

The reaction of the target

Current definitions of workplace bullying can include a reaction by the victim. Most researchers do use some form of self-labelling by respondents, but are vulnerable to methodological problems as a result (e.g. Hubert, 1997). In some studies (e.g. Rayner, 1997; Einarsen et al., 1994), respondents have been presented with a description of bullying (which includes negative reactions such as feeling abused or powerless) and asked if they would label themselves as being bullied. Thus, in this instance, if someone has been the subject of negative acts, but not labelled themselves, they would not be seen as being bullied. Both racial and sexual harassment require the victim to have felt harassed for the harassment to have occurred in law (Painter, 1991), so this approach has merit, but certainly in a legal setting it is a necessary *but not a sufficient* condition (other data, such as demonstration of the negative effect on victims, also need to be presented). In Swedish law, the nature of the defined reaction is potentially being placed outside the work community (SNBOSH, 1993). Hubert (1997) explores how labelling is dependent on accurate classification by the target, and finds a subgroup of targets where others labelled them as being bullied when the targets did not label themselves. Leymann does not incorporate subjective labelling in his definition (Leymann, 1996), relying instead on strict frequency and duration criteria applied to the behaviours reported.

The balance of power between the parties

The Scandinavians (e.g. Leymann; Einarsen) make considerable play of a superior–subordinate relationship between the parties as part of the definition and point out that 'to be a victim of such bullying one must also feel inferiority in defending oneself. Consequently, serious conflicts between parties of "equal" strength . . . are not considered as bullying' (Einarsen & Skogstad, 1996:187). This element of definition has its roots in school bullying work and, where used, has two roles. It effectively acts as a differentiator for bullying from the conflict literature.

Such statements relating to power have a circularity to their argument. What type of power relationship is one referring to? There are many different types of power described in the social psychological literature, for example, French and Raven (1959), Kanter (1984), Handy (1992) which go beyond the simple power of 'status' or positional power. What about 'personal power', the influence people of equal status may exert over each other? The complexity of this point is considered by several writers, for example, Einarsen and Skogstad (1996) and Björkqvist, Österman and Hjelt-Bäck (1994). In many ways the point is only half made; perhaps it may be fair to say that, for this aspect of the definition, bullying exists when someone establishes power over someone else and is perceived to reinforce their superiority unnecessarily (McCarthy, 1996; Sheehan, 1996).

The intent of the perpetrator

Some definitions of bullying, particularly in the context of schools (e.g. Besag, 1989; Tattum & Lane, 1988) include the intent of the perpetrator. This tends to be ruled out in similar areas of experience for adults, such as sexual or racial harassment (Fitzgerald & Shullman, 1993; Jensen & Gutek, 1982) because of the difficulty of measuring intent in the context of litigation. It is discussed by some researchers (e.g. Randall, 1997) and inferred by others (e.g, Björkqvist, Österman & Hjelt-Bäck, 1994). Establishing intent is not operationalized (for example through checking with the perpetrator) and is thus currently of little significance. It does have merit for theorizing, when considering areas such as the dynamics of aggression or perceived intent in attribution theory.

Having reviewed the various elements of the potential definition of bullying at work, imbalance of power and intent of the perpetrator are the weakest aspects. Different contexts (for example research or litigation) may find different definitions appropriate. It is possible, and perhaps advisable, that an organization may *only* look for 'bullying behaviours' as a safe strategy for dealing with bullying. The law requires more tangible parameters than perhaps researchers do, who may be more interested in behaviours which are not so extreme as to be taken to court, but are still damaging. Researchers into incidence have generally used at least two of the parameters, so, for example, Leymann and Vartia focus on frequency and duration alone, but with strict criteria; Einarsen and Rayner look at a combination of frequency and self-report of being bullied against a pre-supplied description. Note that all the operationalized definitions work with self-reports from targets. Self-reports are central to the phenomenon of bullying, but broadening this from the target only to include the alleged perpetrator, witnesses as well as uninvolved outsiders, is important for the future.

DESCRIBING BULLYING

Incidence of Bullying

The incidence of bullying has been studied in different settings in Sweden (e.g. Leymann, 1992b), Norway (e.g. Einarsen & Skogstad, 1996), Finland (e.g. Björkqvist, Österman & Hjelt-Bäck, 1994), Germany (Zapf, Knortz & Kulla, 1996), Austria (Niedl, 1995), the US (Price Spratlen, 1995), and the UK (Rayner, 1997). International comparisons are difficult to establish, as there are subtle but important differences in operational definition used in these countries, thus in Table 5.1 a broad indicator of definition is used. Incidence studies with over 200 respondents have been identified in order to simplify the data presented.

Some efforts have been made to provide international comparators. Leymann estimates that 25% of the Swedish workforce could experience 'mobbing' at some point in their working lives, which is a figure to be compared to 50% within the UK (Rayner, 1997; UNISON, 1997).

Table 2.1 International studies of workplace bullying (see also Niedl, 1995, and Einarsen & Skogstad, 1996)

Author	Date	Country	Method	$n =$	Sample	Incidence	Definition
Lovås	1987	Norway	Telephone interviews	647	Representative of employed but not self-employed		?
Leymann & Tallgren	1990	Sweden	Questionnaire	370	Steelworks employees	4%	1b and 3a
Skogstad, Matthiesen & Hellesøy	1990	Norway	Questionnaire	745	Nurses from 9 hospitals & nursing homes	3%	1a and 4
Einarsen & Raknes	1991	Norway	Questionnaire	2215	Random sample taken from the member register from 7 different specialty unions	1%	
Leymann	1992b	Sweden	Questionnaire	2438	Representative of employed but not self-employed	3.5%	1b and 3a
Paanen & Vartia	1991	Finland	Questionnaire & interviews	984	Female clients of occupational health	10%	1b and 3a
Björkqvist, Österman & Hjelt-Bäck	1994	Finland	Questionnaire & interviews	338	University employees	30% males 55% females	1a + 2
Leymann	1993	Sweden	Questionnaire	610	Political party members		1b and 3a
Lindroth & Leymann	1993	Sweden	Questionnaire	230	Nursery school teachers		1b and 3a
Einarsen & Raknes	1997	Norway	Questionnaire	460	Male industrial workers	7%	1a + 3a +2 +4
Price Spratlen	1995	USA	Questionnaire	806	University employees	23%	2 + 4
Niedl	1995	Austria	Questionnaire	368	Hospital & research institute employees	7.8–26%	1b
Vartia	1996	Finland	Questionnaire	949	Municipal employees	10.1%	4 1 = 'often'
UNISON	1997	UK	Questionnaire	736	Public sector union members	14% 50%	1b + 4 1c + 4
Rayner	1997	UK	Questionnaire	1137	Part time students	53%	1c + 4

Key to 'Definition' symbols:
1 = Frequency of acts: 1a = within last 6 months, 1b = over 6 months, 1c = ever in career; 2 = Type of acts included in judgement; 3 = Duration of acts: 3a = weekly, 3b = less frequently than weekly; 4 = Victims label themselves as bullied

Identifying incidence within a shorter period of time may be useful, and trends may be detected through longitudinal studies. Niedl (1995) used Leymann's 'once a week for six months', *as well as* respondents considering themselves bullied, and found an incidence of 7.8% in Austria, which can be compared with Leymann's incidence of 3.5% in Sweden (Leymann, 1992b) where no subjective judgement is taken into account—the effect of which is unknown. Einarsen and Skogstad (1996) used 'within the last six months' and broader frequency categories, and provide an estimate of 4.5% for Norway, while Rayner following a similar methodology found 14% in the UK.

We can expect this field to develop as definitions converge. The authors consider it is likely that six months will be retained for duration, and that two other measures will emerge in some countries—one for legal purposes (for example once a week in frequency) and the other for research and health purposes, which may include the reaction of the victim as well as the victim's perceived state (i.e. 'bullied') but with a lower requirement on frequency. Where the legal position may be taken from a health and safety point, there will be overlap.

Not only do the differences in definition have an effect on the measurement of incidence between studies, but it is highly likely that cross-cultural differences will exist anyway (Hofstede, 1993; Pavett & Morris, 1995), and be amplified by the use of self-reports in studies. The nature of these differences will hold valuable insight for future cross-cultural work (Leymann, 1996; Niedl, 1995).

The principal methodology used in incidence studies has involved written questionnaires in order to capture data from large samples. Leymann (1990b) developed the LIPT (Leymann Inventory of Personal Terrorization) from several hundred critical incident interviews with targets of bullying. As the range of behaviours is very wide (Zapf, Knortz & Kulla, 1996), how these are configured into categories is a matter of choice, although to date, there has been little debate. Leymann's approach is to group behaviours by the effect on the target—to be able to communicate, maintain social contact and reputation, meaningful work and retain physical health. Zapf, Knortz and Kulla (1996) have applied a factor analysis approach to the items in the LIPT and generated six factors; verbal aggression, rumours, physical violence, attacking with organizational measures, social isolation, and attacking the target's private life and attitudes. Some loadings are low but the factors correspond with previous work done by Vartia (Zapf, Knortz & Kulla, 1996). These categories are coherent in that they focus clearly on behaviour which a person is subjected to rather than the response elicited from the target. Given that the data are derived from target self-reports, which in turn may be affected by many other variables, the validity of the data as an accurate indicator of the actual behaviour of the bully is constrained.

VICTIM PROFILE

Bullying can occur between superiors and subordinates as well as between peers or colleagues. Whilst anecdotal evidence points to a higher number of incidences involving a manager and a subordinate, the evidence is far from conclusive (Björkqvist, Österman & Hjelt-Bäck, 1994; Sjøtveit, 1992; Rayner, 1997; Einarsen & Skogstad, 1996; Leymann, 1992b). Anecdotal evidence identifies the typical target of bullying as being singled out and victimized (Field, 1996; Adams, 1992). National cultural differences may account for some of this variation.

Rayner (1997) found that only 19% of people who considered themselves bullied had been singled out, the rest were bullied in groups. These apparently conflicting data are perhaps resolved through the nature of the samples, and are possibly informative about the type or profile of people who may call 'help-lines'. It may also be argued that some people become reconciled to victimization if others share their fate. This may remove some of the stigma attached to the process of victimization, thereby reducing the adverse effect on self-esteem and self-image frequently identified with bullying.

Most studies conclude that reports of incidence and the nature of the experience are remarkably similar for both men and women. Where differences exist is in 'who is bullying whom', and in examining this feature one must remember that such findings are based on self-reports from the targets of bullying. While men are predominantly bullied by other men, women may be bullied by men or by other women, though more frequently by other women (Leymann, 1992c; Einarsen et al., 1994). Same-sex bullying may reflect the horizontal component of segregation (men work primarily with other men and women with women), whilst the greater likelihood for women of being bullied by a man may be accounted for by women's position in the lower levels of the occupational hierarchy (Hakim, 1979; Einarsen & Skogstad, 1996).

The findings from a study of university employees (Björkqvist, Österman & Hjelt-Bäck, 1994) deviate in some respect from the above conclusions. Their findings suggest that women experience 'work harassment', which is defined as a form of interpersonal aggression, more often and more severely than men. In a separate study, two different types of covert aggression are identified among adults: social manipulation (e.g. insulting comments about one's private life or rumours) and aggressive acts which, on the face of it, appear to be rational (e.g. interrupting or reducing someone's opportunity to express themselves or appraising someone's work unfairly: Björkqvist, Österman, & Lagerspetz, 1994). It is suggested that men and women alike use both forms of covert aggression, but in a selective manner, as a preferred style. Whilst apparently rational covert aggression is the preferred style for both men and women, social manipulation is used more frequently by women than by men.

The relationship between age and bullying finds conflicting data across studies (older employees more vulnerable/frequently bullied in Scandinavia, younger workers in the UK), pointing to cultural as well as labour market differences. Lower age of entry into employment in the UK, higher retirement age in Scandinavia as well as discrepancies in employment protection, may account for part of this variation.

The picture is also inconsistent when it comes to data from the public versus private sector. Whilst a number of studies indicate that public employees and those working in voluntary organizations are particularly vulnerable to bullying (Zapf, Knortz & Kulla, 1996; Adams, 1992; Kile, 1990a), Einarsen and Skogstad (1996) came to the opposite conclusion and Rayner (1997) found no significant differences. In order to explain the presumed overrepresentation of public sector employees among targets of bullying, Zapf, Knortz and Kulla (1996) identify time pressure or restricted control over time as a factor contributing to bullying, as conflicts are frequently left unresolved and are thus in danger of future escalation. Other contributing factors to an overrepresentation of bullying in the public sector may be organizational and managerial shortcomings (Leymann, 1996), and the absence of trade union organizations or lack of a collectivist tradition (Sjøtveit, 1992; Kile, 1990a).

The research on the relationship between bullying and personality is inconclusive. In line with findings from studies into school bullying (Olweus, 1989, 1993; Perry, Kusel & Perry, 1988), bullies have been identified with aggressiveness (Randall, 1996; Crawford, 1992) and victims with low self-esteem and high anxiety levels (Einarsen & Raknes, 1991; Vartia, 1996). However, as far as the bullies are concerned no substantial empirical evidence has been produced to support this claim. Some writers argue that such findings are not indicative of the personality of victims at the time they are being targeted, but a result of the bullying process itself (Leymann, 1996; Groeblinghoff & Becker, 1996). Vartia (1996), for example, identified a significant correlation between being bullied and self-esteem and neuroticism, arguing that when factors relating to the work environment were kept constant, the significance of the personality factors disappeared. One should also bear in mind the argument advanced by Locke, McClear and Knight (1996) that measuring global self-esteem is complicated, as defensive mechanisms frequently make people try to 'fake it' in order to present a better picture of themselves.

THE EFFECTS OF BULLYING

The effects on health most frequently reported are psychosomatic stress symptoms (Leymann, 1992d), musculo-skeletal symptoms (Einarsen & Raknes, 1991), irritability (Niedl, 1996), anxiety (Niedl, 1996) and depression (Björkqvist, Österman & Hjelt-Bäck, 1994). Leymann (1992d) found that 'cognitive effects' (e.g. concentration problems, irritability) and 'psycho-somatic symptoms' (e.g. gastric upset, nausea) accounted for the greatest difference between bullied and non-bullied respondents, whilst Einarsen and Raknes (1991) found the strongest correlation with depression and psychological strain, the latter manifesting itself particularly in anxiety and nervous debility. One should also bear in mind that the effects of bullying on health are not straightforward, as people with health problems may be more susceptible to becoming victims of bullying (Einarsen & Raknes, 1991).

Zapf, Knortz and Kulla (1996), in comparing 'mobbing factors' with psychological health, found that 'attacking the private person' did not only show the most consistent relationship with bullying, but also appeared to have the strongest effect on psychological health.

Women's overrepresentation in studies of bullying (Björkqvist, Österman & Hjelt-Bäck, 1994; Leymann & Gustafsson, 1996; Zapf, Knortz & Kulla, 1996) is matched by greater reported effects of bullying for women than for men (Niedl, 1996; Leymann, 1992d; Einarsen & Raknes, 1991). In particular, women report more somatic problems, musculo-skeletal strain as well as depression. According to Zapf, Knortz and Kulla (1996) such differences may in part be explained by the fact that women generally report higher levels of psychological complaints.

A relationship between bullying and Post-Traumatic Stress Disorder (PTSD) is reported by several writers (Leymann & Gustafsson, 1996; Björkqvist, Österman & Hjelt-Bäck, 1994; Groeblinghoff & Becker, 1996). With reference to the criteria of PTSD laid down by the American Psychiatric Association (APA) (1987), Leymann and Gustafsson (1996) argue that PTSD may result in personality change, with two predominantly anxiety-related effects: serious depression and serious obsession. Furthermore, referring to a study of patients at a rehabilitation clinic for long-term sufferers of bullying, Leymann and Gustafsson point out that compared with patients who had been diagnosed as suffering from PTSD resulting from involvement in traumatic accidents, victims of bullying showed significantly higher values of PTSD.

Whilst the APA definition of PTSD referred to above is concerned with single, acute trauma, Scott and Stradling (1994) suggest, on the basis of an analysis of recent clinical experience with employment-related stressors, that the AMA definition ought to distinguish between acute and enduring psychological stressors, referring to the latter as Post-Traumatic Prolonged Duress (PTPD), and its possible implications for treatment.

Leymann's (1992a) suggestion that bullying may account for a considerable number of suicides is controversial. On the basis of reports from Swedish pastors working in Stockholm and involved in counselling of suicidal persons and families of suicide victims, Leymann hypothesized that annually between 100 and 300 people in Sweden may commit suicide as a result of conditions in their work environment. Einarsen, Raknes, Mathiesen and Hellesøy (1994) refer to such figures as speculative, due to the many uncertainties involved in estimation and the underlying assumption that suicide may be linked to a single cause. However, their own findings suggest that as many as 40% of the most frequently bullied victims in their survey (at least once a week over the last six months) admitted to having contemplated suicide, thereby suggesting that suicide may be a last resort for some victims of bullying.

Reliable figures of the economic impact on organizations, industry and society as a whole are not available. We acknowledge that a large number of uncertain factors will undermine the reliability of any attempt to calculate costs. It appears that a considerable percentage of targets of bullying decide to quit or leave their employment as a result of the bullying process and this alone presents identifiable costs—UK figures show 25% of targets (Rayner, 1997; UNISON, 1997). Other negative cost effects occurred as a result of lower motivation, sickness absenteeism, social-security claims, increased turnover rates and loss of productivity (Rayner & Cooper, 1997; Leymann, 1996; Einarsen et al., 1994; Bassman, 1992).

EXPLAINING BULLYING

Einarsen (1996) has identified three main causal models of workplace bullying, emphasizing: (1) aspects of personality of bullies and victims; (2) inherent characteristics of human interactions in organizations; and (3) contextual or environmental factors related to work organization.

Some longitudinal studies of bullying in school (Perry, Kusel & Perry, 1988) argue that the personality characteristics often identified with bullies and victims are relatively stable personality traits, reaching beyond childhood and adolescence into adulthood (Randall, 1997). It is also common to describe the behaviour of bullies and victims in terms of pathology or various personality disorders (Brodsky, 1976; Crawford, 1992; Randall, 1997). According to this model personality traits associated with bullying and victimization are largely the products of early childhood experience, emphasizing the role of parental style and parent–child interaction. Aided by social learning theory (Bandura, 1973), behavioural patterns observed in adults are seen as reflecting childhood development through processes of positive reinforcement and modelling (Randall, 1997). Supported by some longitudinal studies (Olweus, 1979; Eron, Huesmann, Dubow, Romanoff & Yarnel, 1987), this view gives rise to the idea of a 'life cycle of violence' in which bullying behaviour, established and perfected in childhood and adolescence, continues to express itself in a variety of situations throughout life (Randall, 1997). It is suggested that this topic in particular should be treated with extreme care as the implications are that young people could be labelled very early in their lives with major subsequent consequences. There are also some serious methodological flaws, for example it does not deal with the findings from school research where as many children identify themselves as both bullies *and* targets (but with different people) as identified themselves as bullies only (O'Moore & Hillery, 1988).

Psychoanalytical approaches focusing on inherent characteristics of human interactions view interpersonal conflict, and what is referred to as 'disposal of aggression', as a normal feature of organizational life (Thylefors, 1987; Brodsky, 1976; Crawford, 1992; Stokes, 1994). Thylefors (1987) portrays bullying as a scapegoating process in which frustrations are projected onto individuals, thereby fulfilling the needs of individuals (bullies) and the organization. Here 'frustration' is primarily identified with 'impulses which are perceived as unacceptable to ourselves, conflicts and blame' (Eagle & Newton, 1981), and conflictual thoughts or impulses more than the potential frustration which grows out of alienation from work (Thylefors, 1987). Such processes are seen to reflect coping strategies learnt from dealing with frustration in childhood. It is, above all, those situations which may resemble experiences in childhood which may lead to a reapplication of behavioural patterns, in particular where earlier coping strategies have not been adjusted for later in life (Thylefors, 1987; Crawford, 1992). Typically such approaches rely on the experience of the therapist rather than empirical evidence.

Environmental or contextual factors are identified as causal factors by a number of researchers (Leymann, 1987; Einarsen, Raknes & Mathiesen, 1994; Björkqvist, Österman & Hjelt-Bäck, 1994; Vartia, 1995, 1996; Brodsky, 1976; McCarthy, 1996). Among aspects of the environment which appear to have the strongest influence of bullying are 'quality of leadership' (Vartia, 1996; Einarsen, Raknes & Mathiesen, 1994; Ashforth, 1994), 'work-control' and 'autonomy' (Vartia, 1996; Einarsen, Raknes & Mathiesen, 1994) and 'role-conflict' (Einarsen, Raknes & Mathiesen, 1994). Findings suggesting that time pressure and the presence of a hectic work environment are particularly associated with bullying (Appelberg, Romanov, Honlasalo & Koskenvuo, 1991) are not supported (Einarsen, Raknes, & Mathiesen, 1994). However, combined with lack of work control or autonomy, pressurized work is found to have a bearing upon bullying (Einarsen, Raknes & Mathiesen, 1994). Time-pressure is still seen to affect bullying indirectly as constraints on time impinge upon the possibility of constructive conflict resolution (Zapf, Knortz & Kulla, 1996). As far as 'leadership' is concerned, abuse of power (Einarsen, Raknes & Mathiesen, 1994), communication problems and authoritarian management methods (Vartia, 1996), as well as abdication of leadership responsibility in conflict situations, are seen to be connected with bullying (Ashforth, 1994; Einarsen et al., 1994).

Some factors related to the quality of the work environment were seen to play a moderating role in bringing about bullying, for example, social support (Zapf, Knortz & Kulla, 1996; Einarsen, Raknes & Mathiesen, 1994) and employee involvement in the decision-making process (Vartia, 1996). Einarsen et al. (1994) also found that observers of bullying tend to report a more negative work environment than those reporting no bullying, giving support to the idea that bullying cannot be solely explained as resulting from a general negative mood or 'negative affectivity' in victims (Watson & Clark, 1984).

Aggression Theory

The fact that most theories of aggression come from experimental psychology, primarily from contrived settings between strangers (Geen, 1990), reduces the direct applicability of such theories to situations of bullying, where the individuals involved know each other with all that that entails for past and future interaction. Furthermore, studies of aggression have mainly focused on affective as opposed to instrumental aggression. With these reservations in mind, reference is frequently made to the aggression literature.

According to Geen (1990) the dividing point between present theories of aggression is not the potential role given to social learning theory in explaining initial learning, but on the role of environmental factors in enacting or 'bringing out' aggressive behaviour. What is important is this dynamic between characteristics of person and situation and the cognitive processes which underpins this interaction.

Berkowitz (1989) suggests that frustration may be mediated to cause aggression by negative affect, resulting from arousal derived from external circumstances, for example, stress. In contrast, the 'social interactionist' perspective (Felson, 1992) argues that situational or external factors (in contrast to psychological characteristics of individuals), may affect bullying indirectly by eliciting rule and norm-violating behaviour. Bullying may, therefore, be seen as an intentional response to such behaviour and an instrument for social control.

In evaluating the potential contribution of any of these models in accounting for the relationship between external factors, that is stress and bullying, Einarsen, Raknes and Mathiesen (1994) suggest that both victims and bullies would have to take part in a study where both levels of stress and bullying are measured, in line with Berkowitz (1989), bullies should be identified with particularly high stress levels, whilst the social interactionist model would suggest higher levels of stress for victims.

Linking attribution theory with aggression (Geen, 1990), Zillmann's (1978) theory of 'excitation transfer' may also offer a possible explanation of bullying. Based on the idea that anger may be an intervening variable between frustration and aggression, this theory suggests that when two arousing conditions follow each other sequentially over a limited time span, some of the arousal produced by event one may be transferred and added to event two. In this way, any activity (unconnected to the second event) which raises the level of arousal, when combined with some kind of provocation, can function as an antecedent of aggression if combined with a new provocation. In such situations, the raised arousal level may lead to a cognitive labelling of the first provocation as 'anger'. In a new encounter with the 'provocateur', the anger from the first event may be cognitively reinstated. The time-lag between the events is of importance, as too little time between the events would prevent attribution failure or what is referred to as displaced aggression. In a stressful environment, with many opportunities for arousal, such a theory may explain some cases of bullying which, on the face of it, seem to result from pathological behaviour. In such cases, a relatively minor and harmless provocation could be the first stage in an escalating series of attacks and counterattacks. The targets' perception of such acts as malicious may also strengthen their response (thereby reinforcing the process).

Cox and Leather's (1994) attempt to apply a cognitive behavioural theory of aggression to the concept of 'violence at work' may also prove valuable for workplace bullying. In their view, aggression should be understood as a coping response or problem-solving approach to frustrations. Within this model, aggression is interpreted in the light of the subjective perception of those involved influenced by values and expectations. By emphasizing the importance of identifying the 'structure and dynamics of the cognitive representation underpinning aggression', the concept of aggression may be tied in with the transactional concept of stress (Lazarus, 1976).

Attribution Theory

In understanding bullying, we have been drawing on subjective reports—although it is hoped that in the future these will come from all players other than just the target. In attending to this problem, attribution theory is attractive in that it explores some of the dynamics which may be involved.

Attribution theory (Kelly, 1972) and its applied development (e.g. Weiner, 1990; Baron, 1990) has been recognized by many researchers in the bullying field (e.g. Einarsen et al., 1994; Niedl, 1996; Rayner & Hoel, 1997). Its contribution is at two levels—first in identifying that self-reports can be skewed, and second, in understanding the process itself.

A finding from attribution studies is that individuals tend to project the reasons for positive experiences towards themselves, and for negative experinegative experience, it is likely that we will find 'blame' being placed by targets on their external environment. Björkqvist, Österman and Hjelt-Bäck (1994) found targets assigned more reasons for bullying to the bully than to the target. Candidates for blame could include not only the bully, but the organizational climate and perhaps even the wider societal level.

Jones and Davis (1965) have developed this and refer to a fundamental attribution failure' which can occur when people are in negative dyadic relationships. This suggests that people tend to explain their own behaviour with reference to their environment, whilst explaining the behaviour of others by personality. Kile (1990b) explored this further in the context of bullying at work. He found a progressive situation, where targets consider themselves increasingly less responsible for their own experience over time. This process appears to go hand-in-hand with greater condemnation of the bully or others whom they blame, so that in the end nothing less than a full vindication of their own actions is acceptable to them. It follows that for the severely traumatized targets, as is likely for individuals in samples taken from clinical settings, researchers need to take into account processes of attribution, especially for chronic cases.

In raising the issue of 'blame', attribution theory provides a useful warning against simplistic analyses of bullying situations taken solely from target reports. This is not to say that target reports are inaccurate, but that their cognitive selection of events, and subsequent emphasis placed on some events rather than others to back up a self-vindicating picture, could be an issue. Indeed, the same processes may be applied to all other players including the bully and those within the organization who do or do not help (Kaplan & Miller, 1979).

Anecdotal evidence (e.g. Adams, 1992; Brodsky, 1976) points to the importance of labelling for targets. Through labelling themselves as being bullied, targets apparently start to understand what is happening to them and this affects their future actions (Bassman, 1992; Einarsen & Hellesøy, 1998). What appears to be problematic is that the implicit outcome of the label is to cast the target as a 'victim', and subsequent judgements can be dramatically affected (Zedner, 1994).

Inherent in aggression theory is the concept of 'intent' on the part of the perpetrator, which has already been partly discussed. The original use of intent in aggression theory was to be able to discount 'accidental' acts on the part of a perpetrator. How far one would want to utilize this in a bullying context, where the perpetrator may claim ignorance, has already been mentioned. Attribution theory presents the clearest challenge to using intent, as it can neither be closely defined nor verified—which is well discussed by Tedeschi (Tedeschi, 1984).

In Geen's (1990) words: 'The relationship between an interpersonal attack and aggression is not a simple one. One does not always lead to the other. One important variable that mediates the connection between an attack and subsequent aggression is the victim's interpretation of the meaning and intent of the attack.' Geen's comments were made in the context of retaliatory attacks, and these are seldom documented in the literature. Anecdotal data mention desire for retaliation, for example, murderous thoughts against the bully (Adams, 1992; Field, 1996). American studies of extreme violence at work (e.g. Mantell, 1994), where employees physically attack others, provide a possible thread where some of the perpetrators of the violence appear to have been bullied by those they then attack—in some instances fatally. How far attribution theory can provide insight into retaliatory attacks remains an area for future systematic research.

Linking cognitive attribution theory and the personality literature is the construct of negative affectivity. Burke, Brief and George (1993), for example, have found that people who have high negative affect report stresses and strains more. The implication is that there may be a personality-linked predisposition to assign negative meaning and labels, which could act as a multiplier for an attribution bias, or even as a basis for it. Fundamental to this process is the issue of cause and effect—whether people develop negative affect because of what has happened to them, or whether they interpret what has happened to them as negative because of a predisposition. further work remains to be done in this area, with preliminary work in the pipeline (e.g. Einarsen, 1996).

Bullying and Stress

The relationship between workplace bullying and stress features prominently in most studies into workplace bullying. However, the wide variety of approaches in general use (Beehr, 1995; Sutherland & Cooper, 1990) is reflected also in the bullying literature (Leymann, 1996; Wilkie, 1996).

Stress is understood as the perceived imbalance between internal and external demands facing an individual, and the perceived ability of the individual to cope (Einarsen & Raknes, 1991; Niedl, 1995; Zapf, 1997; Zapf, Knortz & Kulla, 1996). This stress model, referred to as the transactional concept of stress (Cox, 1978, 1993), draws on the concepts of appraisal and coping, acknowledging that stress is a subjective experience based on the person's appraisal of the situation and opportunity for coping (Lazarus, 1966). The transactional concept of stress emphasizes that the experience of stress (in its negative connotation of distress) is dynamic and should be seen as a transaction between individual and situation, rather than either one in isolation (Lazarus, 1966).

The contribution of stress in any causal model of bullying is taken furthest by German and Austrian researchers, who refer to bullying as a form of extreme social stress, a subset of social stressors at work and primarily an indicator of the situation in the workplace (Niedl, 1995; Zapf, 1997). Among Cooper and Marshall's (1976) categories of occupational stressors, bullying fits into 'relationships at work'. Until recently social stress or stressful social relationships at work have received little attention within stress research (Sutherland & Cooper, 1990; Niedl, 1995; Beehr, 1995; Zapf, Knortz & Kulla, 1996). Where social relationships have been examined as part of such research programmes, the emphasis has been largely on the impact of social support as a moderator of stress. Zapf, Knortz & Kulla (1996) emphasize that social stress should not be understood as the opposite of social support. The fact that one may receive social support from someone one does not necessarily like, should emphasize this point (Zapf, Knortz & Kulla, 1996).

In addressing the absence of research into social stressors, it is suggested that, as opposed to stressors arising from the environment and the work-task itself, social stressors are more subjective in character and influenced by the interests and values of the observer (Mergner, 1989). Moreover, their complexity and the fact that social stressors may not be reproduced, as they are unequivocally connected to the particular situation in which they occurred, renders them difficult to study, with implications for methodology (Niedl, 1995).

There are clear advantages in defining bullying as social stress, not least of a methodological nature. It may be argued that by including bullying among recognized work stressors, it may be possible to remove some of the stigma often attached to victims, as well as helping organizations to acknowledge and counteract the presence of bullying.

Management Literature

Managers appear to be a major source of the behaviours that are perceived as bullying (Rayner, 1997; Einarsen, 1996) which is not surprising as it is felt by many that bullying is linked to power relationships (Adams, 1992; Bassman, 1992; Ashforth, 1994; Crawford, 1997). This said, the management literature appears to take little account of management behaviour which may be perceived as negative or destructive. Primarily focusing on effective management, the emphasis within management research has largely been on how to stimulate or improve 'positive' behaviour, rather than reducing behaviour of a negative kind (Yukl, 1994). Ashforth (1994), who refers to those managers who assault subordinates verbally, or are arbitrary in their dealings with employees, who belittle others and whose style of conflict resolution is force, as 'petty tyrants', is among a few notable exceptions.

The extent to which management behaviour may be consistently exhibited in different situations has received some attention, with Rahim and Magner (1995) finding support for such a view, whilst others, for example Van de Vliert, Nauta, Euwema & Janssen (1997), suggest that a variety of styles will be employed by the same person simultaneously. The contradictory nature of these findings appears to support a view that bullying cannot simply be explained in terms of the personality traits of those involved or of the situation (Einarsen et al., 1994).

In contrast to much of the research into conflicts within organizations, Putnam (1997) starts with the assumption that conflict is a normal aspect of organizational life, which should not necessarily be avoided. Supporting such a view, Jehn (1997) makes a distinction between conflicts about task, and what is referred to as emotional or 'affective' conflict, though acknowledging that a clear conceptual distinction between these two constructs is difficult to obtain. With this methodological reservation in mind, Jehn (1997) found task conflict to be related to increased levels of performance, whilst emotional conflict, arguably central to the experience of bullying, appears to have a negative effect on performance as well as on task satisfaction.

Where the conflict literature may inform future bullying research is in respect of conflict escalation and de-escalation (Van de Vliert et al., 1997; Fisher, 1997) as well as the potential role of mediation in the management of conflict (e.g. Fisher, 1997; Donnolen & Kolb, 1997). However, the fact that most studies use contrived situations with students (e.g. Baron, 1988; Jehn, 1994), reflecting the limitations placed by ethical considerations on work of this type (e.g. Guastello, 1995; Geen, 1990), undermines the potential for generalization of results to the context of work. This is particularly true since individuals involved in bullying, in contrast to those participating in experimental conflict studies, have interacted in the past and will continue to co-exist, which would affect the dynamics of the process.

REMEDIAL ACTION

Whilst research into school bullying has produced some useful evidence of the effectiveness of anti-bullying programmes (Olweus, 1991, 1997; Smith & Sharp, 1994; Smith, 1997a), the literature concerning workplace bullying still largely relies on propositions inferred from experience in related areas of study such as stress and violence, as well as more general theories of management, harassment and organizational behaviour. There appears to be a consensus that the main responsibility for preventing bullying has to be with management, which is urged to take a moral stand on the issue (Resch & Schubinski, 1996). The support of senior managers is also seen as a precondition for any successful intervention (Olweus, 1991). For example, Brodsky (1976) argues that bullying ultimately rests on management consent, while Einarsen et al. (1994) suggest that managers take on the responsibility for providing work-cultures free of bullying. The fact that certain negative leadership characteristics have been identified as likely antecedents of bullying (Einarsen, Raknes & Mathiesen, 1994; Vartia, 1996), also suggests that any programme aimed at preventing bullying needs to start with management.

Cox and Cox (1993), discussing possible organizational responses to psycho-social and organizational hazards at work, suggest that management control strategies should be directed at three different levels; prevention, intervention and rehabilitation. We would suggest that this general framework, applied in theory to the prevention of workplace violence (Cox & Leather, 1994) would also be useful in the case of bullying. Their approach acknowledges the need for actions directed at individuals as well as organizations and similarly emphasizes people's perceptions or 'subjective' understanding of the situation, as well as the more 'objective' presence of potential antecedents.

Resch and Schubinski (1996) suggest that preventive strategies should involve management training not least aimed at problem acknowledgement. Some initiatives are arguably a response to research findings indicating that preventive strategies should aim at increasing employees' control over their work situation (e.g. Zapf, Knortz & Kulla, 1996; Einarsen et al., 1994), thereby positively affecting stress levels (Karasek, 1979; Karasek & Theorell, 1990). Whilst there is a danger that such initiatives become nothing more than 'window dressing' exercises, employee involvement aimed at increasing worker control over task, time and situation has proved to be very difficult to implement in practice. Despite statutory support (e.g. Norway), initiatives to involve employees in planning and control of their work have had limited success, not least due to the fact that such initiatives are seen to represent a redistribution of power within the workplace (Gustavsen, 1988). One may also argue that as long as preventive actions hinge on management initiatives, the risk of reinforcing management control appears to be present, thereby possibly increasing rather than reducing the likelihood of bullying.

The selection process has frequently been identified as the proper arena for effective anti-bullying initiatives, by denying potential bullies access (Randall, 1996; Adams, 1992) as well as avoiding inappropriate promotions (Thylefors, 1987). We will argue that the effectiveness of such organizational approaches is likely to be limited, in particular when directed at the pathological bully (Crawford, 1992). The reliability of many selection instruments is weak (Smith & Robertson, 1986). To ensure their effectiveness, ideally they need to be linked to more intrusive investigations of previous employment, which may be unrealistic as well as undesirable. The irony is that such methods are just as likely to hinder the very individuals which they set out to protect. Moreover, such initiatives may simply lead to the promotion of more devious strategies on the part of the bully.

Traditionally, initiatives in the policy area (e.g. grievance and mediation procedures) are recognized as being part of interventionist strategies (Crabb, 1995). Evidence of case studies has given examples of ignorance of bullying amongst doctors, which has led to premature diagnosis of psychiatric illness, thereby adding to the burden of victims (Leymann, 1987; Lennane, 1996). In contrast, well-informed occupational health practitioners may represent a valuable resource, not least in assisting victims in building up their coping resources (Einarsen & Hellesøy, 1998).

However, when conflict is seen as natural and at times even beneficial to organizational effectiveness (Van de Vliert et al., 1997) policies and procedures aimed at resolving conflict before it escalates to a level where victimization is established, may be viewed as a preventive strategy. Mediation, particularly when assessed by neutral third parties (Fisher, 1997), may also provide the opportunity for learning and reflection, as well as reducing feelings of powerlessness by means of employee participation in the development and implementation of such strategies (Donnellon & Kolb, 1997). The mediation process may also hold a potential for revealing underlying causes of conflict, as well as underlying patterns of behaviour, if there is a willingness on the part of the organization to move from individual cases to more general phenomena (Donnellon & Kolb, 1997). Research into 'sexual harassment' has repeatedly acknowledged the individualization of the problem (Fitzgerald & Schullman, 1993; George, 1997). As long as the onus of initiating any organizational response appears to be on victims, individualization becomes a barrier against the revelation of proper knowledge of its prevalence and its various manifestations, as well as an impediment to more wide-reaching organizational responses. The same argument appears to apply to bullying.

Rehabilitation initiatives have largely centred around initiatives aimed at victims of the more extreme cases of bullying, often given the diagnosis Post-Traumatic Stress Syndrome (PTSD) (e.g. Leymann & Gustafsson, 1996). The expressed aim of such strategies has been to establish a therapeutic regime directed at rebuilding a disabled personality. Reinstatement has often been a primary aim and frequently a response to victims' wishes. As a general strategy this appears to be perfectly reasonable. However, there will be situations where it is in the interest neither of the individual nor the organization to return to the past. Moreover, bearing in mind present shortcomings regarding organizational responses to workplace bullying, we tend to agree with Kile (1990a) when he rhetorically asks whether an official apology and occupational reinstatement 'is worth 20 years of someone's life'.

METHODOLOGICAL ISSUES

Despite the fact that anecdotal evidence (e.g. Bassman, 1992; Thylefors, 1987) of bullying is slowly being replaced by more systematic qualitative and empirical evidence, a number of problems of methodological character need to be addressed. As identified in the earlier discussion on defining bullying, there are significant inconsistencies in operationalizing the term 'bullying' across studies. Methodological approaches and measures are contingent upon a more clearly defined bullying construct.

We have already established two distinct approaches in measuring incidence rates and severity of bullying: (1) respondents are presented with a precise definition of bullying and asked to state whether they would label themselves as bullied, given alternatives of duration and frequency of exposure (Einarsen & Raknes, 1991; Rayner, 1997); and (2) respondents rate their own experience against an inventory of behaviour identified with bullying and supplied with alternatives of duration and frequency of exposure. In light of the distinction between subjective versus objective methods, Einarsen (1996) feels that (1) may be referred to as more subjective than method (2). However, if victimization and stress outcomes are an inherent part of the experience being measured in (2), these will also be affected by the subjectivity of reporting, and the results revealed by method (1) may be seen as the more objective measure of bullying (Einarsen, 1996).

The subjectivity–objectivity debate is central to construct development for bullying at work. How far subjective experience should be taken into account is a difficult issue. This problem is intrinsically connected with the extensive reliance on perceptual or 'subjective' data based on self-report in bullying in particular. This distinction between 'subjective' and 'objective' measurement is in need of some clarification. Frese and Zapf (1988) point to the increasing influence of cognitive theory in organizational research, also reflected in this review with the recent progress within stress, conflict and aggression theory. According to Frese and Zapf, individual perception should not be understood as being the opposite of reality, as individuals' perceptions and appraisals 'do not override reality but put reality into perspective' (p.379). In their view 'objective' should be understood in the sense of a measurement of reality not influenced by the cognitive and emotional processing of any particular individual, but as an 'average' person's cognitive and emotional processing, dependent upon contextual factors such as place and time. The implications for bullying research are wide-reaching.

Self-report measures could be seen to be in need of supplementation by more objective data (e.g. observer reports or group ratings—Michela, Lukaszewski & Allegrante, 1995). However, whilst self-reports lead to a confounding of measures and, therefore, inflate correlation between variables, the use of observer data tends to deflate correlations, thereby introducing their own methodological problems (see Frese & Zapf, 1988).

However, the possibility of obtaining more objective measures of bullying by means of peer-observations (Frese & Zapf, 1988) has been questioned by Björkqvist, Österman & Hjelt-Bäck (1994), who doubt that such independent measures can be obtained if full anonymity cannot be guaranteed, and by Einarsen (1996), who in conjunction with Baumeister, Stillwell and Wotman (1990), argues that workplace conflicts seldom allow for neutral or independent positions. This may reflect the fact that workplace conflict frequently takes place against a backdrop of issues of power and control. Einarsen (1996) refers to the substantial overlap between self-report data and teachers' reports in research into school bullying in assessing the validity of their own findings drawn exclusively from self-reports. However, there are significant qualitative differences between the players and the context in these two arenas (i.e. schools and the workplace) for bullying research and they should be acknowledged.

In interpreting the empirical findings (i.e. Table 5.1), many of the problems encountered in the bullying literature are similar to those identified with cross-sectional research design in general (Zapf, 1997; Einarsen, 1996). Among such problems are in particular 'common method variance', which refers to variance in measurement resulting from features of the method employed rather than from the investigated variables (Spector & Brannick, 1995). The effect of common method variance is an inflation of correlations between variables measured by self-report questionnaires (e.g. Schonfeld, Rhee & Xia, 1995; Zapf, Knortz and Kulla, 1996). A number of aspects of the measurement process relevant to bullying may introduce systematic influences on observed scores related to respondents' stimuli, as well as the research procedure itself (Spector & Brannick, 1995). Among such method effects are those connected with 'third variables' which tend to influence both the dependent and independent variables. As far as bullying is concerned, relevant third variables may be negative affectivity (Watson & Clark, 1984), as negative mood may affect perception of the work environment as well as of the experience of being bullied, locus of control (Rotter, 1966) and social desirability effect (Crowne & Marlowe, 1964), which themselves may be interrelated (i.e. mood and social desirability, Spector & Brannick, 1995).

From a procedural (design) point of view, it is suggested that some of the confounding processes may be reduced by measuring the dependent and independent variables separately (Schonfeld, Rhee & Xia, 1995; Frese & Zapf, 1988), and by means of research instruments with neutrally worded items in order to reduce the influence of cognitive and emotional processes (Fitzgerald & Shullman, 1993; Frese and Zapf, 1988), for example, the avoidance of assigning meaning to events after they have taken place. If we apply such rules to bullying research, we will find that Leymann's LIPT approach (Leymann, 1990b) includes emotionally loaded items—perhaps not surprising considering that their source is from in-depth interviews with targets. This situation is not helped by the fact that several studies measuring the relationship between bullying and work environment quality (e.g. Einarsen, Raknes & Mathiesen, 1994; Vartia, 1996) have been criticized for using non-established research instruments (Zapf, 1997). Adaptations of the LIPT have been used by several researchers in an attempt to avoid this very criticism (e.g. Niedl, 1995; Zapf, Knortz & Kulla, 1996).

Operationalizing variables in more than one way might be a way to compensate for some of the shortcomings and weaknesses of cross-sectional design. However, because method variance operates at the level of the specific trait–method combination, the choice of approach is important as methods, which at face value appear to be very dissimilar, may turn out to be influenced by the same third variables (e.g. the influence of social desirability on interviews as well as observation, Spector & Brannick, 1995).

It is widely accepted that cross-sectional designs do not allow robust causality inferences (Zapf, Dormann & Frese, 1996). A further useful distinction highly relevant to studies of bullying, is that between 'real cause' and statistical cause (Zapf, 1997). For example, an overrepresentation of physically disabled people among victims of bullying (e.g. Leymann, 1992e) may appear to suggest that disability is a cause of bullying. However, it is argued that the 'real' cause of bullying should not be sought in the disability itself, which is a variable uninfluenced by psychological factors, but within the actual group or organization (Zapf, 1997; Leymann, 1987).

In order to find a way out of the many problems connected with cross-sectional research design, not least the problem of causality, longitudinal studies have often been seen as a potential solution. However, according to Zapf, Dormann & Frese (1996) this is far from being the case and more attention has to be given to procedural problems concerning such design. Furthermore, as far as bullying is concerned, longitudinal designs will probably prove problematic. Sampling is one such problem. It is argued that in order to ensure results regarding rates of prevalence of bullying of a magnitude of 3.5% (e.g. Leymann, 1992b) you would need an initial sample of 8000 (Zapf, 1997), figures which throw some doubt on the feasibility of such studies. The use of experimental studies, which could otherwise have confirmed direction of causality with greater certainty, are ruled out due to ethical concerns (Zapf, 1997; Einarsen, 1997).

Another key problem related to sampling is the issue of access. It is not a coincidence that the majority of studies have been done within clinical settings (e.g. Leymann, 1990) or in participation with trade unions (Einarsen & Skogstad, 1996). Problems relating to power and politics at the micro level have already been referred to. These are very live issues at the organizational level when attempting to gain access through employers. The use of self-reports of targets reflects an access problem. Researchers seem well aware that a wider scope beyond target self-reports is needed; as shown above, however, finding methodologies to achieve this is extremely difficult with access being pivotal.

A final point regarding methodology connected to quantitative research is that of the scope of the research, which once again reflects conceptualization of the construct. At what level should one be measuring? Zapf (1997) provides four interplaying levels for analysis, and this breadth of approach is reflected in work which extends the bullying at work literature into society (e.g. McCarthy, Sheehan & Kearns, 1995), the organization (e.g. Einarsen & Raknes (1991), the work group (e.g. Hubert, 1997), and at the individual level (e.g. Leymann, 1990a).

The above comments apply largely to quantitative research strategies of a survey or empirical type. In order to capture the subtleties involved with the process of bullying, as well as to reveal more information regarding possible causal links between variables, such studies can be supplemented by other research strategies of a more qualitative nature, employing a range of research instruments such as case studies, semi-structured interviews and focus groups. Whilst the bullying literature refers to a number of such studies (e.g. Adams, 1992; Randall, 1997) criticisms has been forthcoming regarding their methodology. Where case studies have been used, the problem of representativeness due to self-selection is often evident (Randall, 1997), whether the selection method is a direct form of self-selection (e.g. 'help-line'—Field, 1996; Adams, 1992) or more indirectly, by case identification through media, court cases or 'snow-balling' (Zapf, Knortz & Kulla, 1996; Leymann, 1992a). Once again one observes the near total focus on targets or victims of bullying (Rayner & Hoel, 1997; Zapf, 1997).

The emotive aspect of the issue of bullying also appears to have a bearing upon the quality of data, brought about not least by insufficient distance to the cases leading to an intermingling of the 'voice' of the interviewee with that of the interviewer in reports (e.g. Randall, 1997; Field, 1996; Adams, 1992). The remarks made earlier regarding the need for separating information concerning the independent and the dependent variables, in order to reduce the influence of cognitive processes, should also apply to such studies.

Niedl (1996) addresses the problem of the almost complete absence of studies focusing on the complexity of the bullying process, aiming at identifying different strategies for coping with being a target of bullying. However, this study demonstrates that targets of bullying do not choose simple fight or flight reactions when faced with bullying, but try a series of 'constructive strategies' before eventually frequently withdrawing their commitment to the organization or leaving the organization altogether. This underlines Beehr's (1995) point that people are proactive and not just passive with regard to what happens to them.

DISCUSSION

Studies reviewed in this article of bullying at work are generally rather recent—most within this decade. Whilst arguably previous work (e.g. Brodsky, 1976) began to explore this phenomenon, it can be seen as an emergent area of study in the 1990s. Many of the issues brought out in the previous text have highlighted problems which can be seen as typical in such new topics for study (e.g. Gutek, 1985).

The bullying debate has seen significant development in recent years, not least through the ability of researchers to identify high relevance of other areas of study such as sexual harassment, aggression, conflict and stress, which not only provide helpful signposts for possible resolution but also highlight unresolved difficulties within and between such disciplines whose perspectives can confound and complicate their contribution to this field.

The complexity of the problem of workplace bullying is illustrated in complicated models which serve as a framework for conceptual thinking around the processes involved (e.g. Einarsen, 1996; Zapf, 1997). Common to these models is the multiplicity of possible cause and effect relationships and the dynamics of the processes involved, where possible process outcomes may serve as antecedents for further conflict escalation, though at no stage in the process can the next stage or the final outcomes be fully predicted. Therefore, in so far as it makes sense to talk about a concept of bullying, it hinges on the only element common to all cases, that is the victim's perceived experience of being at the receiving end of some form of persistent, harassing behaviour. It follows that simple explanations of any kind, for example viewing bullying as the result solely of the work of pathological minds or the expression of stable personality traits or, likewise, interpreting bullying as purely the result of contextual factors, must, therefore, be rejected. Zapf (1997) captures the complexity nicely. In a study of victims of bullying, four different victim groups are identified, each primarily related to a specific set of antecedents hinging on the characteristics of: the bully, the victim, the work group and the work environment. This suggests that it is critical to identify what part of the problem we are paying attention to (Einarsen, 1997).

As emphasized over the previous pages, these related areas of study appear to have certain elements in common: a focus on the distinction between 'subjective' and 'objective' and a recognition of non-linearity and dynamics associated with process development, both elements mediated by recent development in cognitive theory (Ford & Kraiger, 1995). This development applies not least to stress research. As we have already suggested, there are undoubtedly advantages in defining bullying as 'social stress', for example with regard to the role of the coping process in mediating the relationship between stressors and strain. A focus on the coping process will highlight the impact of coping resources throughout the bullying processes, with implications for both conflict prevention and conflict resolution.

However, whilst stress theory operates at the level of the individual, bullying is most often a complex, dyadic affair, in which the parties share a past as well as a future. This suggests that it may be difficult to identify where the conflict started, as disagreement may exist as to what critical action actually sparked off the conflict, as well as what is to be understood as action and reaction (Mummendey, Linneweber & Loschper, 1984). As we have established, bullying is not to be understood as individual hostile or aggressive acts, but a series of acts or episodes linked together. This suggests a need for theoretical perspectives which acknowledge the role and nature of the dynamics of interaction (Keashly, 1998), which is seen to be 'more than the sum of its parts'. The fact that role reversion may take place during the course of conflict further complicates matters (Einarsen et al., 1994).

The above factors also suggest that the time element in the bullying process is of importance, a fact which is emphasized in construct operationalization (e.g. Leymann, 1992b). The time element is also acknowledged in the stress literature (Frese & Zapf, 1988) where it is seen to affect the relationship between exposure and strain (Zapf, Dormann & Frese, 1996). For example, whilst the 'stress-reaction' model suggests that exposure to stressors will lead to strain after a certain time, though if the stressors are removed the strain would gradually disappear, the 'accumulation' model indicates that an irreversible shift may take place after exposure to stressors over a particular period of time, which in spite of removal of the stressors may become permanent. Depending upon which perspective you take, there are clear implications for organizational intervention and conflict resolution.

The (mediating) role of attributions in bullying has been emphasized and a number of possible attributional processes at work acknowledged. Further studies on how people pass judgement on others' behaviour, not least how weight is assigned to particular information (Mummendey, Linneweber & Loschper, 1984) are needed. This is not least the case in order to establish how victims come to conclude that the bully is 'evil' (Kile, 1990b).

Despite progress, the central problem of construct clarification relating to what constitutes bullying at work is one which remains unresolved and which requires immediate debate by those working in the area. It is our opinion that subjectivity cannot be completely avoided, partly because of methodological problems, but more importantly because perceptions and the process of labelling are seen to be at the heart of the problem (Niedl, 1995). Therefore, in order to embrace the process of bullying at work, one cannot ignore the importance of the subjective element of experience. This is not to say that remedial approaches such as the banning of certain types of behaviour because they 'might' have a negative effect on people is wrong, but that the study of phenomena such as bullying at work is intrinsically caught up with reactions and counteractions typical of 'process' environments. However, whether the subjectivity extends from describing experiences at work as negative and unpleasant to labelling oneself as 'bullied', is crucial—especially in incidence studies. However, there appears to be a consensus that false negative reports (not labelling themselves as being bullied when they were) are more likely than 'false positive' (labelling themselves as being bullied when they were not) (Adams, 1992; Niedl, 1995; Einarsen & Hellesøy, 1998). Criteria to enable participants to label bullying can be generated and are used in studies (e.g. Einarsen & Raknes, 1996; Rayner, 1997), as well as in studies of the related area of sexual harassment (Fitzgerald & Schullman, 1993), but to ask people to reflect on and consider their experience may be inappropriate in the usually short space of time used to complete questionnaires. It is also questionable whether descriptors would apply equally to all contexts of work. Discourse analysis, in which shared ways of thinking, talking and behaving in specific contexts feature, may be a useful source of normative and 'objective' information to the understanding of conflict behaviour and interactions in general (Donnellon & Kolb, 1997), and possibly applicable to this particular problem.

While we are acutely aware of the problems of involving self-labelling as part of a definition, it is important to consider the consequences if one does not use it. Given the use of incidence studies in generating employer-specific policy (e.g. UNISON, 1997) and sometimes national policy (e.g. Leymann's work influencing the establishment of Swedish law), the 'audience' for such research must also be taken into account. If one is in a culture where employers deny or avoid the issue of bullying at work (e.g. Rayner & Cooper, 1997; McCarthy, 1996), the lack of inclusion of both subjective labelling and other criteria (e.g. the number of people who have left their jobs because of bullying at work) may well continue to act as excuse for continuing such tactics.

Given the lack of third-party evidence in incidence studies (which may be present, but not included among survey questions), incidence rates will always be open to question. It is of interest to examine what would make the subjectively reported experience valid in the sceptics' eyes. Third-party reports from within the organization are likely to be tainted by the power and political environment (Zapf, 1997; Björkqvist, Österman & Hjelt-Bäck, 1994). 'Neutral' third-party reports may be assessed by trained counsellors, occupational health practitioners, human resource management professionals or trade union representatives, for example, but probably difficult to assess in sufficient numbers, on a practical basis.

The focus on cognitive processes runs the danger of (increasingly) interpreting the bullying processes through the lens of the victim, thereby indicating that bullying is 'all in the mind'. We will suggest that by removing the issue from its context we may run the risk of cutting ourselves off from proactive responses based on risk assessment and subsequent elimination or reduction of risk (Hoel, 1997; Spurgeon, 1997). Any organizational response to bullying must, therefore, as a starting point, be able to identify and measure with a degree of certainty the risk present, based on instruments which acknowledge the subjective as well as objective elements involved.

Furthermore, one may also argue that a one-sided emphasis on perception and cognitive processes may feed processes of attribution, thereby stimulating victim-blaming. Moreover, whilst a stand against bullying on principle is necessary, the complexity of the issue calls for restraint when it comes to participating in any form of allocation of blame. Victims need our support in all cases without reservation. However, in accepting victims' accounts of what happened as a valid experience, we should neither accept these as the only possible valid accounts, nor moralize when victims vividly deny any responsibility for the situation at the same time as they assess their own competence and performance in an unrealistically positive manner (Zapf, 1997).

Studies of chronic illness have identified similar processes among victims, often referred to as a 'search for credibility' (Eccleston, Williams & Rogers, 1997) and attempts to establish themselves as 'honourable' workers (Reid, Ewan & Lowy, 1991), a point also noted by Kile (1990b) in an early study of victims of bullying. Any attempt to link victimization and ill health to their own private context must be rejected as it is seen as undermining an already faltering self-esteem. According to Eccleston, Williams and Rogers (1997) it is victims' search for meaning for what has happened to them, which leads them to search for a 'story that works', and therefore, they may be in danger of rewriting the past. This leads us to draw two conclusions: first, the primary value of studies of victims of bullying with the diagnosis PTSD/ PTPD is seen as improving diagnostic tools and establishing effective re-habilitative strategies, particularly to connect to their previous environments and roles (Scott, Stradling & Lee, 1997); second, knowledge of the dy-namics of bullying should primarily be drawn from studies of dyadic conflict, where conflict escalation has still not reached the level where the parties, and in particular the victim, are both unwilling and unable to take part in con-structive conflict mediation. The above points place a significant respon-sibility on management to identify conflict at an early stage and to have in place systems which are able to stop destructive conflicts going beyond the point of no return.

The complexity of the process of bullying also suggests that it is pivotal at any time to clarify what level of analysis one is operating at (Einarsen, 1997). So far we have examined issues relating to bullying at the individual level and the dyadic level. A third level of the work group may also be apparent (e.g. Hubert, 1997), and this picture may take very different forms depending on how many people in the working group report being bullied, which can vary from everyone to just one person being singled out and victimized (UNISON, 1977). Also at this level, one would want to investigate further the 'ripple effect' on those who apparently witness others being bullied. It is too early to say whether here we are talking about a series of dyadic inter-actions or whether particular processes are at work.

Few studies have so far directed their attention at the organizational level, with Ashforth (1994) representing an exception. However, in order to get a more accurate picture of the totality of the processes involved with bullying, such studies, searching for underlying factors of contextual and structural nature, need to be undertaken. It is probably at this level that interdisciplin-ary studies may make the greatest contribution.

For organizations seeking remedies an even wider focus is necessary. It is likely that bullies undergo some form of cost-benefit calculation for their action (Björkqvist, Österman & Hjelt-Bäck, 1994). In an organization with no sanctions against bullying, the personal cost to the perpetrator is likely to be low—even though the cost to the organization may be extremely high, with high turnover and possible litigation. Policy formation may be an issue, but a more subtle area for investigation may be the 'psychological contract' which is likely to be partly if not entirely inspired at a corporate level (Mumford, 1991). Such 'implicit' contracts can be seen to penetrate deeply the expectations of employee and employers, and to go well beyond what is written in well-meaning policy statements. It is thus crucial for employers both to act and to be seen to act rather than do nothing, which is not a neutral position as far as bullying is concerned. In countries where the threat of litigation is a key factor for employers to act—for example the UK and Australia—there is an argument to suggest the analysis should go further into a broader discussion at societal level (McCarthy, 1996; Lewis, 1998).

The many shortcomings in this field of study are partly a reflection of insufficient methodological rigour, not least seen in the many publications based on careless case study design or anecdotal evidence. We acknowledge that access and corporate cooperation is a problem. However, this should not prevent us from applying stricter criteria to future studies. At the same time, as is the case in stress research, there is a need for experimentation in research design (Beehr, 1995). Such efforts in the area of research design need to go hand-in-hand with conceptual exploration, the one informing the other.

While experimental studies are ruled out for ethical reasons and particip-ants' observation is difficult, a third avenue/option may prove valuable, that is mediation. With reference to the previous argument, in-depth observation of the mediation process should be able to reveal new knowledge of conflict and conflict escalation. By means of such an approach it would also be possible to examine potential hostile attributions, contribution of the parties involved as well as examining possible underlying causes of the conflict. Such an approach may also, at least in part, fulfil the need to explore both sides of the conflict, an area still largely untouched (Zapf, 1997).

We have in earlier sections indicated that, in spite of significant progress in recent years, the issue of workplace bullying is still in need of further concep-tual clarification. Such clarification appears similarly to be a prerequisite for the type of operationalization which may be successfully applied in cross-cultural studies.

Whilst national cultural differences (Hofstede, 1991; Smith, Dugan & Trompenaars, 1996) may reduce the value of any direct comparison of levels of prevalence, such differences may also impact on the dynamics involved, thereby throwing further light on the totality of processes involved with bully-ing, and possibly opening up new avenues of research. Such expansion of the scope of research also appears to favour the human resource management arena, taking into account the increasing trend in mergers and acquisitions and as far as Europe is concerned, the ongoing processes of integration.

Future work cannot examine all the above perspectives at once, but there is scope for a very wide set of approaches. In bullying at work we hope we have shown that conceptualization of the construct is in central focus, and this impinges on the methodology adopted, and interpretation of results, as well as the ability to compare results across studies. It is important for those working in the field to stay abreast of developments of other work—whatever their level of analysis—in order to inform and evolve a more coalesced view of bullying at work, its prevalence, and the processes involved, and thus find ways to inform practitioners for preventive actions.

REFERENCES

Adams, A. (1992). *Bullying at Work: How to Confront and Overcome It.* London: Virago.
Appelberg, K., Romanov, K., Honlasalo, M.-L. & Koskenvuo, M. (1991). Interpersonal conflicts at work and psychological characteristics of employees. *Social Science Medicine*, **32**, 1051–1056.
Ashforth, B. (1994). Petty tyranny in organizations. *Human Relations*, **47**, 755–778.
Bandura, A. (1973). *Aggression: A Social Learning Analysis.* Englewood Cliffs, NJ: Prentice-Hall.
Baron, R.A. (1988). Negative effects of destructive criticism: Impact on conflict, self-efficacy, and task performance. *Journal of Applied Psychology*, **73**, 199–207.
Baron, R.A. (1990). Attributions and organisational conflict. In S. Graham & V. Volkes (Eds), *Attribution Theory: Applications to Achievement, Mental Health and Interpersonal Conflict.* Hillsdale, NJ: Erlbaum.
Baron, R.A. (1997). Positive effects of conflict: Insight from social cognition. In C. De Dreu & E. Van de Vliert (Eds), *Using Conflict in Organizations* (pp. 177–191). London: Sage Publications.
Bassman, E. (1992). *Abuse in the Workplace* Westport, CT: Quorum Books.
Baumeister, R.F., Stillwell, A. & Wotman, S.R. (1990). Victim and perpetrator accounts of interpersonal conflicts: Autobiographical narratives about anger. *Journal of Personality and Social Psychology*, **59**, 994–1005.
Beehr, T.A. (1995). *Psychological Stress in the Workplace.* London: Routledge.
Berkowitz, L. (1989). The frustration–aggression hypothesis: An examination and reformulation. *Psychological Bulletin*, **106**, 50–73.
Besag, V. (1989). *Bullies and Victims in Schools.* Milton Keynes: Open University Press.
Björkqvist, K., Österman, K. & Hjelt-Bäck, M. (1994). Aggression among university employees. *Aggressive Behaviour*, **20**, 173–184.
Björkqvist, K., Österman, K. & Lagerspetz, K.M.J. (1994). Sex differences in covert aggression among adults. *Aggressive Behaviour*, **20**, 27–33.
Brodsky, C.M. (1976). *The Harassed Worker.* Lexington, MA: D.C. Heath and Company.
Burke, M.J., Brief, A.P. & George, J.M. (1993). The role of negative affectivity in understanding relations between self-reports of stressors and strains: A comment on the applied psychology literature. *Journal of Applied Psychology*, **78**, 193–198.
Cooper, C.L. & Marshall, J. (1976). Occupational sources of stress: A review of the literature relating to coronary heart disease and mental ill health. *Journal of Occupational Psychology*, **49**, 11–28.
Cox, T. (1978). *Stress.* London: Macmillan.
Cox, T. (1993). *Stress Research and Stress Management: Putting Theory to Work.* HSE Contract research report No. 61. London: HMSO.
Cox, T. & Cox, S. (1993). Occupational health control and monitoring of psychosocial and organizational hazards at work. *Journal of the Royal Society of Health*, **221**, 201–205.
Cox, T. & Leather, P. (1994). The prevention of violence at work: Application of a cognitive behavioural theory. In C.L. Cooper & I.T. Robertson (Eds), *International Review of Industrial and Organizational Psychology* (Vol. 9, pp. 213–245). Chichester: Wiley.
Crabb, S. (1995). Violence at work: The brutal truth. *People Management*, **1**(15), 25–29.
Crawford, N. (1992). The psychology of the bully. In A. Adams (Ed.), *Bullying at Work: How to Confront and Overcome It.* London: Virago.
Crawford, N. (1997). Bullying at work: A psychoanalytical perspective. *Journal of Community and Applied Social Psychology*, **7**, 219–225.

Crowne, D. & Marlowe, D. (1964). *The Approval Motive: Studies in Evaluative Dependence*. New York: Wiley.

De Roche, C.P. (1994). On the edge of regionalization: Management style and the construction of conflict in organizational change. *Human Organization*, 53, 209–215.

Donnellon, A. & Kolb, D.M. (1997). Constructive for whom? The fate of diversity disputes in organizations. In C. De Dreu & E. Van de Vliert (Eds), *Using Conflict in Organizations* (pp. 161–176). London: Sage Publications.

Eagle, J. & Newton, P.M. (1981). Scapegoating in small groups: An organizational approach. *Human Relations*, 34, 283–301.

Earnshaw, J. & Cooper, C.L. (1996). *Stress and Employer Liability*. London: IPD.

Eccleston, C., Williams, A.C. De C. & Rogers, W.S. (1997). Patients' and professionals' understandings of the causes of chronic pain: Blame, responsibility and identity protection. *Social Science Medicine*, 45, 699–709.

Einarsen, S. (1996). Bullying and harassment at work: Epidemiological and psychological aspects. PhD thesis, Department of Psychological Science, University of Bergen.

Einarsen, S. (1997). Mobbing i arbeidslivet: Noen teoretiske perspektiver. *Tidsskrift for organisasjonspsykologi*, 6(2), 28–39.

Einarsen, S. & Hellesøy, O.H. (1998). Når samhandling går på helsen løs: Helsemessige konsekvenser av mobbing i arbeidslivet. *Medicinsk årbok 1998*, København: Munksgaard.

Einarsen, S. & Raknes, B.I. (1991). *Mobbing i Arbeidslivet. En undersøkelse av forekomst og helsemessige konsekvenser av mobbing på norske arbeidsplasser*. FAHS, Bergen: Universitetet i Bergen.

Einarsen, S. & Raknes, B.I. (1997). Harassment in the workplace and the victimization of men. *Violence and Victims*, 12, 247–263.

Einarsen, S., Raknes, B.I. & Mathiesen, S.B. (1994). Bullying and harassment at work and their relationships to work environment quality: An exploratory study. *European Work and Organizational Psychologist*, 4(4), 381–401.

Einarsen, S., Raknes, B.I., Mathiesen, S.B. & Hellesøy, O.H. (1994). *Mobbing og Harde Personkonflikter. Helsefarlig samspill på arbeidsplassen*. Bergen: Sigma Forlag.

Einarsen, S. & Skogstad, A. (1996). Bullying at work: Epidemiological findings in public and private organisations. *European Journal of Work and Organizational Psychology*, 5, 185–201.

Eron, L.D., Huesmann, R.L., Dubow, E., Romanoff, R. & Yarnel, P.W. (1987). Childhood aggression and its correlates over 22 years. In D.H. Gowell, I.M. Evans & C.R. O'Donnell (Eds), *Childhood Aggression and Violence*. New York: Plenum.

Felson, R.B. (1992). 'Kick'em when they're down': Explanations of the relationship between stress and interpersonal aggression and violence. *Sociologist Quarterly*, 33, 1–16.

Field, T. (1996). *Bully in sight: How to Predict, Resist, Challenge and Combat Workplace Bullying*. Wantage, UK: Tim Field Success Unlimited.

Fisher, R.J. (1997). Third party consultation as the controlled stimulation of conflict. In C. De Dreu & E. Van de Vliert (Eds), *Using Conflict in Organizations* (pp. 192–207). London: Sage Publications.

Fitzgerald, L.F. & Schullman, S. (1993). Sexual harassment: A research analysis and agenda for the 1990s. *Journal of Vocational Behaviour*, 42, 5–27.

Ford, J.K. & Kraiger, K. (1995). The application of cognitive constructs and principles to the instructional systems model of training: Implications for needs assessment, design and transfer. In C.L. Cooper & I.T. Robertson (Eds), *International Review of Industrial and Organizational Psychology* (Vol. 10, pp. 1–48). Chichester: Wiley.

French, J. & Raven, B.H. (1959). The bases of social power. In D. Cartwright (Ed.), *Studies of Social Power* (pp. 150–167). Ann Arbor, MI: Institute for Social Research.

Frese, M. & Zapf, D. (1988). Methodological issues in the study of work stress: Objective versus subjective measurement of work stress and the question of longitudinal studies. In C.L. Cooper & R. Payne (Eds), *Causes, Coping and Consequences of Stress at Work*. Chichester: Wiley.

Geen, R.G. (1990). *Human Aggression*. Milton Keynes: Open University Press.

George, M. (1997). *Some Fundamental Ethical Flaws in the Design of Sexual Harassment Policies* (pp. 79–83). The National Harassment Network, First Higher and Further Education Branch Annual Conference 1997, University of Lancashire, UK.

Groeblinghhoff, D. & Becker, M. (1996). A case study of mobbing and the clinical treatment of mobbing victims. *European Journal of Work and Organizational Psychology*, 5, 277–294.

Guastello, S.J. (1995). Facilitative style, individual innovation and emergent leadership. *Journal of Creative Behaviour*, 29, 225–239.

Gustavsen, B. (1988). Democratising occupational health: The Scandinavian experience of Work Reform. *International Review of Health Services*, 18, 675–689.

Gutek, B.A. (1985). *Sex and the Workplace*. San Francisco, CA: Jossey-Bass.

Hakim, C. (1979). *Occupational Segregation: A Comparative Study of the Degree and Pattern of the Differentiation between Men's and Women's Work in Britain, the United States and Other Countries*. Department of Employment, research paper no. 9, London.

Handy, C.B. (1992). *Understanding Organizations*, 3rd edn. Harmondsworth: Penguin.

Hickson, D.J., Hinings, C.R., Lee, C.A., Schneck, R.E. & Pennings, J.M. (1971). A strategic contingencies' theory of intraorganizational power. *Administrative Science Quarterly*, 16, 216–229.

Hoel, H. (1997). Bullying at work: A Scandinavian perspective. *Institution of Occupational Safety and Health Journal*, 1, 51–59.

Hofstede, G. (1991). *Cultures and Organizations: Software of the Mind*. London: McGraw-Hill.

Hofstede, G. (1993). Cultural constraints in management theories. *The Executive*, 7(1), 81–94.

Hubert, A. (1997). Untitled paper. Eighth European Congress on work and Organizational Psychology, 2–5 April, 1997, Verona-Bussolengo, Italy.

Jehn, K.A. (1994). Enhancing effectiveness: An investigation of advantages and disadvantages of value-based intragroup conflict. *International Journal of Conflict Management*, 5, 223–238.

Jehn, K.A. (1997). Affective and cognitive conflict on work groups: Increasing performance through value-based intragroup conflict. In C. De Dreu & E. Van de Vliert (Eds), *Using Conflict in Organizations* (pp. 87–100). London: Sage Publications.

Jensen, I. & Gutek, B.A. (1982). Attributions and assignment of responsibility in sexual harassment. *Journal of Social Issues*, 28(4), 121–136.

Jones, E.E. & Davis, K.E. (1965). From acts to dispositions: The attribution process in person perception. In I.L. Berkowitz (Ed.), *Advances in Experimental Social Psychology*, Vol. 2. New York: Academic Press.

Kanter, R.M. (1984). *The Change Masters*. London: Allen & Unwin.

Karasek, R.A. (1979). Job demands, job decision latitude and mental strain: Implications for job redesign. *Administrative Science Quarterly*, 24, 285–308.

Karasek, R.A. & Theorell, T. (1990). *Healthy Work: Stress, Productivity and the Reconstruction of Working Life*. New York: Basic Books.

Keashly, L. (1998). Emotional abuse in the workplace: Conceptional and empirical issues. *Journal of Emotional Abuse*, 1, 85–117.

Kelly, H.H. (1972). Attribution in social interaction. In E.E. Jones (Ed.), *Attribution: Perceiving the Causes of Behaviour*. Morristown, NJ: General Learning Press.

Kile, S. (1990a). *Helsefarlige Ledere og Medarbeidare*. Oslo: Hjemmets Bokforlag.

Kile, S.M. (1990b). *Helsefarleg Leiarskap: Ein Eksplorerande Studie*. Rapport til Norges Almenvitenskapelige Forskningsråd, Bergen.

Kim, H. & Yukl, G. (1990). Relationship of managerial effectiveness and advancement to self-reported and subordinate-reported leadership behaviours from the multiple linkage model. *Leadership Quarterly*, 6, 361–377.

LaBar, G. (1994). Workplace violence: Employees' safety under fire. *Occupational Hazards*, 56(11), 23–28.

Lazarus, R.S. (1966). *Psychological Stress and Coping Process*. New York: McGraw-Hill.

Lazarus, R.S. (1976). *Patterns of Adjustment*. New York: McGraw-Hill.

Lennane, J. (1996). Bullying in medico-legal examination. In P. McCarthy, M. Sheehan & W. Wilkie (Eds), *Bullying: From Backyard to Boardroom* (pp. 97–117), Alexandria, Australia: Millenium Books.

Lewis, D. (1998). Bullying at work. In J. Richardson & A. Shaw (Eds), *The Body in Qualitative Research*. Aldershot, UK: Avebury Press.

Leymann, H. (1987). Sjalvmord til foljd av forhallanden i arbetsmiljon. *Arbete, Manniska, Miljo*, 3, 155–160.

Leymann, H. (1987). *Mobbing i Arbeidslivet*. Oslo: Friundervisningens Forlag.

Leymann, H. (1990a). Mobbing and psychological terror at workplaces. *Violence and Victim*, 5, 119–125.

Leymann, H. (1990b). Presentation av LIPT-formularet. Konstruktion, validering, utfall. Stockholm: Violen inom Praktikertjänst.

Leymann, H. (1992a). *Från Mobbning till Utslagning i Arbeidslivet*. Stockholm: Publica.

Leymann, H. (1992b). *Vuxenmobbning på svenska arbeidsplatser. En rikstäckande undersökning med 2.438 intervjuer*. Delrapport 1 om frekvenser. Stockholm: Arbetarskyddstyrelsen.

Leymann, H. (1992c). *Mannligt og kvinnligt vid vuxenmobbning. En rikstäckande undersökning med 2.438 intervjuer*. Delrapport 2. Stockholm: Arbetarskyddstyrelsen.

Leymann, H. (1992d). *Psyiatriska problem vid vuxenmobbning. En rikstäckande undersökning med 2.438 intervjuer*. Delrapport 3. Stockholm: Arbetarskyddstyrelsen.

Leymann, H. (1992e). *Lönebidrag og mobbad. En rikstäckande undersökning med 2.438 intervjuer*. Delrapport 5. Stockholm: Arbetarskyddstyrelsen.

Leymann, H. (1993). *Mobbing—Psychoterror am Arbeitsplatz und wie man sich dagegen wehren kann*. Hamburg: Rowohlt, Reinbeck.

Leymann, H. (1996). The content and development of mobbing at work. *European Journal of Work and Organizational Psychology*, 5(2), 165–184.

Leymann, H. & Gustafsson, A. (1996). Mobbing at work and the development of post-traumatic stress disorders. *European Journal of Work and Organizational Psychology*, 5, 251–275.

Leymann, H. & Tallgren, U. (1990). *Investigation into the frequency of adult mobbing in a Swedish steel company using the LIPT Questionnaire*. Unpublished manuscript.

Lindroth, S. & Leymann, H. (1993). Vuxenmobbning mot en minoritetsgrupp av män inom barnomsorgen. Stockholm: Arbetarskyddstyrelsen.

Locke, E.A., McClear, K. & Knight, D. (1996). Self-esteem and work. In C.L. Cooper & I.T. Robertson (Eds), *International Review of Industrial and Organizational Psychology* (Vol. 11, pp. 1–32). Chichester: Wiley.

Løvås, S. (1987). *Mobbing på arbeidsplassen*. Oslo: Stensil, Scanfact omibus for mai.

Mantell, M. (1994). *Ticking Bombs: Violence in the Workplace*. Homewood, IL: Irwin.

McCarthy, P. (1996). When the mask slips: Inappropriate coercion in organisations undergoing restructuring. In P. McCarthy, M. Sheehan & W. Wilkie (Eds), *Bullying: From Backyard to Boardroom* (pp. 47–65). Alexandria, Australia: Millenium Books.

McCarthy, P., Sheehan, M. & Kearns, D. (1995). *Managerial Styles and their Effects on Employees' Health and Well-being in Organizations Undergoing Restructuring*. School of

Organizational Behaviour and Human Resource Management, Griffith University, Brisbane.

Mergner, U. (1989). Zur sozialen Konstitution psychischer Belastung durch Arbeit. Konzeptionelle Überlegungen und empirische Konkretionen. *Zeitschrift für Arbeits- und Organisationspsychologie*, **33**(2), 64–72.

Michela, J.M., Lukaszewski, M.P. & Allegrante, J.P. (1995). Organizational climate and work stress: A general framework applied to inner-city schoolteachers. In S.L. Sauter & L.R. Murphy (Eds), *Organisational Risk Factors for Job Stress* (pp. 61–80). Washington, DC: American Psychological Association.

Mumford, E. (1991). Job satisfaction: A method of analysis. *Personnel Review*, **20**(3), 11–19.

Mummendey, A., Linneweber, V. & Loschper, G. (1984). Aggression: From act to interaction. In A. Mummendey (Ed.), *Social Psychology of Aggression: From Individual Behaviour to Social Interaction* (pp. 69–106). Berlin: Springer-Verlag.

Niedl, K. (1995). *Mobbing/bullying am Arbeitsplatz*. Munich: Rainer Hampp Verlag.

Niedl, K. (1996). Mobbing and well-being: Economic and personnel development implications. *European Journal of Work and Organizational Psychology*, **5**, 203–214.

Olweus, D. (1979). Stability of aggressive reactions in males: A review. *Psychological Bulletin*, **94**, 852–875.

Olweus, D. (1991). Bully/victim problems among school children: Basic facts and effects of a school-based intervention program. In D. Pepler & K. Rubin (Eds), *The Development and Treatment of Childhood Aggression* (pp. 411–447). Hillsdale, NJ: Erlbaum.

Olweus, D. (1993). Bullying at school: What we know and what we can do. Oxford: Blackwell.

Olweus, D. (1994). Annotation: Bullying at school: Basic facts and the effectiveness of a school-based intervention programme. *Journal of Child Psychology and Psychiatry*, **35**, 1171–1190.

Olweus, D. (1997). Bully/victim problems in school: Knowledge base and an effective intervention program. *Irish Journal of Psychology*, **18**, 171–201.

O'Moore, A.M. & Hillery, B. (1988). Bullying in Dublin schools. *Irish Journal of Psychology*, **10**, 426–441.

Paananen, T. & Vartia, M. (1991). *Henkinen Väkivalta Työpaikoilla. Kysely-ja haastattelutukimus valtion työterveyshuollossa ja työterveyshullon auttamiskeinot*. Helsinki: Työterveyslaitos, psykologian osasto.

Painter, K. (1991). Violence and vulnerability in the workplace: Psychosocial and legal implications. In M.J. Davidson & J. Earnshaw (Eds), *Vulnerable Workers: Psychosocial and Legal Issues*. New York: Wiley.

Pavett, C. & Morris, M. (1995). Management styles within a multinational corporation: A five country comparison. *Human Relations*, **48**, 1171–1191.

Pelled, L.H. & Adler, P.S. (1994). Antecedents of intergroup conflict in multifunctional product development teams: A conceptual model. *IEEE Transaction Engineering Management*, **41**, 21–28.

Perry, D.G., Kusel, S.J. & Perry, L.C. (1988). Victims of peer aggression. *Developmental Psychology*, **24**, 807–814.

Price Spratlen, L. (1995). Interpersonal conflict which includes mistreatment in a university workplace. *Violence and Victims*, **10**, 285–297.

Putnam, L.L. (1997). Productive conflict: Negotiation as implicit coordination. In C. De Dreu & E. Van de Vliert (Eds), *Using Conflict in Organizations* (pp. 147–160). London: Sage Publications.

Rahim, M.A. & Magner, N.R. (1995). Confirmatory factor analysis of the styles of handling interpersonal conflict: First order factor model and its invariance across groups. *Journal of Applied Psychology*, **80**, 22–132.

Randall, P. (1997). *Adult Bullying: Perpetrators and Victims*. London: Routledge.

Rayner, C. (1997). The incidence of workplace bullying. *Journal of Community and Applied Social Psychology*, 7, 249–255.

Rayner, C. & Cooper, C.L. (1997). Workplace bullying: Myth or reality—can we afford to ignore it? *Leadership and Organization Development Journal*, 18, 211–214.

Rayner, C. & Hoel, H. (1997). A summary review of literature relating to workplace bullying. *Journal of Community and Applied Social Psychology*, 7, 181–191.

Reid, J., Ewan, C. & Lowy, E. (1991). Pilgrimage of pain: The illness experiences of women with repetition strain injury and the search for credibility. *Social Science Medicine*, 32, 600–612.

Resch, M. & Schubinski, M. (1996). Mobbing: Prevention and management in organizations. *European Journal of Work and Organizational Psychology*, 5, 295–307.

Rotter, J.B. (1966). Generalised expectancies for internal versus external control of reinforcement. *Psychological Monographs*, 80(1), 1–28.

Schonfeld, I.S., Rhee, J. & Xia, F. (1995). Methodological issues in occupational stress research: Research in one occupational group and wider applications. In S.L. Sauter & L.R. Murphy (Eds), *Organisational Risk Factors for Job Stress* (pp. 323–329). Washington, DC: American Psychological Association.

Scott, M.J. & Stradling, S.G. (1994). Post-traumatic stress disorder without the trauma. *British Journal of Clinical Psychology*, 33, 71–74.

Scott, M.J., Stradling, S.G. & Lee, S.S. (1997). *Predicting the Long Term Outcome of Posttraumatic Stress Disorder*. Montreal, Canada: International Society for the Study of Traumatic Stress, November.

Sheehan, M. (1996). Case studies in organisational restructuring. In P. McCarthy, M. Sheehan & W. Wilkie (Eds), *Bullying: From Backyard to Boardroom* (pp. 67–82). Alexandria, Australia: Millenium Books.

Sjøtveit, J. (1992). *Når Veven Rakner: Om Samhold og Mobbing på Arbeidsplassen*. Oslo: Folkets Brevskole.

Skogstad, A., Mathiesen, S.B. & Hellesøy, O.H. (1990). *Hjelpepleiernes Arbeidsmiljøkvalitet. En undersøkelse av arbeidsmiljø, helse og trivsel blant hjelpepleierne i Hordaland*. Forskningssenter for Arbeidsmiljø, Helse og Sikkerhet (FAHS), Universitetet i Bergen, Bergen, Norway.

Smith, M. & Robertson, I.T. (1986). *The Theory and Practice of Systematic Selection*. London: Macmillan.

Smith, P.B., Dugan, S. & Trompenaars, F. (1996). National cultures and the values of organizational employees—dimensional analysis across 43 nations. *Journal of Cross-Cultural Psychology*, 27, 231–264.

Smith, P.K. (1997a). Bullying in schools. The UK experience and the Sheffield Anti-Bullying project. *Irish Journal of Psychology*, 18, 191–201.

Smith, P.K. (1997b). Bullying in life span perspective: What can studies of school bullying and workplace bullying learn from each other? *Journal of Community and Applied Social Psychology*, 7, 249–255.

Smith, P.K. & Sharp, S. (Eds) (1994). *School Bullying: Insights and Perspectives*. London: Routledge.

SNBOSH (Swedish National Board of Occupational Safety and Health (1993). Ordinance AFS 1993:17, Provisions on Measures against Victimization at Work and General Recommendations on the Implementation of the Provision. Solna, Sweden: SNBOSH.

Spector, P.E. & Brannick, M.T. (1995). The nature and effects of method variance in organizational research. In C.L. Cooper & I.T. Robertson (Eds), *International Review of Industrial and Organizational Psychology* (Vol. 10, pp. 249–274). Chichester: Wiley.

Spurgeon, A. (1997). Commentary 1. *Journal of Community and Applied Social Psychology*, 7, 241–244.

Stephenson, P. & Smith, D. (1989). Bullying in the junior high school. In D. Tattum & D. Lane (Eds), *Bullying in Schools* (pp. 45–57). Stoke-on-Trent: Trentham Books.

Stokes, J. (1994). Institutional chaos and personal stress. In A. Obholzek & V.Z. Roberts (Eds), *The Unconscious at Work: Individual and Organizational Stress in the Human Services* (pp. 121–128). London: Routledge.

Sutherland, V.J. & Cooper, C.L. (1990). *Understanding Stress: A Psychological Perspective for Health Professionals*. London: Chapman & Hall.

Tattum, D.P. & Lane, D.A. (Eds) (1988). *Bullying in Schools*. Stoke-on-Trent: Trentham Books.

Tattum, D. & Tattum, E. (1996). Bullying: A whole school response. In P. McCarthy, M. Sheehan & W. Wilkie (Eds), *Bullying: From Backyard to Boardroom* (pp. 13–23). Alexandria, Australia: Millenium Books.

Tedeschi, J.T. (1984). A social psychological interpretation of human aggression. In A. Mummendey (Ed.), *Social Psychology of Aggression: From Individual Behaviour to Social Interaction*. Berlin: Springer-Verlag.

Thylefors, I. (1987). Syndbockar. Om utstøtning och mobbning i arbeidslivet. *Natur och Kultur*, Stockholm.

UNISON (1997). *UNISON Members' Experience of Bullying at Work*. London: UNISON.

Van de Vliert, E. (1997). Enhancing performance by conflict stimulation intervention. In C. De Dreu & E. Van de Vliert (Eds), *Using Conflict in Organizations* (pp. 208–222). London: Sage Publications.

Van de Vliert, E., Euwema, M.C. & Huismans, S.E. (1995). Managing conflict with a subordinate or a superior: Effectiveness of conglomerate behaviour. *Journal of Applied Psychology*, **80**, 271–281.

Van de Vliert, E., Nauta, A., Euwema, M.C. & Janssen, O. (1997). The effectiveness of mixing problem solving and forcing. In C. De Dreu & E. Van de Vliert (Eds), *Using Conflict in Organizations* (pp. 38–52). London: Sage Publications.

Vartia, M. (1995). Bullying at workplaces. In R. Bast-Pettersen, E. Bach, K. Lindstrom, A. Toomings & J. Kirviranta (Eds), *Research on Violence: Threats and Bullying as Health Risks Among Health Care Personnel* (pp. 29–33). Proceedings from the Workshop for Nordic Researchers in Reykjavik, 14–16 August 1994, The Nordic Council of Ministers.

Vartia, M. (1996). The sources of bullying: Psychological work environment and organisational climate. *European Journal of Work and Organizational Psychology*, **5**, 203–214.

Wayne, S.J. & Liden, R.C. (1995). Effects of impression management on performance ratings: A longitudinal study. *Academy of Management Journal*, **38**(1), 232–260.

Watson, D. & Clark, L.A. (1984). Negative affectivity: The disposition to experience aversive emotional states. *Psychological Bulletin*, **96**, 465–490.

Weiner, B. (1990). Searching for the roots of applied attribution theory. In S. Graham & V.S. Volkes (Eds), *Attribution Theory: Applications to Achievement, Mental Health and Interpersonal Conflict*. Hillsdale, NJ: Erlbaum.

Wilkie, W. (1996). Understanding the behaviour of victimised people. In P. McCarthy, M. Sheehan & W. Wilkie (Eds), *Bullying: From Backyard to Boardroom* (pp. 1–11). Alexandria, Australia: Millenium Books.

Yukl, G. (1994). *Leadership in Organizations*. Englewood Cliffs, NJ: Prentice-Hall.

Zapf, D. (1997). Organizational, work group related and personal causes of mobbing at work. Eighth European Congress on Work and Organizational Psychology, 2–5 April 1997, Verona-Bussolengo, Italy.

Zapf, D., Knortz, C. & Kulla, M. (1996). On the relationship between mobbing factors and job content, social work environment, and health outcomes. *European Journal of Work and Organizational Psychology*, **5**, 215–237.

Zapf, D., Dormann, C. & Frese, M. (1996). Longitudinal studies in organisational stress research: A review of the literature with reference to methodological issues. *Journal of Occupational Health Psychology*, **1**, 145–169.

Zedner, L. (1994). Victims. In M. Maguire, R. Morgan & R. Reiner (Eds), *The Oxford Handbook of Criminology* (pp. 1207–1246). New York: OUP.

Zillmann, D. (1978). Attribution and misattribution of excitatory reactions. In J.H. Harvey, W.J. Ickes & R.F. Kidd (Eds), *New Directions in Attribution Research* (Vol. 2, pp. 335–368). Hillsdale, NJ: Erlbaum.

Chapter 3

WORKING TIME, HEALTH AND PERFORMANCE

Anne Spurgeon
University of Birmingham

Cary L. Cooper
University of Manchester

INTRODUCTION

During the 1990s substantial changes took place in international legislation on working time. The new European Directive on Working Hours (1993) introduced specific measures relating to the scheduling of shifts and rest breaks and to the maximum number of hours permissible within set periods, whilst more globally, the International Labour Organisation (ILO) introduced radical new standards for working patterns, focusing particularly on night work (1990). These measures reflect an increasing awareness of the potential implications for health and safety of the number and pattern of hours which people are required to work. Moreover there have been marked and rapid changes in these patterns in recent years, most obviously in the area of shiftworking, which in many countries involves up to 25% of the workforce. Shiftwork may be broadly defined as work which takes place either permanently or frequently outside normal daytime working hours. It may, for example, consist of permanent night work, permanent evening work or a rotational pattern where a certain number of days is spent on each shift. Today these patterns are becoming increasingly complex, comprising complicated combinations of different shift times and lengths, which change or rotate according to a variety of schedules. These may be either continuous, running for 24 hours per day and 7 days per week, or semi-continuous, running for two or three shifts per day with or without weekends. An increasingly popular format is the long shift, usually 12 hours, which compresses the working week into fewer days. Added to this are numerous flexible working arrangements which have developed in

Working Time, Health and Performance by Anne Spurgeon and Cary L. Cooper taken from IRIOP 2000 v15, Edited by Cary L. Cooper and Ivan T. Robertson: © 2000 John Wiley & Sons, Ltd

recent years such as flexitime, annualised hours contracts, job sharing and school-term working. Alongside these changes, which are essentially about the way working time is organised, there is a further trend towards extended working hours (Wedderburn, 1996a), either as formally constituted overtime, or as an informal, often unpaid, response to high work demands. In contrast to shiftworking as defined, overtime work consists of extensions to the normal working day which are not part of a predetermined schedule and which may also, for example, include holiday and weekend working. These emerging patterns have developed largely in response to the rapid economic and social change which is taking place in both industrialised and developing countries. New technologies, increased competitiveness and new customer demands for round the clock services have all combined to produce much more irregularity in peoples' working hours. Indeed in some cases the advent of sophisticated communications systems has meant that the distinction between work time and home time is becoming increasingly blurred.

Given these trends, it has become a matter of some importance to understand the potential effects of working time arrangements on the health and well-being of employees, and on their associated work performance. The role of occupational psychology in this process has in the past been somewhat variable. It has always been clear, for example, that psychological methods and tools were central to the assessment of performance decrements resulting from the fatigue and circadian disruption common in shiftworkers. Perhaps less obvious has been the psychologist's role in assessing the risk in terms of the physical health outcomes of particular work patterns and in devising interventions to help reduce those risks. In recent years however, the somewhat artificial distinction between physical and psychological health has been largely replaced by a biopsychological approach which recognises the essential interaction between the two. For example, psychosocial stressors in the working environment may have a significant part to play in the development of health problems such as coronary heart disease and gastrointestinal disorders. Current evidence suggests that the stress derived from the pattern and duration of working time may be particularly important in this respect. Further, the physiological response to potential stressors in the workplace is likely to be mediated by a number of psychological variables, ranging from personality factors, through attitudes and belief systems to the presence of other environmental stressors. From the psychologist's point of view therefore, the subject of working time presents a number of interesting challenges.

The development of human performance testing both in relation to work efficiency and to occupational safety is a continuing requirement, with the need for more sophisticated approaches which closely mimic the real working environment and which also take account of the role of psychosocial mediators. In addition, however, the study of working time may be seen as a particular branch of organisational stress research, where the role of the psychologist is central to the process of assessment and subsequent intervention.

This chapter therefore aims to provide an overview of what is currently known about the effects of different patterns of working time on health, well-being and performance, with a view to defining the future role of psychology in this field. A comprehensive picture of current thinking in this area necessarily involves a multidiscilinary perspective which in particular draws extensively on evidence from occupational medicine and epidemiology, where much of the information is derived from data sets on large populations. However, in recent years more attention has focused on individual differences and vulnerable groups in the workplace and these will also be highlighted. It should also be noted that much of what we know at the moment relates to shiftworking in its various forms, since this has been much more extensively studied than, for example, overtime work. However, as far as possible non-shiftwork issues will also be considered.

It is clear that complex patterns of working time will be an integral part of working life in the future for many people. Yet in the course of this chapter it will also become evident that many of these patterns pose potential problems for peoples' health, well-being and performance. A final section therefore, will deal with the important area of intervention and the various approaches which have been designed to address these problems.

METHODOLOGICAL ISSUES

Research into the potential health effects of working time has been concerned both with short-term complaints about fatigue and general well-being and with longer term risks of more serious disease. Where shiftwork is concerned, most of these problems are thought to relate directly or indirectly to the regular disruption of the body's normal circadian rhythms which involve a range of physiological processes such as changes in heart rate and blood pressure, respiration, temperature, production of certain hormones and digestive and excretory functions. Under normal circumstances these processes function in such a way that individuals are programmed for daytime work and leisure, and for night-time sleep, a pattern which is determined both by endogenous factors, the internal body clock, and by exogenous environmental influences such as daylight, noise and the general social habits of the individual. Regular disturbance of these body rhythms can result in a cumulative sleep deficit, resultant fatigue and symptoms of general malaise. The association between shiftworking and this type of complaint is therefore a fairly direct one. However, in the case of some other aspects of health, notably cardiovascular disease, gastrointestinal disturbance, reproductive effects and mental ill-health, the relationship with shiftworking appears to be mediated by psychological stress, although the precise mechanisms involved remain unclear. The primary means of studying these effects and those relating to other patterns of working time is via large-scale epidemiological studies either on a cross-sectional or a longitudinal basis. Studies of this type can identify an association between working time and certain health outcomes, but not necessarily a causal relationship or an explanatory mechanism.

A reasonably consistent and convincing body of evidence has now accumulated in this area, but there are some well-established methodological problems which need to be borne in mind. The most obvious of these relates to population self-selection, generally termed 'the healthy worker' or 'survivor' effect. Workers who are better able to cope with the problems of shiftwork or overtime are more likely to select themselves into this work initially and are less likely to select themselves out later on as a result of health problems. Consequently both cross-sectional and longitudinal data may be drawn from a population where 'healthy workers' are over-represented and such data may therefore represent an underestimate of the real prevalence of health effects.

Other problems common in epidemiological studies related to the difficulty of establishing appropriate control groups matched for important variables such as age, gender, social class and smoking habits and which differ only in respect of the single variable of work pattern. The influence of a variety of potential confounders is often difficult to control. For example, higher rates of gastrointestinal problems in night workers as compared with day workers may simply reflect a reduction in the quality of catering services available at night. It is well known that in many organisations working conditions at night differ markedly from those during the day, for example in respect of the type of work, the numbers of workers present, the amount of supervision, the application of health and safety procedures and the facilities of all types which are generally available.

Finally, problems have been identified in relation to the definition of outcome measures. A number of categories of disease which have been associated with shiftworking and overtime are not discrete conditions but contain a range of disorders which it may be inappropriate to group together. The most obvious example of this is the case of 'karoshi', a phenomenon identified in Japan, which literally translated means 'death from overwork'. Here a causal link has been postulated between prolonged excessive working hours and sudden death in relatively young and apparently healthy workers. Post-mortem results however, have revealed a range of causes of death in this group, including stroke of various types, acute heart failure, myocardial infarction and aortic rupture (Uehata, 1991), although all would fall under the general heading of 'vascular event'. Similar problems exist in relation to effects on reproductive health and gastrointestinal disturbance, each of which can take many forms.

In the case of shorter term health complaints such as self-reported symptoms of fatigue and depressed mood, investigations in the past have suffered from a lack of standardisation and attention to psychometrics in the questionnaire measures employed. This has recently been addressed, in particular by the development of the Standard Shiftwork Index (Barton, Spelten, Totterdell

et al., 1995) which provides a psychometrically so
the most often reported symptoms in shiftwork 1

Notwithstanding these difficulties there has be
effort directed towards the problem of shiftw(
overtime working, during the last 30 years. E
carried out by Taylor and colleagues who p
studies documenting morbidity and mortality
Taylor, Pocock & Sergean, 1972; Pocock, Ser₋₋
on these data, subsequent researchers have carried out stuu₋₋
served both to define the potential risks to health from shiftwork and overtime
and to inform the development of approaches most likely to reduce those
risks.

SHIFTWORK AND HEALTH

Stress and Mental Health

It is fairly clear that shiftworking constitutes a potential psychosocial stressor.
A number of self-report studies confirm this, using a variety of measures of
perceived stress and well-being (Hurrell & Colligan, 1987; Estryn-Behar, Kaminski, Peigne et al., 1990; Barton & Folkard, 1991; Imbernon, Warret, Roitg
et al., 1993; Cervinka, 1993; Prunier-Poulmaire, Gadbois & Volkoff, 1998).
While shiftworking has been linked to a range of physical health problems,
therefore, its relationship to mental health disturbance is probably the most
direct one. Several studies have used measures of specific mental health outcomes in addition to self-reported strain, and have demonstrated increased
risks of both anxiety and depression in shiftworkers. For example Imbernon et
al. (1993) studied electricity and gas supply workers in France and found
significant levels of disturbance on a measure of 'psychological equilibrium'.
Similarly Estryn-Behar et al. (1990), studying female hospital workers, found
a significant association between job strain due to shiftwork and poor mental
health as measured by a well-established mental health screening tool, the
General Health Questionnaire (GHQ) (Goldberg & Williams, 1988). The
GHQ is a measure of general mental health covering both anxiety and depression. A much earlier study demonstrated in particular an increased incidence
of clinical depression in shiftworkers (Michel-Briand, Chopard & Guiot,
1981). Some recent research has concentrated on the relationship between
shiftwork and personality disturbance. A range of studies in different countries
(reviewed by Cole, Loving & Kripke, 1990) indicate a strong association
between shiftwork and neuroticism. There are some difficulties in interpreting
the direction of causality in this relationship (see later section on Individual
Differences). However, the balance of opinion suggests that neurotics adapt
more poorly to shiftwork than do non-neurotics. In general therefore, current

...ggests that, as a significant source of occupational stress, shift-... likely to increase the risk of mental health problems in all workers, ...t this risk may be magnified in certain vulnerable groups.

Cardiovascular Disorders

The result of early studies on the incidence of cardiovascular disease (CVD) in shiftworkers (reviewed by Harrington, 1978) provided few grounds for concern. Since the early 1980s however, the position has reversed, with the majority of studies indicating a significant association between various types of shiftwork, particularly nightwork, and cardiovascular disorders. The methodology in these more recent studies was considerably better, particularly in respect of the problem of selection. A large-scale longitudinal study carried out on Swedish paper-mill workers (Alfredsson, Karasek & Theorell, 1982; Knutsson, Akerstedt, Jonsson & Orth-Gomer, 1986) followed up workers for 15 years and compared the risk of ischaemic heart disease (IHD) in shiftworkers with that of day workers. Shiftworkers had a significantly elevated risk which rose with increasing duration of shiftworking and which was independent of age and smoking history. Further, it was noted that there were few drop-outs in the study population. Interestingly, however, in those who had been shiftworkers for more than 20 years there was a fall in the relative risk of IHD. The authors attribute this to selection factors since within the group who had begun shiftworking more than 20 years earlier, a large percentage (63%) had selected themselves out of shiftwork within three years, in that they had changed over to day work. This observation underlines the importance of the healthy worker effect which may well account for the negative results of earlier studies. In one of the very few negative studies in recent years (McNamee, Binks, Jones et al., 1996) the authors also cite this factor as a potential explanation for their results. Two further studies in Denmark (Tüchsen, 1993) and in Finland (Tenkanen, Sjoblom, Kalimo et al., 1997) confirmed evidence of an association between shiftworking and cardiovascular disorders, although the Danish data suggested that night work specifically, rather than shiftwork in general, was responsible for a raised risk of IHD. An interesting approach adopted by Olsen and Kristensen in Denmark (1991) involved reviewing existing quantitative epidemiological data concerned with a range of possible causes of coronary heart disease and estimating the aetiological fraction for shiftworking. This fraction is defined as 'the proportion of the disease which would not have occurred if the risk factor had not occurred in the population'. For shiftwork this fraction was calculated to be 7%.

In summary, therefore, the evidence of an association between shiftworking and an increase in CVD is difficult to dismiss. The precise causal mechanism involved in this association is perhaps less clear. However, most hypotheses invoke factors conventionally viewed as resulting directly or indirectly from psychosocial stress. Hence shiftwork and particularly night work is seen as a source of occupational strain which may act to increase physiological risk factors for CVD, notably high arterial blood pressure, increased heart rate, and increased blood lipid concentrations. It may also encourage behaviour patterns associated with increased risk such as poor diet, limited physical activity and smoking. Studies which have investigated blood pressure and heart rate have usually failed to find evidence of increases in shiftworkers as a group compared with the general population (Bursey, 1990; Stoynev & Minkova, 1998). However, individual differences in cardiovascular reactivity to stress are well-established (Carroll, Harris & Ross, 1991) and it is noteworthy that a study in Japan (Kobayashi, Watanabe, Tanaka & Nakagawa, 1992) found significant differences between normotensive and hypertensive workers in the effects of shiftwork on blood pressure and heart rate at different times of the day. A further study in Japan (Nakamura, Shimai, Kikuchi et al., 1997) found that workers on a rotating three-shift system, as compared with day workers, had a higher risk of CVD, higher levels of serum total cholesterol and a greater tendency towards obesity. The authors suggest that these findings may be explained in terms of stress-induced hypercholestrolemia which has been demonstrated in animal experiments (Servatius, Ottenweller & Natelson, 1994). Current data are limited in this area but generally support the view that the demands of shiftwork act both as a direct physiological stressor and as a psychological stressor by encouraging the development of health-threatening coping behaviours.

Digestive Disorders

The most frequently reported health complaints of shiftworkers relate to digestive problems. A number of early studies found an increase of gastroduodenitis and peptic ulcers among those working rotational shifts (reviewed by Vener, Szabo & Moore, 1989). Although many of these studies have been heavily criticised on methodological grounds a more recent review (Costa, 1996) confirms early findings and concludes that there is sufficient evidence to consider shiftwork as an important risk factor for digestive disorders, particularly peptic ulcers. Again night work seems to cause the most problems. In a study of textile workers who developed gastrointestinal problems Costa, Apostoli, d'Andrea and Gaffuri (1981) calculated the time interval between workers beginning a particular type of work and the diagnosis of a digestive disorder. The shortest time interval for both gastroduodenitis and peptic ulcer was repsectively 4.7 and 5.6 years for night workers as compared with 12.6 and 12.2 years for day workers. An important factor in the development of appetite disturbance and gastrointestinal disorders in shiftworkers is likely to be their long-term irregular and inappropriately timed eating habits. For example, physiologically speaking, the body is not geared to cope with the quantity and composition of a normal daytime meal during the night, implying some scope for behavioural modification as an approach to reducing the risk of these problems. In addition, however, gastrointestinal problems have, like CVD, frequently been viewed as resulting at least in part from long-term exposure to occupational stress.

Reproductive Disorders

A number of problems included under the general heading of reproductive disorders have been associated with shiftworking. These include subfecundity (Bisanti, Olsen, Basso et al., 1996, Ahlborg, Axelsson & Bodin, 1996), spontaneous abortion (Axelsson, Ahlborg & Bodin, 1996), pre-term birth and low birthweight (Nuriminen, 1989; Xu, Ding, Li & Christiani, 1994). Although the literature in this area is not large it is fairly consistent and suggests special risks for women of child-bearing age. The suggestion is that negative effects may in part be due to hormonal disturbance (Daleva, 1987), but also to the psychosocial stress which accompanies shiftworking. As with other health outcomes effects appear to derive from an interaction between direct physiological and indirect psychological mechanisms.

Shiftwork and Social Disruption

Running alongside the normal physiological rythms of the body is a societal rhythm which has developed in parallel with the body clock. Hence, most people's activities (sleeping, eating, working, leisure, and family duties) are programmed into blocks of time which appear to be remarkably similar within and even across different cultures (Gadbois, 1984). An important factor is that not all blocks of time are interchangeable and some are much more suited to certain activities than others. For example, time appropriate for spending with children, for certain organised leisure activities or for viewing the most popular TV programmes, is subject to external constraints. Shiftworkers may therefore lose the opportunity for these activities. The importance of this has been demonstrated in studies which have attempted to quantify the value to individuals of having time off at different times of the day (Wedderburn, 1981; Hornberger & Knauth, 1993). Shiftworkers, in common with day workers, tend to place a high value on time off during evenings and weekends and much less value on time off in the daytime. It is unsurprising, therefore, that a number of studies have demonstrated that disturbances of social and family life are at least as important to the overall well-being of shiftworkers as are the physiological effects of circadian disruption.

A large survey of shiftworkers in the UK found that levels of concern about home and family life, and about social life, showed highly significant correlations with feelings of chronic tiredness and general malaise (Smith & Bennett, 1983). Other effects on leisure and social life have been measured either via semi-objective criteria such as participation in specific activities or by self-reports of satisfaction. An early study by Mott, Mann, McLoughlin et al (1965), for example, showed that membership of voluntary organisations averaged 1.4 for day workers as compared with 1.3 for those on nights and rotating shifts and 1.2 for those on fixed afternoon shifts. Similarly Frost and Jamal (1979) found significantly fewer hours were spent on organisational activities by rotating shiftworkers as compared with non-shiftworkers. However, many studies in this area point to the importance of a variety of mediating factors such as the prevalence of shiftwork generally in the geographical area which may promote a culture conducive to adjustment, the compensatory effects of high wages and the availability of choice in shift allocation.

Clearly disruption of family and social life is likely to vary between sub-groups defined by certain demographic characteristics. Several studies have explored the particular problems of women shiftworkers with children. These studies tend to document self-reported problems of reduced time with children (Lushington, Lushington & Dawson, 1997), diminished ability to fulfil the role of parenthood and to maintain family relationships (Greenwood, 1983). However, the findings are not consistent across all shift patterns. Comparisons between women who work night shifts only, with those who work rotating shifts, suggest that the former may experience fewer problems since regular permanent night work enables them to develop a satisfactory pattern of childcare and fulfilment of domestic responsibilities (Alward & Monk, 1990, Barton & Folkard, 1991). Again, an additional important determinant of well-being appears to be the opportunity to choose the preferred shift pattern.

There is some evidence that the self-reported concerns of women shiftworkers may translate into adverse effects on children's development. Studies by Leonard and Claisse in Belgium and by Knauth and by Gadbois in Germany (reported in Wedderburn, 1993) all indicated poorer long-term educational success in the children of shiftworkers as compared with day workers even after taking account of factors such as the qualifications and social class of the parents. A recent investigation by Barton, Aldridge and Smith (1998) also indicated adverse emotional effects on children. However, these studies were concerned with shiftworking parents rather than predominantly shiftworking mothers. While they raise concerns about potential effects on children therefore, the picture is not a straightforward one.

Other family disturbance may relate to effects on the quality of the relationship between partners. A variety of problems have been documented, for example reduced social contacts and joint special activities, different mealtimes and requirements for daytime silence in the house (Nachreiner, Baer, Diekmann & Ernst, 1984) and detrimental effects on sexual life (Wedderburn, 1978; Thierry, 1980). Evidence about actual separation and divorce however, is sparse and somewhat contradictory (Bunnage, 1984).

SHIFTWORK AND PERFORMANCE

Sleep Disturbance

One of the most obvious effects of shiftwork is the disturbance it causes to the length and quality of sleep. Numerous self-report surveys have documented these problems in rotating shiftworkers (Khaleque, 1991; Escriba, Perez-hoyos & Bolumar, 1992; Poole, Evans, Spurgeon & Bridges, 1992; Barak, Achiron, Lampl et al., 1995), in night workers (Chan, Gan, Ngui & Phoon, 1987, Alfredsson, Akerstedt, Mattsson & Wilborg, 1991; Smith & Folkard, 1993; Neidhammer, Lert & Marne, 1994) and in people working other irregular hours (Fletcher, Colquhoun, Knauth et al., 1988; Rutenfranz, Plett, Knauth et al., 1988; Sparks, 1992; Koh, Chia & Lee, 1994). Evidence from the wider literature on sleep research suggests that these effects have two components, firstly a reduction in the actual number of hours of sleep, and secondly fragmentation of sleep, both effects resulting from the requirement to sleep at inappropriate times in the circadian rhythm. Normal sleep appears to consist of two distinct types, predominantly slow wave sleep which is required for brain restitution, and apparently less crucial 'facultative' sleep (Horne, 1985, 1988). The former 'obligatory' sleep tends to occupy the first five hours of the night. Provided individuals are not deprived of 'obligatory' sleep, effects on performance appear to be minimal even where sleep loss extends over several months (Webb & Agnew, 1974). However, displacement of sleep appears to have much more significant effect than does sleep curtailment. Where sleep is displaced to an inappropriate point in the circadian cycle, when hormonal activity in the body is geared to promote wakefulness, sleep is much more difficult to maintain and therefore becomes fragmented. Thus shiftworkers may suffer both from a reduction in hours of sleep, which may extend into the 'obligatory' sleep requirement, and from a lack of sleep continuity. Added to this they are then required to work at a time which is suboptimal from the point of view of their circadian cycle. Taken together, these factors predict that shiftworking is likely to be associated both with a reduction in the quality of performance at work and with an increase in errors and accidents.

Errors and Productivity

Despite a substantial body of laboratory-based research on circadian rhythms, sleep loss and performance (reviewed by Alluisi & Morgan, 1982) workplace-based investigations are relatively rare. This is due in part to the considerable methodological difficulties which arise when attempting to demonstrate intershift differences in performance. These centre on the well-known differences between daytime and night time working environments, which make it very difficult to separate out the effects of time of day per se. Despite this, however, the results are

fairly consistent in demonstrating that errors are more fi
and particularly the night shift when compared with da
been shown in studies assessing real errors in a range of o
readers (Bjerner, Holm & Swensson, 1955), pilots in
Bruner & Holtman, 1970), train drivers (Hildebrandt,
1974) and truck drivers (Harris, 1977). Some more r
laboratory-type tests such as reaction time and mental ar
slower and less accurate performance on the night shift (Tepas, Walsh, Moss &
Armstrong, 1981; Tilley, Wilkinson & Warren, 1982).

Studies which investigate the relationhip between shiftwork schedules and
productivity are particularly scarce. However, again the data which do exist all
appear to point to higher productivity on day shifts. For example, an early
study of shift changes in the UK showed that when the same workers worked
day and night shifts alternately most achieved higher productivity during the
day (Wyatt & Marriott, 1953). A study by Murrel (1965) also noted decreased
productivity in night workers employed in various jobs and a more recent
study in Taiwan showed that optimum performance was achieved on the day
shift and worst performance on the night shift. Within night shifts however,
those that were part of a fixed shift system produced higher productivity than
those that were part of a rotating system (Liou & Wang, 1991).

Accidents

Errors may affect work quality and speed of performance but perhaps more
seriously, they may also cause accidents. Accident investigation data show that
fatigue, defined as 'sleepiness' has contributed to a large number of industrial
and transportation accidents (Mitler, Carskadon, Czeisler et al., 1988). A substantial body of epidemiological evidence exists which links the night shift in
particular to an increased risk of industrial accidents. (Wojtczak-Jaroszowa &
Jarosz, 1987; Ong et al., 1987; Lauridsen & Tonnessen, 1990; Novak, Smolensky, Fairschild & Reeves, 1990; Laundry & Lees, 1991; Gold, Rogacz, Bock
et al., 1992). A recent study in a UK engineering company with three rotating
shifts showed that the relative risk of sustaining an injury at work was 1.23 times
higher on the night shift than on the morning shift (Smith, Folkard & Poole,
1994). These results are despite the fact that in many organisations accidents
and injuries are less likely to be reported at night thus producing a potential
underestimate of the true figure. The evidence that shiftworking results in an
increased risk of accidents at work is therefore a matter of some concern.

COMPRESSED WORKING TIME

Most of the literature on shiftwork is concerned with rotating 8 hour shifts. In
recent years however, work schedules which compress the working week into a

number of longer shifts have become increasingly popular with both employers and employees. By concentrating work into fewer days workers have longer and more frequent rest breaks. For example, a continuously operating 12-hour shift system generates four days off for every four days worked. The advantages for employees include an extended period for leisure or domestic activities, fewer work days with no loss of pay, a reduction in commuting problems and costs and a regular work week. From the employers' point of view these systems provide greater flexibility for covering all jobs at required times and a decrease in start-up times, hence a more efficient continuous stock or service provision flow and a generally better service for customers. In addition more time is available for extra activities such as meetings and training sessions. These are, however, some potential disadvantages which centre on the problem of fatigue which may translate into errors, accidents or health problems. Research on the potential effects of these work schedules has proliferated in recent years. Most has been concerned with evaluating the 12-hour shift system which is by far the most common form of compressed working time.

Initial attention has focused on the workers' general level of satisfaction with 12-hour as opposed to conventional 8-hour shifts. Generally these results have been positive, with workers reporting greater preference for compressed working time, largely on the grounds of the increased leisure time it provides (Ivancevich & Lyon, 1977; Peacock, Glube, Miller & Clune, 1983; Cunningham, 1989; Daniel, 1990; Rosa, 1991; Tucker, Barton & Folkard, 1996). Additional data from Lees and Laundry (1989) indicated a reduction in minor morbidity, especially stress-related complaints associated with a change to 12-hour shifts. However, there are some dissenters to this generally positive view. A survey of nurses in the UK who changed to 12-hour shifts felt that these actually disrupted their social and fmaily life (Thompson, 1989). Similarly a study of nurses in Australia also found more favourable ratings for 8-hour shifts (Kundi, Koller, Stefan et al., 1995). The results of one study of manufacturing workers indicated that while the workers themselves were satisfied with the change to 12-hour shifts, this opinion was not shared by their partners (Wallace, Owens & Levens, 1990). It would seem that attitudes to different shift systems are unlikely to be generalisable across organizations and that numerous demographic and social mediators, including employee choice, need to be taken into account.

Other studies have been concerned with aspects of performance in terms both of productivity and of the potemtial for errors and accidents. The concern here, even when shifts do not rotate is that cumulative fatigue may be engendered by long hours. It should be noted, however, that 12-hour shifts differ markedly from overtime work (discussed below) and that the data are not transferable between the two situations. Unlike overtime, compressed time schedules are predictable in terms of timing and length and do not involve extra remuneration. Further, they continue in the same form for months, or years, rather than involving short periods of extended activity. The attitudes and motivations of employees are therefore likely to differ accordingly.

Studies of potential performance decrements in 12-hour shiftworkers have largely involved self-reports of fatigue or occasionally completion of cognitive tests at different points in the shift schedule. The majority of studies which have used questionnaires indicate that employees do report considerable fatigue towards the end of a 12-hour shift. Daniel (1990) found that workers at a chemical plant reported more fatigue and subsequently slept significantly longer than comparable workers on 8-hour shifts, including night workers. Another study of chemical workers in the UK (Tucker, Barton & Folkard, 1996) which used the Standard Shiftwork Index, found that one of the few differences between those on 8-hour and 12-hour shifts was their self-rated level of alertness, less in the 12-hour shiftworkers, at certain times of the day. By contrast Lowden, Kecklund, Axelsson and Akerstedt (1998), also studying workers at a chemical plant, found that alertness actually increased following a change from an 8-hour to a 12-hour shift system. However, not surprisingly, the particular time of day when reports are recorded appears to be of major importance here. A further study by Tucker, Smith, Macdonald and Folkard (1998) involving manufacturing and engineering companies found that 8-hour workers reported higher levels of alertness in the afternoons, while 12-hour workers were more alert in the mornings. Further, beginning a shift at 6.00 a.m. (a common occurrence in industry) appeared to have particularly deleterious effects on alertness. A study in Sweden also underlines the complexity of the situation. Axelsson, Kecklund, Akerstedt & Lowden (1998) compared sleepiness and physical effort in power plant workers who worked 12-hour shifts during weekends and 8-hour shifts during the week. When 12-hour and 8-hour night shifts were compared sleepiness was greater, and physical effort less, on the 12-hour shift. When morning shifts were compared however, sleepiness was greater on the 8-hour shifts. The authors suggest that reported sleepiness on morning shifts might relate to differences in sleep length prior to the shift, while on the night shift it might relate to differences in physical effort. One cannot conclude therefore, that 12-hour shifts necessarily produce increased sleepiness. In summary, the data on how people actually feel when working on 12-hour shifts are contradictory. Different points in the cycle induce differing levels of fatigue. Further, it has been suggested that the nature of the work, particularly in terms of its physical demands, is an important factor in determining whether or not workers wish to retain a 12-hour system (Wedderburn, 1996b).

Data from actual performance tests are relatively rare. The studies quoted above by Lowden et al. (1998) and Axelsson et al. (1998) also included reaction time, and in the case of the Axelsson study, a vigilance test. In neither study were significant differences in test performance observed between 8-hour and 12-hour shifts. However, an earlier study by Rosa (1991), using a battery of cognitive tests, found performance decrements attributable to 12-hour shiftworking in control room operators who had been working on this schedule for 7 months. These decrements persisted at follow-up 3.5 years later. Unfortunately, time of testing was somewhat variable in these studies and once more the likelihood is that different shift systems produce problems at different points in the cycle.

Whether fatigue problems on 12-hour shifts are translated into increased accident rates is currently unknown. The result of a study by Laundry and Lees (1991) in a yarn manufacturing company supported this view. Further, a recent analysis of 1.2 million accidents in Germany for the year 1994 indicated that there are clear time-related effects on occupational accident risks with the risk increasing exponentially after the ninth hour of work (Hanecke, Tiedemann, Nachreiner & Grzech-Sukalo, 1998). There was also a significant interaction betwen number of hours at work and time of day, data which appear to raise considerable concerns about shiftworking in general, and longer shifts in particular.

Information on productivity relating to 12-hour shifts is largely anecdotal, although some data from Holland did show that operating time in 28 companies studied increased by an average of 15% following the introduction of compressed working weeks (Hoekstra, Jansen & VanGoudoever, 1994). Operating time is not necessarily synonymous with productivity however, a factor of relevance to the next section on extended working hours.

OVERTIME WORK

The tendency to work beyond the length of a regular shift or of a standard (usually 8-hour), working day appears to be increasing in many countries, including developed ones. This is a reversal of previous twentieth century trends, (Wedderburn, 1996a). Much of this overtime, particularly in managerial and professional groups, may be unpaid and in response to increasing workloads and decreasing staff resources. The potential health and safety implications of long working hours were brought into sharp focus by the introduction of the European Directive on Working Time (1993) which among other things introduced a limit of 48 hours per week on working time, unless an alternative agreement had been reached between employer and employees. Certain groups of workers are currently exempt from the directive, notably junior doctors and various types of transport workers, mainly because of practical difficulties in its application. An initial but ultimately unsuccessful challenge to the legislation by the UK government on the grounds that it was not a health and safety issue, prompted a number of reviews of what is actually known about the effects on health and performance of certain patterns of working time, particularly long hours (Harrington, 1994; Spurgeon, Harrington & Cooper, 1997; Sparks & Cooper, 1997). The general consensus view, derived from an admittedly small database, is that the risk to health is sufficient to raise significant concern. As in the case of shiftworking many of the effects of overtime work appear to be mediated by stress. While circadian disruption is not a factor, increasing fatigue and increased duration of exposure to other workplace stressors are important. The current literature on this subject is limited in the main to potential effect on mental health and CVD, with some additional consideration of effects on performance and safety.

Mental Health

The majority of modern studies which explore the association between long working hours and the development of mental health problems have been carried out in the context of occupational stress research, where length of working hours constitutes one potential stressor. Most studies use well-established measures of psychological well-being or mental health. For example, Duffy and McGoldrick (1990) investigated the mental health of urban bus drivers as compared with that of a matched group of general practice patients. Mental health as measured by the Crown–Crisp Experiential Index (Crown & Crisp, 1979) was significantly poorer in the bus drivers, with family problems related to long hours identified as a major source of stress. In a study of UK accountants (Daniels & Guppy, 1995), quantitative work overload of which long hours was a major component, was significantly related to scores on a measure of psychological well-being (Warr, 1990) and on the General Health Questionnaire (GHQ). In Japan a study of factory workers demonstrated that working hours of more than 9 hours a day was significantly related to psychological distress also measured by the GHQ (Ezoe & Morimoto, 1994). Similarly in a UK study, the GHQ scores of junior doctors increased significantly between commencing their first post and eight weeks later during which time they were working on average 73 hours per week (Houston & Allt, 1997). Clearly in all these cases it is not possible to attribute psychological distress solely to the factor of long hours, since overtime work by its very nature tends to occur concomitantly with high levels of other work stressors. Further, some studies have highlighted the importance of individual difference such as gender (Galambois & Walter, 1992), personality type (Watanabe, Torii, Shinkai & Watanabe, 1993) and motivation (Bliese & Halverson, 1996) in moderating the response to long hours. For many workers, however, the demands of excessive overtime may significantly reduce their ability to cope with other occupational stressors.

Cardiovascular Disorders

Unsurprisingly, extended working hours sustained over long periods have also been linked to an increased risk of CVD. Two early studies identified an association between CVD and 'severe occupational strain' which at that time was measured solely in terms of long working hours. Russek and Zohman (1958) found that 71 of 100 coronary patients under the age of 40 had worked more than 60 hours per week over a prolonged period, more than four times the number in the control group. Two years later Buell and Breslow (1960) published the results of a three-year mortality study and concluded that the risk of mortality from CVD in men under the age of 44 was significantly greater in those who worked more than 48 hours a week. Interestingly, heavy physical work seemed to offer some protection from the working hours risk factor. Further support for an association between long hours and CVD has come from another UK study of telephone company employees who were also regular night school attenders (Hinkle, Whitney & Lehman et al., 1968). More recently a study in Japan of men admitted to hospital with acute myocardial infarction demonstrated an increasing trend in the risk of infarction with an increase in working hours (Sokejima & Kagamimori, 1998). Concerns about 'karoshi', which so far seems to be a peculiarly Japanese phenomenon, have already been mentioned.

Other studies, however, have produced contradictory data. For example morbidity and mortality data collected in Sweden over a 20-year period up to 1983 (Starrin, Larsson, Brenner et al., 1990), failed to find any association between CVD-related morbidity in males and long hours, although interestingly, an association was identified in females which may be explained by gender differences in additional domestic workloads. In America no relationship was identified between long hours and risk factors for CVD such as high blood pressure and serum cholesterol concentrations (Sorenson, Pirie, Folsom et al., 1985). Current thinking favours the view that individual differences are important moderators of the relationship between overtime work and CVD. These include factors such as gender (women having dual roles), personality (for example Type A), physiological susceptibility and the presence of other sources of stress. Other, as yet unexplored, factors include differences in attitudes and motivation which are likely to be crucial in determining whether exposure to a potential stressor is translated into a health problem.

Performance Effects

As noted earlier, performance may be assessed in a number of ways, in terms of productivity, errors, accidents or surrogate measures in the form of cognitive tests. In most areas of research there is an understandable preference for data produced from more recent studies, employing as they do the latest methodological approaches. Surprisingly, where long hours and performance are concerned some of the most useful data were collected by an engineering works in the UK at the end of the last century (Mather, 1884). In a series of elegantly designed experiments the management at Mather & Platt in Manchester were able to demonstrate that when weekly hours were reduced from 53 to 48 production levels remained the same. Moreover, absenteeism was reduced. A short time later a German factory producing optical goods reduced daily hours from 9 to 8, resulting in a 3% rise in production (Abbe, 1901). These studies were the first to demonstrate that increased operating time does not necessarily translate into increased production. Since these pioneering experiments a series of others, in different parts of the world, have produced similar findings (reviewed by Alliusi & Morgan, 1982).

In recent years, more attention has focused on the use of performance testing to assess the effects of the fatigue presumed to result from long working hours. In a controlled laboratory experiment student volunteers performed cognitive tests for different time periods (Okogbaa & Shell, 1986). Performance deteriorated with time spent on task and was 6% better with scheduled rest breaks than without such breaks. Performance tests have been applied particularly in the area of driver fatigue (reviewed by Brown, 1994) and to the problems experienced by junior doctors (reviewed by Spurgeon & Harrington, 1989). Data from these studies and from laboratory investigations indicate that, as in the case of CVD, the effects of long working hours are moderated by a range of task-based and individual factors. These include the type of task, for example routine and monotonous versus complex and stimulating (Monk & Folkard, 1985), the motivation of the person, including the perceived cost of errors (Craig, 1984), and the presence or absence of other stressors (Craig, 1984). In common with compressed work schedules therefore, the evidence for performance effects is sufficient to raise concern but proper understanding will require attention to a complex interaction of mediating factors.

INDIVIDUAL AND GROUP DIFFERENCES

Some people seem well able to tolerate the demands of shiftworking and overtime while others seem particularly vulnerable to their effects. Both patterns of work merit study in this respect. However, the information in this section is currently limited to shiftworking since to date no one has studied the particular characteristics of those who respond well to overtime work. Shiftwork tolerance has been defined as 'an absence of complaints with regard to sleep, digestive and nervous disorders or psychological well-being' (Harma, 1993a). Being able to identify the individual and social determinants of increased tolerance or vulnerability is important for two reasons. First, it could be helpful in terms of selecting more suitable people into this kind of work, or at least being in a position to counsel applicants more clearly about the potential risks to their health. Second, it can inform the development of appropriately focused programmes to manage shiftwork problems and thus reduce the risk. A range of factors have been investigated in recent years including age, gender, aspects of lifestyle, health status, personality traits and behaviour patterns.

Age

It is well established that the ability to tolerate shiftwork decreases with age (Oginski, Pokorski & Oginski, 1993; Harma, Hakola, Akerstedt & Laitinen, 1994; Reilly, Waterhouse & Atkinson, 1997; Brugere, Barrit, Butat et al., 1997). Symptoms of intolerance frequently begin to develop around the late forties and early fifties in workers who have often worked on shifts for many years without significant problems. A number of contributory factors have been suggested. First, since age is usually associated with long experience of shiftworking, adverse effects may be cumulative. A study of 750 shiftworkers in an oil refinery was able to show that even in particular age groups, including younger groups, length and quality of sleep decreased with longer experience of shiftwork (Foret, Bensimon, Benoit & Vieux, 1981). Second, there is also a well-documented change or flattening of circadian rhythms as people get older (Czeisler, Dumont, Duffy et al., 1992; Reilly, Waterhouse & Atkinson, 1997). This leads to an increased tendency towards 'morningness', coupled with general phase shifting. Added to this is an increased tendency to shorter sleep and frequent waking with age (Bliwise, 1993). All of these factors make adjustment to any disruption of the normal body clock and compensation for lost sleep more difficult. Harma et al. (1994), in a laboratory-based experiment, showed that older postal workers (mean age 57) were less able to recover from several night shifts than younger subjects (mean age 24) in terms of performance on a letter-sorting task which mimicked their real jobs. Finally, it has been suggested that general deterioration in physical health and the ability to cope with other life stressors may also play a part in the difficulties experienced by older workers.

Health Status

It has often been suggested in the past that those with particular health problems, notably diabetes, thyrotoxicosis, epilepsy, and renal disease should be counselled against shiftworking. Much of this thinking was based on concerns about exacerbating these workers' existing conditions and about disruption of their medication regimes. There is some evidence however, that problems in this area may be much less than was originally thought. For example Poole, Wright and Nattrass (1992) showed that in insulin-dependent diabetes, control of diabetes was no worse in those working shifts than in those who worked days only. In many countries attitudes to physically vulnerable groups are more flexible than hitherto and tend to be based on individual circumstances rather than on blanket policy. This is particularly the case in the UK where the Disability Discrimination Act (HMSO, 1995) now makes it illegal to discriminate against employees on the grounds of physical disability unless it can be demonstrated that employment will significantly increase the risk to their health. This is an issue which tends to be of concern to the occupational physician, specifically in relation to pre-employment screening, rather than to the occupational psychologist, however.

Gender

Traditionally, night work and hence rotating shifts have been discouraged for women. This dates back to an International Labour Organisation convention in 1948 outlawing such work, a convention which is still adhered to in many countries. However, with the emergence of legislation on equality and of a generally anti-discriminatory culture in many developed countries, the number of women involved in shiftwork has gradually increased. In fact for some jobs where shiftwork is unavoidable, notably nursing, women have always been over-represented. There are, however, well-documented differences in the ability of men and women to cope with shiftwork with significantly more problems being experienced by women (Oginski, Pokorski & Oginski, 1993; Beermann & Nachreiner, 1995; Nachreiner, Lubeck-Ploger & Grzech-Sukalo, 1995). Laboratory-based investigations indicate that these findings are not explained by physiological differences (Hakola, Harma & Laitinen, 1995) and it is generally accepted that the problem of women shiftworkers tend to be related to factors such as differences in social and domestic pressures, family and childcare responsibilities and the difficulties of transport and safety during unsocial hours (Hakola, Harma & Laitinen, 1995; Beerman & Nachreiner, 1995). Further, there is evidence that the existence of a partner (Beerman & Nachreiner, 1995), and social support within the family (Louden & Bohle, 1997) are both important moderators of any effect. Interestingly, women over the age of 50 appear to suffer less from shiftwork intolerance than their male counterparts. In one study (Oginski, Pokorski & Oginski, 1993) it was observed that in women, self-reported health complaints decreased significantly in this age group, presumably as a result of a reduction in domestic responsibilities.

Personality Factors

A number of aspects of personality have been investigated in an attempt to predict which types of people are likely to be best suited to shiftwork. The majority of these studies are cross-sectional and product interesting correlational data. However, they raise inevitable questions about causation. Do certain features of personality predict shiftwork tolerance or are they actually an effect of long-term adjustment? The most consistent associations have been obtained in relation to neuroticism which is highly correlated with shiftwork tolerance (Iskra-Golec, Marek & Noworol, 1995; Taylor, Folkard & Shapiro, 1997). However, a rare longitudinal study by Kaliterna, Vidacek, Prizmic and Radosevic-Vidacek (1995) was unable to demonstrate that neuroticism actually predicted shiftwork tolerance and suggested it might be better viewed as a potential confounder in future studies.

Similar problems exist in relation to a number of other factors. Shiftworkers are more likely to have an internal locus of control (Smith, Spelten & Norman, 1995), to be 'flexible' rather than 'rigid' (Gallway & McEntee, 1997) an to be 'evening' rather than 'morning' circadian types (Breithaupt, Hildebrandt & Dohre et al., 1978). Most recently, the concept of 'hardiness' has been investigated (Wedderburn, 1994). In a sample of male and female shiftworkers in a textile and an electronics factory 'hardiness' was positively correlated with increased liking for shiftwork and reduced reporting of physical complaints. Again however, one cannot deduce from these results whether this factor is a predictor or an outcome measure.

The focus in all the above investigations has been on coping styles rather than on actual coping behaviour. Since correlational data provide rather shaky ground on which to base pre-employment selection, recent thinking in this area suggests that the identification of effective patterns of coping behaviour in shiftworkers would be a more useful approach (Nachreiner, 1998). Here the emphasis would be on intervention and training of existing employees to reduce problems and risks rather than attempting to screen out unsuitable individuals. A variety of coping behaviours, particularly the organisation of social, domestic and transport arrangements, appear to be associated with improved attitudes to shiftwork (Greenwood, 1995; Harma, Rosa & Pulli et al, 1995; Blood, Sack, Lewy & Monk, 1995; Pisarski, Bohle & Callan, 1998). There is also evidence that regular exercising and physical fitness are related to shiftwork tolerance in terms of decreased reports of fatigue and of health complaints (Harma, Ilmarinen, Knauth et al., 1988a, b; Harma, 1993b). Predictive data are limited but, as Nachreiner (1998) points out, coping behaviours are amenable to modification and it should therefore be possible to carry out well-controlled intervention studies to inform new approaches to shiftwork management. Current thinking in the area of management and intervention is the subject of the final section of this chapter.

INTERVENTION AND MANAGEMENT

Shiftwork

It is clear from the preceding sections that better adjustment to shiftwork will both enhance the health and well-being of employees and promote safer and more productive work performance. To this end a variety of different approaches to shiftwork management have been introduced with varying degrees of success. Broadly these fall into three categories: (a) interventions which focus on the design of the work/rest schedule itself; (b) interventions which focus on aspects of the work environment in which shiftworking takes place; (c) interventions which focus on the individual, either pharmacologically or in terms of attitudes and behaviour.

Work Schedule Design

Although a large number of shift patterns exist one of the most common is the three 8-hour shift rotation. Consequently most effort in the area of system design has been directed towards this pattern. Essentially two questions have been addressed. First, in what direction should shifts rotate and second, how fast should the rotation occur? Shift systems may rotate in a forward direction (mornings, afternoons, nights), usually called a 'delaying' system or in a backward direction (nights, afternoons, mornings), usually called an 'advancing' system. While there is no ideal shift system, the bulk of evidence suggests that in terms of the health and well-being of the workers a forward rotation which occurs slowly (for example over 3–4 weeks) is preferable (Rosa, Bonnet, Bootzin et al., 1990; Knauth, 1993). This allows the body to adjust fully to each new pattern, a process which normally takes from two to three weeks (Akerstedt, 1985) and ensures that workers are not in a continual state of circadian disruption. In addition, forward rotation is in harmony with the fact that, without external cues which force the body clock into a 24-hour cycle, the normal endogenous period is 25 hours. This has been observed in laboratory situations where external cues are removed (Wever, 1979). Under these circumstances there is a forward moving tendency, with sleep times occurring later and later.

Current data also suggest that night work is best kept to a minimum where possible. Although negative effects on productivity are unproven the evidence for adverse health and social consequences is compelling. In fact only a small minority of employees actually appear to prefer permanent night shifts and an early doctoral thesis on this subject (McDonald, 1958) suggested that night work 'veterans' were a somewhat unusual group both socially and psychologically.

The timing of shifts has also received attention since it has been observed that an early start to the morning shift increases fatigue and errors on this shift (Moors, 1990; Hildebrandt, Rohmert & Rutenfranz, 1974). This is apparently because workers beginning a shift at 6 a.m. tend to go to bed at the usual time the night before. Despite this observation however, optimal timing of shifts depends on a range of local factors from specific elements of the job (for example whether it is the night or the morning shift which is responsible for waking up patients in a hospital ward) to the geography and culture of the area, which may influence optimal times for leisure. These factors point above all to the need for flexibility in shift timing which takes into account local conditions.

In addition to scheduling of the work pattern there have also been suggestions that scheduling of short naps during working hours may offset fatigue effects during night shifts. These have generally been referred to as 'maintenance' naps and have become common practice in Japan where rooms are provided for the purpose. Few evaluations of their effectiveness in terms of increasing alertness have been carried out although one laboratory study (Gillberg, 1984) was able to demonstrate that one hour of sleep, as compared with one hour of rest while awake, improved alertness in an experiment which required subjects to stay awake all night. Currently there is an absence of data on the usefulness of formally sanctioned napping in the workplace and concerns have been raised as to whether napping on successive nights might actually reduce circadian adaptation. As a potentially useful intervention, however, it does merit further investigation.

The Work Environment

In terms of adapting the work environment only two factors have received substantial attention. The first of these is the introduction of bright light during night shifts in an attempt to replicate one of the exogenous factors which encourage wakefulness. The capacity for controlled light exposure to shift the phase of circadian rhythms is well established in animals (Pittendrigh, 1981), but data on humans are contradictory. For example, Costa, Ghirlanda, Minors and Waterhouse (1993) assessed the effects on nurses of short periods of bright light on two consecutive night shifts as compared with two nights with normal lighting. The nurses reported less tiredness and sleepiness and a more balanced sleeping pattern following bright light exposure. In addition, performance on a letter cancelling test was enhanced. No change in physiological correlates of phase shifting (hormonal excretion and body temperature) were observed, however. By contrast Budnick, Lerman and Nicolich (1995) were able to demonstrate significant changes in morning urinary melatonin levels in nightshift workers during a three-month trial of exposure to bright light during the shift. Despite this no significant changes in self-reported alertness were recorded. Current opinion is that more information is needed on the precise timing, intensity and duration of light exposure needed to produce phase shifting but that this intervention holds considerable promise.

The second aspect of the work environment which has been considered is the actual workload both in terms of its physical intensity and its duration. The thinking here is that, for night workers in particular, the activation of body systems conducive to performance via changes in the relationships between cardiac, respiratory and metabolic variables, is much reduced (Rosa et al., 1990). Some studies of energy expenditure in male shiftworkers tend to support this in showing that more energy is expended to achieve a similar level of work on some shifts than on others. For example, a study by Wojtczak-Jaroszowa in Poland (quoted in Rosa et al., 1990) of workers in a glass factory showed that when workers were examined before work and at four points during the work shift, pulmonary ventilation, oxygen uptake and energy expenditure were significantly higher on the night shift than on other shifts. Energy expenditure was 10% higher on this shift despite work speed being slightly slower. It is known that, in any case, under normal daytime conditions, work capacity decreases over the period of an 8-hour shift (Mital, 1986). Therefore for night workers this normal decrease appears to interact with the effects of nocturnal working. These and other data have led to suggestions that in order both to maximise efficiency and to protect the long-term health of the workers different work schedules might be appropriate to different phases in shift cycles. To date, however, there have been no systematic investigations of this approach.

The Individual

Interventions which focus on the individual may be either pharmacologically or behaviourally based. Pharmacological approaches include sedative-hypnotics designed to increase sleep during non-work hours, stimulants to improve alertness during work hours and drugs designed to manipulate the normal circadian sleep/wake cycle. Of these the first two are generally regarded as unhelpful, particularly over the long term since their effectiveness tends to decline with use and the potential for abuse is a significant concern (Kales, Soldatos, Bixler & Kales, 1983; Weiss & Laties, 1962). The effective use of drugs to control the normal sleep/wake cycle, particularly the use of melatonin, which is known to be effective in regulating the sleep patterns of insomniacs (Zhdanova, Wurtman, Lynch et al., 1995), is currently speculative but is regarded as promising. However, the use of this type of drug over a long period, as opposed to its current short-term application for jet-lag sufferers, seems likely to meet with some resistance. For this reason perhaps the most effective long-term interventions are likely to lie in the area of human attitudes and behaviour. Some of these relate simply to improvements in physical fitness and changes in lifestyle patterns and it is these which have so far received the most attention in terms of intervention studies.

The findings relating to energy expenditure discussed earlier have led a number of researchers to investigate the effects of increased regular exercise and physical fitness on adaptation to shiftwork. The results have been generally encouraging. For example Harma et al. (1988a, b) evaluated the effects of a four-month physical training programme on the mood, sleep and symptom reporting of a group of shiftworking nurses. Those participating in the programme showed on average a 5-beat decrease in heart rate and a 5% increase in maximal volume of oxygen as compared with the control group. Importantly, they also reported decreased fatigue, improved sleep and fewer musculoskeletal problems. Disappointingly, manipulation of meal timing and diet content appears to be less successful in terms of promoting circadian adjustment. Much of the early enthusiasm for this approach was based on a study of jet-lag sufferers (Graeber, 1989) which assessed the effects of a particular 'feasting and fasting' regime with positive results. However, it has never been replicated in shiftworkers and the authors of the study have themselves raised doubts about its applicability to patterns of working time. It is perhaps rather too early to dismiss this type of approach completely however, since there have been few well-controlled trials of different regimes.

Manipulation of sleeping patterns in shiftworkers has been similarly limited and current advice seems to centre on avoidance of caffeine near sleep time, advice which is hardly specific to this particular group. However one study by Sharratt and Davis (1991) investigated what was termed a 'chronohygiene programme' for employees on a 12-hour shift system. This incorporated both diet and exercise together with advice about sleep patterns. Workers kept to a specific programme of physical activity and relaxation, together with specific types of food at certain times of the day. After a four-week trial there were several positive results in terms of self-reported increased alertness and decreased fatigue, improved reaction time and reduced errors on a simulated work task. Other evaluative data in this field are limited. However a number of organisations are beginning to introduce such approaches as part of an overall shiftwork policy. The role of the behavioural scientist in introducing and maintaining such programmes is likely to increase.

From the psychologist's point of view perhaps the most interesting possibility lies in the area of individually-based stress management which to date has received very little attention. Rosa et al. (1990) point to several potential applications of different approaches drawn from the psychological literature. They note, for example, that many of the adverse effects of shiftwork are derived from sleep deprivation and that establishing and maintaining good sleep habits would seem to be central to satisfactory adjustment. A number of successful behavioural modification programmes have been developed for the treatment of insomniacs, such as stimulus control instructions (Bootzin & Nicassio, 1978), which simply consist of a set of procedures for optimising the home surroundings for sleep. These might readily be adapted for shiftworkers. In addition, assuming that patterns of working time constitute a potential stressor, a range of well-established stress reduction techniques would also merit exploration in this context. These include for example, relaxation training (Benson, 1975), visualisation training shown to be successful in improving sporting and academic performance (Mahoney, 1984), and biofeedback, also shown to be effective in enhancing alertness and performance (Druckman & Swets, 1988). Finally, and perhaps most importantly, forms of cognitive-behavioural therapy aimed at promoting self-efficacy and positive coping behaviour might be a powerful tool in effecting better adjustment via attitude change. As Rosa and colleagues note, counselling, both for shiftworkers and for their families, is a much neglected area. To date there has been little application of these methods within the workplace to cope with the specific problems of working time. Yet their success in other areas suggests that alongside other organisational interventions they could have an important role to play, not least because of the importance of placing the control of successful adjustment in the hands of the workers themselves.

FUTURE DIRECTIONS

From the evidence presented in this review it is clear that the pattern and length of hours that people work frequently constitute a risk to their health and well-being. Conventional health and safety practice usually prescribes a policy of removal of workplace hazards rather than requiring that the individual employee adjust to those hazards. However, where shiftwork and to a lesser extent overtime work are concerned, it is clear that the hazards in question cannot be removed and are in fact likely to become more pervasive in the future. As a result attention is increasingly turning to the development of policies designed to reduce risks and minimise effects on performance. To date these policies have tended to focus on manipulation of the work enviornment either in terms of optimum shift scheduling or physical interventions such as bright light introduction or workload reduction. While these approaches are of considerable importance and many are derived from a sound evidence base, they have rarely been complemented by attention to the behavioural patterns of the employees themselves. Increasingly, however, the results of studies which investigate the effects of working time are pointing to the importance of attitudes and motivation in promoting satisfactory adjustment to irregular hours. Exploring individual differences in terms of these variables is important to our understanding of some current contradictions in the data on working time in that they supply us with important explanatory mediating factors. Further, they point the way to effective interventions which can enhance those already in place. Epidemiological research can go some way towards defining these factors by careful analysis of the data in terms of age, gender, health status and lifestyle variables. However, an in-depth understanding of how such factors operate requires exploration of the field within a framework which includes the attitude and belief systems of the individuals concerned, their coping strategies and how their working patterns interact with aspects of their domestic and social lives. To date there has been little systematic study in this area either in terms of defining these important psychosocial mediators or in implementing controlled intervention studies. Both aspects will require input from psychological theory and methodology. Further, in the study of lifestyle change, for example, the modification of sleeping and eating patterns, approaches developed within the related fields of health psychology and health promotion, will be of central importance.

Management of working time in its broader sense is currently at an early stage, with some limited attention to better organisation of shiftwork scheduling and virtually none to reducing the risks associated with long, irregular or unsocial hours. Future progress in this area will require a substantial extension of current organisational initiatives but in particular will need a new emphasis on psychosocial issues and on assisting individual employees to develop appropriate adjustment strategies. In this field therefore, as in many others, the biopsychosocial model provides the only meaningful perspective.

REFERENCES

Abbe, E. (1901). Cited in J. Goldmark (Ed.), *Fatigue, Efficiency: a Study in Industry*, 1912, New York: Russell Sage Foundation.

Ahlborg, G., Axelsson, G. & Bodin, L. (1996). Shift work, nitrous oxide exposure and subfertility among Swedish midwives. *International Journal of Epidemiology*, **25**(4), 783–790.

Akerstedt, T. (1985). Adjustment of physiological circadian rhythms and the sleep-wake cycle to shiftwork. In S. Folkard & T. H. Monk (Eds.), (pp. 185–198). New York: Wiley.

Alfredsson, L., Akerstedt, T., Mattsson, M. & Wilborg, B. (1991). Self-reported health and well-being amongst night security guards: A comparison with the working population. *Ergonomics*, **34**(5), 525–530.

Alfredsson, L., Karasek, R. & Theorell, T. (1982). Myocardinal infarction risk and psychosocial work environment: An analysis of the male Swedish working force. *Social Science and Medicine*, **16**, 463–467.

Alluisi, E. A. & Morgan, B. B. (1982). Temporal factors in human performance and productivity. In E. A. Alluisi & A. Fleishman (Eds), *Human Performance and Productivity: Stress and Performance Effectiveness* (pp. 165–247), Vol. 3. A. Erlbaum, Hillsdale, NJ.

Alward, R. R. & Monk, T. H. (1990). A comparison of rotating-shift and permanent night nurses. *International Journal of Nursing Studies*, **27**(3), 297–302.

Axelsson, G., Ahlborg, G. & Bodin, L. (1996). Shift work, nitrous oxide exposure, and spontaneous abortion among Swedish midwives. *Occupational and Environmental Medicine*, **53**, 374–378.

Axelsson, J., Kecklund, G., Akerstedt, T. & Lowden, A. (1998). Effects of alternating 8- and 12-hour shifts on sleep, sleepiness, physical effort and performance. *Scandinavian Journal of Work Environment and Health*, **24**(3), 62–68.

Barak, Y., Achiron, A., Lampl, Y., Gilad, R., Ring, A., Elizur, A. & Sarova-Pinhas, I. (1995). Sleep disturbances among female nurses: Comparing shift to day work. *Chronobiology International*, **12**(5), 345–350.

Barton, J., Aldridge, J. & Smith, P. (1998). The emotional impact of shift work on the children of shift workers. *Scandinavian Journal of Work and Environmental Health*, **24**(3), 146–150.

Barton, J. & Folkard, S. (1991). The response of day and night nurses to their work schedules. *Journal of Occupational Psychology*, **64**, 207–218.

Barton, J., Spelten, E., Totterdell, P., Smith, L., Folkard, S. & Costa, G. (1995). The standard shiftwork index: A battery of questionnaires for assessing shiftwork-related problems. *Work and Stress*, **9**(1), 4–30.

Beermann, B. & Nachreiner, F. (1995). Working shifts—different effects for women and men? *Work and Stress*, **9**(2/3), 289–297.

Benson, H. (1975). *The Relaxation Response*. New York: Morrow.

Bisanti, L., Olsen, J., Basso, O., Thonneau, P. & Karmaus, W. (1996). Shift work and subfecundity: A European multicenter study. *Journal of Environmental Medicine*, **38**(4), 352–358.

Bjerner, B., Holm, A. & Swensson, A. (1955). Diurnal variation in mental performance: A study of three shift workers. *British Journal of Industrial Medicine*, **12**, 103–110.

Bliese, P. D. & Halverson, R. R. (1996). Individual, nomothetic models of job stress: An examination of work hours, cohesion and well-being. *Journal of Applied Social Psychology*, **26**, 1171–1181.

Bliwise, D. L. (1993). Sleep in normal aging and dementia. A review. *Sleep*, **15**, 40–81.

Blood, M. L., Sack, R. L., Lewy, A. J. & Monk, T. H. (1995). Regular social rhythms are associated with circadian phase shifts in night workers. *Shiftwork International Newsletter*, **12**(1), 112.

Bootzin, R. R. & Nicassio, P. M. (1978). Behavioural treatment for insomnia. *Programmes for Behavioural Modification*, **6**, 1–45.

Breithaupt, H., Hildebrandt, G., Dohre, D., Josch, R., Sieber, U. & Werner, M. (1978). Tolerance to shift of sleep as related to the individual's circadian phase position. *Ergonomics*, **21**, 767–774.

Brown, I. D. (1994). Driver fatigue. *Human Factors*, **36**(2), 298–314.

Brugere, D., Barrit, J., Butat, C., Cosset, M. & Volkoff, S. (1997). Shiftwork, age, and health: An epidemiologic investigation. *International Journal of Occupational and Environmental Health*, **3**(2), 15–19.

Budnick, L. D., Lerman, S. E. & Nicolich, M. J. (1995). An evaluation of scheduled bright light and darkness on rotating shiftworkers: Trial and limitations. *American Journal of Industrial Medicine*, **27**, 771–782.

Buell, P. & Breslow, L. (1960). Mortality from CHD in Californian men who work long hours. *Journal of Chronic Disease*, **II**(b), 615–626.

Bunnage, D. (1984). The consequences of shift work on social and family life. In A. Wedderburn & P. Smith (Eds), *Psychological Approaches to Night and Shiftwork*. Edinburgh: Herriot-Watt University.

Bursey, R. G. (1990). A cardiovascular study of shift workers with respect to coronary artery disease risk factor prevalence. *Journal of the Society of Occupational Medicine*, **40**, 65–67.

Carroll, C., Harris, M. G. & Ross, G. (1991). Haemodynamic adjustments to mental stress in normotensives and subjects with mildly elevated blood pressure. *Psychophysiology*, **28**, 438–446.

Cervinka, R. (1993). Night shift dose and stress at work. *Ergonomics*, **36**(1–3), 155–160.

Chan, O. Y., Gan, S. L., Ngui, S. J. & Phoon, W. H. (1987). Health of night workers in the electronics industry. *Singapore Medical Journal*, **28**(5), 390–399.

Chan, O. Y., Gan, S. L. & Yeo, M. H. (1993). Study on the health of female electronics workers on 12 hours shifts. *Occupational Medicine*, **43**, 143–148.

Cole, R. J., Loving, R. T. & Kripke, D. F. (1990). Psychiatric aspects of shiftwork. *Occupational Medicine*, **5**(2), 301–314.

Costa, G. (1991). *Social and Family Life as Important Criteria for the Construction of Shift Systems*. Dublin: European Foundation for the Improvement of Living and Working Conditions.

Costa, G. (1996). The impact of shift and nightwork on health. *Applied Ergonomics*, **27**(1), 9–16.

Costa, G., Apostoli, P., d'Andrea, G. & Gaffuri, E. (1981). Gastrointestinal and neurotic disorders in textile shift workers. In A. Reinberg, N. Vieux & P. Andlauer (Eds) *Night and Shift Work: Biological and Social Aspects* (pp. 215–221). Oxford: Pergamon Press.

Costa, G., Ghirlanda, G., Minors, D. S. & Waterhouse, J. M. (1993). Effect of bright light on tolerance to night work. *Scandinavian Journal of Work and Environmental Health*, **19**, 414–420.

Council of the European Communities (1993). Concerning certain aspects of the organisation of working time. Council Directive 93/104/EC. Luxembourg. *Official Journal of the European Communities*, **L307** (13-12-93), 18–24.

Craig, A. (1984). Human engineering. In J. S. Warr (Ed.), *The Control of Vigilance in Sustained Attention and Human Performance*. Chichester: Wiley.

Crown, S. & Crisp, A. H. (1979). *Manual of the Crown–Crisp Experiential Index*. London: Hodder & Stoughton.

Cunningham, J. Barton (1989). A compressed shift schedule: Dealing with some of the problems of shift-work. *Journal of Organizational Behaviour*, **10**, 231–245.

Czeisler, C., Dumont, M., Duffy, J., Steinberg, J., Richardson, G., Brown, E. et al. (1992). Association of sleep-wake habits in older people with changes in output of circadian pacemaker. *The Lancet*, **340**, 933–936.

Daleva, M. (1987). Metabolic and neurohormonal reactions to occupational stress. In R. M. Kalimo, A. El-Batawi & C. L. Cooper (Eds), *Psychosocial Factors at Work and Their Relation to Health* (pp. 48–63). Geneva: WHO.

Daniel, J. (1990). Sociopyschological studies of operators of 8 and 12 hour shifts in continuous production. *Travail Humain*, **53**(3), 277–282.

Daniels, K. & Guppy, A. (1995). Stress, social support, and psychological well-being in British accountants. *Work and Stress*, **19**(4), 432–447.

Druckman, D. & Swets, J. A. (1988). *Enhancing Human Performance*. Washington, DC: National Academy.

Duffy, C. A. & McGoldrick, A. E. (1990). Stress and the bus driver in the UK transport industry. *Work and Stress*, **4**(1), 17–27.

Escriba, V., Perez-hoyos, S. & Bolumar, F. (1992). Shiftwork: Its impact on the length and quality of sleep among nurses of the Valencian region in Spain. *International Archive of Occupational and Environmental Health*, **64**, 125–129.

Estryn-Behar, M., Kaminski, M., Peigne, E., Bonnet, N., Vaichere, E., Gozlan, C., Azoulay, S. & Giorgi, M. (1990). Stress at work and mental health status among female hospital workers. *British Journal of Industrial Medicine*, **47**, 20–28.

Ezoe, S. & Morimoto, K. (1994). Behavioural lifestyle and mental health status of Japanese factory workers. *Preventive Medicine*, **23**, 98–105.

Fletcher, N., Colquhoun, W. P., Knauth, P., DeVol, D. & Plett, R. (1988). Work at sea: A study of sleep, and of circadian rhythms in physiological and psychological functions, in watchkeepers on merchant vessels. *International Archives of Occupational and Environmental Health*, **61**, 51–57.

Foret, J., Bensimon, G., Benoit, O. & Vieux, N. (1981). Quality of sleep as a function of age and shiftwork. In A. Reinberg, N. Vieux & P. Andlauer (Eds), *Aspects of Human Efficiency* (pp. 273–282). London: English Universities Press.

Frost, P. J. & Jamal, M. (1979). Shiftwork attitudes and reported behavioural individual characteristics and hours of work and leisure. *Journal of Applied Psychology*, **64**, 77–81.

Gadbois, C. (1984). Time budget and strategies regulating off the job activities of night nurses. In A. Wedderburn (Ed.), *Psychological Approaches to Night and Shiftwork*. Edinburgh: Heriot-Watt University.

Galambois, N. L. & Walters, B. J. (1992). Work hours, schedule inflexibility, and stress in dual-earner spouses. *Canadian Journal of Behavioural Science*, **24**(3), 290–302.

Gallway, T. J. & McEntee, J. J. (1997). Effects of individual differences and shift systems on workers' health. *Shiftwork International Newsletter*, **14**(1), 83.

Gillberg, M. (1984). The effects of two alternative timings of a one-hour nap on early morning performance. *Biological Psychology*, **19**, 45–54.

Giovanni, C. (1991). Shiftwork and circadian variations of vigilance and performance. In J. Wise, V. D. Hopkin & M. L. Smith (eds), *Automation and Systems Issues: Air Traffic Control*, Vol. F73, NATO ASI Series edn. Heidelberg, Berlin: Springer-Verlag.

Gold, D. R., Rogacz, S., Bock, N., Tosteson, T. D., Baum, T. M., Speizer, F. E. & Czeisler, C. A. (1992). Rotating shift work, sleep, and accidents related to sleepiness in hospital nurses. *American Journal of Public Health*, **82**(7), 1011–1014.

Goldberg, D. & Williams, P. A. (1988). *Users' Guide to the General Health Questionnaire (GHQ)*. Windsor: Nelson.

Graeber, R. C. (1989). Jet lag and sleep disruption. In M. Kryger, H. T. Roth & W. C. Dement (Eds), *Principles and Practice of Sleep Medicine* (pp. 324–33). Philadelphia: W.B. Saunders.

Greenwood, K. (1983). Report on the SECV quality of life shiftworkers survey. In M. Wallace (Ed.), *Shiftworkers in Australia* (pp. 10–14). Melbourne, Victoria: Brain-Behaviour Research Institute, La Trobe University.

Greenwood, K. M. (1995). Strategies used by shiftworkers to improve sleep following the night shift. *Shiftwork International Newsletter*, **12**(1), 23.

Hakola, T., Harma, M. I. & Laitinen, J. T. (1995). Sex and circadian adjustment to night shifts. *Shiftwork International Newsletter*, **12**(1), 74.

Hanecke, K., Tiedemann, S., Nachreiner, F. & Grzech-Sukalo, H. (1998). Accident risk as a function of hour at work and time of day as determined from accident data and exposure models for the German working population. *Scandinavian Journal of Work Environment and Health*, **24**(3), 43–48.

Harma, M. (1993a). Individual differences in tolerance to shiftwork: A review. *Ergonomics*, **36** (1–3), 101–110.

Harma, M. (1993b). Ageing, physical fitness and shiftwork tolerance. *Applied Ergonomics*, **27**(1), 25–29.

Harma, M. I., Ilmarinen, J., Knauth, P., Rutenfranz, J. & Hanninen, O. (1988a). Physical training intervention in female shift workers: I. The effects of intervention on fitness, fatigue, sleep, and psychosomatic symptoms. *Ergonomics*, **31**(1), 39–50.

Harma, M. I., Ilmarinen, J., Knauth, P., Rutenfranz, J. & Hanninen, O. (1988b). Physical training intervention in female shift workers. II. The effects of intervention on the circadian rhythms of alertness, short-term memory, and body temperature. *Ergonomics*, **31**(1), 51–63.

Harma, M. I., Hakola, T., Akerstedt, T. & Laitinen, J. T. (1994). Age and adjustment to night work. *Occupational and Environmental Medicine*, **51**, 568–573.

Harma, M., Rosa, R. R., Pulli, K., Mulder, M. & Nasman, O. (1995). Individual factors associated with positive attitudes toward later shift start-end times in rotating shift work. *Shiftwork International Newsletter*, **12**(1), 76.

Harrington, J. M. (1978). *Shiftwork and Health: A Critical Review of the Literature*. London: HMSO.

Harrington, J. M. (1994). Shift work and health—a critical review of the literature on working hours. *Annals of the Academy of Medicine*, **23**(5), 699–705.

Harris, W. (1977). Fatigue, circadian rhythms, and truck accidents. In R. Mackie (Ed.), *Vigilance: Theory, Operational Performance and Physiological Correlates* (pp. 133–146). New York and London: Plenum Press.

Hildebrandt, G., Rohmert, W. & Rutenfranz, J. (1974). 12- and 24-hour rhythms in error frequency of locomotive drivers and the influence of tiredness. *International Journal of Chronobiology*, **2**, 175–180.

Hinkle, L. E., Whitney, L. H., Lehman, E. W., Dunn, J., Benjamin, B. & King, R. (1968). Occupation, education, and coronary heart disease. *Science*, **161**, 238–248.

HMSO (1995). Disability Discrimination Act 1995. London: HMSO.

Hoekstra, F., Jansen, B. & VanGoudoever, B. (1994). *The Compressed Working Week*. Dublin: European Foundation for the Improvement of Living and Working Conditions.

Hornberger, S. & Knauth, P. (1993). Interindividual differences in the subjective valuation of leisure time utility. *Ergonomics*, **36**(1–3), 255–264.

Horne, J. (1985). Sleep loss: Underlying mechanisms and tiredness. In S. Folkard & T. Monk (Eds), *Hours of Work: Temporal Factors in Work Scheduling*. New York: Wiley.

Horne, J. (1988). *Why We Sleep: The Functions of Sleep in Humans and Other Mammals*. New York: Oxford University Press.

Houston, D. M. & Allt, S. K. (1997). Psychological distress and error making among junior house officers. *British Journal of Health Psychology*, **2**, 141–151.

Hurrell, J. J. & Colligan, M. J. (1987). Machine pacing and shiftwork: Evidence for job stress. *Journal of Organizational Behaviour*, **8**(2), 159–175.

Imbernon, E., Warret, G., Roitg, C., Chastang, J. & Goldberg, M. (1993). Effects on health and social well-being of on-call shifts: An epidemiologic study in the French national electricity and gas supply company. *Journal of Occupational Medicine*, **35**(11), 1131–1137.

International Labour Organisation (ILO) (1990). *The Hours We Work: New Work Schedules in Policy and Practice*. Geneva: ILO.

Iskra-Golec, I., Marek, T. & Noworol, C. (1995). Interactive effect of individual factors on nurses' health and sleep. *Work and Stress*, **9**(2/3), 256–261.

Ivancevich, J. M. & Lyon, H. L. (1977). The shortened workweek: A field experiment. *Journal of Applied Psychology*, **62**(1), 34–37.

Kales, A., Soldatos, C. R., Bixler, E. O. & Kales, J. D. (1983). Early morning insomnia with rapidly eliminated benzodiazepines. *Science*, **229**, 95–97.

Kaliterna, L., Vidacek, S., Prizmic, Z. & Radosevic-Vidacek, B. (1995). Is tolerance to shiftwork predictable from individual difference measures? *Work and Stress*, **9**(2/3), 140–147.

Khaleque, A. (1991). Effects of diurnal and seasonal sleep deficiency on work effort and fatigue of shiftworkers. *International Archives of Occupational and Environmental Health*, **62**, 591–593.

Klein, D. E., Bruner, H. & Holtman, H. (1970). Circadian rhythm of pilot's efficiency, and effects of multiple time zone travel. *Aerospace Medicine*, **41**, 125–132.

Knauth, P. (1993). The design of shift systems. *Ergonomics*, **36**(1–3), 15–28.

Knauth, P. & Rutenfranz, J. (1987). Shiftwork. In J. M. Harrington (Ed.) *Recent Advances in Occupational Health*, Vol. 3 (pp. 263–281). Edinburgh, London, Melbourne and New York: Churchill Livingstone.

Knutsson, A., Akerstedt, T., Jonsson, B. B. & Orth-Gomer, K. (1986). Increased risk of ischaemic heart disease in shift workers. *The Lancet*, **336**, 89–92.

Knutsson, A., Akerstedt, T. & Jonsson, B. G. (1988). Prevalence of risk factors for coronary artery disease among day and shift workers. *Scandinavian Journal of Work Environment and Health*, **14**, 317–321.

Kobayashi, F., Watanabe, T., Tanaka, T. & Nakagawa, T. (1992). Effect of shift work and time of day on blood pressure and heart rate in normotensive and hypertensive workers. *Journal of Occupational Medicine, Singapore*, **4**(2), 58–63.

Koh, D., Chia, H. P. & Lee, S. M. (1994). Effects of a double day shift system on sleep patterns of hotel workers. *Journal of Occupational Medicine, Singapore*, **6**(1), 27–31.

Kundi, M., Koller, M., Stefan, H., Lehner, L., Kaindlsdorfer, S. & Rottenbucher, S. (1995). Attitudes of nurses towards 8 hour and 12 hour shift systems. *Work and Stress*, **9**(2/3), 134–139.

Laundry, B. R. & Lees, R. (1991). Industrial accident experience of one company on 8- and 12-hour shift systems. *Journal of Occupational Medicine, Singapore*, **33**(8), 903–906.

Lauridsen, O. & Tonnessen, T. (1990). Injuries related to the aspects of shift working: A comparison of different offshore shift arrangements. *Journal of Occupational Accidents*, **12**, 167–176.

Lees, R. & Laundry, B. R. (1989). Comparison of reported workplace morbidity in 8-hour and 12-hour shifts in one plant. *Journal of the Society of Occupational Medicine*, **39**, 81–84.

Liou, T. S. & Wang, M. J. (1991). Rotating-shift system vs. fixed-shift system. *International Journal of Industrial Ergonomics*, **7**, 63–70.

Loudon, R. & Bohle, P. (1997). Work/non-work conflict and health in shiftwork: Relationships with family status and social support. *International Journal of Occupational and Environmental Health*, **3**(2), 71–77.

Lowden, A., Kecklund, G., Axelsson, J. & Akerstedt, T. (1998). Change from an 8-hour shift to a 12-hour shift, attitudes, sleep, sleepiness and performance. *Scandinavian Journal of Work Environment and Health*, **24**(3), 69–75.

Lushington, W., Lushington, K. & Dawson, D. (1997). The perceived social and domestic consequences of shiftwork for female shiftworkers (nurses) and their partners. *Journal of Occupational Health and Safety, Australia and New Zealand*, **13**(5), 461–469.

Mahoney, M. J. (1984). Cognitive skills and athletic performance. In W.F. Straub & J.M. Williams (Eds), *Cognitive Sport Psychology*, Lansing, MI: Sport Science Associates.

Mather, W. (1884). The forty-eight hour week: A year's experiment and its results. Guardian Printing Works.

McDonald, J. C. (1958). Social and psychological aspects of night shiftwork. PhD. Thesis, University of Birmingham.

McNamee, R., Binks, K., Jones, S., Faulkner, D., Slovak, A. & Cherry, N. M. (1996). Shiftwork and mortality from ischaemic heart disease. *Occupational and Environmental Medicine*, **53**, 367–373.

Michel-Briand, C., Chopard, J. L. & Guiot, A. (1981). The pathological consequences of shift work in retired workers. In A. Reinberg, N. Vieux & P. Andlauer (Eds), *Night and Shiftwork: Biological and Social Aspects*, (pp. 399–407). Oxford: Pergamon Press.

Mital, A. (1986). Prediction models for psychophysical lifting capabilities and the resulting physiological responses for work shifts of varied durations. *Journal of Safety Research*, **17**, 155–163.

Mitler, M., Carskadon, M., Czeisler, C., Dement, W., Dinges, D. & Graeber, R. (1988). Catastrophes, sleep and public policy: Consensus report. *Sleep*, **11**(1), 100–109.

Monk, T. H. (1990). Shiftworker performance. *Occupational Medicine: State of the Art Reviews*, **5**(2), 183–198.

Monk, T. H. & Folkard, S. (1985). Individual differences in shiftwork adjustment. In S. Folkard & T. H. Monk (Eds), *Hours of Work: Temporal Factors in Work Scheduling*. Chichester: Wiley.

Moors, S. H. (1990). Learning from a system of seasonally-determined flexibility: Beginning work earlier increases tiredness as much as working longer days. In G. Costa, G. Cesana, K. Kogi & A. Wedderburn (Eds), *Shiftwork Health, Sleep and Performance*. Frankfurt: Peter Lang.

Mott, P. E., Mann, F. C., McLoughlin, Q. & Warwick, D. P. (1965). *Shiftwork: The Social Psychological, and Physical Consequences*, Ann Arbor, MI: University of Michigan Press.

Murrel, K. F. (1965). *Ergonomics: Man in his Working Environment*, Vol. 18. London: Chapman & Hall.

Nachreiner, F. (1998). Individual and social determinants of shiftwork tolerance. *Scandinavian Journal of Work Environment and Health*, **3**, 35–42.

Nachreiner, F., Baer, K., Diekmann, A. & Ernst, G. (1984). Some approaches in the analysis of the interference of shiftwork with social life. In A. Wedderburn & P. Smith (Eds), *Psychological Approaches to Night and Shiftwork*. Edinburgh: Heriot-Watt University.

Nachreiner, F., Lubeck-Ploger, H. & Grzech-Sukalo, H. (1995). Changes in the structure of health complaints as related to shiftwork exposure. *Work and Stress*, **9**(2/3), 227–234.

Nakamura, K., Shimai, S., Kikuchi, S., Tominaga, K., Takahashi, H. & Tanaka, M. (1997). Shift work and risk factors for coronary heart disease in Japanese blue-collar workers: Serum lipids and anthropometric characteristics. *Occupational Medicine*, **47**(3), 142–146.

Niedhammer, I., Lert, F. & Marne, M. J. (1994). Effects of shift work on sleep among French nurses. *Journal of Occuptaional Medicine*, **36**(6), 667–674.

Novak, R. D., Smolensky, M. H, Fairchild, E. J. & Reeves, R. R. (1990). Shiftwork and industrial injuries at a chemical plant in Southeast Texas. *Chronobiology International*, **7**(2), 155–164.

Nuriminen, T. (1989). Shift work, fetal development and course of pregnancy. *Scandinavian Journal of Work Environment and Health*, **15**, 395–403.

Oginski, H., Pokorski, J. & Oginski, A. (1993). Gender, ageing and shiftwork intolerance. *Ergonomics*, **36**(1–3), 161–168.

Okogbaa, G. O. & Shell, R. L. (1986). The measurement of knowledge of worker fatigue. *IIE Transactions*, **18**(4), 335–342.

Olsen, O. & Kristensen, T.S. (1991). Impact of work environment on cardiovascular diseases in Denmark. *Journal of Epidemiology and Community Health*, **45**, 4–10.

Ong, C. N., Phoon, W. O., Iskandar, N. & Chia, K. S. (1987). Shiftwork and work injuries in an iron and steel mill. *Applied Ergonomics*, **18**(1), 51–56.

Peacock, B., Glube, R., Miller, M. & Clune, P. (1983). Police officers' response to 8 and 12 hour shift schedules. *Ergonomics*, **26**(5), 479–493.

Pisarski, A., Bohle, P. & Callan, V. J. (1998). Effects of coping strategies, social support and work-nonwork conflict on shift worker's health. *Scandinavian Journal of Work and Environmental Health*, **24**(3), 141–145.

Pittendrigh, C. S. (1981). Circadian systems: Entrainment. In J. Aschoff (Ed.), *Handbook of Behavioural Neurobiology*, Vol. 4, *Biological Rhythms* (pp. 95–124). New York: Plenum.

Pocock, S. J., Sergean, R. & Taylor, P. J. (1972). Absence of continuous three-shift workers: A comparison of traditional and rapidly rotating systems. *Occupational Psychology*, **46**, 7–13.

Poole, C. J., Evans, G. R., Spurgeon, A. & Bridges, K. W. (1992). Effects of a change in shift work on health. *Occupational Medicine*, **42**, 193–199.

Poole, C. J., Wright, A. D. & Nattrass, M. (1992). Control of diabetes mellitus in shift workers. *British Journal of Industrial Medicine*, **49**, 513–515.

Prunier-Poulmaire, S., Gadbois, C. & Volkoff, S. (1998). Combined effects of shift systems and work requirements on customs officers. *Scandinavian Journal of Work Environment and Health*, **24**(3), 134–140.

Reilly, T., Waterhouse, J. & Atkinson, G. (1997). Ageing, rhythms of physical performance, and adjustment to changes in the sleep-activity cycle. *Occupational and Environmental Medicine*, **54**, 812–816.

Rosa, R. R. (1991). Performance, alertness, and sleep after 3.5 years of 12 hour shifts: A follow-up study. *Work and Stress*, **5**(2), 107–116.

Rosa, R. R., Bonnet, M. H., Bootzin, R. R., Eastman, C. I., Monk, T., Penn, P. E., Tepas, D. I. & Walsh, J. K. (1990). Intervention factors for promoting adjustment to nightwork and shiftwork. *Occupational Medicine: State of the Art Reviews*, **5**(2), 391–415.

Russek, H. I. & Zohman, B. L. (1958). Relative significance of heredity, diet and occupational stress in coronary heart disease of young adults. *American Journal of Medicine*, **325**, 266–275.

Rutenfranz, J., Plett, R., Knauth, P., Condon, R., DeVol, D., Fletcher, N., Eickhoff, S., Schmidt, K. H., Donis, R. & Colquhoun, W. P. (1988). Work at sea: A study of sleep, and of circadian rhythms in physiological and psychological functions, in watchkeepers on merchant vessels. *International Archives of Occupational and Environmental Health*, **60**, 331–339.

Servatius, R. J., Ottenweller, J. E. & Natelson, B. H. (1994). A comparison of the effects of repeated stressor exposures and corticosterone injections on plasma cholesterol, thyroid hormones and corticosterone levels in rats. *Life Science*, **55**, 1611–1617.

Sharratt, M. T. & Davis, S. (1991). The effects of a chronohygiene program on fatigue, alertness and performance levels of 12-hour shift operators. In W. Karwowski & J. W. Yates (Eds) *Advances in Industrial Ergonomics and Safety III* (pp. 669–674). London: Taylor & Francis.

Smith, L. & Folkard, S. (1993). The impact of shiftwork on personnel at a nuclear power plant: An exploratory survey study. *Work and Stress*, **7**(4), 341–350.

Smith, L., Folkard, S. & Poole, C. J. (1994). Increased injuries on night shift. *The Lancet*, **344**, 1137–1139.

Smith, L., Spelten, E. & Norman, P. (1995). Shiftwork locus of control: Scale development. *Work and Stress*, **9**(2/3), 219–226.

Smith, P. & Bennett, S. (1983). Report of the joint University of Bradford and Civil Service Union studies of shiftwork. In A. Wedderburn (Ed.), *Social and Family Factors in Shift Design*, 1993 edn, Vol. 5. Dublin: European Foundation for the Improvement of Living and Working Conditions.

Sokejima, S. & Kagamimori, S. (1998). Working hours as a risk factor for acute myocardial infarction in Japan: Case-control study. *British Medical Journal*, 317, 775–780.

Sorensen, G., Pirie, P., Folsom, A., Luepker, R., Jacobs, D. & Gillum, R. (1985). Sex differences in the relationship between work and health: The Minnesota heart survey. *Journal of Health and Social Behaviour*, 26, 379–394.

Sparks, K. & Cooper, C. (1997). The effects of hours of work on health: A meta-analytic review. *Journal of Occupational and Organizational Psychology*, 70, 391–408.

Sparks, P. J. (1992). Questionnaire survey of masters, mates and pilots of a state ferries system on health, social and performance indices relevant to shift work. *American Journal of Industrial Medicine*, 21, 507–516.

Spurgeon, A. & Harrington, J. M. (1989). Work performance and health of junior hospital doctors: A review of the literature. *Work and Stress*, 9(2/3), 368–376.

Spurgeon, A., Harrington, J. M. & Cooper, C. L. (1997). Health and safety problems associated with long working hours: A review of the current position. *Occupational and Environmental Medicine*, 54(6), 367–376.

Starrin, B., Larsson, G., Brenner, S. O., Levi, L. & Pettersen, I. L. (1990). Structural changes, ill health and mortality in Sweden. *International Journal of Health Services*, 20, 27–42.

Stoynev, A. G. & Minkova, N. K. (1997). Circadian rhythms of arterial pressure, heart rate and oral temperature in truck drivers. *Occupational Medicine*, 47(3), 151–154.

Stoynev, A. G. & Minkova, N. K. (1998). Effect of forward rapidly rotating shift work on circadian rhythms of arterial pressure, heart rate and oral temperature in air traffic controllers. *Occupational Medicine*, 48(2), 75–79.

Taylor, P. J. (1967). Shift and day work: A comparison of sickness absence, lateness and other absence behaviour at an oil refinery from 1962–65. *British Journal of Industrial Medicine*, 24, 93–102.

Taylor, E., Folkard, S. & Shapiro, D. (1997). Shiftwork advantages as predictors of health. *International Journal of Occupational and Environmental Health*, 3(2), 20–29.

Taylor, P. J., Pocock, S. J. & Sergean, R. (1972). Absenteeism of shift and day workers: A study of six types of shift system in 29 organisations. *British Journal of Industrial Medicine*, 29, 208–213.

Tenkanen, L., Sjoblom, T., Kalimo, R., Alikoski, T. & Harma, M. (1997). Shift work occupation and coronary heart disease over 6 years of follow-up in the Helsinki heart study. *Scandinavian Journal of Work Environment and Health*, 23, 257–265.

Tepas, D. I. & Carvalhais, A. B. (1990). Sleep patterns of shiftworkers. *Occupational Medicine: State of the Art Reviews*, 5(2), 199–208.

Tepas, D. I., Walsh, J. K., Moss, P. D. & Armstrong, D. (1981). Polysomnographic correlates of shift worker performance in the laboratory. In A. Reinberg, N. Vieux & P. Andlauer (Eds), *Night and Shift Work: Biological and Social Aspects* (pp. 179–186). New York: Pergamon.

Thierry, H. (1980). Compensation for shiftwork: A model and some results. In W. P. Colquhoun & J. Rutenfranz (Eds), *Studies of Shiftwork* (pp. 449–462). London: Taylor & Francis.

Thompson, J. (1989). Rigour round the clock. *Nursing Times*, 85, 21.

Tilley, A. J., Wilkinson, R. T. & Warren, P. (1982). The sleep and performance of shift workers. *Human Factors*, 24, 629–641.

Tüchsen, (1993). Working hours and ischaemic heart disease in Danish men. A 4-year cohort study of hospitalisation. *International Journal of Epidemiology*, 22(2), 215–221.

Tucker, P., Barton, J. & Folkard, S. (1996). Comparison of 8 and 12 hour shifts: Impacts on health, well-being and alertness during the shift. *Occupational and Environmental Medicine*, **53**, 767–772.

Tucker, P., Smith, L., Macdonald, I. & Folkard, S. (1998). Shift length as a determinant of retrospective on-shift alertness. *Scandinavian Journal of Work and Environmental Health*, **24**(3), 49–54.

Uehata, T. (1991). Karoshi due to occupational stress-related cardiovascular injuries among middle-aged workers in Japan. *Journal of Science of Labour*, **67**, 20–28.

Vener, K. J., Szabo, S. & Moore, J. G. (1989). The effect of shiftwork on gastrointestinal function: A review. *Chronobiology*, **12**, 421–439.

Wallace, M., Owens, W. & Levens, M. (1990). Adaptation to twelve hour shifts. In G. Costa, G. Cesana, K. Kogi & A. Wedderburn (Eds), *Shiftwork: Health, Sleep and Performance*. Frankfurt am Main: Peter Lang.

Warr, P. B. (1990). The measurement of well-being and other aspects of mental health. *Journal of Occupational Psychology*, **63**, 193–210.

Watanabe, S., Torii, J., Shinkai, S. & Watanabe, T. (1993). Relationships between health status and working conditions and personalities among VDT workers. *Environmental Research*, **61**, 258–265.

Webb, W. & Agnew, H. (1974). The effects of a chronic limitation of sleep length. *Psychophysiology*, **11**(3), 265–274.

Wedderburn, A. (1978). Some suggestions for increasing the usefulness of psychological and sociological studies of shiftwork. *Ergonomics*, **21**, 827–833.

Wedderburn, A. (1981). Is there a pattern in the value of time off work? In A. Reinberg, N. Vieux & P. Andlauer (Eds), *Night and Shift Work: Biological and Social Aspects*. Oxford: Pergamon Press.

Wedderburn, A. (Ed.) (1993). *Social and Family Factors in Shift Design*, 1st edn, Vol. 5. Dublin: European Foundation for the Improvement of Living and Working Conditions.

Wedderburn, Z. (1994). Shiftwork, health and personality hardiness: An apparent double link. Paper presented at the 1994 Occupational Psychology Conference, London.

Wedderburn, A. (Ed.) (1996a). 'Statistics and News', *Bulletin of European Studies on Time*, Vol. 9. Dublin: European Foundation for the Improvement of Living and Working Conditions.

Wedderburn, A. (ed.) (1996b). 'Compressed Working Time', *Bulletin of European Studies on Time*, Vol. 10. Dublin: European Foundation for the Improvement of Living and Working Conditions.

Weiss, B. & Laties, V. G. (1962). Enhancement of human performance by caffeine and the amphetamines. *Pharmacological Review*, **14**, 1–36.

Wever, R. A. (1979). *The Circadian System of Man*. New York: Springer Verlag.

Wojtczak-Jaroszowa, J. & Jarosz, D. (1987). Chronohygienic and chronosocial aspects of industrial accidents. *Programmes in Clinical and Biological Research*, **227B**, 415–426.

Wyatt, S. & Marriott, R. (1953). Night work and shift changes. *British Journal of Industrial Medicine*, **10**, 164–172.

Xu, X., Ding, M., Li, B. & Christiani, D. C. (1994). Association of rotating shiftwork with preterm births and low birth weight among never smoking women textile workers in China. *Occupational and Environmental Medicine*, **51**, 470–474.

Zhdanova, I. V., Wurtman, R. J., Lynch, H. J., Ives, J. R., Dollins, A. B., Morabito, C. et al. (1995). Sleep inducing effects of low doses of melatonin ingested in the evening. *Clinical Pharmacological Theories*, **57**, 552–558.

Chapter 4

UNDERSTANDING ACTS OF BETRAYAL: IMPLICATIONS FOR INDUSTRIAL AND ORGANIZATIONAL PSYCHOLOGY

Jone L. Pearce and Gary R. Henderson
University of California, Irvine

Because it is an air of all-pervading bitterness that lingers over what has been one of Asia's most successful brokerage operations following the June departure of five of Morgan Grenfell Asia's (MGA's) top six Singaporean directors including Chairman NG Soo Peng and managing director Hsieh Fu Hua). Accusations of betrayal from the Singaporeans and counter-accusations from MGA's London-based parent Morgan Grenfell are still flying with stinging ferocity (Shale, *AsiaMoney*, 1993).

As interest has grown in complex organizational forms and contractual arrangements, industrial/organizational (I/O) psychologists throughout the world have directed their attention to interpersonal relations as the foundation for successful organization. As the above quotation illustrates, when these relationships flounder, feelings of betrayal often follow. In today's more fluid organizational environment trust has become both more important and more problematic. Trust is more important because it cannot rest on stable hierarchies and functional relationships among people who work together their entire careers. Trust is more difficult because the growth of international networked organizations, cross-cultural teams and new forms of contingent employment make building and sustaining such relationships more difficult. We believe that for a better understanding of interpersonal relations in complex forms of interdependent organizations we can better understand these relationships by knowing more about betrayal. Our own interest reflects others' growing interest: industrial and organizational psychologists increasingly talk of betrayal. Reflecting this burgeoning interest, betrayal appears in scattered subdisciplines, for example, betrayal has been mentioned by scholars of trust, workplace justice and by those studying violations of psychological contracts. We also find that betrayal is at the intersection of several important scholarly trends in I/O psychological research; yet it is an ill-lit crossing.

Understanding Acts of Betrayal: Implications for Industrial and Organizational Psychology by Jone L. Pearce and Gary R. Henderson taken from IRIOP 2000 v15, Edited by Cary L. Cooper and Ivan T. Robertson: © 2000 John Wiley & Sons, Ltd

This is so for two reasons. First, the concept of betrayal is being used in a multitude of ways, most of them quite narrow, some of them implicit, and with differing implications for theory and practice. In part this reflects the study of betrayal in the larger world of behavioral and social science, where the term has many meanings and uses. The growth of interest in topics of networks, trust, justice and psychological contracts, matters in which a betrayal is a key feature, suggests that there is need to clarify and organize what we do know about betrayal in its workplace forms. Second, a closer examination of betrayal helps illuminate other contemporary concerns in the field of I/O psychology. These include questions about intra-psychic processes, assumptions that more explanation will mitigate unwelcome organizational acts, how emotions affect behavior at work, and cross-national differences in interpretations of others' actions. This chapter begins with a wide-ranging review of the social and behavioral science conceptualizations of betrayal. Then we discuss several contentious issues from the literature that are most relevant to workplace psychology. We conclude by summarizing the implications of our discussion for several of those contemporary conceptual issues in international I/O psychology.

BETRAYAL IN INDUSTRIAL/ORGANIZATIONAL PSYCHOLOGY

Betrayal is a difficult topic to embrace adequately because it has been touched on in work as old as the I/O field itself. In Roethlisberger and Dickson's (1939) classic Hawthorne Studies, for example, the workers of the Bank Wiring Room attempted to restrain the high productivity of the Room's rate-buster; they saw his violation of their informal quota as a betrayal likely to lead to them all having to work harder for the same pay. This study of betrayal of a work group's own normative expectations formed the basis for several decades of research on workplace rewards, work-group norms, and interpersonal influence. More recently betrayal has been noted by those seeking to understand the role of trust in organizational settings, those studying workplace justice, and theorists of psychological contracts.

Betrayal of Trust

Two sets of scholars seeking to understand workplace trust have discussed betrayal in depth. They see betrayal as integral to an understanding of trust (Elangovan & Shapiro, 1998; Morris & Moberg, 1994), and consider betrayal to be the risk one runs when trusting another, the inherent vulnerability people have when they must place their fortunes in the uncertain hands of others (cf., Bigley & Pearce, 1998). They note that workplace trust is necessary because tasks are ambiguous and changing, and others' actions and the outcomes of those actions are often difficult to observe. Both works distinguish personal betrayal from impersonal betrayal and focus on the former. As Morris and Moberg (1994) state their case, personal betrayal is situated in the relationship between two people and a betrayal occurs when the expectations of a specific person for the actions of another person are not met. For example, the Bank Wiring Room rate-buster described above personally betrayed his coworkers. In contrast, impersonal betrayal is when a normative expectation or expectations pertaining to an office or to membership in a group are violated. If a government official accepts a bribe for a favorable decision, this is a violation of impersonal trust pertaining to that person's membership in the organization and occupation of a particular office or role. Similarly, if a general sells his army's battle plans to the enemy that is impersonal betrayal. Morris and Moberg (1994) developed a theoretical framework of personal betrayal in work settings. They focused on conditions leading individuals to perceive that they have been betrayed by another, and suggested that betrayal will be felt if the act was perceived as intentional, and if it was 'personal' (intentionally directed at the victim), rather than accidental.

The second set of scholars is Elangovan and Shapiro (1998), who provide a comprehensive theoretical model of personal betrayal in organizations. In contrast to others in industrial/organizational psychology they focused on why the perpetrator betrays rather than on the circumstances under which a breach or transgression is interpreted as a betrayal by the victim. Elangovan and Shapiro took a utilitarian approach to explaining why someone would betray others at work. They suggested that a person at work is more likely to betray others if the act is likely to be personally beneficial, the penalties or possibility of detection are low, other principles supporting the betrayal can be evoked, and if the perpetrator has a personal propensity to betray. Morris and Moberg (1994) and Elangovan and Shapiro (1998) have contributed to our understanding of workplace trust by articulating the circumstances that would lead victims to classify a transgression as a betrayal and that might cause perpetrators to violate others' trust in them.

Workplace Injustice

In much work on injustice the word betrayal is rarely mentioned but descriptions of reactions to felt injustice reflect many elements of betrayal. For example, Bies (1987) reported the results of programmatic research on how argumentation lessens others' perceived moral outrage. He examined how offending acts could be reframed so they no longer seemed morally culpable, eliciting moral outrage in the victim. Outrage at perceived injustice has also been examined by Bies and Tripp (1998) and Bies, Tripp & Kramer (1997). This work has helped to counterbalance the excessive emphasis on cognitive calculation in much justice research by highlighting that a perceived injustice can elicit very strong emotions. In these works 'moral outrage' appears to be a synonym for betrayal. If anything, one might assume that some offending acts might be relatively mild, provoking sorrow, perhaps, but not moral outrage. Yet in the injustice literature the examples provided (e.g. underpayment) include unmet expectations which can be merely inconvenient or irritating rather than the kind of morally outrageous acts characterized as betrayals. That is, those studying injustice appear to address a broad range of workplace unmet expectation, from the trivial to the most extreme. Yet, we would not expect perpetrators' attempts to mitigate with self-justifying explanation to apply equally to a wide range of transgressions. For example, argumentation may only be effective for ambiguous acts, or mild transgressions, ones that have little chance of evoking moral outrage in the first place. Certainly, the excuses of perpetrators of genuinely morally outrageous acts are likely to be greeted with scorn. Differences in degree do matter, and so a better understanding of betrayal can help in understanding the boundary conditions for social accounts in mitigating reactions to transgressions with the potential to outrage.

Breach of Psychological Contract

The growing interest in reframing employees' relationships with their organizations as psychological contracts has led to inquiry into the consequences of a breach of the psychological contract. A psychological contract is a set of beliefs, held by the employee, about what the employee and employer are obliged to give and receive in the relationship (Morrison & Robinson, 1997; Robinson, Kraatz & Rousseau, 1994; Robinson, 1996; Rousseau, 1995). Sandra Robinson (Morrison & Robinson, 1997; Robinson, 1996) has developed a model of the circumstances under which a breach of the psychological contract leads employees to experience the emotion of violation. She noted that a perception of a breach of psychological contract does not necessarily lead to 'feelings of betrayal and psychological distress', what she called perceived violation. Robinson suggested that a breach will be experienced as a violation if it is of sufficient magnitude, has important implications, is purposeful, is unfair, and violates the prevailing social contract. Her theoretical and empirical work makes an important contribution by emphasizing that all breaches of expectations do not necessarily result in strong feelings of violation or betrayal. However, in contrast to Elangovan and Shapiro's suggestion that betrayal is experienced only in personal relationships, Robinson includes an impersonal partner—the organization.

Like Morris and Moberg (1994) and Bies (1987), Robinson's work provides a basis for a more comprehensive examination of issues they introduce. These include determining which expectations are important enough to evoke feelings of betrayal if violated, a re-examination of the exclusion of impersonal betrayal from I/O psychology, the necessity of perpetrator intent to betray, the role of third parties, and necessity of shared knowledge, among others. We hope to build on this work with a comprehensive examination of betrayal. It begins with a discussion of what betrayal is, with particular attention to what leads certain transgressions to be more likely to be perceived as betrayals. This is followed by an analysis of areas in which theorists differ in their description of betrayal or its consequences. The paper concludes with a discussion of the implications of this conceptualization of betrayal for research in I/O psychology.

UNDERSTANDING ACTS OF BETRAYAL

There are widely differing definitions of betrayal depending on the focus of the scholar. It is necessary to gain clarity on two defining features of betrayal before proceeding. First, to some betrayal is an individual's perception of another's act since, following Robinson, any given act may be perceived to be a betrayal or not. Others view betrayal as the action itself. Here, the latter act-based focus is adopted. This is because it is the most widely adopted definition, avoids a potentially autistic focus solely on individuals' potentially idiosyncratic perceptions, and directs attention to the question of why an act may or may not be interpreted as a betrayal.

Second, once we understand betrayals as acts defined as transgressing important expectations, we are free to treat the acts of groups, organizations or other collective entities as having the potential to be perceived as betrayals. Individuals have expectations for collective groupings as well as for individuals. Psychological contracts, for example, involve an individual's expectations for organizations' obligations to them. Certainly, there is widespread agreement on the importance of trust in and trust created by institutions (e.g., North, 1990; Zucker, 1986), and where there is trust there is the potential to betray the trust. Yet, before examining the characteristics of acts of betrayal we begin with the point of widespread agreement.

Betrayal Enrages

When a transgression is categorized as a betrayal, strong negative emotions are aroused (Bateson, 1977). Åkerström (1991) suggested that an act of betrayal arouses intense sentiments such as indignation, contempt, revenge, and rage that can continue long after the event took place. As an illustration, Hansson, Jones and Fletcher (1990) reported that adults over age 60 stated that half of the incidents of betrayal at work they recalled had occurred more than twenty years before. The perception of being betrayed can unleash powerful emotions and so can have severe and potentially lasting consequences. It is this potentially powerful emotional quality and motivating potential of felt betrayal that attracts the interest of industrial/organizational psychologists. In organizations not all transgressions will enrage, yet when individuals experience a transgression as a betrayal the effects are potentially grave.

Transgressions that Betray

If a violation is perceived to be a betrayal when it transgresses important expectations, what makes some expectations important while others are not? As Shackelford (1997, p. 73) notes, 'The actions or events that constitute betrayal in one relationship context may not constitute a betrayal in another such context'. Robinson noted that to qualify as a betrayal the trust violated needs to be important—what Elangovan and Shapiro called 'pivotal expectations'. Yet labeling transgressions which evoked feelings of betrayal as important after the fact has little predictive value. It would be more useful to have some guidance regarding which expectations are likely to be important or pivotal. Fortunately, many researchers in social psychology, sociology and political science have sought to distinguish betraying transgressions from others. While there is much overlap in the ideas of these theorists from different disciplines, each perspective is worth exploring.

Violations of a constitutive rule

Metts (1994) argued that a transgression is more likely to be perceived as a betrayal if it violates a 'constitutive rule'. These are rules about what actions must occur if the relationship is going to continue. If constitutive rules are seen to be violated the relationship becomes meaningless or incoherent. The relationship or group must cease to exist in its present form (cf., Jones & Burdette, 1994). Constitutive rules are contrasted with 'regulative rules' which govern how interdependence will be managed. Thus, a constitutive rule for physicians may be to recommend only those procedures and drugs they believe will help the patient, while a regulative rule might be to see patients at their appointed times. A perceived violation of the constitutive rule (only beneficial treatment) goes to the heart of the nature of the relationship and so its violation is more likely to be seen as a betrayal than is a 30-minute delay in seeing the doctor.

In organizations constitutive rules would be those necessary to the coherence of the relationship with another individual, group or organization. For organizations these would be role requirements necessary to the functioning of the organization, and would be expected to vary depending on the context. For example, we would consider a colleague's 'selling' a good grade to a student at our university to be a violation of a constitutive rule and thus a betrayal. However, we are familiar with universities elsewhere in which such acts have occurred and the transgressions were treated more as a regulative-rule violation than a betrayal. Doesn't the assignment of grades based solely on students' performance constitute a core function of a university? It did appear that grades in those settings did not have the same constitutive meaning as they do in ours. There students obtained jobs and other opportunities based on who they knew, and their intellectual prowess was judged from personal interaction. Grades had no use as signals of intelligence or conscientiousness or knowledge because they all knew one another in these small intellectual circles, and so selling university grades was not a constitutive rule transgression.

Revelations of group-defining secrets

Another approach to identifying why certain transgressions constitute betrayals is offered by Åkerström (1991). While having many similarities to the above arguments on constitutive rules, he examines one kind of constitutive rule in some depth—secrecy. He argues that betrayal involves overstepping a 'We-boundary'. A 'We' consists of relations ranging from a pair of friends to a nation (Åkerström, 1991, p. 2). He suggests that secrets and confidences exchanged are the creators of social bonds, the necessary component to the creation of a We. Åkerström echoes Simmel's (1994) contention that without secrets many aspects of social life would be impossible. Secrets divide those who know from those who do not. Such We-groupings can vary in size and intimacy and may be quite unstable. Thus, betrayal is a dishonoring of the We.

Åkerström goes on to note that in times of conflict or when individuals or groups have invested a great deal in their secrecy the betrayal can become very threatening. He distinguishes 'telling' betrayals from 'leaving' betrayals. On the one hand, telling betrayals may divulge information which is harmful in the hands of the outsider (i.e., the planned product innovation in the hands of a competitor) or may simply be mundane information that symbolizes the 'specialness' of the relationship or group. Nevertheless, it violates the We bond. On the other hand, leaving the group, occupation or organization can be seen as betrayal, as is desertion during war. Sometimes there are instrumental reasons for treating leaving as a betrayal—as violent underworld association members are concerned that a deserter is a potential informer. Alternatively, leaving may simply be interpreted as a rejection of the values of the We.

Applying his ideas to organizational settings helps illustrate why it is often so difficult to determine which acts will be seen as betrayals there. Both telling and leaving are a normal part of many career patterns. The skills and practices one learns on the job become the person's own foundation for a successful career. Employees often occupy explicitly 'boundary spanning' roles in which information exchange with their counterparts in other organizations is encouraged, and employees are frequently hired from other companies so that the hiring firm can learn new practices. Thus, telling and leaving may be expected activities at work, and not viewed as betraying acts. However, whether an act of employee telling or leaving is an act of betrayal can be a matter of great dispute. Following Åkerström, we suggest this is when such telling and leaving threatens the group or organization's values or survival. The fact that such expectations can be very contentious is reflected in the numerous lawsuits regarding 'no compete' clauses in employment contracts which bind employees after they have left an employer. Certainly, we would expect tellings and leavings that threaten the organization, occupation, or group to be more likely to evoke feelings of betrayal. Thus, we might expect participants to develop normative expectations about which leavings and tellings are an expected part of work and which ones would be betrayals.

Threats to security

Transgressions that threatens the relationship, group, occupation or organization's security are likely to be seen as betrayals (Shackelford, 1997). Different acts pose security threats to different relationships, so the same acts may be seen as a betrayal in one relationship or setting but not in another. Shackelford (1997) provides insights into distinguishing acts that are betraying transgressions in one relationship from the same acts which do not evoke that judgement in another. He suggests that over evolutionary history human beings have adapted to relationships with different specific functions, and that a betrayal will be perceived as a transgression that threatens the viability of that specific relationship. He uses the contrast between same-sex friendships with mateships, producing evidence that extra-relationship intimate involvement is more threatening to a security in mateships than friendships and so more likely to be perceived as a betrayal.

Certainly, organizations and work groups will differ in the acts which might threaten their security. For example, in some organizations trade secrets pose a real threat to the continued viability of the organization while in others there are no real trade secrets. Some organizations working at the leading edge of internet or other software technology will not even disclose the kind of projects they are developing, whereas teachers do not have any trade secrets from one another. So we would expect the internet product developer to be more likely to see a software writer's departure for a competitor as a betrayal, but the principal would host a party to wish the departing teacher good luck.

Threats to identity

Finally, transgressions that threaten one's identity are more likely to be seen as betrayals (Jones & Burdette, 1994). In their discussion, Morris and Moberg (1994) argue that in order to be felt as a betrayal a transgression must be personalized such that 'the victim's sense of self-legitimacy or social identity' is threatened (p. 180). Likewise, Afifi and Metts (1998) suggest that 'many of the examples of betrayal provided by participants are directly related to identity attacks' (p. 386). For example, not receiving an expected promotion may threaten one person's self-image as an upwardly mobile, successful manager while for another it may be disappointment but poses no threat to self-identity.

In the former case the victim is more likely to see the non-promotion as a betrayal. Thus, personal relationships, groups and organizations will vary in the extent to which membership is important to an individual's identity and for those individuals transgressions of constitutive rules would strike at the core of one's self-image (Metts, 1994).

In summary, transgressions are more likely to lead to classification as betraying acts if the expectations transgressed are pivotal or important. What leads some transgressions to be important enough to be judged betrayals are violations of those rules or normative expectations that govern the very purpose of the relationship, or if they violate secrets that support the relationship, or if they threaten the victim's basic security or sense of identity. These are the sorts of transgressions that evoke feelings of betrayal in either personal or impersonal relationships. Further, such betrayals also reflect disruptions in what the victim had assumed or taken for granted, introducing uncertainty about one's security and sense of self. The foregoing discussion is summarized in Table 4.1.

Table 4.1 Understanding organizational betrayal

Betraying acts enrage those betrayed.

Transgressions will be classified as betrayals if they:

- violate expectations serving as constitutive rules for the relationship, or
- violate expectations protecting relationship-defining secrets, or
- threaten members' security, or
- threaten members' identities

Betrayals:

- may be transgressions of impersonal role obligations to groups or organizations as well as personal obligations to other individuals
- may be perceived whether or not the perpetrator intended to betray the victim or victims
- involve implicit or explicit third parties
- do not necessarily involve shared expectations
- may be situationally or dispositionally driven.

DIFFERING PERSPECTIVES OF BETRAYAL

Despite general consensus on the characteristics of those acts likely to be seen as betrayals, there remain several equivocal issues. A discussion of these differences helps to highlight several current issues in I/O psychology, and so we briefly address questions such as: Can transgressions of impersonal role obligations be perceived as betrayals? Is it a necessary condition that an act of betrayal be intentionally harmful? Must all participants agree on the meaning and interpretation of acts of betrayal? What is the role of emotion in reactions to betrayals?

Personal and Impersonal Betrayal

In I/O psychology theorists vary as to whether transgressions of expectations regarding impersonal relationships may be experienced as acts of betrayal. Recall that personal betrayal occurs when the expectations of a specific person for the actions of another person are not met, while impersonal betrayal is when a normative expectation or expectations pertaining to an office or to membership in a group are violated. Personal betrayals concern only the relationship between two people—their expectations for one another based on the relationship they have built—while impersonal betrayal is violation of role expectations as a member of a collective entity such as a group or organization. Morris and Moberg argue that individuals will seek to distinguish actions intended to harm them personally from accidental harm as a byproduct of something else in deciding whether or not they have been personally betrayed. This is because harmful events at work can happen for many reasons. Thus a focus on personal betrayal alone allows them to focus on the victims' search for intent in deciding how to classify a transgression.

Similarly, Elangovan and Shapiro (1998) argue that transgressions of obligations owed to impersonal entities such as groups or organizations would not be viewed as betrayals by employees. While Elangovan and Shapiro (1998) provide an articulate defense of their reason for considering violations of impersonal trust to be deviations rather than betrayals, we contend that a better understanding of why acts may be classified as betrayals makes the elimination of impersonal betrayal unnecessary. A deviation is a violation of a group's normative expectation for members. We contend that a betrayal may be a type of deviation, but it is a special type of deviance. Deviance can include such mild acts as wearing a suit on Casual Friday or eating at your desk. Clearly, some violations of collective norms are serious and threatening enough to be seen as betrayals, and therefore to enrage. While Elangovan and Shapiro's (1998) restriction to personal betrayals assists them in maintaining clarity in their discussion of why perpetrators betray, we believe that limiting I/O psychology solely to the study of personal betrayals in the workplace unnecessarily neglects an important aspect of work and forgoes insights that can be gained from understanding impersonal betrayal. This is so for several reasons.

First, other theorists include impersonal entities as parties to betrayal and trust. Robinson considers violations when the perpetrator is a collective (the organization) and so a strict focus on personal betrayals alone would exclude her work. Similarly, organizations, groups and institutional arrangements may be trusted in the course of conducting organizational work (cf., Bigley & Pearce, 1998) and where trust exists it can be betrayed.

Second, in practice, it may not be possible to clearly distinguish personal from impersonal transgressions in organizational settings. The general selling secret battle plans to the enemy is violating impersonal role expectations, but those of his colleagues who knew him would very likely consider it a personal betrayal. Similarly, did the rate-buster in the Bank Wiring Room violate his personal relationship with each of his coworkers, or did he betray a normative expectation pertaining to his work group? Organizations are mixes of role and personal obligations, and transgressions of role obligations that threaten individuals' understanding of their workplace, threaten their security or their own identities are as likely to be seen as betrayals as are violations of informal personal understandings.

Finally, members of organizations certainly may experience an enraging sense of betrayal from another's betrayal of the organization. Examples might include a colleague you do not know personally agreeing to testify for the government in its lawsuit against the company, or when a fellow employee (who is a stranger to you) gets caught accepting a bribe and brings embarrassment to everyone working for the organization. Transgressions of impersonal role obligations can be the most stinging of betrayals—those which endanger the safety of the group.

After all, the term betrayal was first applied to selling secrets which harmed the clan; the word betrayal comes from the Latin word *tradere*, 'to hand over', as in secrets to an enemy. The application of this concept to personal relationships, such as friendships or marriage, is a comparatively recent attempt to indicate that threatening transgressions can occur at the personal as well as the collective level. (And perhaps reflects the fact that in modern societies our personal security is dependent on smaller groupings—couples rather than clans.) Individuals who work enter into obligations to organizations, occupations, and work groups; obligations to these entities, if violated, may be very threatening and so may be seen by their fellows as betrayals. Therefore, we suggest that acts which transgress expectations regarding both personal and impersonal relationships can be perceived as betrayals.

The Necessity of Intent

It is generally agreed that betrayal harms the victim in some way (hence the term victim). However, less clear is whether the perpetrator must intend to harm the victim. Harm, in the sense used here, can refer to any negative outcome of the betrayal episode from physical forms of betrayal (e.g. abuse) to psychological outcomes (e.g. loss of self-identity). Does it matter whether the employees who sell secret product innovations to the company's competitor do so in a deliberate attempt to harm the organization, or are they just indifferent to the harm their greed may cause? To be seen as a betrayal must the act be calculated to harm the victim? It turns out that one's answer to this question rests on the theoretical perspective one takes and, empirically, who is studied.

The most ardent claims for the necessity of intentional harm-doing in determining whether an action is a betrayal comes from research on the victim's interpretive or sense-making process (Bies, 1987; Morris & Moberg, 1994; Robinson, 1996). Each of these theorists agreed that betrayal must be perceived by the victim as an act whereby the perpetrator intentionally causes harm. Thus Morris and Moberg argued that 'the victim must convince himself or herself not only that it was the violator who caused the harm but also that he or she did so freely and deliberately' (1994, p. 179).

However, theorists from other disciplines suggest that it isn't necessary to require perpetrators' intention to harm, simply that they intend to behave opportunistically. As Elangovan and Shapiro stated, 'although violations of trust need to be voluntary to be considered betrayal, some of them may be unintentional' (1998, p. 551). These authors used both the presence of intent and the timing of intent (whether prior to or after the initiation of a relationship) to develop a typology of betrayal which distinguishes between acts of 'accidental' betrayal—the absence of intent—from 'intentional', 'premeditated,' and 'opportunistic' types. For example, numerous accounts of studies of espionage highlight the idealistic motives of the perpetrator—selling intelligence for the common good—and not their intent to harm the unfortunate victims (Åkerström, 1991).

Finally, there is considerable ambiguity about intent when perpetrators and victims are directly queried. Jones and Burdette (1994) provided evidence gleaned from retrospective narratives that both perpetrators and victims perceive opportunistic motives yet differ in their attributions of cause. That is, while both agreed that the act of betrayal was intentionally performed, perpetrators overwhelmingly attribute their own motives to unstable causes (e.g. fit of rage). Victims, on the other hand, were much more likely to perceive the motives of the perpetrator as intentional, stable, and internal (e.g. dispositional character flaw). In addition, Baumeister, Stillwell and Wotman (1990) discovered that victims and perpetrators have substantially different subjective interpretations of the consequences of betrayals. Perpetrators are more likely to see the incident as isolated and without lasting implications, while the victims believed it caused lasting harm and continuing grievance. Such differing subjective perceptions of betrayal are not surprising—a betrayal is such an extreme violation that we would expect perpetrators to minimize and mitigate it if at all possible. As Jones and Burdette reasoned, 'Perhaps such explanations reduce one's sense of moral responsibility for undesirable behaviors' (1994, p. 258).

Thus, requiring intent to harm victims probably is too strict a requirement. Particularly when we consider impersonal betrayals, it seems clear that many betrayals are undertaken for gain and the harm to the victim is a byproduct rather than the primary purpose of the act. Anyway, perpetrators can always claim they meant no harm or hadn't realized the implications (and we really cannot read their thoughts). As Elangovan and Shapiro (1998) suggested, it is not the intent to harm which leads an act to be seen as a betrayal but an indifference to the harm caused to those who placed their trust in the perpetrator. We recognize that many actions which victimize individuals in organizational settings are compelled by circumstances or are accidental and participants do seek to differentiate those from betrayals. However, future work would benefit from a more precise focus on indifference to or devaluing of harm, rather than intent to harm, as the requirement for eliciting feelings of betrayal.

Victim, Perpetrator, and Third Parties

In industrial/organizational psychology the focus has been on the victim–perpetrator dyad. Typically, third parties are incidental to the betrayal episode, relegated instead to the status of a comparison standard (Morrison & Robinson, 1997) or a source of influence (Morris & Moberg, 1994). Yet theorists in other disciplines focus on the role of third parties, some insisting that acts of betrayal inherently require third parties (Baxter, Mazanec, Nicholson et al., 1997).

Shackelford and Buss (1996) suggested that betrayal involves the potential threat of diverting valued resources to persons outside the primary relationship. Likewise, Argyle and Henderson (1984) hypothesized that relationship rules are created to deal with potentially negative consequences related to third parties (e.g. ensuring that self-disclosures are kept in confidence). Their research suggests that the violation of rules concerning third parties is one of the most crucial in terms of the consequences to the relationship, with over one-third of the respondents rating them as either 'moderately' or 'very important' in the relationship's subsequent dissolution.

Some theorists require that any act of betrayal involve a third party. Baxter et al. examined betrayal from a dialectic perspective—that loyalty is meaningful only in unity with its opposite, disloyalty (or, the act of betraying)—and argued that third parties are required in any account of betrayal: 'There are always three parties, A, B, C, in a matrix of loyalty. A can be loyal to B only if there is a third party C who stands as a potential competitor . . . thus the concept of loyalty becomes meaningful to us only when united conceptually with the possibility of betrayal' (1997, p. 656). Thus, third parties are central to many scholarly theories of what it means to betray.

Industrial/organizational psychologists probably also should recognize the implicit and sometimes explicit third party in acts of betrayal. For example, as members of social groups, third parties are implicated to the extent that shared norms, agreements, and expectations concerning appropriate conduct are developed. In this way third parties constitute a powerful source of influence (Morris & Moberg, 1994), or 'clan control' (Ouchi, 1980). Yet typically I/O psychologists place the role of third parties outside the primary betrayal episode. For example, Robinson (1996) limited the role of third parties to a source of comparative information in the victim's sense-making process of a potential violation. For others, third parties are implicit at best. Bies, for example, focused on outrage over underpayment of expected compensation. Third parties would be implicit in this betrayal, in the form of alternative employers forgone, based on the false promise of high compensation. An explicit recognition of the role of third parties would help enrich our understanding of the kind of reactions individuals may have to violated expectations. Who those third parties are and how they are involved in workplace betrayals would be a fruitful area for future research.

The Necessity of Shared Knowledge

To what extent must the victim and perpetrator share knowledge concerning expectations and their importance to the relationship? Here again there appears to be little consensus in the literature. Robinson (1996) argued that the lack of mutuality concerning the content of expectations is a common condition. Alternatively, Elangovan and Shapiro (1998) stated that both must agree on the contents of expectations but may disagree on the extent to which these are important to the relationship. Still others, such as Bies (1987) and Metts (1994), suggested that knowledge of the facts is negotiated between the victim and perpetrator through social accounts or other remedial efforts.

Robinson did not require that the victim and perpetrator agree on expectations for the relationship. Commensurate with the current definition of the psychological contract as individual employees' perception of their own and their organization's reciprocal obligations (Rousseau, 1989, 1995), Robinson focused exclusively on the individual employee's perception that they are a victim of a psychological contract breach. Since psychological contracts are inherently perceptual and idiosyncratic to each individual, it follows that 'an employee's beliefs about the obligations underlying his or her employment relationship are not necessarily shared by agents of the organization' (Robinson, 1996, p. 228). She based her model in part on the possibility of 'incongruence' because each may have divergent schemata by which to interpret expectations, many expectations are complex and ambiguous, and the level of communication will vary. What matters is that the employee perceives a breach and, through an interpretative process, comes to feel that it constitutes a violation of an important promissory agreement. Thus, the victim and perpetrator need not agree on the contents, importance, or even the behaviors involved for a breach to be classified as a betrayal.

Elangovan and Shapiro (1998) disagree. Arguing from the perpetrator's perspective, they stated that mutuality is a precondition for betrayal. They require that both victim and perpetrator be 'mutually aware' of the expectations, otherwise there could be no intent on the part of the perpetrator, hence no actual betrayal. This definitional condition allows for the distinction between an act of opportunistic betrayal and an oversight or accident. If both agree on the expectations the transgression cannot be attributed away as an accident, misunderstanding, or other mere disappointment. However, the two parties do not have to agree on the extent to which the expectations are pivotal or important to the relationship. Thus, they may still disagree on whether an act of betrayal occurred. In fact, the victim need not even be aware of the betrayal, since Elangovan and Shapiro focused exclusively on the perpetrator's decision to betray.

Further, Metts (1994) and Bies (1987) proposed that expectations are negotiated, sometimes even after the transgression has occurred. Both Metts and Bies focused on how the knowledge of a betrayal episode may be altered through social accounts or other remedial efforts. In both cases, the perpetrators use any inherent ambiguity concerning the contents of expectations to ameliorate the harm or intention attributed to them and their act. In Metts' (1994) discussion of relational transgressions, the consequences of a particular transgression are largely the outcome of a negotiation process consisting of several factors: severity of offence, explicitness, motivations, attributions, understanding, and insight. Similarly, Bies (1987) discussed the social accounts provided by perpetrators that served to mitigate the negative implications for the harm-doer.

Like intent to harm, the requirement for mutuality seems too strict for workplace settings. There is simply too much that is ambiguous, so many ways in which behavior can be compelled by changing circumstances. Acts which are serious threats to an employee's security or identity can occur because the market for the company's product has collapsed. Employees may have worked for many years for a public utility that has now been privatized and finds that it must operate in a more efficient manner than the employees had expected. Or an unexpected opportunity for a better job may induce an engineer to leave the project at a critical time. While there will always be mutual agreement that a general's selling secrets to the enemy is a betrayal, many of the changes organizations and individuals working in them undertake cannot be so unambiguously understood by all to be betrayals. There seems to be no way to escape the fact that what are betrayals in work settings will often be matters of dispute.

Dispositional vs. Situationally Driven Betrayal

There has been a long-standing tension between dispositional theories, on the one hand, and situational theories, on the other, in social science. Despite widespread agreement that, in the famous equation of Lewin (1951), behavior is a function of both the person and the environment there remains only a limited number of truly interactionist models (see Eoyang, 1994, for a notable exception). The same pattern exists among those studying betrayal.

The clearest example of the dispositional approach to betrayal is provided by Jones and Burdette (1994) who conceptualized betrayal as driven by a personality trait; in addressing betrayal from this perspective they have developed a measure of an individual's propensity to betray, called the Interpersonal Betrayal Scale. In contrast, several other scholars have embraced the notion of situational relativity and argue for differences in interpretations of acts as betrayals as dependent on the nature of the relationship (Baxter et al., 1997; Clark & Waddell, 1985; O'Connell, 1984; Shackelford & Buss, 1996). For example, Baxter and colleagues argued that perceptions of an act as a betrayal will vary from one context to the next depending on the loyalty demands present. Similarly, Clark & Waddell (1985) examined differences in betrayal as a function of the type of relationship. According to their previous research (Clark & Mills, 1979) they argued that the rules concerning the benefits one expects to give and receive will vary depending on the type of relationship. Using the distinction between communal—whereby 'members feel a special obligation for the other's welfare' (Clark & Waddell, 1985, p. 404)—and exchange-based relationships (defined by the lack of this special obligation) these authors argued that 'behaviors considered unjust in one relationship may be considered perfectly acceptable in another' (p. 403). Echoing this sentiment, Shackelford and Buss (1996, p. 1152), argued from an evolutionary perspective to suggest, 'one way to predict and explain which behaviors will be interpreted as a betrayal of a relationship is to identify the adaptive benefits that might have accrued to ancestral humans forming that relationship'. From Baxter et al., Clark and Waddell, and Shackelford and Buss's perspectives different relationships are developed to reap different benefits and to the extent that the expected benefits differ across relationships there should be different perceptions of what constitutes a betrayal in the various contexts.

In order to better understand workplace betrayal we can draw on both perspectives. For example, research might seek to establish the validity of Jones and Burdette's (1994) Interpersonal Betrayal Scale for selection decisions. Similarly, we might be able to begin to identify those situations where perception of betrayal is a possibility by learning more about the loyalty demands in different situations, or the importance of different relationships and memberships to participants' self-identity. To assist the latter work, Baxter et al. (1997) reported a measure that can be used to determine the importance of relationships to one's sense of self, the Inclusion-of-Other-in-the-Self Scale (Aron, Aron & Smollan, 1992) and Luhtanen and Crocker (1992) have developed a measure of the importance of various social-group identities to the individual.

IMPLICATIONS

As complex, global organizational forms and contractual relationships increase in importance questions of trust, injustice and psychological contracts become more salient to the organizational enterprise. We identified betrayal as a concept central to these fields of study and to a better understanding of interpersonal relationships that was ill-understood. This review sought to introduce industrial/organizational psychologists to the wider literature on betrayal and to clarify its applications to the workplace. These arguments have several implications for current issues in research and practice in industrial/organizational psychology, which are elaborated below.

Clarifying Workplace Betrayal

First, we discovered that there are several different and conflicting understandings of workplace betrayal. We drew on the more extensive literatures on betrayal in social psychology, sociology, and political science to develop a more comprehensive understanding of workplace betrayal. First, we saw that simply stating that a transgressed expectation must be important or pivotal to elicit feelings of betrayal provides insufficient guidance. Specifying what is important and why, as social psychologists such as Shackelford and Buss have done, is necessary to theory development. Here we provided those features other scholars have said characterize important expectations and applied them to organizational settings, proposing that transgressions which violate constitutive expectations, violate a We-boundary, threaten a victim's sense of security, or threaten self-identity are more likely to be seen as betrayals. We hope these can provide a basis for theory development and testing of what leads to feelings of betrayal in the workplace.

Second, we suggested that defining impersonal betrayal as outside the scope of workplace betrayal was both misguided and unnecessary. Impersonal betrayals can be every bit as threatening as personal ones. Further, concerns about having one party to the transgression be a collective fade once we relax the requirement that a perpetrator must intend to harm the victims. If the perpetrator is aware of and indifferent to the potential harm he or she may cause, impersonal betrayal can be accommodated. Role obligations are simply too important to industrial/organizational psychology, to define them out of consideration.

Third, in industrial/organizational psychology normative advice on averting moral outrage has centred on admonitions to provide explanations and information to prevent an interpretation of the act as a betrayal. Yet this work suggests that transgressions of constitutive, relationship-forming rules that threatens one's security or identity are not likely to be mitigated with soothing words. Most people aren't going to be talked out of their perception that an action threatens the very basis of the relationship or is not a threat to their security or identity. Once such suspicions are engaged it would be difficult to present any sort of argumentation that would not be viewed as cravenly self-serving. Rather we would suggest that ambiguous acts which may or may not be interpreted as betrayals are comparatively rare in organizational settings. In functioning organizations many participants have extensive experience with one another and the setting and the areas of ambiguity are concomitantly small. This is not to say that explanation would not help to support employees' perceptions that they are respected and have standing (Tyler, 1998) or perhaps shift blame elsewhere, just that it would probably not lead individuals to be less likely to interpret an act as a betrayal, or to mitigate their rage once they have done so. Thus, at best, forestalling perceptions of betrayal would depend more on an advance understanding of employees' perceptions of their We-groups, their constitutive rules governing their relationships and memberships, and which relationships are important to their senses of security and self-identity. Only such foreknowledge would provide the information necessary to either shift expectations before the act or gird for the consequences if that is not possible.

Finally, we know too little about cross-cultural differences in perceptions of acts of betrayal or in reactions to felt betrayal. The extent to which culture influences the rules of relationships and perceptions of betrayal remains an as yet unexplored area of inquiry (Argyle & Henderson, 1984; Clark & Waddell, 1985). If transgressions are subject to ambiguity in a single organization in one society, the potential for differences in what constitutes a betrayal in cross-cultural settings is immense. For example, the first author has conducted research in formerly communist countries in transition to market economies, and she has found that newly installed American and British managers were engaging in what their subordinates believed to be acts of betrayal: violations of their employees' expectations that bosses should act as caring parents (e.g., Pearce, 1995). Even when these expatriate executives understood their subordinates' expectation they tended to dismiss them as wrong, expecting the employees to adopt their own constitutive rules once they had been shown their 'errors'. Clearly, constitutive rules are not so easily changed, and these subordinates' feelings of betrayal certainly were not mitigated by such instruction. Helping to identify differences in constitutive rules, We-boundaries, sources of security and the importance of memberships to self-identity could prove useful in averting serious breakdowns of trust in cross-cultural collaborations.

Extreme Emotions as Motivators of Workplace Behavior

One of the defining aspects of betrayal is that it evokes strong negative emotions. These strong emotions, in turn, hold great motivating power. As Ellsworth (1994, p. 25) has stated, 'many scholars believe that the primary function of emotion is to move the organism to appropriate action in circumstances consequential for its well-being.' We have argued that betrayal often involves a fundamental threat to one's security (i.e. well-being). As such, it provides a unique opportunity to examine the motivating potential of emotions. Given industrial/organizational psychology's long-standing interest in motivation, it is surprising that the emotions and the behaviors thereby motivated are only now coming under scrutiny.

Betrayal forms the basis for two suggestions for future research with respect to betrayal and the emotions evoked. First, research on betrayal has been relatively silent about the actual emotion elicited by an act interpreted as a betrayal. While almost everyone would agree that betrayal evokes strong negative emotions (Bateson, 1977) the actual form taken may vary considerably from feelings of sorrow to extreme rage. Åkerström (1991) uses a host of terms to express the negative emotions aroused, including indignation, contempt, revenge, and rage. Morrison and Robinson suggest that 'central to the experience of violation are the feelings of anger, resentment, bitterness, indignation, and even outrage' (1997, p. 231). It would be useful to illuminate the various scope conditions concerning the manifestation of the negative emotions involved in betrayal. For example, when will a terminated employee who had expected lifetime employment feel outrage versus bitterness? Perhaps the research on betrayal in I/O psychology has gotten ahead of itself by focusing on how to mitigate the consequences of the resultant negative emotions (e.g. Bies, 1987), while neglecting the various forms and consequences of negative emotion that may occur in the first place.

Attribution theories of emotion (e.g. Smith & Ellsworth, 1985; Ortony, Clore & Collins, 1988; Scherer, 1984; Weiner, 1985) could provide a useful starting point for understanding the workplace consequences of strong negative emotion. According to these attribution theorists, emotions result from an individual's appraisal of their environment along a number of dimensions. It is noteworthy that our review of the defining features of acts that elicit betrayal reflects some of the more general dimensions proffered by attribution theorists of emotion. That is, attribution theorists discuss the dimensions of novelty, agency, and norm/self-concept compatibility (see Ellsworth, 1994) which correspond to our discussions of security, intent, and identity centrality, respectively. For example, Ellsworth discussed evidence that the attribution of agency plays a crucial role in differentiating the resultant negative emotion. Thus, the employee who attributes the cause of her or his termination to fate or market conditions may feel bitterness, whereas an attribution of cause to a manager's betrayal may engender extreme feelings of outrage (cf. Frijda, 1986; Scherer, 1984).

This also illustrates the influential role of culture. For example, Matsumoto, Kudoh, Scherer & Wallbott (1988) reported that Japanese were less likely to assign blame to individuals than were American participants. When asked to assign responsibility, these participants were more likely to respond 'non-applicable' than were their American counterparts. This is particularly important with respect to betrayal, since research generally supports the notion that without blame there is generally little anger (Mesquita & Frijda, 1992). Indeed, there is some evidence provided by cultural psychologists suggesting that a situation that would evoke anger in more individualist cultures may actually evoke feelings of shame in more collectivist or interdependent cultures (e.g. Markus & Kitayama, 1991). Thus, the interdependence of emotion and culture suggests a variant of our situational argument concerning betrayal. To what extent does knowledge of betrayal developed in the more individualist cultures of North America and Northern Europe apply to cultures with different value systems? The role of culture suggests a host of scope conditions that need to be explored with increasing urgency in the globally integrated workplace.

Our second suggestion for future research has to do with the behaviors which result from an experienced emotion. That is, there is surprisingly little empirical research or theory in I/O psychology that predicts the actions of those who experience different emotions. Instead, most research and theory concerning the role of emotions at work has focused predominantly on their expression as distinct from their experience (e.g. Hochschild, 1983; Rafaeli & Sutton, 1989). Unfortunately, to our knowledge no one has yet conducted systematic empirical research about reactions to the experience of different workplace emotions (Jones and George, 1998, presented persuasive theory but, as yet, no empirical tests). How does the victim respond to the rage engendered by betrayal? How does the perpetrator respond to the guilt they feel upon their act of betrayal? When will the doctoral student who feels betrayed murder the offending professor (or himself)? These are just some of the questions that a review of betrayal suggests. The time is ripe to begin to develop a more nuanced understanding of the behavioral reactions to emotions at work.

CONCLUSIONS

Betrayal is vital to an understanding of the more interpersonally based networked organizational forms, and also is a surprisingly versatile reflection of many of the current interests of industrial/organizational psychologists. The concept is central to theories of trust, justice, and psychological contracts, and suggests productive areas of research in cross-cultural normative expectations, the efficacy of mitigating accounts in workplace settings, and the effects of strong emotion on workplace action. This review suggests that if it is something we are talking about more, such a conversation can be illuminating.

ACKNOWLEDGEMENTS

The authors wish to thank Greg Bigley, Marta Elvira, Gil Geis, Paul Olk, Amy Randel, and Chris Zatzick for their penetrating comments on an earlier draft.

REFERENCES

Afifi, W. A. & Metts, S. (1998). Characteristics and consequences of expectation violations in close relationships. *Journal of Social and Personal Relationships*, **15**, 365–392.

Åkerström, M. (1991). *Betrayal and Betrayers: The Sociology of Treachery*. London: Transaction.

Argyle, M. & Henderson, M. (1984). The rules of friendship. *Journal of Social and Personal Relationships*, **1**, 211–237.

Aron, A., Aron, E. N. & Smollan, D. (1992). Inclusion of other in the self scale and the structure of interpersonal closeness. *Journal of Personality and Social Psychology*, **63**, 596–612.

Bateson, G. (1997). *About Bateson: Essays on Gregory Bateson*. New York: Dutton.

Baumeister, R. F., Stillwell, A. & Wotman, S. R. (1990). Victim and perpetrator accounts of interpersonal conflict: Autobiographical narratives about anger. *Journal of Personality and Social Psychology*, **59**, 994–1005.

Baxter, L. A., Mazanec, M., Nicholson, J., Pittman, G., Smith, K. & West, L. (1997). Everyday loyalties and betrayals in personal relationships. *Journal of Social and Personal Relationships*, **14**, 655–678.

Bies, R. J. (1987). The predicament of injustice: The management of moral outrage. *Research in Organizational Behavior*, **9**, 289–319.

Bies, R. J. & Tripp, T. M. (1998). Revenge in organizations: The good, the bad, and the ugly. In R. W. Griffin, A. O'Leary-Kelly & J. M. Collins (Eds), *Dysfunctional Behavior in Organizations: Non-violent Dysfunctional Behavior* (pp. 49–67). Greenwick, CT: JAI Press.

Bies, R. J., Tripp, T. M. & Kramer, R. M. (1997). At the breaking point: Cognitive and social dynamics of revenge in organizations. In R. A. Giacalone & J. Greenberg (Eds), *Antisocial Behavior in Organizations* (pp. 18–36). Thousand Oaks, CA: Sage.

Bigley, G. A. & Pearce, J. L. (1998). Straining for shared meaning in organization science: Problems of trust and distrust. *Academy of Management Review*, **23**, 405–421.

Clark, M. S. & Mills, J. (1979). Interpersonal attraction in exchange and communal relationships. *Journal of Personality & Social Psychology*, **37**, 12–24.

Clark, M. S. & Waddell, B. (1985). Perceptions of exploitation in communal and exchange relationships. *Journal of Social and Personal Relationships*, **2**, 403–418.

Elangovan, A. R. & Shapiro, D. L. (1998). Betrayal of trust in organizations. *Academy of Management Review*, **23**, 547–566.

Ellsworth, P. C. (1994). Sense, culture, and sensibility. In S. Kitayama and H.R. Markus (Eds), *Emotion and Culture: Empirical Studies of Mutual Influence* (pp. 23–50). Washington DC: American Psychological Association.

Eoyang, C. (1994). Models of espionage. In T. R. Sarbin, R. M. Carney & C. Eoyang (Eds), *Citizen Espionage* (pp. 69–92). London: Praeger.

Frijda, N. H. (1986). *The Emotions*. Cambridge: Cambridge University Press.

Greenberg, J. & Scott, K. S. (1996). Why do workers bite the hands that feed them? Employee theft as a social exchange process. *Research in Organizational Behvavior*, **18**, 111–156.

Hansson, R. O., Jones, W. H. & Fletcher, W. L. (1990). Troubled relationships in later life: Implications for support. *Journal of Social & Personal Relationships*, **7**, 451–463.

Hochschild, A. (1983). *The Managed Heart*. Berkeley, CA: University of California Press.

Jones, G. R. & George, J. M. (1998). The experience and evolution of trust: Implications for cooperation and teamwork. *Academy of Management Review*, **23**, 531–546.

Jones, W. H. & Burdgette, M. P. (1994). Betrayal in relationships. In A. L. Weber & J. H. Harvey (Eds), *Perspectives on Close Relationships* (pp. 243–262). Boston: Allyn & Bacon.

Lewin, K. (1951). *Field Theory in Social Sciences*. New York: Harper & Row.

Luhtanen, R. & Crocker, J. (1992). A collective self-esteem scale: Self-evaluation of one's social identity. *Personality and Social Psychology Bulletin*, **18**, 302–318.

Markus, H. R. & Kitayama, S. (1991). Culture and the self: Implications for cognition, emotion and motivation. *Psychological Review*, **98**, 224–253.

Masumoto, D., Kudoh, T., Scherer, K. & Wallbott, H. (1988). Antecedents of and reactions to emotions in the United States and Japan. *Journal of Cross Cultural Psychology*, **19**, 267–286.

Mesquita, B. & Frijda, N. H. (1992). Cultural variations in emotions: A review. *Psychological Bulletin*, **412**, 179–204.

Metts, S. (1989). An exploratory investigation of deception in close relationships. *Journal of Social and Personal Relationships*, **6**, 159–179.

Metts, S. (1994). Relational transgressions. In W.R. Cupach and B.H. Spitzberg (Eds), *The Dark Side of Interpersonal Communication* (pp. 217–239). Hillsdale, NJ: Erlbaum.

Morris, J. H. & Moberg, D. J. (1994). Work organizations as contexts for trust and betrayal. In T. R. Sarbin, R. M. Carney & C. Eoyang (Eds), *Citizen Espionage* (pp. 163–201). London: Praeger.

Morrison, E. W. & Robinson, S. L. (1997). When employees feel betrayed: A model of how psychological contract violation develops. *Academy of Management Review*, **22**, 226–256.

North, D. (1990). *Institutions, Institutional Change and Economic Performance*. London: Cambridge University Press.

O'Connell, L. (1984). An exploration of exchange in three social relationships: Kinship, friendship, and the marketplace. *Journal of Social and Personal Relationships*, **1**, 333–345.

Ortony, A., Clore, G. & Collins, A. (1988). *The Cognitive Structure of Emotions*. New York: Cambridge University Press.

Ouchi, W. G. (1980). Markets, bureaucracies and clans. *Administrative Science Quarterly*, **25**, 129–141.

Pearce, J. L. (1995). A reviewer's introduction to staging the new romantic hero in the old cynical theatre: On managers, roles and change in Poland. *Journal of Organizational Behavior*, **16**, 628–630.

Rafaeli, A. & Sutton, R. I. (1989). The expression of emotion in organizational life. In L. L. Cummings & B. M. Staw (Eds), *Research in Organizational Behavior*, Vol. 11 (pp. 1–42). Greenwich, CT: JAI Press.

Robinson, S. L. (1996). Trust and breach of the psychological contract. *Administrative Science Quarterly*, **41**, 574–599.

Robinson, S. L., Kraatz, M. S. & Rousseau, D. M. (1994). Changing obligations and the psychological contract: A longitudinal study. *Academy of Management Journal*, **37**, 137–152.

Roethlisberger, F. J. & Dickson, W. J. (1939). *Management and the Worker*. Cambridge, MA: Harvard University Press.

Rousseau, D. M. (1989). Psychological and implied contracts in organizations. *Employee Responsibilities and Rights Journal*, **2**, 121–139.

Rousseau, D. M. (1995). *Psychological Contracts in Organizations*. Thousand Oaks, CA: Sage.

Scherer, K. R. (1984). On the nature and function of emotions: A component process approach. In P. Ekman & K. Scherer (Eds), *Approaches to Emotion* (pp. 293–317). Hillsdale, NJ: Erlbaum.

Shackelford, T. K. (1997). Perceptions of betrayal and the design of the mind. In J. A. Simpson and D. T. Kenrick (Eds), *Evolutionary Social Psychology* (pp. 73–107), Hillsdale, NJ: Erlbaum.

Shackelford, T. K. & Buss, D. M. (1996). Betrayal in mateships, friendships, and coalitions. *Personality and Social Psychology Bulletin*, **22**, 1151–1164.

Shale, T. (1993). What went wrong? *AsiaMoney*, **4**(6), 14–16.

Simmel, G. (1964). *The Sociology of Georg Simmel*. Trans., ed. K. Wolff. Part 4, *The Secret and the Secret Society* (pp. 307–355). New York: Free Press.

Smith, C. A. & Ellsworth, P. C. (1985). Patterns of cognitive appraisal in emotion. *Journal of Personality and Social Psychology*, **48**(4), 813–838.

Tyler, T. R. (1998). The psychology of authority relations. In R. M. Kramer & M. A. Neale (Eds), *Power and Influence in Organizations*. Thousand Oaks, CA: Sage.

Weinber, B. (1985). An attributional theory of achievement motivation and emotion. *Psychological Review*, **92**, 548–573.

Zucker, L. G. (1986). The production of trust: Institutional sources of economic structure 1840–1920. *Research in Organizational Behavior*, **8**, 53–111.

Chapter 5

THE INTERFACE BETWEEN JOB AND OFF-JOB ROLES: ENHANCEMENT AND CONFLICT

Michael P. O'Driscoll
University of Waikato, New Zealand

INTRODUCTION

Since 1977, when Rosabeth Kanter debunked the 'myth of separate worlds', growing interest and concern has been expressed by academics and practitioners alike for the interaction between job experiences and life off the job. As noted by Burke and Greenglass (1987), there are several possible reasons for the burgeoning literature on this topic. Changing family structures and orientations toward parenthood, greater participation by women in the workforce, increasing linkages between people's jobs/careers and their family lives, and changing work values and aspirations have highlighted the mutual interaction between job and off-the-job experiences. In addition, technological developments over the past decade (for example, portable computers and mobile telephones) have facilitated a blurring of boundaries between these two domains, to the point where for many workers they have become virtually inseparable. As a result, it can no longer be presumed that workers are able to compartmentalize their job and off-job lives into distinct, non-overlapping categories (Wiley, 1991).

As well as changes in technology and other job-related characteristics (such as work schedules), another major source of influence has been the evolution of family structures. The traditional model of the family, with males providing the financial foundation and females occupying the role of homemaker and childcarer, is in many societies 'becoming a vestige of the past' (Aryee, 1993). While it is still the case that women assume the major family responsibilities, there is a growing trend for household and family tasks to be shared among men and women.

Interest in the interplay between the job and off-job domains has not been limited to academics conducting research in industrial and organizational

The Interface Between Job and Off-Job Roles: Enhancement and Conflict by Michael P. O'Driscoll taken from IRIOP 1996 v11, Edited by Cary L. Cooper and Ivan T. Robertson: © 1996 John Wiley & Sons, Ltd

psychology. Managers in organizations have also begun to show concern for the effects of off-the-job experiences on variables such as job performance and work-related attitudes. From an organizational standpoint, knowledge about factors outside the workplace which may influence relevant job attitudes and behaviours can provide valuable information for the development of human resource management policies and practices. Reducing costs of absenteeism and increasing employee commitment to the organization, which in turn is associated with reduced turnover, are important considerations for managers wishing to optimize the utilization of their human resources.

At a societal level, too, social analysts, decision makers and politicians are becoming increasingly aware of the implications of the interaction between the worlds of 'work' and 'non-work'. For example, the continuing rise in many countries of the proportion of women engaged in full-time paid employment has engendered many governmental and legislative policy changes in areas such as parental leave (for both mothers and fathers!), recognition of the importance of providing facilities for the care of dependants (whether they be children or elderly relatives), and more flexible work schedules to accommodate the needs of employees with family responsibilities (Kalleberg & Rosenfeld, 1990). While many of these changes have occurred in reaction to demands from particular pressure groups within society, they have brought with them significant changes in societal attitudes about the role of paid employment in people's lives and the desirability of maintaining a balance between job demands and responsibilities and commitments and interests outside the work environment.

Researchers interested in these issues have sought to identify the nature of the interface between people's job and off-job lives and to describe the processes which account for the influence of each domain upon the other. The aim of the present chapter is to outline major theoretical explanations for the interaction between job and off-job experiences, to overview recent research on the antecedents and consequences of this interaction, and to discuss implications for both individual coping strategies and organizational human resource management policies and practices.

THEORETICAL PERSPECTIVES

Several perspectives have been developed to examine and explain the interplay between job and off-job experiences. Zedeck and Mosier (1990), for example, have noted that there are five main models of the association between job experiences and life off the job. An early view, which was prevalent in the 1950s and 1960s, is the *segmentation* hypothesis, which proposes that the worlds of work and family are quite distinct and that there is no influence from one domain to the other. In other words, experiences and behaviours related to one's job have no bearing on these variables outside of work, and vice versa. Currently, however, this perspective has little credibility among researchers in the field. In contrast, the *spillover* model assumes that domain boundaries are permeable and that the impact of experiences in one domain (for example, the job context) will influence attitudes and behaviours in the other (for instance, family interactions). While much research has focused on positive spillover of attitudes and satisfactions from one sphere to the other, there is also evidence of negative emotional spillover, especially from the job context to the off-job domain (Bartolome & Evans, 1980; Jackson, Zedeck & Summers, 1986).

A third model is based upon the notion of *compensation*, whereby deficits within one domain (for example, in satisfaction) are compensated for in the other. It is assumed that individuals invest differential levels of energy into their work and off-the-job activities, and derive satisfaction from one sphere to compensate for lack of satisfaction in the other.

In contrast to both this view and the segmentation hypothesis, a fourth model, referred to by Zedeck and Mosier (1990) as *instrumental* theory, suggests that involvement in one role can provide resources for the person to be successful or achieve his/her goals in the other setting. For example, the job serves as a source of income which can then be used to acquire material resources needed for family life. This perspective focuses attention primarily on material resources which may be desirable or even necessary for effective functioning in each domain, but the logic can be extended to include non-material resources (such as emotional support from family members or supervisors at work).

The final model outlined by Zedeck and Mosier (1990) is the *conflict* approach to the job/off-job relationship. This view holds that individuals have finite time and energy, such that satisfaction or success in one environment entails some sacrifice in the other. In essence, according to this perspective engagement in multiple roles necessarily entails some degree of interrole conflict, either because of time constraints or because behavioural norms and expectations in the two domains may be incompatible. Conflict between the two domains is presumed to generate stress and hence detract from psychological well-being.

The above models have dominated the literature on job/off-job relationships and extensive research has been conducted to establish their respective validities. Many of the early studies in this field compared predictions from the spillover hypothesis with those derived from the compensation and segmentation perspectives, and focused almost exclusively on satisfaction levels as the criterion variable. By and large, the weight of evidence favoured spillover, although some studies demonstrated that it is not impossible for spillover and compensation to exist concurrently (Miller & Weiss, 1982).

More recently, however, efforts have been directed toward investigating the mechanisms underlying the occurrence of spillover. Rather than simply gauging the size and sign of correlations between job-related and off-job behaviours and satisfaction, researchers have become more interested in exploring the social and psychological conditions under which there is positive and negative spillover. Studies are also being conducted to determine whether the job and off-job domains compete with each other for a person's attention and energy or whether they are complementary.

The present discussion focuses on these latter issues. Following numerous demonstrations that the job and off-job spheres do interact, it is argued here that the important agenda for research now and in the future is to determine the processes by which these domains overlap. A primary aim of this research must be to explore strategies which facilitate a positive and constructive interaction between job and off-job experiences, leading to enhancement of individual well-being and organizational productivity.

Conflict Between Competing Roles

The *conflict* hypothesis, mentioned above, represents one current line of thought on the relationship between the worlds of paid employment and life off the job. A fundamental issue for this hypothesis is that individuals engage in several roles in life, some of which are associated with their job while others (such as family activities) fall outside the work environment. The conflict hypothesis states that individuals have finite resources in terms of time and energy, and that demands from different roles will tax those resources (Tiedje, Wortman, Downey, Emmons, Biernat & Lang, 1990).

Gutek, Searle and Klepa (1991) have labelled this the *rational* view, because it presumes that the extent of interrole conflict is directly proportional to the amount of time (or energy) expended in each domain. It has also been referred to as the *utilitarian* approach (Lobel, 1991), since it focuses upon the rewards and costs of investing time and energy into specific roles. The utilitarian model depicts life as a struggle between competing roles which have differential reward:cost ratios (Lobel, 1991). The common theme in each of these characterizations is that conflict between roles is inevitable—the more time and energy required to perform specific roles successfully, the greater the extent of interrole conflict. Obtaining balance between role demands is considered to be an ongoing task for people occupying multiple roles, especially those connected with paid employment and with family activities. As noted by Lambert (1990), individuals may have to engage in a process of accommodation, where they limit or modify their involvement in one sphere to accommodate the demands of the other. For instance, intensive demands from the job may require the person to significantly reduce his or her input into family life.

In addition to time-based conflict, Greenhaus and Beutell (1985) have highlighted two other sources of interrole conflict. One which is mentioned less often in the literature is the potential for conflict between role norms and expectations. Greenhaus and Beutell referred to this as behaviour-based conflict. As well as competing for one's time and physical energy, the attitudes, values and behaviours required in one role may be incompatible with those needed in another. For example, in the work context an employee may be expected to be aggressive, ambitious, hard-driving and task-oriented. Successful job performance (and the rewards associated with such performance) may be contingent upon demonstration of these behavioural characteristics. In the home situation, however, being loving, supportive, accommodating and relationship-oriented may be regarded as essential to the development of a positive family life. Clearly these oppositional behavioural expectations may create tension within individuals as they make the transition from one environment to another.

A third source of potential conflict between roles is strain-based conflict, which is induced by emotional interference from one domain to the other (Greenhaus & Beutell, 1985; Jackson, Zedeck & Summers, 1985; Small & Riley, 1990). In particular, job conditions (such as work overload, poor interpersonal relations, job insecurity, and lack of opportunity to exercise control and self-direction) can produce negative emotional consequences (reduced self-esteem, feelings of uncertainty, loss of a sense of competence) which impinge upon interactions within the family (Menaghan, 1991). These negative emotional reactions within the work environment can lead to expressions of irritability toward family members or withdrawal from family interaction in order to recuperate (Menaghan, 1991). Similarly, it is possible that the stresses and strains of family life might carry over into the work context, although evidence of this is less conclusive (Higgins & Duxbury, 1992; Jackson, Zedeck & Summers, 1985; Williams & Alliger, 1994).

Enhancement Effect of Multiple Role Involvements

In contrast to the assumptions underlying the notion of interrole conflict, some theorists and researchers have emphasized the benefits which may accrue from involvement in multiple roles (Kirchmeyer, 1992a,b; Tiedje et al., 1990; Wiersma, 1990). The *enhancement* hypothesis suggests that involvement in several roles can energize individuals and provide them with resources (for instance, skills and social support) that they may not acquire from engagement in a single role. According to this view, multiple role involvement enhances, rather than detracts from, their role performances.

An early formulation of the enhancement hypothesis was articulated by Sieber (1974), who argued that there are many rewards associated with role 'accumulation' which can offset the strain arising from interrole conflict. Involvement in multiple roles can 'make life more varied and therefore more interesting and purposeful, bring extra money, and provide a buffer against distress generated in one particular role' (Wiersma, 1990, p. 233). More extensive social interaction and social support may be available to individuals who engage in several roles, and skills developed in one role may transfer to other roles. For instance, parenting skills may be applicable to supervision of subordinates in the work context (Tiedje et al., 1990). Finally, consistent with the compensation hypothesis mentioned earlier, individuals may be buffered from disappointments and failures in one role by receiving gratification from other roles.

Another early contributor to the debate over enhancement versus conflict was Marks (1977), who noted that time and commitment are critical elements of role involvement. According to one viewpoint (the 'scarcity' perspective), time and energy are limited resources (Ilgen & Hollenbeck, 1991; Kirchmeyer, 1992b; Wiley, 1991) and hence commitment to one role necessarily means less available time and energy for other roles. In contrast, the 'expansion' approach suggests that energy is an abundant and expandable commodity, and that some activities may in fact produce energy, rather than sapping it. For instance, Marks suggests, involvement in family relationships, while time-consuming, can create satisfaction and psychological energy which carries over to the work setting. Such transfer of energy represents an illustration of positive spillover.

Clearly the scarcity and expansion viewpoints generate contradictory hypotheses about the relationship between time and energy devoted to one sphere and levels of involvement (and satisfaction) in the other (Kirchmeyer, 1992b). The scarcity hypothesis predicts negative spillover and hence conflict between the job and off-job domains, whereas the expansion model indicates that positive spillover and enhancement can occur. In other words, while interrole conflict has been presumed to induce dissatisfaction and stress among individuals as they endeavour to balance competing demands, it is also possible that (in some cases at least) the positive benefits of role accumulation may outweigh the burdens of multiple role involvement.

The following sections of this chapter outline empirical evidence relating to the conflict/enhancement debate. Over the past 20 years considerable research evidence has been gathered on the job/off-job interface. Earlier reviews (see, for example, Burke & Greenglass, 1987; Greenhaus & Parasuraman, 1987; Lambert, 1990; Lobel, 1991) have summarized research conducted up to the late 1980s, hence the primary focus here will be on empirical findings reported more recently (over the past five years), although earlier investigations will also be referred to. Studies of the antecedents of conflict and enhancement will be discussed first, followed by an overview of outcomes. Given the centrality of gender roles in the interaction between job and off-the-job roles, findings relating to gender differences in interrole conflict will also be highlighted. Finally, strategies for coping with this form of conflict and facilitating a positive relationship between the job and off-job domains, along with implications for organizational policies and practices, will be considered.

Before we examine the findings and conclusions from empirical research in this field, two brief comments on methodology are needed. First, many studies have been conducted to assess interrelationships between job satisfaction, off-job (usually family) satisfaction, and overall life satisfaction. While the findings of these studies are pertinent to the current topic, the focus in this review is on research which has directly assessed interference or enhancement between roles. Secondly, a major constraint on drawing definitive conclusions and comparing data across studies is that different, and sometimes non-equivalent, measures of interrole spillover have been utilized. In particular, while some studies have assessed bi-directional interference between the job domain and life off the job (e.g. Frone, Russell & Cooper, 1992a,b; Gutek, Searle & Klepa, 1991; O'Driscoll, Ilgen & Hildreth,1992; Williams & Alliger, 1994), others have measured either non-directional conflict (e.g. Goff, Mount & Jamison, 1990; Wiersma & van den Berg, 1991) or have examined interference in one direction only (e.g. Aryee, 1993; Small & Riley, 1990; Kirchmeyer, 1992a,b). In addition, most research in this field has restricted its focus to job–family interactions, although some investigators (e.g. Kirchmeyer, 1992a,b; O'Driscoll, Ilgen & Hildreth, 1992) have included a broader range of areas in the off-job domain (such as community, political and recreational activities). Although all of these studies purportedly investigate interrole spillover (either positive or negative), lack of equivalence in foci and measurement instruments limits the extent to which generalizations can be made.

ANTECEDENTS OF CONFLICT AND ENHANCEMENT

Prior to the late 1980s, most empirical studies on the job/off-job interface concentrated on describing the relationships between job and off-job roles, rather than assessing antecedents of those relationships. In more recent years, however, greater attention has been given to exploring predictors of interrole enhancement or conflict.

Time Demands

Based on the scarcity model of interrole interactions, a few studies have focused on time demands from the two domains as predictors of interrole conflict. For example, Wiersma and van den Berg (1991) found that time spent on domestic responsibilities correlated with interrole conflict for women, whereas for men time devoted to the job was the more significant predictor of conflict. As noted above, however, Wiersma and van den Berg measured undifferentiated interrole conflict, which precludes analysis of the direction of interference (job to family or vice versa).

Using separate indices of job→family and family→job conflict, Gutek, Searle & Klepa (1991) reported that time devoted to activities in one sphere (e.g. family) was not necessarily linked with time spent in the other (e.g. paid work). In addition, they observed an asymmetry in the impact of time demands, indicating that interference of the job with family commitments and responsibilities is not the same as interference in the other direction.

Picking up on this issue, O'Driscoll, Ilgen and Hildreth (1992) conducted a path analysis of the linkages between time demands (from both job and off-the-job activities), bi-directional interrole conflict, and affective experiences (job satisfaction, off-job satisfaction, organizational commitment, and psychological strain). Consistent with Gutek, Searle and Klepa's data (and those reported in an earlier study by Kopelman, Greenhaus & Connolly, 1983), O'Driscoll, Ilgen and Hildreth found that time devoted to work-related activities was a predictor of interference between the job and life off the job, but off-job time demands did not show a corresponding effect. In a further study of managerial women, O'Driscoll and Humphries (1994) observed a significant correlation between hours spent on the job and job interference (with off-job activities), but only a small (and non-significant) relationship between off-job hours and off-job interference with work. Kirchmeyer (1992a) also found no spillover from off-job time commitments to the job. Together, the findings of these studies suggest that it is important to differentiate between various sources of time demands, as well as examining possible differences between the experiences of men and women.

Role Overload

Another way of considering the effects of limited time is to examine overload in one or more roles that an individual occupies. It is logical to surmise that excessive demands or pressures from one role would impinge upon the individual's capacity to function effectively in others, and would reduce the amount of energy available to perform other roles (Greenhaus & Parasuraman, 1987). Surprisingly, however, although some studies (e.g. Frone, Russell & Cooper, 1992a) have included role overload as part of a set of job and off-job stressors, relatively few researchers have directly assessed the unique contribution of this variable to interrole conflict.

Greenhaus, Parasuraman, Granrose, Rabinowitz and Beutell (1989) explored sources of work–family conflict among dual-career couples, finding that role overload predicted both time-based and strain-based conflict. On the other hand, Bacharach, Bamberger and Conley (1991) obtained a role overload effect in only one of the two samples they investigated. In their study, overload was a strong predictor of conflict between the job and home life for engineers, but not for nurses. Bacharach, Bamberger and Conley speculated that perhaps role overload is expected by nurses (but not by engineers); because it is anticipated and 'routine', steps may be taken to minimize its effects on life outside the job.

While they did not measure interrole conflict directly, Bolger, DeLongis, Kessler and Wethington (1989) found that role overload may lead to stress 'contagion', that is a carry over of psychological strain from one domain to another. Their research revealed that overload at home predicted job-related stress for men, but not women, while work overload was associated with stress at home for both men and women. As with the findings on time demands discussed above, Bolger et al.'s results illustrate that it is important to distinguish between the sources of overload when examining its impact on affective experiences.

These few examples provide suggestive evidence that role overload may be a potential contributor to conflict between job and off-job activities, although clearly more systematic exploration is needed to determine how overload influences interrole conflict. In particular, it would be informative to ascertain whether the effect of overload in one domain (e.g. the work context) is due to a reduction in overall energy levels of the individual, distraction of attention away from activities in the other domain (e.g. family responsibilities), or some other process (such as stress contagion, as suggested by Bolger et al., 1989). Further research should identify the unique contribution of overload, as well as its additive influence when combined with other role stressors.

Psychological Involvement

The extent to which individuals devote their time and physical energy to performance of a particular role is, of course, just one indicator of their involvement in that role. Another important element is the psychological investment they make in the role. This is sometimes referred to as 'commitment', although 'involvement' has also been commonly used to describe cognitive and emotional attachment to one's job or roles in the off-job domain, such as parenting and marriage. Psychological investment or involvement can lead to a preoccupation with the demands and responsibilities of a particular role, 'even when physically attempting to fulfill the demands of a second role' (Frone, Russell & Cooper, 1992a, p. 67).

Most research on involvement has focused on the implications of high levels of job involvement for engagement in roles outside work, such as marital functioning. Several studies have shown that high job involvement is frequently associated with work–family conflict, that is interference of the job with family commitments and responsibilities (e.g. Frone & Rice, 1987; Greenhaus et al., 1989; Wiley, 1987). However, some recent investigations have also reported on linkages between off-job (usually family) involvement and interrole conflict. Kirchmeyer (1992a) assessed the impact of off-job experiences on the job domain, and found that high off-job involvement was associated more with enhancement than with interrole conflict, although the type of spillover varied for different off-job activities. Specifically, involvement in parenting and recreational activities was more likely to lead to positive than negative spillover from the off-job domain into the work context, whereas the opposite was true for community involvement. Kirchmeyer suggested that both the benefits and the burdens of specific roles might become more accentuated with increasing levels of involvement, potentially leading to positive and negative spillover simultaneously.

Higgins, Duxbury and Irving (1992) and Williams and Alliger (1994) also explored the association between high levels of both job and family involvement and work–family conflict. Williams and Alliger (1994) observed complementary effects of job and family involvement on job interference (with family life) and family interference (with the job). In the Higgins, Duxbury and Irving (1992) study, job involvement significantly predicted interrole conflict, but levels of family involvement were not linked with conflict. Some caution is required in comparing these findings with other studies, however, since Higgins, Duxbury and Irving used a global measure of interrole conflict which did not distinguish between the type of interference (that is, job→family or family→job).

Frone, Russell and Cooper (1992a) have conducted the most direct assessment of the contributions of both job and family involvement to interrole conflict. In a longitudinal study of over 1600 workers, Frone and his colleagues found that psychological involvement in the family induced family-→work conflict, whereas high job involvement did not have a significant bearing on work→family conflict. These findings are of interest because they appear to be at odds with research discussed earlier on time demands, which suggested more interference from job-related time demands than from time devoted to off-job activities. One explanation for this apparent discrepancy might be that levels of family involvement reported by Frone, Russell and Cooper's respondents were notably higher than corresponding levels of job involvement, while the extent of family→work conflict was somewhat lower than work→family conflict.

Within-role Ambiguity and Conflict

In addition to role overload, ambiguity and conflict within roles (especially in the work context) have been associated with job-off-job interference. Of the two role strains, within-role *conflict* has been assessed more frequently as a predictor of interference. Earlier studies, although few in number, illustrated that the experience of conflict with supervisors, subordinates and peers in the work setting was significantly associated with greater interference between work and family (see Higgins, Duxbury & Irving, 1992). Recent investigations, especially those which have distinguished between job→family and family→job interference, have yielded less definitive results. Bacharach, Bamberger and Conley (1991), and Higgins and his colleagues (Higgins & Duxbury, 1992; Higgins, Duxbury & Irving, 1992) observed that role conflict in the job was strongly linked with interrole conflict, and Barling and MacEwen (1992) indirectly demonstrated the salience of role conflict. On the other hand, in their studies of dual-career couples Aryee (1993) found no significant influence of work-related conflict and Greenhaus et al. (1989) observed an effect for women but not men. Hence, although the literature on role stressors provides substantial support for the notion that job-related conflict is a powerful predictor of psychological strain and job dissatisfaction (O'Driscoll & Beehr, 1994), evidence for its contribution to interrole conflict between work and family is less conclusive.

Role *ambiguity* on the job has been explored in three recent studies of work–family conflict. Frone, Russell and Cooper (1992a) included ambiguity in their set of role stressors which were significantly linked with work→family conflict, although they did not explore the specific impact of ambiguity itself. Greenhaus et al. (1989) and Aryee (1993) did examine the unique contribution of role ambiguity to interrole conflict. Aryee (1993) found that the relationship between ambiguity and interrole conflict was stronger for men than for women, while Greenhaus and his colleagues observed a significant link for men only. These findings suggest that 'role ambiguity is a more potent source of work–family conflict for men than for women . . . (and) that the stress produced by role ambiguity intrudes more severely into the family lives of men than women' (Greenhaus et al., 1989, p. 149). Unfortunately, no studies have been conducted to determine whether the influence of ambiguity on interrole conflict is direct or mediated by job-related strain or other variables.

Other Predictors

In addition to the variables discussed above, several other potential predictors of job/off-job conflict have been explored. Given a lack of systematic replication, findings for these variables must be treated with caution, but they do offer suggestive evidence on their possible contribution and highlight themes for further investigation.

Some studies have focused on family variables as potential sources of interrole conflict or enhancement. Aryee (1993) and Frone, Russell and Cooper (1992a), for example, found that family stressors (such as the number of young children, lack of spouse support, and parental workload) predicted conflict between family and job, while Wiersma and van den Berg (1991) found that family climate and domestic responsibilities (number of family and household chores) also influenced the degree of interrole conflict experienced. Similarly, Williams and Alliger (1994) observed that family intrusions into work time and distress within the family contributed to family→work interference. On the other side of the coin, Tiedje et al. (1990) reported that social support from one's spouse was a significant predictor of interrole enhancement among professional women. Although not discussed in detail by Tiedje and her colleagues, it is likely that practical assistance with the management of daily household and family tasks, plus empathic consideration from one's partner or spouse, will facilitate the balancing of job/career and family responsibilities (O'Driscoll & Humphries, 1994).

Within the job domain, several task attributes have been implicated as sources of interrole conflict. In addition to the variables mentioned above, lack of autonomy at work (Greenhaus et al., 1989; Thomas & Ganster, 1995) and task complexity (Greenhaus et al., 1989) have been found to induce conflict, while supervisor support for accommodating family responsibilities and perceived control over the job (Thomas & Ganster, 1995) may alleviate perceptions of conflict. Flexible time schedules can have a positive impact, presumably because they create feelings of greater control (Thomas & Ganster, 1995). On the other hand, following an earlier study by Cooke and Rousseau (1984), Higgins, Duxbury and Irving (1992) showed that an expectation that the job will expand beyond normal hours and may entail extra duties can heighten a sense of conflict with off-job commitments and responsibilities.

In sum, a complex array of factors may function to influence the degree of conflict or enhancement experienced by individuals as they endeavour to fulfil multiple roles. Consistent with earlier research, recent studies outlined above illustrate that variables within both the job and off-job domains can make a substantial contribution to perceptions of the interface between these two spheres of life. It is clear that job-related demands and overload can induce interrole conflict, while support from the organization (for example, supervisors) can serve to reduce or alleviate it. The effects of other role variables, such as ambiguity and conflict, are less clearcut and require further investigation. Characteristics of the off-job environment, such as family stressors, also may contribute to increased conflict, although there is no systematic evidence that the amount of time devoted to activities in the off-job sphere will increase the degree of interference with job performance. Support from one's partner or spouse, along with flexibility in fulfilling commitments (on and off the job), can have a positive effect on a person's ability to balance multiple roles.

OUTCOMES OF CONFLICT AND ENHANCEMENT

As with research on antecedents, investigations of outcomes relating to the job/off-job interface have been scattered in terms of their foci. A 1987 review by Greenhaus and Parasuraman highlighted several possible consequences of conflict between job and off-job roles, including dissatisfaction (with the job and life in general), along with psychological strain and somatic problems. These reviewers noted, however, that evidence is by no means conclusive that involvement in multiple roles is necessarily detrimental to mental and physical health. More recent research has attempted to clarify the relationship between interrole conflict or enhancement and specific outcome variables.

Satisfaction

Several researchers have examined the impact of interrole conflict on job satisfaction, as well as satisfaction with off-job roles (such as parenting and marriage). For instance, O'Driscoll, Ilgen and Hildreth (1992) and Thomas and Ganster (1995) observed a direct relationship between levels of job/off-job conflict and dissatisfaction with the job, and Rice, Frone and McFarlin (1992) found direct paths between conflict and both job and off-job satisfaction. On the other hand, while Tiedje et al. (1990) noted that women who experienced high conflict/low enhancement reported significantly less satisfaction with parenting than did women with high enhancement and low conflict, they obtained no differences between these groups in levels of job satisfaction. Finally, consistent with findings from two earlier studies (Cooke & Rousseau, 1984; Kopelman, Greenhaus & Connolly, 1983), Bacharach, Bamberger and Conley (1991) reported that the effect of interrole conflict on job satisfaction was mediated by burnout, rather than being direct.

Although she did not directly measure interrole conflict, Kirchmeyer (1992b) obtained data suggesting that time devoted to off-the-job roles such as parenting and community work can actually increase, rather than detract from, job satisfaction. In keeping with the enhancement hypothesis, involvement in these roles may enrich personal resources (e.g. competencies, self-esteem) which carry over into the job domain and 'enhance the person's capacity to meet work demands and his or her importance to the organization' (Kirchmeyer, 1992b, p. 790).

Rather than focusing on job or off-job satisfaction *per se*, Higgins and his colleagues examined quality of work and family life as criterion variables. In two studies (Higgins & Duxbury, 1992; Higgins, Duxbury & Irving, 1992), they found that job–family conflict predicted reductions in both quality of work life and quality of family life, although there was more effect on family life. These findings indicate that spillover into the off-job domain is due to inflexibility in work schedules, outdated organizational policies which reinforce the myth of separate worlds (Kanter, 1977), and lack of social support for individuals who choose to be involved in both career and family responsibilities. Other commentators have suggested that, compared with the job, family boundaries may be more permeable, and hence more readily disrupted by job–family conflict, whereas job-related expectations concerning work hours and commitments are relatively inflexible in many occupations (Frone, Russell & Cooper, 1992b; Lobel, 1991; Wiley, 1991). Similarly, employees may believe they have more control over family activities than over the time they can devote to their job (Gutek, Searle & Klepa, 1991; Frone, Russell & Cooper, 1992a), which they might view as the organization's rather than their own responsibility.

Health Consequences

Other studies have explored the effects on mental and physical health of being engaged simultaneously in several roles. Considerable evidence is now available that where there is a high degree of conflict between these roles, negative

emotional outcomes are more likely. Confirming the findings of earlier research (e.g. Cooke & Rousseau, 1984), recent studies have illustrated that
interrole conflict generates *psychological strain* (Frone, Russell & Cooper,
1992a; O'Driscoll, Ilgen & Hildreth, 1992; Small & Riley, 1990), although it
is not yet clear which direction of interference (job→family or family→job)
has more impact on strain. Whereas Frone, Russell and Cooper (1992a)
reported that only family→job conflict induced strain, O'Driscoll and his
colleagues found the converse.

Additional indicators of mental health, such as *anxiety* and *depression*, have
also been explored. Small and Riley (1990) found that negative spillover from
the job was associated with anxiety, while Frone, Russell and Cooper (1992a),
Thomas and Ganster (1995), and Tiedje et al. (1990) have observed higher
levels of depression among individuals who experienced interrole conflict.
Frone and his colleagues noted, however, that this relationship was indirect,
being mediated by job-related psychological strain.

Another index of mental health and psychological well-being is *burnout*,
which is a chronic affective response to very extreme emotional demands both
on and off the job (Jackson, Schwab & Schuler, 1986). Only a few recent
studies have assessed burnout in relation to interrole conflict. Bacharach,
Bamberger and Conley (1991) obtained a direct link between job→family
conflict and burnout, and Ray and Miller's (1994) measure of non-directional
work–home conflict predicted scores on all three dimensions of the Maslach
Burnout Inventory (emotional exhaustion, depersonalization, lack of personal
accomplishment). In contrast, Izraeli (1989) found that job–family conflict
was not strongly related to burnout for either men or women, while in Aryee's
(1993) Singaporean sample job–parent conflict predicted burnout for wives,
but not husbands, and job–spouse conflict was not associated with burnout
for either group. Consistent with earlier findings reported by Sekaran (1985),
Aryee's results suggest that multiple role stressors may be more detrimental to
the mental health of women than of men. Nevertheless, while existing data
illustrate that interrole conflict may make some contribution to the experience
of burnout, further confirmation of the relationship between these variables is
required.

Although more attention has been given to relationships with mental
health, the impact of interrole conflict on *physical health* has also been
investigated. While she did not directly measure job–family conflict,
Verbrugge (1986) found that having numerous roles was associated with
good physical health, but variables related to conflict (such as time
constraints and irregular work schedules) predicted poor health. These data
offer support for both the scarcity model and the enhancement hypothesis.
Thomas and Ganster (1995) explored the effect of (undifferentiated) work–
family conflict on three indices of physical health: diastolic blood pressure,
cholesterol level, and somatic complaints. Conflict had direct positive
linkages with the last two of these health indicators. Further research is

needed to examine more closely the specific physiological and physical reactions which are influenced by job/off-job conflict and to determine whether these relationships are mediated by psychological variables, such as levels of strain and dissatisfaction.

A somewhat different angle on health issues has been taken by Bromet, Dew and Parkinson (1990) and Frone, Russell and Cooper (1993), who examined the impact of interrole conflict on *alcohol abuse*. Bromet, Dew and Parkinson found a positive link between job–family conflict and alcohol consumption among female blue-collar workers. However, their study was limited by the use of single-item measures of both these variables. In a more rigorous assessment of the relationship between conflict and alcohol use, Frone, Russell and Cooper (1993) obtained strong support for a positive connection between alcohol use/abuse and work–family conflict. They noted, however, that 'this relationship is found almost exclusively among individuals who believe that alcohol promotes relaxation and tension reduction' (p. 553), suggesting that job/off-job interferences may lead to alcohol usage problems among 'vulnerable' individuals. In a more recent article, Frone and his colleagues (Frone, Barnes & Farrell, 1994) have related work–family conflict to substance abuse among employed mothers.

Organizational Outcomes

Almost all of the research on the job/off-job interface has focused on consequences for individuals, whether they be job-related (such as job satisfaction) or off-the-job variables (e.g. marital satisfaction, quality of life, overall well-being). Given the potential implications for organizations of high levels of job/off-job conflict or enhancement among their employees, in terms of (for example) job attitudes and performance, absenteeism and turnover, it is surprising that there has been almost no research on organizationally-relevant outcomes. Despite prevailing beliefs among many employers and managers that commitments to family and other off-job responsibilities could interfere with an individual's capacity to perform his/her job satisfactorily and could result in absence from work, there is in fact no empirical substantiation of these assumptions.

Some of these studies mentioned earlier have included organizationally-relevant variables in their analyses. *Job satisfaction* is one salient outcome which has been explored in some depth; studies examining this variable have been reviewed above. *Organizational commitment* has also been investigated as a potential outcome in two studies. O'Driscoll, Ilgen and Hildreth (1992) found that interference from off-job activities did contribute to reduced organizational commitment, both directly and indirectly via job satisfaction. Kirchmeyer (1992b), on the other hand, observed that both job satisfaction and organizational commitment were positively correlated with the amount of time spent in parenting and community work, suggesting a lack of interference from these off-job spheres. Furthermore, in Kirchmeyer's (1992a) investigation of positive and negative spillover, there was stronger agreement with statements reflecting positive spillover into the job context, suggesting that respondents believed their involvement in off-the-job activities enhanced the development of job-related skills, energized them to tackle challenges on the job, and provided them with ideas that could be applied at work.

To date there has been just one study which has directly assessed the impact of work–family conflict on *absenteeism* among employees. Goff, Mount and Jamison (1990) surveyed over 900 employees in a single company to determine the benefits of employer-supported childcare facilities. The average number of hours absent each month due to illness, personal business and absence without leave was calculated and path analysis utilized to identify significant contributors to absenteeism. Work–family conflict was a strong predictor of absenteeism levels in this study. It might be presumed that the interrole conflict effect can be attributed more to family→work than work-→family interference, but the authors did not separate these variables in their analyses, even though both were measured.

In sum, evidence from the studies outlined here provides support for the notion that conflict between job and off-job roles will have an adverse impact on individuals' satisfaction with their job and lives outside the work context, as well as on their physical health and psychological well-being. Nevertheless, the data also indicate that involvement in multiple roles does not necessarily induce conflict, and that benefits may also accrue from engagement in a range of job and off-job activities. However, little research has been conducted to determine the actual costs for organizations of high levels of employee involvement in multiple roles.

GENDER AND THE INTERFACE BETWEEN JOB AND OFF-JOB ROLES

In addition to the direct association between the job/off-job interface and other variables, several other factors have been implicated as moderators of these relationships, including personal characteristics (such as role salience), and environmental factors (for instance, social support at home and in the workplace). Of all these, however, the variable which has received most attention and been accorded greatest significance is gender. In the context of the present review, two questions are particularly relevant to research on interrole conflict and enhancement: (a) Are there differences between men and women in the extent of conflict and/or enhancement experienced as a result of their involvement in job and off-the-job roles? and (b) Do the processes linking interrole conflict/enhancement with other variables (such as satisfaction and well-being) vary between men and women?

There is no doubt that, despite widespread changes in many countries in the configurations of roles occupied by males and females, significant differences still exist in the activities which men undertake and those in which women are engaged. Women, for example, still assume primary responsibility for child-care and household management, even in many situations where both they and their partner or spouse have professional careers. Certainly there is evidence that the level of men's involvement in these activities is increasing and that there is, at least in some countries, greater sharing of these responsibilities. Despite these shifts, in both ideology and practice, the predominant pattern has altered only marginally over the past 20 or so years (Kalleberg & Rosenfeld, 1990).

One major shift which has occurred, of course, is that more and more women are participating in the workforce and greater proportions are now engaging in professional careers (Burke & Greenglass, 1987). This has entailed substantial modification to women's perceptions of their roles in society, as well as considerable effort to achieve success in the employment domain, and at the same time develop strategies for balancing the demands of the job or career with home and family responsibilities.

Research on gender issues relating to job/off-job interactions has concentrated primarily on the number of roles and role configurations of men and women (Voydanoff & Donnelly, 1989). Typically it has been suggested that men occupy a greater number of roles, and that occupancy of several major life roles generally tends to enhance well-being (Gove & Zeiss, 1987; Verbrugge, 1986). These findings run counter to the scarcity hypothesis, which would suggest that involvement in several roles should increase the demands on a person's time and energy, leading to conflict between roles and hence increased psychological strain. As suggested earlier, multiple role involvement may provide benefits which offset the pressures and demands on time and energy.

Whether women experience greater levels of interrole conflict than men has been a topic of much debate in recent years. Wiley (1991) argued, for instance, that women operate under greater constraints from having to juggle role responsibilities and have less opportunity to compartmentalize their job and off-job roles. This proposition has been supported in studies which utilized non-directional measures of interrole conflict (e.g. Greenglass, Pantony & Burke, 1989; Wiersma, 1990; Wiersma & van den Berg, 1991), which have typically found higher interrole conflict among women.

More fine-grained assessments have been less clear-cut in their conclusions. According to the gender role perspective, for example, women should report more job→family interference than men, whereas the opposite should hold for family→job conflict. In other words, while job and family boundaries may be asymmetrically permeable for both genders, this perspective suggests that the permeability operates in opposite directions for men and women (Gutek, Searle & Klepa, 1991). Some jobs clearly illustrate this pattern. In managerial and professional occupations, there is often an implicit or even explicit expectation that males will allow their work responsibilities to infringe upon their personal lives, whereas for women the demands and responsibilities of family life do not permit such intrusion (Wiley, 1991).

However, research differentiating job→family from family→job interference has yielded less support for the asymmetric permeability hypothesis. Greenhaus et al. (1989) obtained no differences between men and women on their measure of strain-based conflict, and an initial gender difference on time-based conflict (males higher than females) was eliminated once other demographic and work role characteristics were controlled for. Frone, Russell and Cooper (1992b) also found no evidence of gender differences in patterns of asymmetry. Williams and Alliger (1994), on the other hand, recorded higher levels of both forms of interference in women than in men, while Bolger et al. (1989) observed that stress at home had more effect on job-related stress for men than for women. Consistent with this last finding, Kirchmeyer (1992a) reported that negative spillover from parenting to work was less pronounced among women in her research. However, as pointed out by Kirchmeyer, these findings leave unanswered the question as to whether women experience fewer role burdens or if they are simply able to cope better with multiple role demands.

In sum, recent studies do not uniformly confirm the existence of gender differences in the amount and direction of interrole conflict. While statistical data indicate that women still take the major share of responsibility for household and family tasks (even when they are also engaged in paid employment), there is no compelling evidence that they always experience higher levels of interrole conflict. Furthermore, contradicting popular mythology that family responsibilities are more likely to intrude upon women's role performance and satisfaction on the job, some research has illustrated that in some situations there is little difference between men and women, or even that men experience more interference from their off-job commitments.

These results indicate the need to explore the processes, and not just the level, of interrole conflict among men and women. Few researchers have tackled this issue directly. The notion of compartmentalization (Wiley, 1991) suggests that men can more readily segregate their job and off-job experiences, but recent investigations mentioned above (e.g. Bolger et al., 1989; Gutek, Searl & Klepa, 1991) question this generalization. Furthermore, there is little reason to presume that men and women respond differently to interrole conflict (Lambert, 1990) or that relationships between interrole conflict and other variables (such as job and off-job satisfaction, and psychological well-being) will vary between males and females. As noted by several authors (e.g. Frone, Russell & Cooper, 1992a; Greenhaus et al., 1989; O'Driscoll & Humphries, 1994; Verbrugge, 1986; Wiersma, 1990), factors such as job level, the accessibility of financial and other resources, and the level of practical and emotional support available both at home and in the workplace, will have a significant bearing on the amount of interrole conflict experienced by individuals and on the types of outcomes they report.

COPING WITH INTERROLE CONFLICT

Another issue which it is clearly important to examine in relation to interrole conflict is how people endeavour to deal with the problems generated by this stressor. As with other sources of stress, the impact of interference between the job and off-job domains depends to a large extent on the behaviours employed by individuals to cope with this form of conflict (White, Cox & Cooper, 1992). However, while there has been considerable discussion in the literature of the need for effective coping strategies, little empirical research has been conducted to investigate the extent of utilization of different methods of coping with interrole conflict and the effectiveness of these methods.

The earliest attempt to describe the range of potential responses which might be used to cope with interrole conflict was by Epstein (1970), who identified nine mechanisms which people might employ to manage the conflicting demands of multiple roles. These include the elimination of certain roles or activities, redefinition of roles, delegation of tasks, and selective involvement in particular roles. Epstein's list of strategies was classified by Hall (1972) into three primary coping mechanisms: (a) changing role demands (e.g. employing a child-carer); (b) setting priorities (redefining personal roles); (c) reactive role behaviour, which entails increasing one's efforts to meet the demands of all roles (White, Cox & Cooper, 1992).

In their review of the literature on job/off-job conflict and stress, Greenhaus and Parasuraman (1987) adopted Lazarus and Folkman's (1984) typology of coping to elucidate various strategies which might be utilized in both the job context and in the off-job domain. Lazarus and Folkman referred to three forms of coping behaviour: problem-focused, emotion-focused, and symptom management. Among problem-focused coping strategies, Greenhaus and Parasuraman (1987) discussed changing the work environment to clarify expectations about performance, increasing or reducing levels of responsibility, plus obtaining more practical help with demanding tasks. In the off-job sphere, deriving a more effective division of labour, eliminating burdensome roles, improving communications with family members to clarify expectations, and seeking outside help for domestic chores and childcare represent possible conflict-reducing mechanisms.

Emotion-focused coping with interrole conflict includes seeking emotional support, reassessing the importance of job or career success, and redefining internal standards of performance, as well as recognizing limits to one's ability to achieve perfection in all areas of life, and resetting priorities in family goals. Finally, managing the symptoms of psychological strain, which is Lazarus and Folkman's third category of coping strategies, typically entails the use of exercise, relaxation, and other forms of physical or psychological refocusing, to maintain a healthy lifestyle and to obviate the potentially damaging consequences of excessive strain.

As noted by Voydanoff (1987), there has been limited research on the frequency of usage of various coping strategies. In one of the few systematic investigations of coping with interrole conflict, Gray (1983) surveyed professional women about their roles and how they dealt with conflicts between them. She found that only 16% reported that they kept their job and family roles separate, and that attempting to achieve segregation was generally associated with dissatisfaction. Many women endeavoured to avoid limitations to their professional development, by soliciting help from family members with household tasks and responsibilities, reducing their expectations of what they could achieve in particular roles (for instance, the standard of household maintenance), organizing and scheduling activities (especially those in the off-job domain) to avoid conflicts between them, and ensuring that their personal interests were not overlooked.

Elman and Gilbert (cited in Voydanoff, 1987) conducted a survey of mothers in dual-career relationships, where the most frequently used strategies were increasing role behaviour (working harder, planning, and organizing), cognitive restructuring, and redefining the personal meaning of roles. More recently, O'Driscoll and Humphries (1994) also surveyed women in professional and managerial positions to explore how they managed the potentially conflicting demands of their careers and off-the-job responsibilities. Both job interference (with off-job commitments) and off-job interference were measured, along with utilization of problem-focused and emotion-focused coping behaviours. Many of the women sampled in this study appeared to maintain their involvement in off-the-job activities and commitments, even when they experienced the strain of interrole conflict. While some made efforts to reschedule their job hours and reduce their workload, this was not always a feasible option. Most continued to take primary responsibility for home and family commitments, sacrificing leisure time to accommodate demands from both spheres of their lives. O'Driscoll and Humphries commented that employers cannot assume that individuals will always be able to develop effective ways of coping with incompatible pressures, and that organizations need to give more serious consideration to career development policies which take account of individuals' (especially women's) life circumstances (see also Anderson-Kulman & Paludi, 1986).

One factor which has been implicated as a possible moderator of the negative effects of interrole conflict is *social support*. Utilization of support from both the family and the workplace has been suggested as an effective coping strategy for dealing with stress generally and there is evidence that support from others can offset many of the negative effects of stressful working environments (Cooper, 1987; Kahn & Byosiere, 1990). However, there is mixed evidence for the buffering influence of social support in work situations (Beehr, King & King, 1990). While some investigators have reported that social support moderates the impact of work-related stressors, others have found no evidence of buffering, and yet others have obtained a 'reverse' buffering effect, whereby utilization of support exacerbates the amount of strain experienced (Ganster, Fusilier & Mayes, 1986).

Although the research literatures on job stress and 'non-work' stress indicate that social support should have a significant bearing on the experience of interrole conflict and on the outcomes of this stressor, only two studies have directly investigated these issues. MacEwen and Barling (1988) assessed the direct and moderating effects of support from the family on the marital adjustment of full-time employed mothers with young children. These researchers found a reverse buffering effect for social support—mothers scoring high on both interrole conflict and support from the family experienced more negative change in marital adjustment than did mothers with low support from their family. MacEwen and Barling suggested that emotional support may not necessarily help people to resolve conflict demands from their job and family roles, and may even lead to feelings of guilt for dividing one's attention between job and family responsibilities. In these circumstances, emotional support may be less effective for resolving interrole conflict than instrumental (practical) support.

A more recent study by Ray and Miller (1994) also obtained evidence of a reverse buffering effect. In contrast to MacEwen and Barling (1988), Ray and Miller examined support from both job-related sources (e.g. supervisors, co-workers, management) and from family sources, to assess effect of support on burnout (measured via the Maslach Burnout Inventory). Supervisor support made a direct contribution to reduced emotional exhaustion and depersonalization, while administrative support was linked with greater personal accomplishment. On the other hand, high levels of family support contributed to increased emotional exhaustion. Furthermore, significant interaction effects on emotional exhaustion were obtained between home–work conflict and co-worker support, such that employees experiencing high levels of both interrole conflict and support reported more emotional exhaustion.

Ray and Miller (1994) posit several suggestions for the reverse buffering effect observed in their study. First, developing and maintaining support from co-workers may in itself be stressful, requiring the investment of time and energy. Also, as has been observed in previous research on burnout (e.g. O'Driscoll & Schubert, 1988), discussions with colleagues of work conditions and the difficulties of balancing job and home responsibilities may simply reinforce one's already negative view of these conditions, hence leading to more rather than less perceived conflict and strain. Finally, as noted by MacEwen and Barling (1988), emotional support from family members or co-workers may be ineffective in helping to change the situation, if the conflict is due to structural conditions beyond the individual's control (such as inflexible job hours which conflict with childcare or other home responsibilities).

In summary, data on the contribution of social support from others in either the workplace or the family context do not point to a uniformly positive influence. Emotional support from the family or from work colleagues may not have the intended effect of reducing the strain caused by conflict and overload from competing roles. Clearly there is a need for further systematic investigation of behavioural strategies and support mechanisms which will be effective in either alleviating interrole conflict between the job and off-job domains, or at least in minimizing its negative consequences. The studies referred to above have highlighted behaviours which are frequently engaged in by individuals in an effort to combat potential interference between their job/career and off-job interests and commitments, and some researchers have examined the utilization of support from significant others in the home and work environments. However, there has been little confirmation of which responses will be most effective and how social support can be harnessed most profitably.

One issue which research to date has highlighted is that individuals by themselves may not always be able to alleviate the strain caused by job/off-job interference. No matter how much effort is invested into coping with interrole conflict, the structure of jobs and career development are often inherently competitive with commitments and responsibilities outside the work environment. As mentioned earlier, inflexible work hours, expectations from management about 'out-of-hours' contributions, and inaccessibility of family-supportive facilities (such as childcare) represent some of the structural incompatibilities which prevent individuals from creating a balance between their jobs and life outside the work context. To address these problems, it is also important to consider how organizational practices and policies affect employees, not just in terms of their work attitudes and job performance, but also their well-being and overall quality of life.

ORGANIZATIONAL POLICIES AND PRACTICES

Although research to date has concentrated primarily on the experiences and reactions of individuals, the recognition that employees may have limited control over the structure of work conditions (for example, hours of work and the location of the work environment) has led to increasing debate over the role and responsibilities of employing organizations in relation to the interface between job demands and individuals' off-job commitments. Do existing organizational policies and workplace practices assist or impede employees in their endeavours to balance job and off-job (especially family) commitments? Do organizations have a responsibility to assist their employees to achieve this balance, or does this responsibility lie solely with individuals? These are issues which have social and moral as well as practical implications, and which raise questions about the role of organizations in society and the exchange relationship between individual employees and their employing organization.

From the research cited in this and other reviews (e.g. Burke & Greenglass, 1987; Greenhaus & Parasuraman, 1987), there is substantial evidence that both the structure of jobs and organizational expectations concerning role performance can induce feelings of conflict between job demands and activities and commitments outside of the job. As discussed earlier in this chapter, although increased involvement in both the job and off-job domains can provide benefits for individuals (Kirchmeyer, 1992a,b; Tiedje et al., 1990; Wiersma, 1990), there can be no doubt that work conditions which are incompatible with family and other off-job responsibilities do create interrole conflict which leads to increased psychological strain and reduced satisfaction with both the job itself and life off the job.

Many commentators have suggested that organizations do carry some responsibility for the impact of work conditions on employees' off-job lives. Higgins and Duxbury (1992), for instance, indicated that negative spillover from the job domain is due to a lack of flexibility in the workplace, for example in work hours, vacation periods, and allowing for variable conditions in people's lives. As noted by these and other authors (e.g. Smith, 1992; Thomas & Ganster, 1995), many organizational policies still subscribe to the myth of separate worlds, and treat the off-job sphere as infinitely permeable. Finally, the continuation of stereotypical attitudes and values reinforces lack of support for individuals (both men and women) engaging in roles which are not entirely consistent with societal norms and expectations (Major, 1993).

In contrast to the prevailing managerial stance, there have been calls for greater recognition by management of the spillover between job and off-the-job activities, and consideration of how workplace policies might help employees to balance job and family commitments (Lambert, 1990). Greenhaus and Parasuraman (1987) outlined several approaches which might be adopted by organizations, including: (a) modifying stressful work environments (for example, through job redesign or elimination of aversive elements in the workplace); (b) providing employees with accurate information to clarify their job-related responsibilities; (c) offering support services for employees who are experiencing specific forms of job/off-job interference; and (d) developing alternative career development programmes which allow more versatility for employees who do not wish to pursue a linear career pathway.

There is no doubt that many organizations have already embarked upon some of these initiatives. Some companies have responded with maternity/paternity leave programmes for their employees, provided childcare facilities, derived alternative work schedules, and experimented with 'home-based work' (Zedeck & Mosier, 1990). Unfortunately, there is little empirical data on the benefits and limitations of these developments. For instance, while some authors have highlighted the positive benefits of on-site childcare facilities, for both employees and employers, extant research does not consistently demonstrate that such facilities are perceived as beneficial or even necessary, especially if viable alternatives are available (Goff, Mount & Jamison, 1990, Gonyea & Googins, 1992). However, as discussed earlier, the lack of differentiation between job→family and family→job conflict in many of these studies means that it is not possible to draw conclusions about the relationship between family→job conflict and utilization of childcare and other facilities. In a study which did discriminate between the two sources of interference, Frone and Yardley (1994) found that employees who experienced high levels of family→work conflict had a greater need for and were more likely to benefit from family-supportive programmes than individuals who were less affected by family→work conflict.

Despite efforts on the part of some organizations to alleviate some of the job/off-job interface problems confronted by employees, there are no consistent guidelines for the development and widespread implementation of policies and practices which will benefit organizations and their employees alike. Two reasons for the absence of a concerted response from organizations are the costs of implementation and a wariness of becoming too involved in the off-job lives of employees. As noted by Zedeck and Mosier (1990), although the provision of facilities such as childcare centres may generate benefits for an organization, such as reduced absenteeism and tardiness, many companies are yet to be persuaded that these benefits are not outweighed by the costs of establishing and maintaining such facilities. In addition, organizations may be 'wary of treading in the personal area of their employees' lives' (Zedeck & Mosier, 1990, p. 248).

CONCLUSION

This chapter has endeavoured to summarize findings from recent research examining the interplay between roles on and off the job. Much of this work has concentrated predominantly on the potential conflict between job and off-job roles, although there has also been some attention to the possibility that roles may be mutually enhancing. The prevailing view among researchers is that multiple role involvement can lead to both conflict and enhancement, sometimes simultaneously. Two characteristics of role involvement which may be relevant in this regard are (a) whether participation in specific roles is voluntary or involuntary, and (b) the extent to which a person feels in control. Activities which are engaged in voluntarily may be perceived by an individual as challenging and rewarding, whereas involuntary roles may be viewed as demanding and competing with other more preferred activities. Similarly, perceived control over one's involvement in and performance of different roles may also contribute to feelings of enhancement rather than conflict. Future research may help to clarify the salience of choice and control as critical predictors of interrole conflict versus enhancement.

Studies which have explored antecedents and consequences of multiple role involvement have been discussed, along with research on how individuals attempt to cope with the problems of interrole conflict. The conditions under which job/off-job conflict occurs and the consequences for individuals experiencing conflict were highlighted, but there is clearly a need for further systematic investigation of interactions between job-related and off-job variables.

In particular, it is important that research in this field distinguish between job interference with off-job activities (job→off-job conflict) and off-job interference with job commitments (off-job→job conflict). Failure to examine the direction of interference in much research to date has limited the conclusions which can be drawn from these studies.

It would also be informative to focus on off-job activities other than those directly associated with family roles. Although a few researchers have explored involvement in the community, recreational, and (to a lesser extent) social and political arenas, the large majority of studies have concentrated solely on job–family conflict. Examining a broader range of off-job activities would provide a more comprehensive picture of the kinds of job/off-job interference which are commonly experienced.

Finally, because this issue is relevant for organizations as well as individual employees, and indeed has ramifications for society as a whole, mechanisms for alleviating interrole conflict or at least minimizing its negative consequences must be founded upon both individual and organizational responsibility. It can no longer be presumed, if it ever could be, that employees can segregate their job and off-the-job lives such that the two worlds do not overlap. The availability of sophisticated technology which is readily transportable is one of many 'forces' blurring the boundaries between the job and off-job domains, to such an extent that for many individuals they are no longer separable. Given their knowledge and expertise in this field, organizational scientists have a particular responsibility to investigate the personal and social consequences of these transformations, with a view to promoting policies and practices which enhance, rather than detract from, the quality of life and individual well-being.

REFERENCES

Anderson-Kulman, R. & Paludi, M. (1986) Working mothers and the family context: Predicting positive coping. *Journal of Vocational Behavior*, **28**, 241–253.

Ayree, S. (1993) Dual-earner couples in Singapore: An examination of work and nonwork sources of their experienced burnout. *Human Relations*, **46**, 1441–1468.

Bacharach, S., Bamberger, P. & Conley, S. (1991) Work–home conflict among nurses and engineers: Mediating the impact of role stress on burnout and satisfaction at work. *Journal of Organizational Behavior*, **12**, 39–53.

Barling, J. (1994) Work and family: In search of more effective workplace interventions. In C. L. Cooper and D. M. Rousseau, (eds), *Trends in Organizational Behavior*, vol. 1 (pp. 63–73). New York: Wiley.

Barling, J. & MacEwen, K. (1992) Linking work experiences to facets of marital functioning. *Journal of Organizational Behavior*, **13**, 573–583.

Bartolome, F. & Evans, P. (1980) Must success cost so much? *Harvard Business Review*, **58**(2), 137–148.

Beehr, T., King, L. & King, D. (1990) Social support and occupational stress: Talking to supervisors. *Journal of Vocational Behavior*, **36**, 61–81.

Bolger, N., DeLongis, A., Kessler, R. & Wethington, E. (1989) The contagion of stress across multiple roles. *Journal of Marriage and the Family*, **51**. 175–183.

Bromet, E., Dew, M. & Parkinson, D. (1990) Spillover between work and family: A study of blue-collar working wives. In J. Eckenrode & S. Gore (eds), *Stress Between Work and Family*. New York: Plenum Press.

Burke, R. & Greenglass, E. (1987) Work and family. In C. Cooper & I. Robertson (eds), *International Review of I/O Psychology 1987* (pp. 273–320). Chichester, UK: Wiley.

Cooke, R. & Rousseau, D. (1984) Stress and strain from family roles and work-role expectations. *Journal of Applied Psychology*, **69**, 252–260.

Cooper, C. (1987) The experience and management of stress: Job and organizational determinants. In A Riley & S. Zaccaro (es), *Occupational Stress and Organizational Effectiveness* (pp. 53–69). New York: Praeger.

Epstein, C. (1970) Encountering the male establishment: Sex-status limits on women's careers in the professions. *American Journal of Sociology*, **75**, 965–982.

Frone, M., Barnes, G. & Farrell, M. (1994) Relationship of work/family conlifct to substance use among employed mothers: Examining the mediating role of negative affect. *Journal of Marriage and the Family*, **56**, 1019–1030.

Frone, M. & Rice, R. (1987) Work–family conflict: The effect of job and family involvement. *Journal of Occupational Behavior*, **8**, 45–53.

Frone, M., Russell, M. & Cooper, M. (1992a) Antecedents and outcomes of work–family conflict: Testing a model of the work–family interface. *Journal of Applied Psychology*, **77**, 65–78.

Frone, M., Russell, M. & Cooper, M. (1992b) Prevalence of work–family conflict: Are work and family boundaries asymmetrically permeable? *Journal of Organizational Behavior*, **13**, 723–729.

Frone, M., Russell, M. & Cooper, M. (1993) Relationship of work–family conflict, gender, and alcohol expectancies to alcohol use/abuse. *Journal of Organizational Behavior*, **14**, 545–558.

Frone, M. & Yardley, J. (1994) Predictors of employed parents' desire for workplace family-supportive programs. Manuscript submitted for publication.

Ganster, D., Fusilier, M. & Mayes, B. (1986) Role of social support in the experience of stress at work. *Journal of Applied Psychology*, **71**, 102–110.

Goff, S., Mount, M. & Jamison, R. (1990) Employer supported child care, work/family conflict and abstenteeism: A field study. *Personnel Psychology*, **43**, 793–810.

Gonyea, J. & Googins, B. (1992) Linking the worlds of work and family: Beyond the productivity trap. *Human Resource Management*, **31**, 209–226.

Gove, W. & Zeiss, C. (1987) Multiple roles and happiness. In F. J. Crosby (ed.), *Spouse, Parent, Worker: On Gender and Multiple Roles* (pp. 125–137). New Haven, CT: Yale University Press.

Gray, J. (1983) The married professional woman: An examination of her role conflicts and coping strategies. *Psychology of Women Quarterly*, **7**, 235–243.

Greenglass, E., Pantony, K. & Burke, R. (1989) A gender-role perspective on role conflict, work stress and social support. In E. B. Goldsmith (ed.), *Work and Family: Theory, Research and Applications* (pp. 317–328). London: Sage Publications.

Greenhaus, J. & Beutell, N. (1985) Sources of conflict between work and family roles. *Academy of Management Review*, **10**, 76–88.

Greenhaus, J. & Parasuraman, S. (1987) A work-nonwork interactive perspective of stress and its consequences. *Journal of Organizational Behavior Management*, **8**, 37–60.

Greenhaus, J., Parasuraman, S., Granrose, C., Rabinowitz, S. & Beutell, N. (1989) Sources of work–family conflict among two-career couples. *Journal of Vocational Behavior*, **34**, 133–153.

Gutek, B., Searle, S. & Klepa, L. (1991) Rational versus gender role explanations for work–family conflict. *Journal of Applied Psychology*, **76**, 560–568.

Hall, D. (1972) A model of coping with role conflict: The role behavior of college-educated women. *Administrative Science Quarterly*, 17, 471–486.

Higgins, C. & Duxbury, L. (1992) Work–family conflict: A comparison of dual-career and traditional-career men. *Journal of Organizational Behavior*, 13, 389–411.

Higgins, C., Duxbury, L. & Irving, R. (1992) Work-family conflict in the dual-career family. *Organizational Behavior and Human Decision Processes*, 51, 51–75.

Ilgen, D. & Hollenbeck, J. (1991) Job design and roles. In M. Dunnette and L. Hough (eds), *Handbook of Industrial and Organizational Psychology*, 2nd edn, vol. 2 (pp. 165–208). Palo Alto, CA: Consulting Psychologists Press.

Izraeli, D. (1989) Burning out in medicine: A comparison of husbands and wives in dual-career families. In E. B. Goldsmith (ed.), *Work and Family: Theory, Research and Applications* (p. 329–346). London: Sage Publications.

Jackson, S., Schwab, R. & Schuler, R. (1986) Toward an understanding of the burnout phenomenon. *Journal of Applied Psychology*, 71, 630–640.

Jackson, S., Zedeck, S. & Summers, E. (1985) Family life disruptions: Effects of job-induced and emotional interference. *Academy of Management Journal*, 28, 574–586.

Kahn, R. & Byosiere, P. (1990) Stress in organizations. In M. Dunnette and L. Hough (eds), *Handbook of Industrial and Organizational Psychology*, 2nd edn, vol. 2, (pp. 165–208). Palo Alto, CA: Consulting Psychologists Press.

Kalleberg, A. & Rosenfeld, R. (1990) Work in the family and in the labor market: A cross-national, reciprocal analysis. *Journal of Marriage and the Family*, 52, 331–346.

Kanter, R. (1977) *Work and Family in the United States: A Critical Review and Agenda for Research and Policy*. New York: Russell Sage Foundation.

Kirchmeyer, C. (1992a) Perceptions of nonwork-to-work spillover: Challenging the common view of conflict-ridden domain relationships. *Basic & Applied Social Psychology*, 13, 231–249.

Kirchmeyer, C. (1992b) Nonwork participation and work attitudes: A test of scarcity vs. expansion models of personal resources. *Human Relations*, 45, 775–796.

Kopelman, R., Greenhaus, J. & Connolly, T. (1983) A model of work, family and interrole conflict: A construct validation study. *Organizational Behavior & Human Decision Processes*, 32, 198–215.

Lambert, S. (1990) Processes linking work and family: A critical review and research agenda. *Human Relations*, 43, 239–258.

Lazarus, R. & Folkman, S. (1984) *Stress, Appraisal and Coping*. New York: Springer.

Lobel, S. (1991) Allocation of investment in work and family roles: Alternative theories and implications for research. *Academy of Management Review*, 16, 507–521.

MacEwen, K. & Barling, J. (1988) Interrole conflict, family support and marital adjustment of employed mothers: A short term, longitudinal study. *Journal of Organizational Behavior*, 9, 241–250.

Major B. (1993) Gender, entitlement and the distribution of family labor. *Journal of Social Issues*, 49, 141–159.

Marks, S. (1977) Multiple roles and role strain: Some notes on human energy, time and commitment. *American Sociological Review*, 42, 921–936.

Menaghan, E. (1991) Work experiences and family interaction processes: The long reach of the job. *Annual Review of Sociology*, 17, 419–444.

Miller, L. & Weiss, R. (1982) The work–leisure relationship: Evidence for the compensatory hypothesis. *Human Relations*, 35, 763–772.

O'Driscoll, M. & Beehr, T. (1994) Supervisor behaviors, role stressors and uncertainty as predictors of personal outcomes for subordinates. *Journal of Organizational Behavior*, 15, 141–155.

O'Driscoll, M. & Humphries, M. (1994) Time demands, interrole conflict and coping strategies among managerial women. *International Journal of Employment Studies*, 2, 57–75.

O'Driscoll, M., Ilgen, D. & Hildreth, K. (1992) Time devoted to job and off-job activities, interrole conflict, and affective experiences. *Journal of Applied Psychology*, 77(3), 272–279.

O'Driscoll, M. & Schubert, T. (1988) Organizational climate and burnout in a New Zealand social service agency. *Work & Stress*, 2, 199–204.

Ray, E. & Miller, K. (1994) Social support, home/work stress, and burnout: Who can help? *Journal of Applied Behavioral Science*, 30, 357–373.

Rice, R., Frone, M. & McFarlin, D. (1992) Work–nonwork conflict and the perceived quality of life. *Journal of Organizational Behavior*, 13, 155–168.

Sekaran, U. (1985) The paths to mental health: An exploratory study of husbands and wives in dual-career families. *Journal of Occupational Psychology*, 58, 129–137.

Sieber, S. (1974) Toward a theory of role accumulation. *American Sociological Review*, 39, 567–578.

Small, S. & Riley, D. (1990) Toward a multidimensional assessment of work spillover into family life. *Journal of Marriage & Family*, 52, 51–61.

Smith, C. (1992) Dual careers, dual loyalties: Management implications of the work/home interface. *Asia Pacific Journal of Human Resources*, 30(4), 19–29.

Thomas, L. & Ganster, D. (1995) The impact of family-supportive work variables on work–family conflict and strain: A control perspective. *Journal of Applied Psychology*, 80, 6–15.

Tiedje, L, Wortman, C., Downey, G., Emmons, C., Biernat, M. & Lang, E. (1990) Women with multiple roles: Role-compatibility perceptions, satifaction, and mental health. *Journal of Marriage & Family*, 52, 63–72.

Verbrugge, L. (1986) Role burdens and physical health of men and women. *Women & Health*, 11, 47–77.

Voydanoff, P. (1987) *Work and Family Life*. Newbury Park, CA: Sage.

Voydanoff, P. (1988) Work role characteristics, family structure demands and work/family conflict. *Journal of Marriage and the Family*, 50, 749–762.

Voydanoff, P. & Donnelly, B. (1989) Work and family roles and psychological distress. *Journal of Marriage & Family*, 51, 923–932.

Wiersma, U. (1990) Gender differences in job attribute preferences: Work–home role conflict and job level as mediating variables. *Journal of Occupational Psychology*, 63, 231–243.

Wiersma, U. & van den Berg, P. (1991) Work–home role conflict, family climate, and domestic responsibilities among men and women in dual-earner families. *Journal of Applied Social Psychology*, 21, 1207–1217.

White, B., Cox, C. & Cooper, C. (1992) *Women's Career Development: A Study of High Flyers*. Oxford: Blackwell.

Wiley, M. (1987) The relationship between work/nonwork role conflict and job-related outcomes: Some unanticipated findings. *Journal of Management*, 13, 467–472.

Wiley, M. (1991) Gender, work and stress: The potential impact of role-identity salience and commitment. *The Sociological Quarterly*, 32, 495–510.

Williams, K. & Alliger, G. (1994) Role stressors, mood spillover, and perceptions of work–family conflict in employed parents. *Academy of Management Journal*, 37, 837–868.

Zedeck, S. & Mosier, K. (1990) Work in the family and employing organization. *American Psychologist*, 45, 240–251.

Part II

GENDER IN ORGANIZATIONS

Chapter 6

WOMEN'S CAREERS AND OCCUPATIONAL STRESS

Janice Langan-Fox
University of Melbourne, Australia

INTRODUCTION

Work and Health

By the year 2005, 60% of all adult women are expected to participate in the Australian labour force (ABS, 1993). This shows substantial growth from the reported 53% who participated in the labour force in 1995 (ABS, 1995). Similar growth in labour force participation has been predicted for American women. In the USA, in 1986, two-thirds of all adult women were in the workforce with this figure expected to reach 81% by the year 2000 (Matthews & Rodin, 1989). White males are expected to comprise only 15% of the new entrants into the workforce in the decade leading up to the year 2000, down from 46% at the start of the decade (Rodin & Ickovics, 1990), while almost two-thirds of entrants into the workforce during this decade will be women.

These statistics appear to be good news for women in terms of health and well-being. Compared to non-employed women, employed women have more favourable health profiles (LaCroix & Haynes, 1987), a weaker association between family-role stress and negative health outcomes (Baruch, Biener & Barnett, 1987), fewer sick days, and better psychological well-being (LaCroix & Haynes, 1987). Women's traditional role (i.e. marriage, family and domestic duties) is thought to contribute to dependence, isolation, low status, negative emotions, and the suppression of initiative (Helson & Picano, 1990). However, the direction of causality in the relationship between employment and health is not completely known since many studies are cross-sectional, and it is unclear whether employment promotes health or whether women in poor health and different circumstances are unable to work, or prefer other alternatives (Sorensen & Mortimer, 1988).

Women's Careers and Occupational Stress by Janice Langan-Fox taken from IRIOP 1998 v13, Edited by Cary L. Cooper and Ivan T. Robertson: © 1998 John Wiley & Sons, Ltd

Support for the health-promoting effects of employment was provided by a San Antonio Heart Study where employed women were found to be at a lower risk of cardiovascular illness (Hazuda, Haffner, Stern et al., 1986). Furthermore, the benefits of employment on physical and mental health have been illustrated by controlled studies (McDaniel, 1993), with the advantages especially strong for women in higher status careers. Baruch, Biener and Barnett (1987) claimed that employment achieves health benefits by encouraging 'challenge, control, structure, positive feedback, and self-esteem and to provide a valued set of social ties' (p. 132).

However, the quality of employment is now considered more important than simply occupying an employment role. O'Brien and Feather (1990) found that individuals with 'high-quality' employment had lower depressive affect, with higher life satisfaction, internal control and personal competence than unemployed or 'low-quality' employed individuals. 'Low-quality' working life can stem from lower pay, job insecurity, poor mobility prospects, and sexual harassment (McDaniel, 1993). Nevertheless, while the bulk of research points to the positive benefits of employment, especially 'high-quality' employment, employment status does impact on lifestyle and quality of life, and recent statistics suggest that health and well-being benefits may be increasingly compromised.

Emerging patterns of gender differences in health

For many years, statistics collected in most Western nations confirmed that women and men possess different health outcomes, with women at a higher relative risk of morbidity and a lower risk of mortality (Rodin & Ickovics, 1990). Records have shown that women have increased incidence of reporting non-life-threatening illness, whereas males tend to report a higher rate of chronic illnesses that lead to mortality (AIHW, 1996). In recent years, gender differences in morbidity and mortality have declined. Women are no longer dying from infectious or parasitic diseases or from childbirth. This may be due to increased hygiene and awareness of risk factors and improved nutrition and medical technology (ABS, 1994) but the primary cause of death is thought to be the so-called 'lifestyle' diseases (ABS, 1994): heart disease, cancer and stroke. While it has been reported that men have disproportionately higher morbidity and premature mortality from heart disease than women, according to the National Heart Foundation half of women's deaths are related to cardiovascular disease, and one-third of these are premature (Broom, 1996). Hibbard and Pope (1993) found that for women, 'particular qualities of marital and work roles were predictive of subsequent morbidity' (p. 217). Death, malignancy and stroke were decreased among employed women with social support structures, while work-related stress increased working men's risk of heart disease. Rodin and Ickovics (1990) suggested that the causes for these changes include women's increased substance use (e.g. alcohol, tobacco), which in combination with oral contraceptives multiplies the risk of heart attack and stroke by 10.

Thus, there seems to be a pattern emerging whereby women's advantageous health position relative to men is declining. This makes the well-being–stress–career linkage in women of particular importance and worthy of review. With an ever-increasing proportion in the workforce, it is timely to query the costs and benefits of women's careers and to examine the relationship with occupational stress.

This chapter aims to draw together the recent literature on stress and careers and indicate some features for future study. Attention will be given to the effects of workforce participation on women's health: in particular multiple roles and dual-earner couples; stress transmission; the physiological and psychological antecedents/consequence of stress; the effects of occupations; and coping with stress.

Some general assumptions and predictions

From an initial overview of the literature on stress and careers, some general assumptions of stress and career were hypothesized. First, it could be expected that the more jobs or roles an individual is involved in, the greater the potential for stress to occur, such that past or current roles would be difficult to relinquish whilst new roles were added. This would mean that multiple roles would cause difficulty and stress, and that women in dual-career situations would experience more stress than men. Second, that in general women in non-traditional jobs would experience more stress than those in traditional jobs. The problem here is that such women are 'pioneers' in changing workplace attitudes, whereby they are seen to be different in jobs once dominated by men. The potential then is that discrimination, sexual harassment and workplace pressures are experienced as stress. Third, women in jobs experiencing large advances in technological innovation would be under pressure to adapt to whole-scale change—new equipment, organizational structure, job loss (or the threat of it), and so on—and would report a wide variety of stressors. Fourth, that women will demonstrate effective coping strategies, especially in comparison to men. Women have been traditionally 'good' at seeking out support structures of friends, relatives and others in helping them meet the demands of family and work. Since the major stimulus to stress has been thought to be the onset of multiple-role occurrence, the impact of such roles is discussed below.

MULTIPLE ROLES AND STRESS

Multiple roles include those of wife, mother and worker. Increasingly, married women are working through the child-caring years. Statistics show that in

1995, the overall participation rate of married women was 50%, a slight increase from 1991, and was similar to that of unmarried women (52%). However, in the peak child-bearing years (ages 20–34) the participation rate for unmarried women was 10% higher than for married women (ABS, 1995). For the age group 25–29, the participation rate for working married mothers (43%) was half that of employed married women without children (88%). This difference decreases with increases in the mother's age (i.e. as children get older), such that in the age group 40–44 years, 70% of married women with children and 75% of married women without children participate in the labour force (ABS, 1995). Thus women's workforce participation is still sizeably keyed to the development and care of their children.

Most literature has concentrated on the constraints on professional attainment for females undertaking dual roles of worker and homemaker, a combination which has been thought to cause psychological stress such as role conflict. Research has found (Cleary & Mechanic, 1983) that females possess greater interrole conflict and overload than males, but 10 years later a more detailed picture emerged when Rankin (1993) reported that the major stresses for women in multiple roles included lack of time, child-related problems, and maternal guilt. The adverse health effects of competing time demands and role conflict associated with multiple roles include the presence of stress-related illnesses traditionally associated with men. Early in the 1980s, a study by the National Heart, Lung and Blood Institute found that the risk of coronary heart disease (CHD) increased in employed women and decreased in non-employed women as their number of children increased (1980). In contrast, Langan-Fox and Poole (1995) stated that the physical health of married women with three or more children was reported to be poorer than other marital and parental groups. An important buffer was reported by Facione (1994) who found that women who expressed subjective losses in work and interpersonal relationships experienced more major cardiovascular diseases, and that those who lacked spouse and social support had a direct connection to diminished mental health. Nonetheless, Reifman, Biernat and Lang (1991) in surveying 200 married professional women with at least one child found that contrary to expected results, social support yielded no stress-buffering effects.

Although multiple roles may create competing demands which result in role conflict and strain (McBride, 1990), considerable research suggests that involvement in multiple roles provides substantial personal benefits, such as expansion of resources and rewards, provision of alternate sources of self-esteem, support, and control (Sorensen & Vebrugge, 1987), improved family life (Rankin, 1993), and job satisfaction (Pietromonaco, Manis & Frohardt-Lane, 1986), and that in general, the more roles a woman occupies, the better her health status (Baruch, Biener & Barnett, 1987). Research findings have not been entirely consistent—Nelson, Quick, Hitt and Moesel (1990) found that for women, work–home conflicts were associated with role strain but were unrelated to organizational (i.e. 'extra') resources, a 'benefit' of the multiple-role syndrome.

Yet marriage, family and organizations do not, *per se*, act as stressors, as shown in a study of female Australian managers and professionals where the roles of marriage and family were related to job satisfaction and reduced work 'overload' (Langan-Fox, 1996) and where occupational stress was most strongly associated with the desire for promotion. What is needed in research, are discriminations made on the basis of the quality of various roles. For instance, it has been found that employed women with low levels of marital and employment strain possess lower depression levels than non-employed wives with low marital strain. Non-employed wives with high levels of marital strain experienced higher levels of depression than women who had both high marital and high employment strain (Aneshensel, 1986). Hemmelgarn and Laing (1991) examined the relationship between situational and background factors, especially individual attitudes and perceptions, and role strain experienced by women returning to work following the birth of their first child, and found that high maternal identity scores were related to lower role strain scores. Thus, even changes in role which spell the onset of multiple roles, such as the birth of a child, need not predict role strain.

Role Quality

It has been argued that when evaluating the effects of multiple roles the qualitative aspects of roles are more important than role occupancy (Barnett, Davidson & Marshall, 1989a; Baruch, Biener & Barnett, 1987). Low-quality roles often involve time constraint, irregular schedules and low control, and result in a deterioration of health (Vebrugge, 1986). High-quality roles may maintain or enhance health, and continue to do so even when these roles are numerous, such that physical symptoms are higher for women with children, only when work-role quality is low (Barnett, Davidson & Marshall, 1989a). From research by Lennon and Rosenfield (1992), family demands (children) are associated with distress only among women who have low job autonomy role-quality effect. Thus, the role-quality research suggests that more children does not straightforwardly equal poor mental health. Other research by Langan-Fox (1996) found that women with three or more children were job-motivated and had high job satisfaction.

High work-quality roles, such as hours worked, and skill utilization, influence women's health. Partner- and parent-role quality have been shown to influence psychological distress and physical symptoms, with the relation between partner-role quality and physical symptoms being enhanced in women who help others (Barnett, Davidson & Marshall, 1989b). In a sample of health-care providers, work-role quality influenced psychological distress, subjective well-being, physical health symptoms, and risk of cardiovascular disease. The impact of work-role quality on psychological distress was lower in employed women who were married than in unmarried women, perhaps providing support for the benefits of social support and multiple-role occupancy. As reported in the mid 80s (Barnett & Baruch, 1985), research supports the view that the quality of roles is the main predictor of role overload, role conflict and anxiety.

However, a complex four-way interaction, role quality × age × parental status × career development, can occur, reducing the benefits of a quality role. It is possible that mothers with young children who are also trying to establish their careers will experience stress from multiple low-quality roles because the 20s and 30s are peak years for family establishment, occupational advancement and the attainment of life goals (Levinson, 1986). The statistics mentioned earlier on the phases of childcare years for employed women indicate that it would not be surprising that employed women in their mid-30s have been found to experience difficulty in finding a balance between their family/ personal and work lives (Gallese, 1985, cited in Hall, 1987), whereas successful family executives who are at a stage where their role conflicts are minimized, report adequate time for their personal lives (Hennig & Jardim, 1977). Interestingly, although the parent-role is potentially a major source of stress for women in their middle years, Langan-Fox and Poole (1995) reported that in managerial and professional women, the role of spouse was the 'most stressful role'.

Even though the proportion of women entering the workforce has continued to increase, women's employment still dominates in traditional occupations such as clerical, teaching and nursing (Herr & Cramer, 1988). This trend has begun to decline in recent years, although it still presents a problem with women experiencing limited or poor work-role quality in traditionally male-dominated careers (Herr & Cramer, 1988). For instance, Lorber and Ecker (1983) found that the professional attainment of female physicians was significantly lower than that of their male counterparts over a 16-year period. Ten years later, Burlew and Johnson (1992) reported that marriage was still more of a career barrier for non-traditionals than for traditionals, and that non-traditionals found more career-related marital discord, barriers to career success (racial and gender discrimination), limited opportunities to develop political skills, colleagues' doubts about competence, and lack of peer support.

Dual-earner Couples

Balancing two-person multiple roles

The quality of roles becomes even more crucial in couples with multiple roles. The importance of sustaining a delicate balance of power in dual-earner relationships was revealed by Starkey (1991) who explored the role of a wife's earnings, a husband's interpersonal competence and interaction with a wife's earnings and labour supply. This major study used a sample of 1855 married males (aged 16–54 yrs) from the Panel Study of Income Dynamics for the years 1968–1972. The marginal impact of a wife's earnings on the risk of marital instability was highly variable, depending on the state of risk of the marriage and the interpersonal competence of the husband. Findings revealed that a wife's earnings tended to destabilize marriages, and that the interpersonal competence of the husband was important to maintain a stable marriage, especially when the wife was employed. Rosenfield (1992) examined the effects of the wife's employment on the husband's psychological well-being and showed that in so far as it decreases husbands' relative income, and increases their share of domestic labour, women's employment was still negative for husbands' mental health. In a series of interviews, Poole and Langan-Fox (1997) reported that men's concern about changed home circumstances led many women to deliberately 'size-down' their career expectations. One possible explanation for these findings could be found in research by Greenberger and O'Neil (1993) who reported that women's psychological state was associated with a wider circle of support but that men's states relied more on their wives. Not surprisingly, Gupta and Saini (1993) found that when wives' traditional husbands approved of their employment, anxiety was greater than when they did not approve of it.

Izraeli (1994) examined earnings ratios and the division of family work and gender-role (GR) attitudes among 136 physician couples. Consistent with resource theory, 'moderns' (husbands and wives earned the same) and 'innovatives' (wives earned more than husbands) had a more egalitarian division of labour in the home and GR ideology, than did 'conventionals' (husbands earned more than wives). Among the husbands, the lower their relative earnings, the greater their participation in childcare and housework and the relative importance they attributed to their wives' career success. The impact of family stress in a dual-career family does appear to be influenced by the division of household labour and childcare, which tends to be based on the spouse's expectancies or attitudes (Hiller & Philliber, 1986). Evidence to support the importance of attitudes comes from Silver (1993) who contrasted male and female homeworkers (HWs) with their counterparts working outside the home. Working at home did not break down gender roles in domestic life, and despite time saved from commuting, male HWs performed no more housework than comparable men working outside the home.

Domestic responsibilities and family climate have been shown to significantly correlate with work–home role conflict (Wiersma & van den Berg, 1991), and dual-earner couples who are contemplating having children need to consider whether they are willing, and able, to redefine their roles. Women and men need to reconsider their expectations of their own and their partners' roles. Wainrib (1992), in a number of interviews, identified various issues in women's expectations of male behaviour: women's ambivalence toward their source of power in the home being usurped by men; and performance of housework compared with wives' performance. Hall (1992) reported that higher levels of role strain were experienced by working women as a direct consequence of their guilt, awareness of unmet household needs, denial of their own needs, and perceptions of others' expectations. Similar to that reported earlier, workload and the quality of work and home experiences were major predictors of work–family strains (Marshall & Barnett, 1993). These authors reported that, regardless of gender, negative job and marital experiences were associated with high levels of psychological distress (PDS). In other research, no gender differences were found (Barnett, Brennan & Marshall, 1994) in the associations between parent-role quality (PRQ) and PDS, although women reported somewhat higher levels of distress than their husbands.

Besides role and partner expectations, the meanings that women attach to their provider-role responsibilities also appear to be related to their psychological well-being, family relationships and the division of labour in the home. Perry, Seery and Crouter (1992) reported that wives who were ambivalent about their provider responsibilities or who saw their employment role as secondary to their husbands', reported higher levels of depression, overload, and lower marital satisfaction. Similarly, Nathawat and Mathur (1993) found that women working outside the home had higher negativity scores than housewives. Despite the stress of separation from very young children, regret at missing the early developmental years, and social pressure to return to a more traditional role, none of the women in Grbich's study (1994) took up this option, and many of them significantly improved their career options and came to perceive themselves as more assertive.

Controlling for socio-economic status (SES), Galambos and Walters (1992) found that husbands' schedule inflexibility and long work hours (LWHs) were related to stress in husbands, and that LWHs by wives were associated with husbands' anxiety and depression. Research suggests that men and women who are similar in their occupational status and place of employment are also similar in the sources of work–family conflict (Izraeli, 1994) but that time spent on family work at weekends, and being troubled about work performance, had a greater conflictual effect on men.

In the past, the view has been that the job role is the 'add-on' role for women and that it is this role which causes their stress, while for men the work role is the main role and is also likely to be a major stressor. However, in research on role quality in dual-earner couples by Barnett, Marshall, Raudenbush and Brennan (1993) and Barnett, Brennan, Raudenbush and Marshall (1994), job-role quality and marital-role quality were negatively associated with psychological distress for women as well as for men and the magnitude varied little with gender. These results cast doubt on the widely held view that job experiences more significantly influence women's mental health states than men's.

Stress Contagion

The ill-health reported above associated with multiple-role occupancy may be explained by spillover. This is a form of stress contagion, where stress experienced in one domain (home or work) creates stress in the other domain. Another form of stress contagion is crossover, where a spouse's work stress creates stress for the other partner.

Burley (1991) examined two types of time-related independent variables used to predict family–work spillover in dual-career couples (role overload and equity). Family work-time was associated with higher spillover for the women. In contrast, time spent in family work, whether considered in the form of raw hours or in conjunction with a partner's family work-time, did not predict men's spillover. A three-stage spillover process in which parents' stress and parent–adolescent relations can mediate a link between parents' work overload and adolescent problem behaviour was drawn by Galambos, Sears, Almeida and Kolaric (1995) who found that parent–adolescent conflict was highest when both parents were stressed. As well, Repetti (1994) reported that after a demanding day at work, evidence showed a direct spillover of negative feelings associated with distress at work, and behavioural and emotional withdrawal of parents with their children at home, an increase in expressions of parental anger and greater use of discipline during interactions with a child later in the day. Williams and Alliger (1994) found that unpleasant moods spilled over from work to family and vice versa, but pleasant moods had little spillover. Mood states, role juggling, and daily levels of role involvement predicted end-of-day ratings of work–family conflict. Specific gender differences were found by Chan and Margolin (1994) who reported support for the crossover hypothesis as seen in the effect of wives' negative work mood and fatigue on husbands' reactions at home and spouses' home affect on partners' subsequent work mood.

Unlike the work of Williams and Alliger (1994), Barnett and Marshall (1989) reported no negative spillover effects from parenting to work, or work to parenting, but positive spillover effects from work to parenting. Supporting the health advantages of women engaged in multiple roles, Barnett and Marshall (1992a) found nurses and social workers reported no negative-spillover effects, but many positive-spillover effects from job to parenting. Kirchmeyer (1993) stated that professionals agreed more strongly with items about positive non-work-to-work spillover than with those about the negative side and that women and men reported largely the same levels of non-work involvement, time commitment, satisfaction, positive spillover, and use of coping strategies. Although, compared with men, women reported lower negative spillover overall, and greater use of strategies when they were parents.

Some support for the role-stress model, but no support for the role-enhancement model, was found by Barnett and Marshall (1992b) where the relationship between job stress and psychological distress was exacerbated among men who had troubled relationships with their partners. A study by Bolger, DeLongis, Kessler and Wethington (1989) reported that home-to-work stress contagion occurred more frequently among males than females, but that both sexes experienced stress contagion from the workplace to the home. It should be noted that older research found evidence of negative spillover effects from work to home (Evans & Bartolome, 1980) and from home to work (Crouter, Perry-Jenkins, Huston & Crawford, 1989). Jones and Fletcher (1993) investigated the extent and direction of occupational stress transmission and its possible psychological mechanisms in a survey of working couples. Transmission of stress from men to women was particularly evident where men had high-strain jobs (high in demand and low in support). In a similar vein, Higgins and Duxbury (1992) reported that dual-career men appeared to experience a significant negative spillover from their work domain, which may have been due to lack of structural flexibility in the work-place, or of social support for the male dual-career role. Amongst career counselling clients, men have reported high levels of occupational stress (OS) in the form of role insufficiency, high levels of vocational, psychological and physical strain, higher stress, and lower coping scores than women (Niles & Anderson, 1993).

The degree of control at work experienced by an individual has been found to moderate the effect of demands within the family (Lennon & Rosenfield, 1992). Further, the reward experienced from assisting others at work seems effective in reducing the influence of home relationship problems on physical health (Barnett, Davidson & Marshall, 1989b). Westman and Etzion (1995) investigated the crossover of burnout and of coping resources between male Israeli military officers and their spouses. For both sexes, sense of control had the highest impact on their burnout and on their spouse's burnout, after controlling for their own job stress and resources. Thus, the spouse's sense of control was an additional 'resistance resource' working to the benefit of the other partner. Similarly, employed mothers with troubled mother–child relationships had higher levels of psychological distress, unless they were in rewarding jobs (Barnett, Marshall & Sayer, 1992) where the positive-spillover from work to home was attributable to the presence of rewards from challenging work.

In the 1980s, structurally induced strains associated with the conflicting demands of occupational and childcare roles produced performance decre-ments in both domains (Dunlop, 1981, cited in Richardson & Johnson, 1984) and it was noted that at the time, the extent of organizational changes, such as flexitime, had been too minor to reduce the stress levels associated with women's combined roles (Bohen & Viveros-Long, 1981, cited in Richardson & Johnson, 1984). In 1994, Duxbury and Higgins stated that it was still necessary to recommend that organizational interventions are needed to alleviate multiple-role stress.

The multiple effects of various interacting constructs have been illustrated, and desirably could be integrated to form a dynamic predictive model of stress.

MODELLING STRESS

A good descriptive model of occupational stress which has been used with women subjects is that by Davidson and Cooper (1985). However, the full model and its predictive power remain untested. Long, Kahn and Schutz (1992) developed and tested a model of managerial women's stress from Lazarus's (1966) framework of stress/coping and found it accounted for 56% of the total variance among the constructs, with agentic traits and sex-role attitudes having both direct and indirect effects on outcome variables. Other work with this model by Spielberger and Reheiser (1994), with 922 women and 859 men working in university and corporate settings, showed that stress levels were similar for men and women, but that women reported higher scores on perceived severity and frequency of occurrence of individual stressor events.

Hendrix, Spencer and Gibson (1994) examined the effects of different sources of job and life stress on emotional and physical well-being, and in turn on absenteeism. Using a sample of 170 males and 204 females they indicated that females experienced higher levels of job stress, absenteeism, and poorer emotional well-being, and therefore required a more complex descriptive model. Raphael (1992) described the distribution of women in the workforce in Australia and the general sources of stress in the workplace, including factors that add stress to the job, role in the organization, career development, relationships at work, organizational structures, and work pressures on the family. The effects of pressure in each of these areas may lead to stress, burnout and stress-related symptoms for 'either the organisation or the individual' (p. 25).

While work sources appear to be a primary determinant of burnout in men, predictors of women's burnout include *both* work and family variables such as role conflict and marital satisfaction, as well as work stress and quality of spouse experience (Aryee, 1993; Greenglass, 1991). Thus, the influence and predictive power of numerous variables, for both women and men, need to be considered in the development of future models. Variables discussed in the multiple-roles section and in the following section on determinants could be useful in this endeavour.

Determinants and Consequences of Stress

Physiological determinants of stress

In a respect of physiological factors, research has tended to find that women react to stress in a more hyporeactive manner compared to males, especially with respect to adrenalin secretion. Since stress is believed to produce cardiac heart disease (CHD) through adrenergic mechanisms, it appears likely that female employees will be at a lower risk of CHD and may experience different stress symptomatology (Houtman, 1990). Dixon, Dixon and Spinner (1991) used the Career–Life Balance Inventory (CLBI) to survey a wide variety of tensions between careers and interpersonal commitments among a group of professional women to determine potential risk factors of cardiovascular disease. Subjective experience of life tensions appeared to be important in discriminating people who were likely to experience heart disease. In a Swedish study (Lundberg, 1996), women's role conflict and work overload were reflected in elevated psychophysiological arousal not only at work but also outside work. Such arousal may induce psychosomatic symptoms (e.g. cardiovascular and musculoskeletal disorders). In a review of studies on the physiological and endocrine mechanisms by which psychosocial factors influence health and behaviour in men and women, Frankenhaeuser (1991) illustrated how the neuroendocrine and cardiovascular reactions which are triggered by work overload and underload can be modulated by social support systems and opportunities for personal control. Johansson, Laakso, Peder and Karonen (1989) also examined gender differences in the hormone levels of 29 male and 27 female medical students before and after a stressful exam. Their results indicated slight differences between the sexes in the behaviour of some hormones when the homeostatic balance of the body was upset by psychological stress factors.

It appears that sex differences in catecholamine reactivity have emerged in that the low catecholamine response to achievement demands, characteristic of women in the past, has been replaced by 'male-like' stress responses in women who occupy traditionally male occupations and managerial positions.

Psychological determinants and consequences of stress

Stress can produce many adverse effects, with its impact on physical health, injury, job satisfaction, commitment, absenteeism, turnover, performance, sabotage, interpersonal aggression, hostility, and complaints (Chen & Spector, 1992; Jamal, 1990), yet there are a number of individual factors mediating the effects of stress. In fact few studies have investigated sex differences in the career–personality–stress relationship. Various research findings show that psychological reactions mediate the relationship between stressor and outcome (Jex, Baldwin, Hughes, Storr & Sheehan, 1991), and that the perception of occupational stress as a threatening or challenging situation varies between individual employees (Gadzella, Ginther, Tomcala & Bryant, 1991). Hardiness has been considered a variable which moderates the effect of stress (Nowack, 1989; Wiebe, 1991). Also an optimistic orientation creates more effective strategies for coping with stress (Lee, Ashford & Jamieson, 1993). Individuals who have a tendency to be optimistic use 'active' coping strategies rather than 'avoidant' methods, resulting in enhanced coping and defensive pessimism which can also reduce the impact of stressors (Scheier & Carver, 1992). An interesting source of stress in employed women has been identified as the 'imposter phenomenon' whereby stress is caused by attributing success to factors other than competence (Hirschfeld, 1982; Terzella, 1986). Type A and Type B behaviour are important personality variables in employee health and performance (Lee, Ashford & Jamieson, 1993). In a study of nurses (Jamal, 1990), Type A behaviour was 'associated with high job stress, high role ambiguity, conflict, resource inadequacy, and psychosomatic health problems' (p. 727). Gender differences have been identified in the correlation between Type A behaviour and coping styles (Houtman, 1990), and with women managers having higher Type A coronary-prone behaviour patterns than their male counterparts (Cooper & Davidson, 1982).

Sex-role orientation determines levels of psychological distress, and early in 1980, Collins, Reardon and Waters argued that sex-role orientation, rather than the gender dominance of an occupation, was the primary influence on perceived success in non-traditional occupations. In women, a negative relationship between masculinity and psychological distress has been accounted for by an association between masculine attributes and a rejection of defensive styles. Self-esteem, interpersonal self-confidence and self-concepts contribute to stress levels in both sexes (Zuckerman, 1989). However, Sekaran (1986) reported that career orientation rather than gender more strongly influenced job satisfaction, life satisfaction and mental health. Stickel and Bonnet (1989) suggested that females may avoid non-traditional, male-dominated careers, not only because their perceived self-efficacy is low but also because of concerns about simultaneously meeting the demands of the family role. Perhaps for these and other reasons, it has been found that females report lower performance expectations in male-dominant occupations than in female-dominant occupations (Betz & Hackett, 1986; Bridges, 1988).

STRESS IN THE OCCUPATIONS

Traditional/Non-traditional Jobs

Previous research has been limited by a neglect of the effects of occupational structure and culture on stress. A study of nurses and engineers found that occupation-specific models of stress were more representative than the conventional generic model (Bacharach & Bamberger, 1992), with results showing that current role stressor models did not possess cross-occupational generalizability, and that the characteristics of a particular occupation were important influences on the antecedents and consequences of role stressors. For example, for women, research suggests that the non-traditional job sphere holds potentially 'more' stress than for those in 'traditional' jobs (Koch, Boose, Cohen et al., 1991).

Developing career paths in management

Managerial and some professional occupations are still considered non-traditional for women, and have received considerable attention in research. Some of the first work in this area was conducted by Davidson and Cooper (1985) who found that compared to male managers, women managers experienced more pressures at work and at home, and possessed a greater number of stress manifestations. Women managers have also been found to be at risk of work underload, resulting in fewer promotion opportunities and dissatisfaction, with female employees being more qualified than male employees at similar management levels (Davidson & Cooper, 1985). Other potential sources of stress which have been identified for managers and professionals include 'factors intrinsic to the job, role based stress, relationships, career development factors, organizational structure and climate, and the work: family interface' (Glowinkowski & Cooper, 1987, p. 177). Specifically, discrimination is perceived to be an obstacle to career development in terms of daily working lives, on-the-job training and education (Nykodym & George, 1989). Renault de Moraes, Swan and Cooper (1993) reported that female white-collar government employees experienced a greater number of stress sources, poorer health and lower job dissatisfaction than male employees, and for professional women, many female employees have expressed concern that males were given 'priority' in large organizations (Watson & Hodgson, 1984).

Hochwarter, Perrewe and Dawkins (1995) examined gender differences in stress amongst managers employed in predominantly male, predominantly female, or integrated occupations with respect to perceptions of job demands, work control, and stress. Women perceived more job demands in male-dominated occupations and female-dominated occupations than men; however, no gender differences were found in integrated occupations. Males in both female-dominated and integrated occupations perceived more job control than females. Even in non-Western societies, Beena and Poduval (1992) found that female executives had greater stress than males. However, a study of Australian managerial and professional women (Langan-Fox & Poole, 1995) showed that there were no significant organizational difficulties for this group of women.

The negative consequences that are associated with career success have been termed as 'career success/personal failure' (Westman & Etzion, 1990). Aspirations for promotion, power and income in managerial employees, and the associated stress and strain, produce deleterious effects on the quality of the family role (Westman & Gafni, 1987). Female managers have been thought to be particularly susceptible to stress-related problems since they often have overextended emotional demands and experience conflicting time-tables for the work and family roles (Etzion & Pines, 1986). In Israel and the United States, burnout produced by the conflicting demands of work and family roles was considerably higher in females than males (Etzion, 1987), and in non-management and management men and women in the telecommunications industry, women and men did not share the same environmental vulnerabilities to burnout, with female non-managers reporting the highest levels of all burnout (Pretty, McCarthy & Catano, 1992). Similarly, Kahn and Cooper (1992) found that amongst currency traders, sources of females' anxiety appeared job-related, while that of males was related to dealing and personality factors.

Support structures and processes

The importance of mentors and role models for women in alleviating stress and improving performance has been documented in several studies. The benefits of mentoring appear to be influenced by organizational climate, with outcomes being most positive when there is open communication, high trust and value of employee development in the organization. Bahniuk, Dobos and Hill (1990) surveyed male and female managers and found that both men and women with mentors scored higher on informal and formal communication variables than did subjects without mentors. The benefits of mentoring for women in managerial careers have been reported by McKeen and Burke (1989) where the experienced senior mentors assisted employees to learn the politics, encounter opportunities, receive support and reach career aspirations. Women involved in mentor relationships experienced enhanced self-esteem, feedback, rapid promotion, and management skills (Reich, 1986). Similarly, Gaskill and Sibley (1990) found that mentored female mid-level executives in the retail industry reported significantly more promotions over 5 years than did non-mentored executives and that upper-level women experiencing mentoring relationships reported higher levels of job motivation than did their non-mentored counterparts. Interestingly, Gaskill and Sibley (1990) found that female upper-level executives were more likely to be mentored by men and more often than mid-level executives. Lower-level employees have also benefited from mentoring among 208 male and female bank officers—mentoring was associated with job satisfaction and with not having reached a 'career plateau' (Corzine, Buntzman & Busch, 1994). Additionally, it has been suggested that managerial career success is influenced by practical, or tacit, knowledge which is primarily acquired through mentoring (Wagner, 1987, cited in Horgan & Simeon, 1990). However, the effect of a mentor on improved tacit knowledge has been identified for male, but not for female, managers (Horgan & Simeon, 1990), and also that tacit knowledge has not influenced career success or higher levels of perceived competency in women. Furthermore, Goh (1991) found that women perceived male supervisors as exhibiting less mentoring behaviour toward them and had lower job satisfaction when compared with males, under male supervision.

Organizations encounter barriers when finding a mentor for a female employee, such as the lack of access to information networks, tokenism, stereotypes, norms regarding cross-sex relationships and the reliance on ineffective power bases in women (McKeen & Burke, 1989) but in general, the performance advantages of mentoring emphasize the importance of further research to encourage organizations to implement programmes.

Impact of new technology in offices and on the shopfloor

Between 1981 and 1984, 35% of office workplaces introduced computers (Daniel, 1987, cited in Liff, 1990), but surprisingly the impact of such dramatic changes on employees, especially clerical and secretarial workers, has not been well documented. Furthermore, the need for research is even more pressing when taking into account the fact that women now share over 50% of technical jobs in Canada, the Nordic countries, the United States, and Poland (UNDP, 1995).

Some work by Garrison and Eaton (1992) showed that secretaries were significantly more depressed than other women, but this was not investigated with respect to new technology. Amick and Celentano (1991) examined the stress of postal clerks (42.5% female) in a mail-sorting environment after the introduction of new technology. They found that technology was indirectly associated with job satisfaction and psychosomatic symptoms by virtue of job structure, and that a machine-paced technological system of work was associated with greater job demands, less control in the job, and less co-worker support. While gender differences were found for psychosomatic symptoms and autonomy, no specific hypotheses relating to the direction of these gender differences were proposed. Nevertheless, this type of research should be supported in future work.

A study conducted by Liff (1990) found that female office workers reported an increase in workload due to computer installation and one-third of respondents had an increase in stress levels, with many related health problems such as eye-stain, headaches, tiredness, depression and backaches. Similarly, Collins (1988) found that a sample of operators (over 75% women) who spent more than two-thirds of their working time using new equipment believed they had lower levels of skill utilization, variety and influence in their work than previously, and higher levels of pressure and work-related health problems. These changes led to a low level of job satisfaction. Further, a study by Schalk and van den Berg (1993) established that the mental health of information technology employees is more strongly influenced by work and health perceptions than work characteristics, personality or activities outside work. Obviously, the full effect of technology has yet to be documented and much more intensive research needs to be conducted.

The specific aspects of occupations influencing stress and which have been a focus for research include teaching and other jobs which have high interpersonal impact.

The effects of teaching

Women have dominated the teaching profession for many years and in 1995, 66% of employees in education were women (ABS, 1995). However, different patterns of stress can be detected between the sexes in teaching, with many studies showing that men suffer more stress and depersonalization than women. Long and Gessaroli (1989) surveyed 164 male and 617 female elementary school teachers in Canada and found that males felt more stressed than females, and that males felt that avoidance, and females that problem-solving, was a more effective coping style. Beer and Beer (1992) reported that stress scores were significantly higher for male SPE high school teachers than for female SPE high school teachers and male SPE grade school teachers. Ogus, Greenglass and Burke (1990) compared female and male teachers and found that men scored significantly higher than women on depersonalization and stress and also had a lower quality of daily life than women. Women tended to put more energy into their friendships and to value them more. In other research, Greenglass, Burke and Ondrack (1990) reported that in school personnel, compared with women, men scored significantly higher on deper-sonalization and work stress, but were less likely to employ coping techniques, particularly with regard to their quality of daily life, investment in friends, and cultural activities. Women were better able to use coping strategies to reduce burnout. In men, burnout appeared to be a joint function of work stress and children, with the presence of children significantly raising a man's level of burnout over that associated with work stress.

Fontana and Abouserie (1993) investigated the stress of 95 teachers but found no significant gender differences in stress levels, concluding that personality di-mensions contributed more to stress than gender. Similarly, a study of Jamaican science teachers found no significant differences in the degree of stress experi-enced by teachers, based on gender (Soyibo, 1994). Amongst health education specialists though, women have displayed a higher degree of emotional exhaustion symptoms than men (Chen & Lu, 1993–4). In the higher education sector, where women are outnumbered by men, female university teachers have been found to have higher misfit scores than their male counterparts, to perceive stress at work at least 50% of the time, and to be more likely to consider job change as a result of job stress (Blix, Cruise, Mitchell & Blix, 1994).

Besides their domination in teaching, women also make up 75% of all em-ployees in the caring professions, typically in hospitals and dental nursing (ABS, 1995). In recent years, the helping professions have experienced significant organ-izational, structural and professional changes, which could easily affect stress.

Demands in the helping professions

Cushway and Tyler (1994) investigated levels and sources of stress in clinical psychologists, and found that women reported higher stress levels and somatic symptoms at a higher rate than men. Coping strategies most frequently reported were behavioural, for example, talking to others, but an avoidance coping strategy was associated with poorer mental health outcomes. Other research by Nowack and Pentkowski (1994) has also reported frequent use of avoidant coping strategies. These authors explored differences in self-reported lifestyle habits, substance use (alcohol, drugs, and smoking), and predictors of job burnout in 879 professional working women (aged 20–65 yrs) employed in dental health offices. Subjects with higher levels of drinking, smoking and drugs reported significantly lower quality lifestyle practices, nutrition habits, and more frequent use of avoidant coping strategies in the face of work and life hassles, compared to non-drinkers. In drug and alcohol counselling employees (57% women) Price and Spence (1994) investigated the relationship between work and non-work stressors to determine burnout, with results showing that daily hassles contributed to employee burnout reactions for both men and women. Turner, Tippett and Raphael (1994) interviewed 11 women holding senior positions in medicine—one factor that significantly affected these women's careers included the stress that resulted from conflicting family and career priorities. Olkinuora, Asp, Juntunen et al. (1992) examined whether specialists and non-specialists experience stress and burnout differently, using 2671 physicians (aged <66 years). Among male physicians, the highest burnout scores were found for those in general practice, occupational health, and psychiatry. For female physicians, those in general practice and occupational health had the highest burnout scores. Tendencies toward suicidal thoughts were high among subjects, especially women. On the other hand, job stressors did not vary by gender in a study of job-stress among physicians by Simpson and Grant (1991), and Sutherland and Cooper (1990) found that compared to females, male general practitioners had higher levels of anxiety and depression, whereas female GPs compared favourably to the population norm. Similarly, male mental health professionals have been reported to be somewhat more stressed, to have poorer relationships with their co-workers and to have greater negative spillover than women (Kirkcaldy & Siefen, 1991). General practice and occupational health seem to have high burnout scores with heavy work loads, hectic work tempos, and problems with professional identity. VanYperen, Buunk and Schaufeli (1992) investigated whether burnout symptoms (emotional exhaustion, depersonalization, and reduced personal accomplishment) occurred among male and female nurses who were low in communal orientation. While men seemed more inclined to respond to patients in a non-personal way, independent of stress, depersonalization served women as a coping mechanism. Fine differences in the structure of the working day can affect stress, particularly in the health professions where shiftwork is common. Kandolin (1993), studying mental health nurses, reported that female nurses in three-shift work reported more stress symptoms and had generally ceased to enjoy their work more than women in two-shift work.

Other jobs which require shift work by employees are those which are dominated by men, and these are the 'para-professional' occupations.

Experiencing the 'masculine' occupations

In occupations, probably the last bastion of male domination can be found in the police, fire, prison and military services. Much of the research suggests that the problem for women is with personal relationships with colleagues, and in general that there is widespread harassment and discrimination.

Brown and Fielding (1993) investigated differences in police officers' experience of occupational stress in 358 male and 139 female English police constables engaged in uniformed patrol or detective duties. Women uniformed constables were less likely to be exposed to police operational stressors involving violence, but if exposed, reported more adverse reactions than did uniformed policemen. Norvell, Hills and Murrin (1993) assessed male and female officers of a state highway patrol agency. Male officers experienced a greater degree of perceived stress and emotional exhaustion and dissatisfaction with their work than did women, and while such stress was influenced by symptoms of job dissatisfaction in women, higher levels of perceived stress in women were associated with dissatisfaction with co-workers, also evident in Brown and Fielding's (1993) study. It seems that women uniformed officers and detectives are more likely to be involved in dealing with victims of violence or sexual offences and the former more likely to report higher levels of associated self-perceived stress than their male counterparts. There have been few differences in exposure to organizational stressors, except that women detectives and uniformed officers have reported higher rates of sex discrimination and prejudice than did policemen (Brown & Fielding, 1993). To a large extent, women seem to experience the same stressors as men in small-town policing (Bartol, Bergen, Volckens & Knoras, 1992), with the exception of task-related stressors, for which women reported more stress when exposed to tragedy, and feeling more stress associated with responsibility for the safety of the public and their professional colleagues. Women also reported stress associated with working in a male-dominated occupation. Although there are reported gender differences in types of stressors, Alexander and Walker (1994) found that police officers' methods of coping with occupational stress were not particularly successful and were independent of gender, rank, and duties. However, other research by Langan-Fox, Deery and van Vliet (in press) supported the view that both male and female police trainees used the more effective 'problem focused' coping strategy rather than 'emotion-focused' coping.

Murphy, Beaton, Cain and PIke (1994) investigated gender differences in 700 firefighters' job stressors and symptoms of stress. Male and female subjects reported highly similar patterns of job stress and symptoms of stress; however, males reported tedium and family financial strains more frequently than females. Female subjects reported higher scores on job discrimination (job stressor) and higher rates of depression (symptoms of stress). In surveying gender differences in occupational stress among correctional officers Gross, Larson, Urban and Zupan (1994) found that women were more likely to have been absent and tardy and to have taken sick leave, than men. Similarly, Nice and Hilton (1994) showed that women in non-traditional occupations visited sick bay at a significantly higher rate than women in traditional occupations.

A study by Hammelman (1995) examined the extent to which certain stressors influenced male and female US Army soldiers. Results revealed that female soldiers were influenced less by stressors than their male counterparts were. Leiter, Clark and Durup (1994) used LISREL analysis to investigate similarities and differences in the way men and women experience the military as a workplace. They found that 232 men and 241 women in the Canadian Forces demonstrated considerable differences in levels of burnout, organizational commitment, and psychosomatic symptoms, with women finding that these environments provide fewer coping resources. Results supported the prediction that supportive collegial relationships are of greater salience to women than to men, and that women are more concerned with issues of powerlessness when confronting organizational problems.

Some additional occupations considered in the stress literature include bus and tram drivers (Kuhlmann, 1990) and transit workers (Mansfield, Koch, Henderson & Vicary, 1991); tradeswomen (Mansfield et al., 1991); women workers in a microelectronics plant (Bromet, Dew, Parkinson & Cohen, 1992); garment assembly plants (Pines & Guendelman, 1995); married clergy (Rogers, 1991); female ministers (Eaton & Newlon, 1990); and farmers' wives. These studies present small but important inroads into jobs which are unusual for women and much more research of this type is needed.

In general, the picture presented by research in the male-dominated occupations suggests that the experiences of women are 'different' and probably do not reflect the true extent of problems women face in these occupations. These are jobs where substantial assistance is required if women are to cope and flourish in what seems to be a hostile environment.

COPING WITH OCCUPATIONAL STRESS

Coping Strategies and Stress-Management Interventions

In general, the literature reviewed suggests that men and women use different coping resources. As to whether 'strategies' or styles (an individual difference variable) are different, remains to be seen.

The coping management skills of 100 Indian Navy wives experiencing stress due to the prolonged absence of their husbands was examined by Thomas and

Sudhakar (1994). Subjects with an androgynous gender role orientation, or equally high masculine and feminine traits, showed a positive correlation with coping styles of developing interpersonal relations and social support. Either women develop appropriate coping strategies or they have husbands who help facilitate them. Kirchmeyer (1993) identified the successful strategies used by managers (35% women) to cope with the many demands and responsibilities of multiple domains. Compared with men, women reported lower negative spillover overall, and greater use of the strategies when they were parents. Husbands' psychological support for wives' dual role, and husbands' participation in family work were most strongly associated with the ability to cope with stress and life satisfaction in research by Gray, Lovejoy, Piotrkowski and Bond (1990).

Consistent with other research by Langan-Fox and Poole (1995), Fong and Amatea (1992) reported that single women sometimes have significantly higher levels of stress symptoms than married-parent women. In this research, single women more often used passive coping strategies. One explanatory view could be that single women have fewer support structures by virtue of their status and are therefore more likely to suffer stress. Alternatively, it is possible that the effects of marital and parental status could 'force' women into various 'search' behaviours in an effort to find solutions to their multiple-role demands, which could result in providing women with an army of diverse skills, making them adept at changing between environmental, work and family demands.

FEATURES OF PAST RESEARCH, AND KEY ISSUES FOR THE FUTURE

Up until the early part of this century, years of conservatism kept women out of the paid workforce. Thus, we could say that in terms of education, work and quality of lifestyle, women living in Western, post-industrialized nations have made great leaps forward in the world of work, especially in the past 40 years. The statistics on job participation suggest that this pattern of participation will not change. As we approach the new millenium, what then is the picture that emerges of recent research on women's careers and occupational stress?

The belief that if women enter the workforce they will automatically develop stress, psychological or physical ill-health, has proved to be ill-founded. Role strain, role overload and role conflict are the potential negative consequences of multiple-role occupancy for both women and men, and these have been reported, but the benefits of role expansion appear to be more prominent, and furthermore, women themselves choose multiple roles. They want a career, and a family. The role expansion model suggests that the health benefits of employment provide opportunities for individuals to access alternative sources of self-esteem, satisfaction and personal identity. In addition, individual difference variables mediating the stress–outcome relationship, such as Type A behaviour, hardiness, an optimistic orientation, 'active' coping strategies, and sex-role orientation, have been identified, although their degree of influence warrants further research.

Moderators of stress in women's careers appear to be role quality which is now considered to be more important than role occupancy. There are grounds for rejecting Assumption 1, mentioned in the early part of this review. High-quality roles enhance health and buffer stress. An individual's sense of control and work reward in a given career is an additional 'resistance resource'. Given the importance of timing in careers, role quality might only act as a moderator when considered in relation to other variables such as age, parental status and career development.

The growth in dual-earner couples indicates too, that a linchpin in a woman's capacity to attain her goals for work and family, and maintain a healthy lifestyle, is her spouse or partner. Some research suggests that women's employment is 'still negative for husbands' mental health' and that women's work destabilizes a marriage. This suggests that women are 'at fault'. The converse could be true: a crucial moderator in ameliorating stress for women in dual-career relationships is a range of personality variables belonging to the husband—interpersonal competence, perceptions of threat, and capability of responding appropriately to domestic responsibilities. Women's perceptions of their provider role in the relationship are influential, as are more diffuse contextual variables such as family climate, ratio of husband–wife earnings, and jointly determined variables such as the 'at-risk' status of the marriage. In other words, the dual-career couple have before them a delicate and complex set of factors which require a high level of skill to negotiate. The more recent research on stress contagion indicates that women are less likely than men to report negative spillover overall, but that parent–child relationships are predictably poor at the end of many work-days. Dual-career men may be suffering adversely either through a lack of structural flexibility and support in organizations, and/or through poor synchronization of their career to their family life. There is no overwhelming evidence suggesting that women suffer more stress than men. It seems that both partners experience stress, in *varying types and degrees*. Given that groups are chosen for research because it is thought there might be a 'problem', a more rounded approach needs to be taken about the whole circumference of family life, how it changes, over different periods, and over the course of other family and life changes. On the basis of the research findings which indicate that the whole family is affected by stress (e.g. end-of-day stress), it is now timely to suggest that research should involve the whole family—not just couples or partners.

An important task to be tackled is the development of models of stress suitable for women and men. Such models would factor in physiological conditions, and may show that the determinants of stress may be changing for men and women, such that there is high convergence amongst women who have occupations traditionally held by men, but that this convergence could spread to other occupations as well.

A focus needs to be given to specific occupations, beyond the professions—managers and professionals which have been the subject of much research—to blue-collar jobs—manufacturing areas such as the automobile and aviation industries. Also there appears to be a great gap in our knowledge about work stress amongst ethnic groups. In terms of burnout, there seem to be different environmental factors facilitating stress in men and women. A more recent innovation in the last 10 years or so, has been the development of mentoring schemes, especially in male-dominated jobs, and it appears that the benefits of these are yet to be fully recognized both by organizations and by women themselves. More research is needed to substantiate the glowing reports of scheme success, perhaps having stronger research designs, before-and-after, and comparing organizations with and without schemes.

In some of the female-dominated professions such as teaching, it seems that men fare less well than women and suffer considerably more stress through their coping strategies, and negative spillover, although a small amount of research contradicts this view. Some areas dominated by men—the university sector—suggest that women suffer stress more than men, but this is an underresearched area. Other areas dominated by women—the helping professions—suggest that hectic work tempos, shiftwork and high workloads result in a pattern of high stress and burnout amongst women and that the ability to juggle home–work obligations is difficult. Women do report extreme stress when working in male-dominated occupations, evident in a range of negative reactions: taking more sick leave; more adverse reactions (than men) to violence and tragedy; more stress associated with responsibility to the public and colleagues. Other negative experiences include job discrimination, perceived hostile work environments, lack of support from colleagues, and powerlessness. These male-dominated power-professional jobs require intense investigation to analyse their cultures and their effects on the career progress of women. To a large extent, Assumption 2 was supported. In the area of new technology, although research has been conducted into ergonomic features of work-stations, little work has been done to assess the effects of psychological and occupational stress on women in particular jobs. This is a vast undertaking, given the pace of technological change, but a necessary and important one for future researchers. Assumption 3 remains untested. Instructional techniques in coping strategies could be an important first step for induction in certain work environments and the research suggests that both men and women—in different occupations—would benefit from such interventions. On the whole, Assumption 4 was supported. The literature in general shows that there is a body of scattered research suggesting that women employ coping strategies more often, and are more effective in implementing them.

Finally, the important trends which were mentioned early in this chapter, women's mortality and morbidity rates, need to be monitored and researched.

In this regard, a major challenge for women into the twenty-first century will be to develop and maintain control over all those influences affecting the quality of their lifestyle.

ACKNOWLEDGEMENT

Grateful thanks is given to Kim Albert, who assisted in reviews of the literature.

REFERENCES

ABS (1993). Women in Australia. Australian Bureau of Statistics. Catalogue: 4113.0.

ABS (1994). Women's Health. Australian Bureau of Statistics. Catalogue: 4365.0.

ABS (1995). Australian Women's Yearbook. Australian Bureau of Statistics. Catalogue: 4124.0.

AIHW (1996). Australian Institute of Health & Welfare, *Australia Health*. Canberra, ACT: Australian Government Publishing Service.

Alexander, D. A. & Walker, L. G. (1994). A study of methods used by Scottish police officers to cope with work induced stress. *Stress Medicine*, **10**(2), 131–138.

Amick, B. C. & Celentano, D. D. (1991). Structural determinants of the psychosocial work environment: Introducing technology in the work stress framework. *Ergonomics*, **34**(5), 625–646.

Aneshensel, C. S. (1986). Marital and employment role-strain, social support, and depression among adult women. In S. E. Hobfell (Ed.), *Stress, Social Support, and Women*. Washington, DC: Hemisphere.

Aryee, S. (1993). Dual earner couples in Singapore: An examination of work and nonwork sources of their experienced burnout. *Human Relations*, **46**(12), 1441–1468.

Bacharach, S. & Bamberger, P. (1992). Causal models of role stressor antecedents and consequences: The importance of occupational differences. *Journal of Vocational Behavior*, **4**, 13–35.

Bahniuk, M. H., Dobos, J. & Hill, S. K. (1990). The impact of mentoring, collegial support, and information adequacy on career success: A replication. *Journal of Social Behavior and Personality*, **5**(4), 431–452.

Barnett, R. C. & Baruch, G. K. (1985). Women's involvement in multiple roles and psychological distress. *Journal of Personality and Social Psychology*, **49**, 135–145.

Barnett, R. C., Brennan, R. T. & Marshall, N. L. (1994). Gender and the relationship between parent role quality and psychological distress: A study of men and women in dual earner couples. *Journal of Family Issues*, **15**(2), 229–252.

Barnett, R. C., Brennan, R. T., Raudenbush, S. W. & Marshall, N. L. (1994). Gender and the relationship between marital role quality and psychological distress: A study of women and men in dual earner couples. *Psychology of Women Quarterly*, **18**(1), 105–127.

Barnett, R. C., Davidson, H. & Marshall, N. L. (1989a). *Occupational stress and health of women LPN's and LSW's: Final project report*. Working Paper No. 202, Wellesley College, Center for Research on Women, Wellesley, MA 02181.

Barnett, R. C., Davidson, H. & Marshall, N. L. (1989b). *Physical symptoms and the interplay of work and family roles*. Working Paper No. 201, Wellesley College, Center for Research on Women, Wellesley, MA 02181.

Barnett, R. C. & Marshall, N. L. (1989). *Multiple roles, spillover effects and psychological distress.* Working Paper No. 200, Wellesley College, Center for Research on Women, Wellesley, MA 02181.

Barnett, R. C. & Marshall, N. L. (1992a). Men's job and partner roles: Spillover effects and psychological distress. *Sex Roles,* 27(9–10), 455–472.

Barnett, R. C. & Marshall, N. L. (1992b). Worker and mother roles, spillover effects, and psychological distress. *Women and Health,* 18(2), 9–40.

Barnett, R. C., Marshall, N. L., Raudenbush, S. W. & Brennan, R. T. (1993). Gender and the relationship between job experiences and psychological distress: A study of dual earner couples. *Journal of Personality and Social Psychology,* 64(5), 794–806.

Barnett, R. C., Marshall, N. L. & Sayer, A. (1992). Positive spillover effects from job to home: A closer look. *Women and Health,* 19(2–3), 13–14.

Bartol, C. R., Bergen, G. T., Volckens, J. S. & Knoras, K. M. (1992). *Criminal Justice and Behaviour,* 19(3), 240–259.

Baruch, G. K., Biener, L. & Barnett, R. C. (1987). Women and gender in research on work and family stress. *American Psychologist,* 42, 130–136.

Beena, C. & Poduval, P. R. (1992). Gender differences in work stress of executives. *Psychological Studies,* 37(2–3), 109–113.

Beer, J. & Beer, J. (1992). Burnout and stress, depression and self esteem of teachers. *Psychological Reports,* 71(3), 1331–1336.

Betz, N. E. & Hackett, G. (1986). Applications of self-efficacy theory to understanding career choice behaviour. *Journal of Social and Clinical Psychology,* 4, 279–289.

Blix, A. G., Cruise, R. J., Mitchell, B. & Blix, G. G. (1994). Occupational stress among university teachers, *Educational Research,* 36(2), 157–169.

Bolger, N., DeLongis, A., Kessler, R. C. & Wethington, E. (1989). The contagion of stress across multiple roles. *Journal of Marriage and the Family,* 51, 175–183.

Bridges, J. S. (1988). Sex differences in occuptaional performance expectations. *Psychology of Women Quarterly,* 12, 75–90.

Bromet, E. J., Dew, M. A., Parkinson, D. K. & Cohen, S. (1992). Effects of occupational stress on the physical and psychological health of women in a microelectronics plant. *Social Science and Medicine,* 34(12), 1377–1383.

Broom, D. (1996). Gendering health, sexing illness. In *Changing Society for Women's Health* (pp. 22–26). Canberra: Australian Government Publishing Service.

Brown, J. & Fielding, J. (1993). Qualitative differences and women police officers' experience of occupational stress. *Work and Stress,* 7(4), 327–340.

Burlew, A. K. & Johnson, J. L. (1992). Role conflict and career advancement among African American women in nontraditional professions. *Career Development Quarterly,* 40(4), 302–312.

Burley, K. A. (1991). Family work spillover in dual career couples: A comparison of two time perspectives. *Psychological Reports,* 68(2), 471–480.

Chan, C. J. & Margolin, G. (1994). The relationship between dual earner couples' daily work mood and home affect. *Journal of Social and Personal Relationshps,* 11(4), 573–586.

Chen, P. Y. & Spector, P. E. (1992). Relationships of work stressors with aggression, withdrawal, theft and substance use: An exploratory study. *Journal of Occupational and Organizational Psychology ,* 65, 177–184.

Chen, W. W. & Lu, L. P. (1993–94). Assessment of job-related burnout among health education specialists in Taiwan. *International Quarterly of Community Health Education,* 14(2), 207–214.

Cleary, P. D. & Mechanic, D. (1983). Sex differences in psychological distress among married people. *Journal of Health and Social Behaviour,* 4, 111–121.

Collins, J., Reardon, M. & Waters, L. K. (1980). Occupational interest and perceived personal success: Effects of gender, sex-role orientation, and the sexual composition of the occupation. *Psychological Reports,* 47, 1155–1159.

Collins, M. (1988). *The Impact of New Office Technology on Clerical Workers in Queensland*. Canberra: Australian Government Publishing Service.

Cooper, C. L. & Davidson, M. J. (1982). The high cost of stress on women managers. *Organizational Dynamics*, Spring, 44–53.

Corzine, J. B., Buntzman, G. F. & Busch, E. T. (1994). Mentoring, downsizing, gender and career outcomes. *Journal of Social Behavior and Personality*, **9**(3), 517–528.

Crouter, A. C., Perry-Jenkins, M., Huston, T. I. & Crawford, D. W. (1989). The influence of work-induced psychological states on behaviour at home. *Basic and Applied Social Psychology*, **10**(3), 273–292.

Cushway, D. & Tyler, P. A. (1994). Stress and coping in clinical psychologists: *Stress Medicine*, **10**(1), 35–42.

Davidson, M. & Cooper, C. (1985). Women managers: Work, stress and marriage. *International Journal of Social Economics*, **12**, 17–25.

Dixon, J. P., Dixon, J. K. & Spinner, J. C. (1991). Tensions between career and interpersonal commitments as a risk factor for cardiovascular disease among women. *Women and Health*, **17**(3), 33–57.

Duxbury, L. & Higgins, C. (1994). Interference between work and family: A status report on dual career and dual earner mothers and fathers. *Employee Assistance Quarterly*, **9**(3–4), 55–80.

Eaton, K. F. & Newlon, B. J. (1990). Characteristics of women ministers in Arizona. *Counselling and Values*, **34**(3), 205–208.

Etzion, D. (1987). Burning out in management: A comparison of women and men in matched organizational positions. *Israel Social Science Research Journal*, **5**, 147–163.

Etzion, D. & Pines, A. (1986). Sex and culture as factors explaining coping and burnout among human service professionals: A social psychological perspective. *Journal of Cross-Cultural Psychology*, **17**, 191–209.

Evans, P. & Bartolome, F. (1980). The changing pictures of the relationship between career and family. *Journal of Occupational Behavior*, **5**, 9–21.

Facione, N. C. (1994). Role overload and health: The married mother in the waged labor force. *Health Care for Women International*, **15**(2), 157–167.

Fong, M. L. & Amatea, E. S. (1992). Stress and single professional women: An exploration of causal factors. Special Issue: Women and health. *Journal of Mental Health Counselling*, **14**(1), 20–29.

Fontana, D. & Abouserie, R. (1993). Stress levels, gender and personality factors in teachers. *British Journal of Educational Psychology*, **63**(2), 261–270.

Frankenhauser, M. (1991). The psychophysiology of sex differences as related to occupational status. In U. Lundberg & M. Chesney (Eds), *Women, Work and Health*. New York: Plenum.

Gadzella, B. M., Ginther, D. W., Tomcala, M. & Bryant, G. W. (1991). Educators' appraisal of their stressors and coping strategies. *Psychological Report*, **68**, 995–998.

Galambos, N. L., Sears, H. A., Almeida, D. M. & Kolaric, G. C. (1995). Parents' work overload and problem behaviour in young adolescents. *Journal of Research on Adolescence*, **5**(2), 201–223.

Galambos, N. L. & Walters, B. J. (1992). Work hours, schedule inflexibility, and stress in dual earner spouses. *Canadian Journal of Behavioural Science*, **24**(3), 290–302.

Garrison, R. & Eaton, W. W. (1992). Secretaries, depression and absenteeism. *Women and Health*, **18**(4), 53–76.

Gaskill, L. R. & Sibley, L. R. (1990). Mentoring relationships for women in retailing: Prevalence, perceived importance, and characteristics. *Clothing and Textiles Research Journal*, **9**(1), 1–10.

Glowinkowski, S. P. & Cooper, C. L. (1987). Managers and professionals in business/industrial settings: The research evidence. In *Organizational Studies in Stress*, New York: Haworth Press.

Goh, S. C. (1991). Sex differernces in perceptions of interpersonal work style, career emphasis, supervisory mentoring behaviour, and job satisfaction. *Sex Roles,* 24(11–12), 701–710.

Gray, E. B., Lovejoy, M. C., Piotrkowski, C. S. & Bond, J. T. (1990). Husband supportiveness and the well-being of employed mothers of infants. Special Issue: Work and family. *Families in Society,* 71(6), 332–341.

Grbich, C. (1994). Women as primary breadwinners in families where men are primary caregivers. *Australian and New Zealand Journal of Sociology,* 30(2), 105–118.

Greenberger, E. & O'Neil, R. (1993). Spouse, parent, worker: Role commitments and role related experiences in the construction of adults' well-being. *Developmental Psychology,* 29(2), 181–197.

Greenglass, E. R. (1991). Burnout and gender: Theoretical and organizational implications. *Canadian Psychology,* 32(4), 562–574.

Greenglass, E. R., Burke, R. J. & Ondrack, M. (1990). A gender role perspective of coping and burnout. *Applied Psychology. An International Review,* 39(1), 5–27.

Gross, G. R., Larson, S. J., Urban, G. D. & Zupan, L. L. (1994). Gender differences in occupational stress among correctional officers. Special Issue: Personnel issues in criminal Justice. *American Journal of Criminal Justice,* 18(2), 219–234.

Gupta, A. & Saini, I. (1993). Anxiety and health problems in traditional and dual career couples. *Pharmacopsychoecologia,* 6(1), 21–26.

Hall, D. T. (1987). Careers and socialization. *Journal of Management,* 13, 301–321.

Hall, W. A. (1992). Comparison of the experience of women and men in dual earner families following the birth of their first infant. *IMAGE Journal of Nursing Scholarship,* 24(1), 33–38.

Hammelman, T. L. (1995). The Persian Gulf conflict: The impact of stressors as perceived by Army Reservists. *Health and Social Work,* 29(2), 140–145.

Hazuda, P. H., Haffner, S. M., Stern, M. P., Knapp, J. A., Eifler, C. W. & Rosenthal, M. (1986). Employment status and women's protection against coronary heart disease. *American Journal of Epidemiology,* 123, 623–640.

Helson, R. & Picano, J. (1990). Is the traditional role bad for women? *Journal of Personality and Social Psychology,* 59, 311–320.

Hemmelgarn, B. & Laing, G. (1991). The relationship between situational factors and perceived role strain in employed mothers. *Family and Community Health,* 14(1), 8–15.

Hendrix, W. H., Spencer, B. A. & Gibson, G. S. (1994). Organizational and extra-organizational factors affecting stress, employee well-being, and absenteeism for males and females. *Journal of Business and Psychology,* 9(2), 103–128.

Hennig, M. & Jardim, A. (1977). *The Managerial Woman.* New York: Pocket Books.

Herr, E. L. & Cramer, S. H. (1988). *Career Guidance and Counselling Through the Life Span.* Glenview, IL: Scott, Foresman.

Hibbard, J. H. & Pope, C. R. (1993). The quality of social roles as predictors of morbidity and mortality. *Social Science and Medicine,* 36(3), 217–225.

Higgins, C. A. & Duxbury, L. E. (1992). Work–family conflict: A comparison of dual career and traditional career men. *Journal of Organizational Behavior,* 13(4), 389–411.

Hiller, D. V. & Philliber, W. W. (1986). The division of labor in contemporary marriage: Expectations, perceptions and performance. *Social Problems,* 33, 191–201.

Hirschfeld, M. M. (1982). *The Imposter Phenomenon in Successful Career Women.* New York: Fordham University.

Hochwarter, W. A., Perrewe, P. L. & Dawkins, M. C. (1995). Gender differences in perceptions of stress related variables: Do the people make the place or does the place make the people? *Journal of Managerial Issues,* 7(1), 62–74.

Horgan, D. D. & Simeon, R. J. (1990). Gender, mentoring, and tacit knowledge. *Journal of Social behaviour and Personality,* 5, 453–471.

Houtman, I. L. (1990). Personal coping resources and sex differences. *Personality and Individual Differences,* **11**(1), 53–63.

Izraeli, D. N. (1994). Money matters: Spousal incomes and family/work relations among physician couples in Israel. *Sociological Quarterly,* **35**(1), 69–84.

Jamal, M. (1990). Relationship of job stress and Type-A behaviour to employees' job satisfaction, organizational commitment, psychosomatic health problems, and turn-over motivation, *Human Relations,* **43**, 727–738.

Jex, S. M., Baldwin Jr, D. C., Hughes, P., Storr, C. & Sheehan, D. V. (1991). Behavioural consequences of job-related stress among residents physicians: The mediating role of psychological strain. *Psychological Reports,* **69**, 339–349.

Johansson, G. G., Laakso, M., Peder, M. & Karonen, S. L. (1989). Endocrine patterns before and after examination stress in males and females. *Activities-Nervosa- Superior,* **31**(2), 81–88.

Jones, F. & Fletcher, B. C. (1993). An empirical study of occupational stress transmission in working couples. *Human Relations,* **46**(7), 881–903.

Kahn, H. & Cooper, C. L. (1992). Anxiety associated with money market dealers: Sex and cultural differences. Special Issue: Occupational stress, psychological burnout and anxiety. *Anxiety, Stress and Coping. An International Journal,* **5**(1), 21–40.

Kandolin, I. (1993). Burnout of female and male nurses in shiftwork. Special Issue: Night and shiftwork. *Ergonomics,* **36**(1–3), 141–147.

Kirchmeyer, C. (1993). Nonwork to work spillover: A more balanced view of the experiences and coping of professional women and men. *Sex Roles,* **28**(9–10), 531–552.

Kirkcaldy, B. D. & Siefen, G. (1991). Occupational stress among mental health professionals: The relationship between work and recreational pursuits. *Social Psychiatry and Psychiatric Epidemiology,* **26**(5), 238–244.

Koch, P. B., Boose, L. A., Cohen, M. D., Mansfield, P. K. et al. (1991). Coping strategies of traditionally and nontraditionally employed women at home and at work. *Health Values. Health Behaviour, Education and Promotion,* **15**(1), 19–31.

Kuhlmann, T. M. (1990). Coping with occupational stress among urban bus and tram drivers. *Journal of Occupational Psychology,* **63**, 89–96.

LaCroix, A. Z. & Haynes, S. G. (1987). Gender differences in the health effects of workplace roles. In R. C. Barnett, L. Biener & G. K. Baruch (Eds), *Gender and Stress.* New York: Free Press.

Langan-Fox, J. (1996). Validity and reliability of measures of occupational stress using samples of Australian managers and professionals. *Stress Medicine,* **12**, 211–225.

Langan-Fox, Deery, J. & Van Vliet (in press). Stress, illness, coping strategies and need for power in police trainees. *Work and Stress.*

Langan-Fox, J. & Poole, M. E. (1995). Occupational stress in Australian business and professional women. *Stress Medicine,* **11**, 113–122.

Lazarus, R. S. (1966). *Psychological Stress and the Coping Procedure.* New York: McGraw-Hill.

Lee, C., Ashford, S. J. & Jamieson, L. F. (1993). The effects of Type A behaviour dimensions and optimism on coping strategy, health and performance. *Journal of Organizational Behavior,* **14**, 143–157.

Leiter, M. P., Clark, D. & Durup, J. (1994). Distinct models of burnout and commitment among men and women in the military. *Journal of Applied Behavioral Science,* **30**(1), 63–82.

Lennon, M. C. & Rosenfield, S. (1992). Women and mental health: The interaction of job and family conditions. *Journal of Health and Social Behaviour,* **33**, 316–327.

Levinson, D. J. (1986). A conception of adult development. *American Psychologist,* January, 3–13.

Liff, S. (1990). Clerical workers and information technology; Gender relations and occupational change. *New Technology, Work and Employment,* **5**, 44–55.

Long, B. & Gessaroli, M. E. (1989). The relationship between teacher stress and perceived coping effectiveness: Gender and marital differences. *Alberta Journal of Educational Research*, **35**(4), 308–324.

Long, B. C., Kahn, S. E. & Schutz, R. W. (1992). Causal model of stress and coping: Women in management. *Journal of Counselling Psychology*, **39**(2), 227–239.

Lorber, J. & Ecker, M. (1983). Career development of female and male physicians. *Journal of Medical Education*, **58**, 447–456.

Lundberg, U. (1996). Influence of paid and unpaid work on psychophysiological stress: Responses of men and women. *Journal of Occupational Health Psychology*, **1**(2), 117–130.

Mansfield, P. K., Koch, P. B., Henderson, J. & Vicary, J. R. (1991). The job climate for women in traditionally male blue-collar occupations. *Sex Roles*, **25**(1–2), 63–79.

Marshall, N. L. & Barnett, R. C. (1993a). Variations in job strain across nursing and social work specialities. Special Issue: Work stressors in health care and social service settings. *Journal of Community and Applied Social Psychology*, **3**(4), 261–271.

Marshall, N. L. & Barnett, R. C. (1993b). Work–family strains and gains among two earner couples. *Journal of Community Psychology*, **21**(1), 64–78.

Matthews, K. A. & Rodin, J. (1989). Women's changing work roles: Impact on health, family, and public policy. *American Psychologist*, **44**(11), 1289–1393.

McBride, A. B. (1990). Mental health effects of women's multiple roles. *American Psychologist*, March, 381–384.

McDaniel, S. A. (1993). Challenges to mental health promotion among working women in Canada. *Canadian Journal of Community Mental Health*, **12**(1), 201–210.

McKeen, C. A. & Burke, R. J. (1989). Mentor relationships in organisations: Issues, strategies and prospects for women. *Journal of Management Development*, **8**, 33–41.

Murphy, S. A., Beaten, R. D., Cain, K. & Pike, K. (!994). Gender differences in fire fighter job stressors and symptoms of stress. *Women and Health*, **22**(2), 55–69.

Nathawat, S. S. & Mathur, A. (1993). Marital adjustment and subjective well-being in Indian educated housewives and working women. *Journal of Psychology*, **127**(3), 353–358.

Nelson, D. L., Quick, J. C., Hitt, M. A. & Moesel, D. (1990). Politics, lack of career progress and work/home conflict: Stress and strain for working women. *Sex Roles*, **23**(3–4), 169–185.

Nice, S. D. & Hilton, S. (1994). Sex differences and occupational influences on health care utilization aboard US Navy ships. Special Issue: Women in the Navy. *Military Psychology*, **6**(2), 109–123.

Niles, S. G. & Anderson, W. P. (1993). Career development and adjustment: The relation between concerns and stress. *Journal of Employment Counselling*, **30**(2), 79–87.

Norvell, N. K., Hills, H. A. & Murrin, M. R. (1993). Understanding stress in female and male law enforcement officers. *Psychology of Women Quarterly*, **17**(3), 289–301.

Nowack, K. M. (1989). Coping style, cognitive hardiness, and health status. *Journal of Behavioural Medicine*, **12**, 145–158.

Nowack, K. M. & Pentkowski, A. M. (1994). Lifestyle habits, substance use and predictors of job burnout in professional working women. *Work and Stress*, **8**(1), 19–35.

Nykodym, N. & George, K. (1989). Stress busting on the job. *Personnel*, July, 56–59.

O'Brien, G. E. & Feather, N. T. (1990). The relative effects of unemployment and quality of employment on the affect, work values and personal control of adolescents. *Journal of Occupational Psychology*, **63**, 151–165.

O'Neil, J. M. & Carroll, M. R. (1983). A gender role workshop focused on sexism, gender role conflict, and the gender role journey. *Journal of Counselling and Development*, **67**, 193–197.

Ogus, E. D., Greenglass, E. R. & Burke, R. J. (1990). Gender role differences, work stress and depersonalisation. *Journal of Social Behaviour and Personality,* **5**(5), 387–398.

Olkinuora, M., Asp, S., Juntunen, J., Kauttu, K. et al. (1992). Stress symptoms, burnout and suicidal thoughts in Finnish physicians. Fifth US Finnish Joint Symposium on Occuptaional Safety and Health: Occupational epidemics on the 1990s, Cincinnati, Ohio. *Scandinavian Journal of Work, Environment and Health,* **18**(2), 110–112.

Perry, J. M., Seery, B. & Crouter, A. C. (1992). Linkages between women's provider role attitudes, psychological well-being, and family relationships. *Psychology of Women Quarterly,* **16**(3), 311–329.

Pietromonaco, Manis & Frohardt-Lane, P. R. (1986). Psychological consequences of multiple social roles. *Psychology of Women Quarterly,* **10**, 373–382.

Pines, A. & Guendelman, S. (1995). Exploring the relevance of burnout to Mexican blue-collar women. *Journal of Vocational Behavior,* **47**(1), 1–20.

Poole, M. E. & Langan-Fox, J. (1997). *Australian Women's Careers: Psychological and Contextual Influences over the Life Course.* Cambridge: Cambridge University Press.

Pretty, G. M., McCarthy, M. E. & Catano, V. M. (1992). Psychological environments and burnout: Gender considerations within the corporation. *Journal of Organizational Behaviour,* **13**(7), 701–711.

Price, L. & Spencer, S. H. (1994). Burnout symptoms amongst drug and alcohol service employees: Gender differences in the interaction between work and home stressors. *Anxiety, Stress and Coping. An International Journal,* **7**(1), 67–84.

Rankin, E. D. (1993). Stresses and rewards experienced by employed mothers. *Health Care for Women International,* **14**(6), 527–537.

Raphael, B. (1992). Pressures on women at work. *Mental Health in Australia,* **4**(1), 20–27.

Reich, M. H. (1986). The mentor connection. *Personnel,* **63**, 50–56.

Reifman, A., Biernat, M. & Lang, E. L. (1991). Stress, social support, and health in married professional women with small children. *Psychology of Women Quarterly,* **15**(3), 431–445.

Renault de Moraes, L. F., Swan, J. A. & Cooper, C. L. (1993). A study of occupational stress among government white-collar workers in Brazil using the Occupational Stress Indicator. *Stress Medicine,* **9**, 91–104.

Repetti, R. L. (1994). Short term and long term processes linking job stressors to father–child interaction. *Social Development,* **3**(1), 1–15.

Richardson, M. S. & Johnson, M (!984). Counselling women. In S. D. Brown & R. W. Lent (Eds), *Handbook of Counselling Psychology.* New York: Wiley.

Rodin, J. & Ickovics, J. R. (1990). Women's health. Review and research agenda as we approach the 21st century. *American Psychologist,* **45**(9), 1018–1034.

Rogers, A. L. (1991). Stress in married clergy. *Psychotherapy in Private Practice,* **8**(4), 107–115.

Rosenfield, S. (1992). The costs of sharing: Wives' employment and husbands' mental health. *Journal of Health and Social Behaviour,* **33**(3), 213–225.

Schalk, M. J. D. & van den Berg, P. T. (1993). Mental health in information work. *European Work and Organizational Psychologist,* **3**, 181–190.

Scheier, M. F. & Carver, C. S. (1992). Effects of optimism on psychological and physical well-being: Theoretical overview and empirical update. *Cognitive Therapy and Research,* **16**, 201–228.

Sekaran (1986). Significant differences in quality-of-life factors and their correlates: A function of differences in career orientations or gender? *Sex Roles,* **14**, 261–279.

Silver, H. (1993). Homework and domestic work. *Sociological Forum,* **8**(2), 181–204.

Simpson, L. A. & Grant, L. (1991). Sources and magnitude of job stress among physicians. *Journal of Behavioral Medicine,* **14**(1), 27–42.

Sorensen, G. & Mortimer, J. T. (1988). Implications of the dual roles of adult women for their health. In J. T. Mortimer & K. M. Borman (Eds), *Work Experience and Psychological Development Through The Life Span* (pp. 157–197). American Association for the Advancement of Science.

Sorensen, G. & Vebrugge, L. M. (1987). Women, work and health. *American Review of Public Health*, **8**, 235–251.

Soyibo, K. (1994). Occupational stress factors and coping strategies among Jamaican high school science teachers. *Research in Science and Technological Education*, **12**(2), 187–192.

Spielberger, C. D. & Reheiser, E. C. (1994). The Job Stress Survey: Measuring gender differences in occupation stress. *Journal of Social Behaviour and Personality*, **9**(2), 199–218.

Starkey, J. L. (1991). The effects of a wife's earnings on marital dissolution: The role of a husband's interpersonal competence. *Journal of Socio-Economics*, **20**(2), 125–154.

Stickel, S. A. & Bonett, R. M. (1989). *Sex differences in career self-efficacy.* Paper presented at the Annual Meeting of the American Educational Research Association, San Francisco, California, 30 March.

Sutherland, V. J. & Cooper, C. L. (1990). *Understanding Stress. A Psychological Perspective for Health Professionals.* London: Chapman & Hall.

Terzella, M. E. (1968). How you see success . . . *The Executive Female*, March/April, 25–29.

Thomas, S. & Sudhakar, V. U. (1994). Gender role orientation and coping repertoire of women in the management of military induced stress. *Journal of Indian Psychology*, **12**(1–2), 49–61.

Turner, J., Tippett, V. & Raphael, B. (1994). Women in medicine: Socialization, stereotypes and self perceptions. *Australian and New Zealand Journal of Psychiatry*, **28**(1), 129–135.

UNDP (1995). *Human Development Report, 1995.* United Nations Development Program. Oxford University Press.

Van Yperen, N. W., Buunk, B. P. & Schaufeli, W. B. (1992). Communal orientation and the burnout syndrome among nurses. *Journal of Applied Social Psychology*, **22**(3), 173–189.

Vebrugge, C. (March, 1986). *Sex differences in physical health: Making good sense of empirical results.* Paper presented at the meetings of the Society of Behavioural Medicine, San Francisco, CA.

Wainrib, B. R. (1992). Successful women and househusbands: The old messages die hard. 99th Annual Meeting of the American Psychological Association (1991), San Francisco, California. *Psychotherapy in Private Practice*, **11**(4), 11–19.

Watson, E. D. & Hodgson, R. C. (1984). Women in management: Reducing the price of success. *Business Quarterly*, **34**, 137–143.

Westman, M. & Etzion, D. (1990). The career success/personal failure phenomenon as perceived in others: Comparing vignettes of male and female managers. *Journal of Vocational Behavior*, **37**, 209–224.

Westman, M. & Etzion, D. (1995). Crossover of stress, strain and resources from one spouse to another. *Journal of Organizational Behavior*, **16**(2), 169–181.

Westman, M. & Gafni, A. (1987). Hypertension labelling as a stressful event leading to an increase in absenteeism: A possible explanation for an empirically measured phenomenon. In S. Meital (Ed.), *Applied Behavioural Economics*, (Vol. 2), New York: New York Unviersity Press.

Wiebe, D. J. (1991). Hardiness and stress moderation: A test of proposed mechanisms. *Journal of Personality and Social Psychology*, **60**, 89–99.

Wiersma, U. J. & Van den Berg, P. (1991). Work–home role conflict, family climate, and domestic responsibilities among men and women in dual earner families. *Journal of Applied Social Psychology*, **21**(15), 1207–1217.

Williams, K. J. & Alliger, G. M. (1994). Role stressors, mood spillover, and perceptions of work–family conflict in employed parents. *Academy of Management Journal,* **37**(4), 837–868.

Zuckerman, D. M. (1989). Stress, self-esteem, and mental health: How does gender make a difference? *Sex Roles,* **20**, 429–443.

Chapter 7

ORGANIZATIONAL MEN: MASCULINITY AND ITS DISCONTENTS

Ronald J. Burke
York University, Canada

and

Debra L. Nelson
Oklahoma State University, USA

Guys are in trouble these days. Years ago, manhood was an opportunity for achievement, and now it is a problem to be overcome. Plato, St Francis, Michelangelo, Mozart, Leonardo da Vinci, Vince Lombardi, VanGogh—you don't find guys of that calibre today, and if there are any, they are not painting the ceiling of the Sistine Chapel. They are training to be Mr OK, All-Rite, the man who can bake a cherry pie, go play basketball, come home, make melon balls and whip up a great souffle, converse easily about intimate matters, participate in recreational weeping, laugh, hug, be vulnerable, be passionate in a skilful way . . . A guy who women consider acceptable (Kiellor, 1993, p. 11).

INTRODUCTION

Why do we need a chapter on men in organizations? Don't we know enough about them, since the practice of management was once largely a male endeavour? It is true that although management has historically been a male endeavour, the experiences of men as men have been virtually ignored (Cheng, 1996). In the 1970s and 1980s, attention was focused on women, spearheaded by scholars who called attention to the fact that increasing numbers of women were entering the workforce and women's roles were changing. In the mid-1990s the focus has shifted to men and men's roles, which are undergoing sweeping changes (Levant, 1996).

The popular press has suggested that there is considerable confusion currently about men's roles (Kimmel & Messner, 1989). Such questions as 'What

Organizational Men: Masculinity and Its Discontents by Ronald J. Burke and Debra L. Nelson taken from IRIOP 1998 v12, Edited by Cary L. Cooper and Ivan T. Robertson: © 1998 John Wiley & Sons, Ltd

are men supposed to do?' and 'What do women want from men?' convey the general tenor of this uncertainty (Kimmel, 1993). It is not clear though how widespread or deep this confusion may really be. Part of the confusion may be the result of pressures on men to exhibit behavior that conflicts with traditional notions of masculinity. Such pressures include those to commit to relationships, communicate one's deepest feelings, share in household responsibilities, nurture children, and to limit aggression and violence (Levant, 1996).

In addition, many men find it increasingly difficult to fulfil the expectations of the provider role. Historically, men have defined themselves by their work, a profession, and a paycheck (Kimmel, 1993, 1996). Men are having to redefine themselves in the 1990s as a result of women's influx into the workplace and the greater difficulties men face in working (providing) as a result of corporate downsizing and restructuring. These forces are requiring men to re-evaluate what it means to be a success at work and in the home, because the worker/provider role isn't what it use to be (Cohen, 1993). Most men today still consider their work/career to be important and they do not want to ignore their families (Daly, 1993). Some of these men hold very demanding jobs. In the same way as some women, many men want it all. Men aspire to be fully involved with their families with no loss of income, prestige and organizational support and no loss of a sense of manhood (Gerson, 1993).

There have been recent efforts to bring the issue of men and masculinity to the forefront; the objects for theory, research and critique. Recent feminist writings have revealed the existence of masculine values in the structure, culture and practices of organizations (Acker, 1990). This work has identified the gendered nature of power relations, the importance of paid work as an important source of masculine identity, status and power (personal success in the workplace) and the importance of the breadwinner/provider role for men. This work also provides considerable evidence of the ways power and status are denied to women.

There is an increasing hunger in North American society for a greater understanding of men's development. This is witnessed by the commercial success of recent literary contributions (Bly, 1990; Keen, 1991) and interest in the popular press (e.g. *Newsweek*, 1991). Researchers, with only a few notable exceptions (Valliant, 1977; Levinson, Darrow, Klein, Levinson & McKee, 1978; Maccoby, 1976) have devoted little attention to the development and total life experience of adult men.

Hearn (1994) proposes that it is necessary to begin to devote research attention to men and management because the practice of management is too often oppressive to both men and women. A focus on men and management may foster changes in management as currently practiced towards a more empowering experience. Men's roles in organizations are changing from the experience of being the majority to, in some cases, being the minority—and some would argue, a disenfranchised minority.

Our intent in this chapter is to explore the topic of men and masculinity in organizations by focusing both on scholarship and on activism. Research provides a basis for activism, which is critical given the importance of the subject matter for men, women, families, organizations and society. The subject cuts across many areas of industrial/organizational psychology: careers, adult development, work and family, organizational change and human resource management, among others. We are concerned that the chapter should not come across as 'male bashing', because that is not our intent. Instead, we advocate a careful examination of the research evidence to help men and women wipe away denial and consider the issue part of men's life planning in the broadest sense. Our objectives are several: to review and integrate an incredibly diverse body of research and writing; to identify what we know and don't know about men and masculinity in organizations; and to suggest a research agenda for this underresearched area.

The chapter will address the following content: What is masculinity? looking at the social construction of gender and the multiple forms of masculinity; going on to discuss the gendered nature of organizations, covering dimensions of corporate masculinity, masculinity and management, femininity and androgyny.

It next deals with the implications for men, women and children: including gender role strain; male privilege; the costs of corporate masculinity; the Type A experience; the problems of workaholics/corporate bigamists; work and the experience of children; and the power-motivated man and his relationships with women.

It goes on to consider men and stress, discusses career success and personal failure, and the antecedents of such situations and both individual and organizational solutions. Finally, the chapter sums up the progress made by organizational men, looks at what needs to be done in the future, and discusses future lines of research.

WHAT IS MASCULINITY?

The central construct in research that examines men and men's roles is masculinity ideology, which views masculinity as a socially constructed gender ideal for men (Thompson & Pleck, 1995). The roots of the masculine gender ideal are instilled through the socialization process.

The Social Construction of Gender

West and Zimmerman (1991) describe gender as an achieved status, or an accomplishment constructed through psychological, cultural and social means. While the terms 'male' and 'masculine' are used interchangeably, there is a critical distinction between maleness, as a biologically determined state, and masculinity, a socially constructed state. In Western societies, the shared cultural perspective of gender views women and men as naturally and clearly defined categories having distinctive psychological and behavioral characteristics based on their sex. Differences between women and men are seen as fundamental and enduring, supported by sexual division of labor, and clear definitions of women's work and men's work. This division follows as a natural consequence of biological differences which form the basis for the observed differences in psychological, behavioral and social outcomes.

West and Zimmerman (1991) suggest that gender is the product of 'social doings'; it is actually created through interaction. Gender is observed in interaction but is actually being produced in the larger context of a social system (society). The process by which gender roles are acquired is typically invisible, resulting in a 'normal' pattern of behaviors that others perceive as normative gender behavior. The social influences and interactions are so subtle, yet pervasive, we take the results as natural and are oblivious to the underlying process. Gender work refers to the processes by which gender is individually acquired; the development of what might be termed 'normal' manhood is a social process existing within a patriarchal family structure.

These processes place unique pressures and expectations on men (and on women) that influence men's work and private lives. For example, men have been viewed historically on their ability to fill the breadwinner role, as a money-making machine (Ehrenreich, 1983, 1989), and by the size of their paychecks (Gould, 1974). With the movement of women into the paid work-force, women have become less economically dependent on their husbands; the breadwinner/provider role has become less central to man's identity. Men will be less likely to be evaluated by their ability to earn income and support a family.

Men and women acquire appropriate sex roles through socialization. These sex roles encompass the attitudes, behaviors and attributes that are seen as appropriate for males, and appropriate for females. Masculinity emphasizes technical mastery, competitiveness, aggression, logic and rationality; femininity encompasses emotionality, nurturance, connectedness and passivity. Masculinity serves as the standard against which both men and women are compared.

Tannen (1990) identifies differences in women and men's conversational styles resulting from their distinctive sex role socialization. For men, communications are negotiations to achieve or maintain the upper-hand in a hierarchical social order. Life is a constant struggle to preserve independence and avoid failure. For women, communications are negotiations for closeness seeking and giving confirmation and support in efforts to reach consensus. Life is a struggle to preserve intimacy and avoid isolation. Men lecture; women listen. Men want respect; women want to be liked.

Boys play in large groups, hierarchically structured. There is a leader telling boys what to do. There are winners and losers, and rules for their contests. Boys jockey for status, boast and compete with one another. Girls play in small groups, often in pairs with a best friend. They take turns; intimacy is observed. There are no winners or losers, order giving, or boasting or jockeying for position. Girls cooperate with each other, and are concerned with being liked.

Contemporary adult men, as boys, were socialized to learn risk-taking, teamwork, assertiveness, and calmness in the face of danger, which are action skills. In contrast, contemporary adult women were socialized to learn emotional skills such as empathy, the ability to access and feel intense emotions, and the ability to express those emotions through both verbal and nonverbal means (Levant, 1995). Thus, traditional masculine and feminine ideology prevailed in the socialization process, and became reflected in adult behavior.

Spence and Helmreich (1978), in their measure of masculinity, consider such characteristics as: independent, active, competitive, persistent, self-confident and feels superior. Rosencrantz, Vogel, Bee, Broverman and Broverman (1968) include aggressive, independent, dominant, self-confident and unemotional. Women on the other hand, value love, communication and relationships. They spend time supporting, helping and nurturing one another. Women's self-concept is defined through emotions and the quality of their relationships. Women are relationship oriented.

Gender is thus a socially constructed phenomenon. Male gender role socialization is the primary influence on men's views of masculinity.

Masculinity in Multiple Forms

Because masculinity is a social construction, men's views of what constitutes masculinity vary widely. Some writers acknowledge the variety in men's experiences, attitudes, values, behaviors and situations as a function of social class, race, sexual preferences, age, ethnicity, intelligence and many other categories used to describe individuals and their experiences (Cheng, 1996). All of these factors influence men's conceptions of masculinity. Despite this range of views, it is possible to identify what some refer to as traditional masculine ideology (Pleck, 1995).

Brannon (1976) identified four themes in traditional masculine ideology.

1. *No sissy stuff*—avoid anything feminine.
2. *Be a big wheel*—be powerful, strong and competitive since men must be admired to be real.
3. *Be a sturdy oak*—show no emotion.
4. *Give 'em hell*—take risks, go for it, face danger and demonstrate bravado.

Thompson and Pleck (1987), building on Brannon's four themes of the male role, developed and validated a 57-item self-report questionnaire of the male sex role. Data were obtained from male college students. Factor analysis of their data yielded three factors: *status*—achieve status and others' respect; *toughness*—mentally, physically and emotionally tough and self-reliant; and *anti-femininity*—avoid stereotypically feminine attitudes and occupations. They concluded that men in their sample did not fully endorse traditional male norms.

More recently, Levant, Hirsch, Celantano et al. (1992) described traditional male ideology as having seven dimensions: avoid anything feminine; restrict one's emotional life; display toughness and aggression; be self-reliant; work to achieve status above all else; adopt non-relational, objectifying attitudes toward sexuality; and fear and hate homosexuals.

David and Brannon (1976) define role as 'any pattern of behaviors which a given individual in a specified set of situations is both expected and so encouraged and/or trained to perform' (p. 5). Roles are therefore related to stereotypes, stereotypes being cultural expectations for individuals in certain categories and situations. Roles tend to offer *general guidelines* on how individuals should conduct themselves instead of *specific behaviors*.

Pleck (1995) provided an update on research relating to his 'gender role strain' model for masculinity (Pleck, 1981). The gender role strain model involved ten different propositions:

1. Gender roles are operationally defined by gender role stereotypes and norms.
2. Gender role norms are contradictory and inconsistent.
3. The proportion of individuals who violate gender role norms is high.
4. Violating gender role norms leads to social condemnation.
5. Violating gender role norms leads to negative psychological consequences.
6. Actual or imagined violation of gender role norms leads individuals to overconform to them.
7. Violating gender role norms has more severe consequences for males than females.
8. Certain characteristics prescribed by gender role norms are psychologically disfunctional.
9. Each gender experiences gender role strain in its paid work and family role.
10. Historical change causes gender role strain. (Pleck, 1995, p. 12)

Three broad ideas underlie these propositions. First, a considerable number of males experience long-term failure to fulfil male role expectations, which is termed gender role discrepancy or incongruity. Second, even if male role expectations are fulfilled, the process and/or the fulfilment itself is traumatic. Third, the successful fulfilment of work role expectations leads to undesirable side-effects for men or for others (e.g. low family involvement). Three types of strain result: discrepancy, trauma and dysfunction strain. We will elaborate on gender role strain as a cost of masculinity when we consider implications later in the chapter.

Kimmel (1996) believes that manhood is less about dominating others than it is about the fear men have about being dominated by other men. Men defend their masculinity in relation to other men. At the beginning of the seventeenth century, American manhood was defined by land ownership or self-sufficient occupations such as being artisans, farmers or shopkeepers. Then towards the middle of the nineteenth century, with the appearance of the industrial revolution, manhood was linked to financial success achieved through position in a turbulent marketplace.

Hegemonic masculinity is the definition of masculinity that serves as the standard for all men against which they are measured and often found wanting. It defines white, middle-class, early middle-aged, heterosexual men. Hegemonic masculinity is the maintenance of practices that institutionalize men's dominance over women. It is comprised of three shared meanings: emotional detachment, competitiveness, and the sexual objectification of women (Bird, 1996). It is important to recognize that hegemonic masculinity may either be internalized (central to one's core self) or interiorized (simply acknowledged by the self). Thus men may hold socially shared meanings of masculinity and their own individual views as well. Male homosocial heterosexual interactions work to maintain hegemonic masculinity, despite individuals' views that may not agree. Those who do not agree suppress their views, or suffer penalties if they violate hegemonic norms.

Kimmel (1996, p. 120) defines masculinity 'as a constantly changing collection of meanings that we construct through relationships with ourselves, with each other and with our world.' Masculinity is neither static nor timeless; it is historical, socially constructed and created in the culture in which a man lives. Collinson and Hearn (1994) propose that one can consider different types of masculinity without minimizing the importance of the power of hegemonic masculinity.

Although appreciative of the fact that there are many and varied masculinities, this chapter will focus on hegemonic masculinity because of its dominance in men's lives. This masculinity is typified by white, heterosexual, dominant and powerful middle-class men (Bird, 1996).

THE GENDERED NATURE OF ORGANIZATIONS

There is a gendered substructure that characterizes organizational life (Collinson & Hearn, 1995, 1996; Maier, 1996, 1997; Mills & Tancred, 1992). Traditional organizational views assumed that workers were male. Women's positions and roles in organizations, which were support roles with lower salaries, mirrored the positions and roles women held in society at large. As Kanter (1977) observed, the numbers, power and opportunity structures of organizations, which favored men, conveyed a negative picture of the worth and contributions of women. Women performed what Kanter called 'office housework'. Kanter showed the sex segregation and sex polarization of occupations and presented an historical overview of how modern management theory took on a masculine/paternalistic bias. The masculine bias in organizations limits women's progress through making developmental opportunities harder to obtain (Burton, 1992; Maier, 1992).

Gender can be similarly used as a metaphor for characterizing organizations (Alvesson & Billing, 1992). Such an approach does not treat masculinity (or femininity) as homogeneous; instead, various forms of organizational masculinity are distinguished. Patriarchy and technocracy, for example, are two different forms of masculinity. By considering 'genderness' of organizations, it becomes possible to recognize a continuum of masculine organizations from those that are feminine-friendly, to gender neutral, to less well-intentioned.

Dimensions of Corporate Masculinity

Organizations are made up of cultures, social relationships, and practices that are dominated by male perspectives. As a result, they are characterized by rationality, instrumentality, analysis, emotional restraint, competitiveness, and self-sufficiency (Burrell, 1984). The work culture is rooted in these masculine norms. Since managers have traditionally been men, the qualities and traits associated with management fit society's definition of the masculine role. These norms highlight objectivity, competition and a task orientation. Men must put work first. They must act as though they have no competing loyalties. Work and family roles are assumed to be structurally compatible for men.

Maier (1991) used the term 'corporate masculinity' to describe men's behavior in organizations (objectivity, competitive, adversarial, logic, task-oriented). Men believe that this masculine model of management, rewarded in most organizational cultures, is the best and right way to manage. As a result, women's approaches to management are devalued. Corporate masculinity requires men to consider all other life roles as less important than the work role and to act as though 'they had no other competing demands' (Kanter, 1977).

Collinson and Hearn (1994) identified five practices of masculinity that are widespread and dominant in organizations. These were: authoritarianism, paternalism, entrepreneurialism, informalism and careerism.

- *Authoritarianism*—characterized by an intolerance of dissent, a rejection of dialogue, use of coercive power based on dictatorial control and unquestioned obedience (an aggressive masculinity).
- *Paternalism*—exercising power based on the protective nature of authority, an authoritative, benevolent and wise father.
- *Entrepreneurialism*—competitive, hardworking, under tight deadlines, and totally dedicated to their work.
- *Informalism*—the old boy network, socializing.

- *Careerism*—preoccupation with upward mobility, a successful career, division between work and home/family life.

Maier (1991) sees corporate masculinity as having several kinds of dysfunctions. First, the masculine corporate culture limits men's effectiveness and potential as managers. There is increasing evidence that while the typical manager is seen to possess masculine characteristics, the best manager is described as having both masculine *and* feminine characteristics. Effective managers support and develop staff; they make staff powerful. They do more than simply get the job done. Second, men get most of their satisfaction and psychological rewards from work. Managers must exhibit complete dedication, resembling workaholics in many cases, to be and feel successful. Working long hours, and putting the organization first, are measures of this commitment. Since men are socialized into breadwinner and protector roles, such commitments come easy.

Our society has a narrow definition of success, typically viewed in career advancement and occupational achievement. This is a male model of work which favors men and overvalues traditional masculine characteristics. Men need to be liberated from sex roles and the masculine values which exist in our culture. As Maier notes (1991) men are seen, and see themselves as 'success objects' whose masculinity is measured by the size of their paychecks. Male socialization leads to an excessive attachment to achievement. Managerial and professional men are rewarded by their employing organizations for enhancing addictive work systems.

Masculinity and Management

Surprisingly—or perhaps not so surprisingly—the predominance and dominance of management by men has been relatively ignored. Instead, early management writings implicitly assume men/masculinity in prevailing models, styles, theories, language (e.g. military, sports) and culture (Collinson & Hearn, 1995). Management is, by default, a description of men and the behavior and values of men. Management is, by extension, a reflection of the larger male-dominated social structure. Managers are assumed to be men; management and leadership approaches are assumed to be masculine. As a consequence, women in management are disadvantaged from the outset.

Maier (1992) outlines the role of gender in management theories from 1900 to the present. Organizations are constructed in ways that exemplify male behaviors, validating masculine approaches in the process while excluding feminine approaches. Initially organizations/business were seen as the purview of men. With the entrance (and increasing numbers) of women, women were expected to compete with men on 'men's terms' by adopting/exhibiting the traditional management style (masculine).

Requiring women to imitate male behavior to be effective managers is problematic for both women and men (Collinson & Hearn, 1995). Women are criticized for behaving like men; they are damned if they do, damned if they don't, and thus encounter a double bind. Masculine management styles also limit men. Masculine management tends to be associated with qualities of average/typical managers, whereas androgynous management—a combination of both masculine and feminine behaviors—is often associated with qualities of effective managers.

The major challenge to men—and men in management—has come from feminism (Ferguson, 1984). Feminism has concerned itself with the oppression of women, and power and authority relations in the paternalistic society at large. The feminist critique has cast men in management/masculine management as problematic. The presence of men in management, and masculine management, is less likely now to be accepted as 'natural' as in the past. Men in management have responded to the feminist critique with a wide range of responses. These include hostility, coupled with backlash (Burke & Black, 1997), indifference and, in some quarters, an openness to the possibilities for change or even a motivation to change. Part of the impetus for this change has come from a growing literature that examines gender-related leadership styles.

Masculinity, Femininity and Androgyny

Bem (1974) developed a theory of sex role orientation in which masculinity and femininity are seen as two uncorrelated bi-polar dimensions. Masculinity is associated with task orientation, agency and instrumentality; femininity is associated with emotions and interpersonal relationships. Traditional sex-typed persons have more of one dimension than the other (masculine males have more masculine and fewer feminine characteristics; feminine females have more feminine than masculine characteristics). A balance of both masculine and feminine characteristics, termed androgyny, is potentially advantageous since it allows individuals the freedom and flexibility to exhibit male- or female-typed attributes in response to a given situation.

Starting with the early work of Bem (1974), the extensive writing on androgyny takes the position that both extreme masculine and feminine sex roles are harmful and have limited effectiveness. This writing proposed that an androgynous combination is the most effective and is associated with psychological health. Recent critiques of this body of work have concluded that androgyny itself involves valuing stereotypically masculine characteristics in the very nature of the term itself, and that the operationalization of the concept treats stereotypes of what masculinity and femininity mean as real, thereby reinforcing these stereotypes rather than destroying them.

More recently, Spence and Helmreich (1978) proposed that androgyny involved high levels of both masculine (instrumental/assertive) and feminine (expressive/empathetic) behaviors. They used the terms 'instrumental' and 'expressive' (instead of masculine and feminine) to reduce the perpetuation of stereotypes and false dichotomies that overemphasize gender differences.

Lagace and Twible (1990), in a sample of 177 retail and industrial sales-people, found that these salespeople were androgynous, with saleswomen being more androgynous than salesmen. Motowidlo (1982) found highly an-drogynous individuals were active listeners, and Gayton, Havo, Baird and Ozman (1983) reported that androgynous individuals were assertive.

Early research treated biological sex and sex role orientation as one and the same. They may overlap to some degree, but not all males are masculine and not all females are feminine. Consider, for example, research reported by Maupin and Lehman (1994). In a study of male and female auditors, they found that a high stereotypical masculine sex role orientation was significantly and positively related to higher organizational level, job satisfaction and lower turnover. The study involved 461 auditors followed over a 5-year period. Some changed jobs/firms during this time period, permitting an examination of turnover. Female auditors at higher organizational levels were more mas-culine and more androgynous. Similar findings were observed among male partners, as well as lower levels of masculinity at lower organizational levels. Turnover among male and female auditors was lowest among androgynous groups followed by masculine, undifferentiated and feminine groups (the highest turnover). Among men, both masculinity and femininity levels were significantly associated with job satisfaction; among women, only the mas-culinity score was related (positively) to job satisfaction. Maupin and Lech-man concluded that a high stereotypic masculine orientation is a critical ingredient to advancement, job satisfaction and long tenure in accounting organizations (a traditional male occupation).

Several studies have found a relation between gender role orientation and women's career pursuits (Betz & Fitzgerald, 1987). Thus instrumentality has been found to be related to a stronger career orientation (Marshall & Wijting, 1980), career achievement (Wong, Kettlewell & Sproule, 1985) and achieve-ment motivation (Orlofsky & Stake, 1981) among women. There is also re-search evidence that instrumentality and androgyny may be related to successful performance outcomes for women in male-dominated professions (Scandura & Ragins, 1993). Thus, Jagaciniski (1987) found that masculine and androgynous women engineers reported greater levels of performance, salary and satisfaction than feminine engineers. Maupin (1986) reported a significant relationship between organizational level and gender role orienta-tion among women accountants. Women accountants at higher organizational levels (partners) described themselves as androgynous or masculine whereas women at entry levels described themselves as feminine. Interestingly, Maupin (1986) observed gender differences in reports of job satisfaction; androgyny was significantly related to job satisfaction for men while mas-culinity was significantly related to job satisfaction for women. Fagenson (1989), in a study of outcomes of protégés and non-protégés, reported that mentored individuals were significantly more masculine and feminine than non-mentored individuals. Fagenson (1990) found that women and men at higher organizational levels were also significantly higher on measures of masculinity than were respondents at lower organizational levels, controlling for a number of important demographic variables.

Researchers have found that either masculine or androgynous managers have higher levels of supervisory responsibility, satisfaction and career success than feminine managers (Jagaciniski, 1987; Wong, Kettlewell & Sproule, 1985) and that respondents consistently rated 'good' managers as masculine (Powell & Butterfield, 1979, 1984, 1989). Since women are more often feminine and men are often masculine, women may receive lower pay as a result (Bem & Lenney, 1976). In addition, men may get more benefits from masculine characteristics than women do. Falbo, Hagen and Linimon (1982) found that respondents rated speakers who used a style consistent with their sex role as more competent and qualified than those who behaved inconsistently.

Johnson and Scandura (1994) examined the effect of mentorship and sex-role style, on male–female wages and wage differentials among certified public accountants (CPAs). Johnson and Scandura reported data obtained from 571 male and 293 female CPAs. Women reported significantly lower salaries than men, significantly less work experience, being at significantly lower organizational levels, being significantly more feminine, significantly less masculine and significantly more androgynous. The sex-role results varied by gender. For men, masculinity was significantly and positively correlated with earnings. For women, levels of femininity were significantly and negatively correlated with earnings. Masculine men received higher wages; masculine women did not. Feminine women had lower wages; feminine men did not.

Korabik (1990) reported that masculinity was correlated with use of an initiating structure leadership style, and femininity was correlated with use of consideration. Androgyny was found to be related to using both initiating structure and consideration. In addition, sex-role orientation was a better predictor of leadership style than biological sex was. In laboratory studies, Korabik found that masculine women and men preferred the task-oriented role while feminine women and men preferred the social-emotional role. Androgynous women and men fulfilled both.

Korabik and Ayman (1989) suggest that masculine qualities are impediments to effectiveness, sometimes leading to career derailment (e.g. insensitivity to others, arrogance, too ambitious, cold). Feminine characteristics (e.g. sensitivity to feelings, open communication, building support and trust) are associated with greater managerial effectiveness. Masculine competitiveness can be problematic when problem-solving and cooperation are called for.

In summary, the issue of gender in organizations is a complex one. Masculinity and masculine management styles, which were once dominant and assumed effective, are being subjected to scrutiny, and researchers are delineating the limitations of these styles. Recognizing that gender may exist in a continuum from feminism to masculine, androgyny has been proposed as including high levels of both.

IMPLICATIONS FOR MEN, WOMEN AND CHILDREN

Masculinity ideology affects not only men, but women and children as well. In this section, we review the consequences of masculinity ideology, both positive and negative. Kaufman (1993) observes that the ways in which societies have defined male power for thousands of years has brought potentially great power and privilege to men but also great pain and insecurity. This pain had remained hidden until the emergence of feminism. As women began to identify and challenge men's power and privilege, men have felt under attack, vulnerable, confused, empty, and introspective.

There are many virtues to be found in men's masculinity: physical and emotional strength, sexual desire, ability to operate under pressure, courage, creativity, intellect, self-sacrifice, and dedication to the task (Kaufman, 1993). Although these qualities exist in all humans, too many of them become distorted in men. Some men work too hard, drink too much, are isolated and alienated from other men, distant from their children, and present a façade that all is well. Men's power is a source of both privilege and pain, and of loneliness.

Kaufman further contends that society's definition of masculinity creates a shell which protects men from the fear of *not* being manly. Ironically, it is almost impossible to live up to our society's image of masculinity/manhood. It should come as no surprise that so many men have concerns about their ability to 'measure up' to this image. The development of a sense of what constitutes masculinity starts early in life in the family. It entails a learning to discipline one's body and unruly emotions. Men eventually come to accept relationships built on power and hierarchy (Butts & Whitty, 1993). Men learn to become leery of emotions, to deny feelings and needs that are not considered masculine. Men come to suppress a range of emotions, needs and possibilities such as nurturing, receptivity, empathy and compassion which are seen as inconsistent with power of manhood. These are suppressed because they are associated with femininity. The standards of masculinity are almost impossible to reach, so many men fail. This failure is driven by the fear of not measuring up. With the passing of time, men lose the ability to identify and express emotions. And sadly men are unaware of behaving in this way (Jourard, 1964).

Brod (1987) also weighs the costs to men and the benefits (economic, legal, social, political) obtained from patriarchy. The male role is associated with heart attacks, hypertension, ulcers, suicide, early death and greater dissatisfaction (Harrison, 1978). Brod, like Kaufman, sees the possession of power (and privilege) as double-edged. Yet there are vested interests of the powerful/privileged in keeping the roots of their power/privilege secretive, since this is one way to remain powerful/privileged. Leaving men's lives unexamined is one way to keep men's power/privilege unexamined.

Kaufman (1993) cautions that there is a danger in placing undue emphasis on the costs rather than the benefits of masculinity. These benefits include the freedom to fully commit to the workplace, the luxury of a back-up resource (in many cases), basking in the perception of a strong father figure, and achieving comfort and stability in their lives (Weiss, 1990), the exclusion of women; and the availability of privilege more broadly. Focusing on the downside of masculinity diverts attention away from the ways in which masculinity excludes and burdens women.

It is curious that men have all the power, yet many men feel powerless. There are two basic reasons for this apparent contradiction. On the one hand, only a small proportion of men meet the definition of masculinity. In addition, there is discrimination among men on the basis of race, age, ethnicity, class and sexual preference. Kaufman (1993) asserts that men's power comes with a high price in terms of pain, isolation and alienation from both women and men. Yet an appreciation of this pain is important in order to understand men and masculinity. In addition, it sheds light on ways men are socialized in society and on the process of gender acquisition.

The masculine role has been implicated in men's health. For example, the gap in life expectancy between males and females increased from 2 years in 1900 to 8 years in 1988. Men also suffer heart attacks and ulcers at a consistently higher rate than women. Harrison, Chin and Ficarrotto (1989) conclude that three-quarters of men's early deaths are related to the male sex role. Men rarely ask for help with physical or emotional problems. Men internalize stress; men cope with stress through use of alcohol, tobacco and drugs; men take more unnecessary risks, therefore having higher rates of accidental injury; and men are more successful at committing suicide (Jourard, 1964).

In many problem groups, males make up the majority. Such groups include perpetrators of violence, sex offenders, substance abusers, victims of homicide, suicide, and fatal auto accidents, parents estranged from their children, and victims of stress-related illnesses (Levant, 1996). These problems affect not only men, but society as a whole. Many of these problems may be related in part to gender role strain.

Gender Role Strain

Pleck's (1981) gender role strain paradigm spawned research that identified three distinct types of male gender role strain. Discrepancy strain occurs when an individual fails to live up to his internalized masculine ideal. Among contemporary men, this ideal is that of traditional masculinity. Discrepancy strain has been associated with anxiety and depression (O'Neil, Good & Holmes, 1995) and with cardiovascular reactivity (Eisler, 1995).

A second form of male gender role strain is dysfunction strain, which occurs when men meet the requirements of traditional masculinity. Masculine traits often have negative side-effects both for men and for those around them. Dysfunction strain includes violence, rape and sexual harassment, sexual excess, socially irresponsible behaviors (including absent fathering), and relationship dysfunctions (Brooks & Silverstein, 1995).

Trauma strain is the third form of male gender role strain, which results from the male role socialization experience. Trauma strain has many consequences, including alexithymia (the absence of words for emotions), defensive autonomy (feeling safer being alone rather than close to someone), and destructive entitlement (the unconscious belief that people in one's adult life should make up for what one failed to receive as a child) (Levant, 1996).

All three forms of male gender role strain have dysfunctional consequences that stem from traditional masculinity ideology. We next consider the effects of the privilege of males in the workplace and find that this privilege is both enabling and constraining. Privilege has many benefits but also carries with it many pressures and costs.

Male Privilege

Men are usually unwilling to admit that they are overprivileged though many agree that women are disadvantaged (McIntosh, 1989). These men might work to improve women's status providing it won't lessen their own, and they seem unwilling to discuss the advantages men gain from women's disadvantages. Crowley (1993) writes about the lie of entitlement he lived as a man. By being silent, accepting this legacy and saying nothing about its costs to women's lives, men accrue privilege. As a result, male privilege is protected from being fully acknowledged, diminished, or ended. A man must give up the myth of meritocracy should he admit male privilege (Maier, 1994).

McIntosh (1989) makes a distinction between earned strength entitlements and unearned strength entitlements. Male privilege, the conferred dominance of men because of their sex, is an example of the latter. Male privilege is 'like an invisible weightless knapsack of special provisions, assurances, tools, maps, guides, cookbooks, passports, visas, clothes, compass, emergency gear and blank checks' (McIntosh, 1989, p. 10). Some common aspects of male privilege are presented in Table 7.1.

Once male privilege is described and acknowledged, men become accountable (Maier, 1994). What will men do to reduce male privilege? Common rationalizations from men are given to maintain 'business as usual'.

1. Male privilege exists, but it hasn't helped me.
2. Male privilege alone cannot explain the central roles men play in the world.
3. Male privilege exists, but the system is thousands of years old and cannot be changed.
4. I will make efforts to help women, but I won't work to lessen men's privilege.

McIntosh (1989) questions whether the term privilege creates too favorable an image of the conditions and behaviors created by systems of privilege. Everyone would be interested in achieving a privileged state. Male privilege

Table 7.1   Facets of male privilege

1. I can turn on the television or open to the front page of a newspaper and see men widely represented.
2. When I am told about our rational thinking, I am shown that men made it what it is.
3. I can be sure that my children will be given educational materials that highlight men's contributions.
4. I am never asked to speak for all men.
5. I can do well in a challenging situation without being called a credit to my sex.
6. I can speak in public to a powerful male group without putting my sex on trial.
7. I can take a job with an affirmative action employer without having co-workers think I got it because of my sex.
8. I can be pretty sure that if I ask to speak to 'the person in charge' I will be talking to a person of my sex.
9. I can go from most organizations I belong to feeling somewhat tied in, rather than isolated out-of-place, outnumbered, unheard or had at a distance.
10. If my day or week is going badly I don't have to wonder whether each negative episode or situation has sexual overtones.
11. I can benefit from a system that assigns domestic responsibilities to women.
12. I can benefit from a system that historically has not encouraged women to enter my profession (i.e. little competition).
13. When I go for a job interview, it is unlikely that the fact I am a male will be held against me. I will not be taken less seriously because I am male; I will not be presumed to be less competent or less committed because I am male.
14. If I accept a position, I am unlikely to worry about 'fitting in' on account of my sex.
15. I am unlikely to be restricted from business-related networking opportunities because of my sex.
16. My physical appearance will likely be an asset.
17. When I look at the people in senior management I am likely to see other men.
18. When I set in ways that are managerial, I will be seen as behaving in ways consistent with my gender.
19. When I walk through my organization I am unlikely to be mistaken for support staff.
20. When I travel on company business I am unlikely to be mistaken for support staff.
21. I will see people like me well represented in official company literature (annual reports, advertising) indicating I belong.
22. I will not have to work harder to prove myself because I'm a man.
23. I can expect that most of the people I interact with on business—clients, colleagues, customers—will be people of my own gender.
24. I am unlikely to be referred to as the male manager in my unit—the implicit/unspoken norm is that management is male.
25. If I don't do well at work, it is unlikely that people will say we shouldn't have hired a man for the job.
26. As a male, my marital status won't reduce my prospects for promotion.
27. As a male, I will not generally be worried about sexual harassment.
28. As a male, it is likely that my mentoring relationships will be professionally focused—not sexualized.
29. As a male, I will not be patronized or pitied because of my gender.
30. If there are men already in top-level positions, it is unlikely this will reduce my chances for promotion.
31. If, as a male, I get promoted, it is unlikely this will reduce the chances of other men's promotion.
32. I can, as a male, assume my wife/partner will defer to my career enhancing my advancement over her own.
33. As a male, I have legitimate excuses for limiting my involvement and participation in parental or domestic roles.
34. As a man, at company social functions, it is unlikely I will be mistaken for 'just a spouse', and ignored.
35. As a male in a male-dominated organization, I will not be referred to as the 'other male who works here'.
36. I can congregate with the men without being accused of segregating.
37. I can talk to other men without being accused of gossiping.

Source: Based on McIntosh (1989) and Maier (1994).

confers dominance, the right to control. Such privilege may serve no useful role to society, however.

Costs of Corporate Masculinity

By the time boys reach the age of five, they are socialized into masculine role behavior (Paley, 1984). Boys should be controlled, aggressive, competitive, loud, loyal and self-directed. As boys move into their teens, they learn that to fill the masculine role they must also be providers and protectors of their families. These values are consistent with a social commitment to work and the tenets of corporate masculinity (Maier, 1991).

As a consequence, men come to put work first and family second (Bardwick, 1984). They experience tension and stress from work overload, work–family conflict, and the discrepancy between what they say is important (family) and what they put energy towards (work). Men are sometimes unaware of their internal states and personal needs, given their market orientation (Fromm, 1974, 1976). A majority of corporate men seem to be satisfied with their lives and life experiences but a minority feel trapped, alienated and victimized. There is widespread pressure to achieve and to accumulate materialistic possessions in a capitalistic society. Corporate men's feelings of self-worth become linked to successfully meeting tests along the path of upward career mobility. These men must be valued by others before they can value themselves (Korman & Korman, 1980).

Corporate masculinity is becoming an increasing liability for managers in the 1990s (Maier, 1991). First, changes in the demographic make-up of the workforce (more women, more non-traditionals) has made it more difficult for more employees to fit the masculine model and made it more difficult for men to manage these employees in traditional ways. Second, issues of fairness and ethics are raised when the masculine culture is found to advantage men while making it more difficult for women. Third, masculine management approaches reduce the effectiveness of managers (the typical manager, but not the best manager) since the best managers tend to be androgynous. Fourth, the masculine model, focusing on successfully fulfilling the breadwinner/provider role, results in work-addictive behaviors.

The answer lies in freeing men from the requirements to be 'success objects' while filling the provider role. This involves breaking the masculine mold. This is challenging for a variety of reasons. Some men are unaware of how strongly they have been socialized. For them, giving up masculinity is a sign of weakness. The new behavior will also be uncomfortable for these men. But there are some benefits to men in freeing themselves from the masculine role. These include becoming a more effective manager, obtaining career and family balance, and becoming less work-addicted.

Maier (1991) identifies four reasons for men to change corporate masculinity.

1. The limitations of masculine management styles.
2. The ethical concerns of maintaining male privilege while disadvantaging females (unfairness).
3. Changing demographics of the workforce necessitates developing effective relationships with others who are different.
4. Escaping organizational achievement addiction, part of the male breadwinner/provider role.

Corporate masculinity requires that managers act as though they have no conflicting loyalties, a requirement that may be more difficult for men than women since a greater proportion of men than women are married and have children.

Maier (1993, 1996) challenges the assumption that both men and women should assimilate to corporate masculinity. Using the Space Shuttle Challenger disaster, Maier proceeds to show how masculine norms and behaviors were dysfunctional in this organizational fiasco. Building on David and Brannon's four core dimensions of hegemonic masculinity (1976), Maier showed how these dimensions operated in the Challenger decision-making. Implicating corporate masculinity as a source of the Challenger disaster might cause some managers and organizations to question their views on what it means to 'be a man' in our society. Questioning the value of living up to the masculine standard may encourage some men to acknowledge, value and express their feminine qualities. In so doing these men can redefine masculinity. After all, typical masculine practices are considered masculine only because men have exhibited them more than women have.

Luthans (1988) undertook a study of 'real' managers and observed that managerial *effectiveness* and managerial *success* were not necessarily synonymous. Success was defined in terms of career advancement (promotions, upward mobility). Effectiveness involved the manager's ability to get the job done through high quality and quantity standards of performance and through satisfied and committed people. The more strongly one embraces the values and behaviors of hegemonic masculinity, the more likely one will pursue advancement (successful managers) and the less likely one will focus on human resources activities (more feminine oriented behaviors such as mentoring and service to the organization) associated with effectiveness.

Corporate masculinity thus has costs not only for individual men but for organizations as well. Another consequence of masculinity in organizations is Type A behavior.

The Type A Experience

The Type A behavior syndrome has captured considerable attention in medical and psychological research circles over the past two decades. An important series of studies (Rosenman, Friedman, Strauss et al., 1966; Rosenman,

Friedman, Strauss et al., 1970; Rosenman, Brand, Jenkins et al., 1975) has strongly implicated the Type A pattern in the pathogenesis of coronary heart disease (CHD) independent of standard risk factors such as age, hypertension, diet and heredity generally associated with the condition. Research evidence finds that the risk in Type A individuals of developing CHD and of having fatal heart attacks is approximately twice that risk in Type Bs in the population.

In its broadest sense, the Type A pattern is a psychological and behavioral style of certain individuals in meeting challenges, demands, and obstacles in their environment. The set of behaviors involved reflects the interaction of psychological predispositions and environmental conditions. The pattern is more prevalent in industrialized countries and in urban rather than rural communities, which leads to the speculation that values and reward systems of societies such as ours (particularly those of institutions and organizations) play a significant role in promoting the expression of Type A behavior in susceptible individuals.

Certain identifying elements of the Type A pattern are exaggerated expressions of achievement striving, a strong sense of time urgency and competitiveness, and an aggressive style. The Type A individual is described as an unrelenting worker, dominated by the success ethic, ambitious to outperform others and to constantly better his/her productivity. A psychological vigilance, hurried and restless movements, polyphasic behavior and overtones of free-floating hostility are other Type A features (Friedman & Rosenman, 1974). Type Bs are individuals who display opposite characteristics of behavior, having a more relaxed, calmer approach to life in general.

Cardiovascular disease is a major cause of death in many industrialized countries. It is the leading cause of death in the United States, accounting for about half of all deaths (American Heart Association Heart Facts, 1979). Although coronary heart disease (CHD) is but one of the many cardiovascular diseases, it is the largest single contributor to the overall cardiovascular death rate. Heart attacks alone cause three times as many deaths as all other cardiovascular diseases combined. Almost 650 000 Americans die each year from heart attacks, and about a quarter of these individuals are under 65 years of age.

Friedman and Ulmer (1984) refer to Type A behavior as 'a continuous struggle, an unremitting attempt to accomplish or achieve more and more things or participate in more and more events in less and less time, frequently in the face of opposition—real or imagined—from other persons. The Type A personality is dominated by covert insecurity of status or hyperaggressiveness, or both' (p. 31).

One or both of these components cause the struggle to begin resulting in a third personality characteristic, time urgency or hurry sickness. With continued struggle, hyperaggressiveness is evidenced in easily aroused anger, which they term free-floating hostility. Finally, persistent and protracted struggle leads to a fifth characteristic, the tendency toward self-destruction. The unconscious drive toward self-destruction shows itself in men yearning for a heart attack and covertly destroying their careers as a way to get out from under overwhelming stresses and strains.

Type A behavior poses a threat to carers, personality and life itself. Type A behavior threatens careers through impatience, anger and burnout. Type A threatens personality by increasing interpersonal conflict, narrowing the possibilities for joys (limiting oneself to things that can be counted—becoming boring and dull). Finally Type A threatens life by fostering the development of arterial disease and its association with cigarette smoking.

As opposed to their Type B counterparts, Type As work more hours per week, travel more days per year, take less vacation and sick time off work, are more job involved and organizationally committed (Howard, Cunningham & Reichnitzer, 1977). Type As are more likely to experience high self-esteem at work (Burke & Weir, 1980). Thus, Type As are more invested and committed to their work than are their Type B counterparts. But they are not necessarily more satisfied in their jobs. Type A behavior has typically been found to bear no relationship to job satisfaction (Burke & Weir, 1980; Howard, Cunningham & Rechnitzer, 1977).

Two questions still remain unanswered: (a) Are Type As more productive or effective in their jobs than Type Bs? (b) Are Type As more likely to be promoted (or found) at the top of organizations? The limited data that are available suggest that Type As are in fact more likely to receive greater organizational rewards than Type Bs (Mettlin, 1976). In addition, Type As are more likely to be promoted and to have higher performance ratings than Type Bs (Chesney & Rosenman, 1980). But in spite of this, Type As are not more satisfied in their jobs. Burke and Deszca (1982) reported that Type As were more likely to report mid-career experiences of personal and social alienation and pessimism, which Korman and Korman (1980) refer to as 'career success and personal failure,' than Type Bs. Thus, although Type As invest more of themselves in the work role and report greater occupational self-esteem, they are not necessarily more satisfied in their jobs and run the risk of increased feelings of personal failure later in their careers.

Type As report less marital satisfaction, and a more adverse effect of their job demands on personal, home and family lives (Burke & Weir, 1980). Spouses of Type A job incumbents agree with their husbands. They also report less marital satisfaction, and a more adverse effect of their partner's job demands on personal, home and family lives (Burke, Weir & DuWors, 1979). Thus, there probably is a link between Type A behavior and marital distress, and ultimately marital dissolution. It is also likely that Type A individuals are less involved with their children (Burke & Bradshaw, 1981). Friedman and Rosenman (1974) provide anecdotal information that is consistent with these research conclusions. Thus Type A individuals, and their partners, report a less satisfying home and family life.

It is interesting to note that the facets of Type A behavior are almost synonymous with traditional masculine ideology. Aggressiveness, competitiveness, and achievement striving are part of traditional masculinity. Anger and hostility, perhaps the most noxious components of Type A, are the common pathways for all strong feelings among men (Pollack, 1995). Male gender role stress has been associated with anger and anxiety, which is consistent with higher Type A risk (Eisler, 1995; Price, 1982). Type A might well turn out to be 'Type M' for men because of its association with masculinity (Pollack, 1995).

Workaholics/Corporate Bigamists

Male socialization contributes to an excessive attachment to achievement. Not only is the work ethic alive and well, some writers believe that it may be too alive (Frost, Mitchell & Nord, 1986). They write:

> We fear that many individuals are so fully indoctrinated with work values and routines that psychologically they are not free to make reasonable choices about how much work to do, how hard to work, and how central a role to let work play in their lives. . . .
> The virtues of performing work roles are so deeply ingrained in people and the costs of commitments to work, and careers so little considered, that individuals appear to play work roles compulsively, without considering how they might allocate their time and energies in a more fully satisfying manner. (Frost, Mitchell & Nord, 1986, p. 265)

Schaef and Fassel (1988) conclude that addictive (greedy) organizations promote workaholism. Many men (and women) are structurally rewarded for colluding with addictive work systems and in these addictive organizations, destroying one's life and loved ones is acceptable if it produces something useful in the society. Schaef and Fassel argue that denial about workaholism is pervasive because of an attachment to an economically based system, capitalism, and a social structure that undergirds this system.

Shortened work weeks coupled with increased leisure time have not been realized (Kiechel, 1989). In fact the opposite is true. With increases in single-parent households and dual-income families, more people are caught in a time-squeeze (Schor, 1991; Rifkin, 1987). The consequences of busy time-pressured lives, while often ignored, are significant. 'Time-pressured lives are competent and productive. But they don't foster satisfaction; only more work requiring more dutifulness . . . If we can run our own lives, we can accomplish a great deal. And should we accomplish a great deal, perhaps we won't even care. For ultimately, time isn't money or status; time is life itself' (Cunningham, 1986, p. 260).

Porter (1996) defines workaholism as 'excessive involvement with work evidenced by neglect in other areas of life and based on internal motives of behavior maintenance rather than requirements of the job or organization'

(p. 71). She takes the position that an addictive pattern of excessive work impairs both immediate and long-term performance at work. Consistent with other addictions such as alcoholism, Porter's review includes material on identity issues, rigid thinking, withdrawal, progressive involvement and denial. Her definition has two elements: (a) excessive involvement with work, and (b) neglect of other areas of life. Workaholism makes it difficult to even think about anything other than work—family, friends and self are neglected (Naughton, 1987; Woititz, 1987).

Machlowitz (1980) conducted interviews with 100 'workaholics'—mostly male, with professional/managerial careers. Her study indicated that the workaholics were obsessive–compulsive, exhibited Type A behavior, were unable to delegate, were hard on staff, absent from home lives and obsessed with work. She concluded that well-springs of workaholism begin with children while they are at home with their families. Parental love is contingent on achievement, and behavior is then rewarded in school. Workaholic parents frequently serve as models. Contrary to stereotype (her words), she found her sample to be overwhelmingly happy. Spence and Robbins (1992), besides developing interesting measures of workaholism, have provided empirical support for several hypothesized correlates and consequences of workaholism.

Feinberg (1980) coined the term 'corporate bigamist' to refer to men married both to spouse and to career. Such men usually put their careers first, to the neglect of their families, sometimes viewing home life as a threat to their careers. These men worked 60–100 hours per week. Feinberg identified six 'alibis' used by corporate bigamists to justify their behaviors.

1. 'I'm really doing it for you and the kids.'
2. 'You have everything you want—money, a nice house, every advantage for the kids. What more do you want?'
3. 'You aren't interested in my career.'
4. 'When I'm home, you try to turn me into a day laborer, handyman or garbage man.'
5. 'I'm a very busy man. The company demands every waking moment I can spare, you know that. I just can't give you and the children the time that you insist that I should spend—much as I'd like to.'
6. 'I can't reason with you anymore. Every time I try to talk to you about my work, you turn it into a terrible argument.'

Each of these alibis is consistent with men fulfilling the provider/ breadwinner role, women filling the homemaker role, the separation of the work and home fronts, men's reluctance to undertake 'second shift ' work (Hochschild, 1989), and the conflict that may be acknowledged but is never really addressed.

Both workaholism and corporate bigamy reflect imbalances between work and home lives. Kofodimos (1993) suggests that the imbalance in the lives of

American managers results from their basic character (masculinity). She notes the similarity of the character structure of male managers and the values and beliefs of organizations, which are consistent with a male model of success. Both external and internal forces operate so that individuals who capably manage large organizations lose control of their own lives. External forces include organizational pressures, values, and rewards. These forces are seductive, resulting in more time and energy being devoted to work with the accompanying neglect of family life. Internal forces include needs, wants and drive.

Kofodimos implicates two broad polarities in the experience of men—striving for mastery and avoidance of intimacy—to explain the escalating commitment of time and energy to work to the neglect of personal and family life. *Striving for mastery* shows up for men in both work and family life. It embodies an emphasis on task accomplishment, rationality in decision-making, and viewing other people as resources for getting the job done. *Avoidance of intimacy* includes a lack of empathy and compassion, an unawareness of own and other's feelings, an unwillingness to be spontaneous and playful, and an inability to admit weakness.

Kofodimos proposes that issues of identity and self-work are the wellsprings of striving for mastery and avoidance of intimacy. Although she does not refer specifically to masculinity or manhood, her notions are consistent with prevailing views of traditional masculinity. She, consistent with other writings on the socialization of masculinity, suggests that men acquire these two orientations early in their lives from parents and schools, and they become further developed through organizational rewards.

Over the long term, imbalance resulting from mastery-striving and intimacy-avoidance has costs. These include difficulties in one's personal life (family crises, distant relationships) as well as failures in management (anger, intimidation, overcontrol, not asking for help, avoiding feedback), ultimately increasing stress levels and health care costs. Imbalances such as workaholism and corporate bigamy affect entire families, with particular consequences for children.

Work and the Experiences of Children

Pleck (1981) provides an historical perspective on fathering in America. He notes slow change in the direction of an enlarged father role. The eighteenth and early nineteenth centuries revealed fathers as moral overseers; the nineteenth century until the mid-twentieth century showed fathers as distant breadwinners; and fathers serving as sex role models emerged during the 25 years from 1940 to 1965. While the father as provider/breadwinner is still the most dominant father role, a 'new' father role has appeared. New fathers are likely to be present at the birth of their children, to be involved with children as infants, participate in the day-to-day work of childcare, and be involved equally with daughters and sons. This new father role has been supported by increasing numbers of wives in employment as well as recent views on human development suggesting that men are impoverished by not being fathers. The quality of men's parental role is a significant predictor of their overall physical health (Barnett, Davidson & Marshall, 1991).

In a chapter entitled 'The Children of "God"', Feinberg (1980) indicated some of the difficulties that children of driven high achievers must endure. These included the experience of excessively high standards, an inability to please or be good enough, and stinging criticism. A common reaction of this kind of environment is to try to get back at the father. One tragic symptom of such 'revenge' may be reflected in the frightening growth in the number of teenage suicides. A 1979 report in the *Journal of the American Medical Association* revealed an increase in the rate of suicide among 15–24 year olds of 124% since 1961, making it the third ranking cause of death in that age group.

Sostek and Sherman (1977) published the results of an 8-year study of executives' children which examined their attitudes toward parents and their behavior. The reaction of most of these children to their extremely successful parents and to parental authority was bitter resentment. The self-confidence, achievement orientation, and pride in workmanship of this group was significantly lower than in control groups of children with less affluent or important parents. The biggest complaint of the children of executives was about the rigid, non-negotiable demands for compliance with the point of the view of parents who at the same time showed little interest in or understanding of the children's views. These children often chose failure rather than aggressive, socially acceptable goal-seeking behavior. According to Sostek and Sherman, over half of the children of upper-middle-class families choose the failure route. Thus, the factors which enable the male executive to achieve financial success at the same time contribute to the development of a non-academic, suffering child with a fear of failure and a low aspiration behavior pattern.

Another outcome may be that few of the children of executives are interested in pursuing the same career as their fathers (Brooks, 1977). In a study of children whose fathers were in top or upper-middle management in a *Fortune* 500 US corporation, only 15% planned a corporate or business career. At the same time, the children may have been rejecting a particular set of values— those typically held by executives, such as the pursuit of money, status, and power. It is conceivable that high-achieving parents may pursue other goals, including service to others and intellectual accomplishment. Given a greater congruence between the values held by parent and offspring, children should be less likely to reject parents and their values.

Other research has examined the support mothers, fathers, and peers give to adolescents in dealing with their problems and anxieties (Burke & Weir, 1977). The sample consisted of 273 adolescents ranging in age from 13 to 20, and represented diverse backgrounds. Adolescents were least likely to inform their fathers (as opposed to mothers or peers) about their problems and anxieties, and were least satisfied with the help they received from their fathers.

What seemed particularly noteworthy was that fathers were more frequently seen as uninterested, unresponsive, unapproachable, and likely to be embarrassed by the discussion of certain problems. In addition, the adolescents reported being more embarrassed about talking over particular problems with fathers than with mothers and peers. The helping style offered by fathers was seen as one of lecturing their children; trying to influence them with facts, arguments, and logic; ordering or commanding them to do something; and criticizing or blaming them. Fathers were seen as responding in ways which diminished or 'put down' the adolescent and which acted to control or exhibit authority. The relatively poorer performance of the fathers as helpers was not affected very much by fathers' age, education, and income.

It is interesting that the behavior attributed to fathers in their helping relationships with their adolescents is behavior which is prevalent in most work environments. The work world tends to be characterized by impersonal relationships, and respect is granted on the basis of power, authority, logic, and facts. It is possible that fathers may be attempting to relate to their adolescents and their personal problems in the same way as they relate to co-workers and handle problems at work. The latter type of behavior in a personal life context may do little but set up barriers between fathers and their children.

In her study of work and family in which she conducted interviews and family observations, Piotrkowski (1978) reported that children connected their fathers' jobs to their fathers' bad moods. When unable to do this, children blamed themselves for difficulties with their fathers and they also got angry with them. Three other areas in which work influenced children's reactions were: they connected work (income) and family financial security; they worried about their fathers' physical safety;' and father absence negatively affected the process of identification by which young boys acquired their mature masculine identity.

O'Reilly (1990) also makes the point that the qualities that make for corporate success are often not what are needed to be an effective mother or father. The intensity and single-mindedness that contribute to corporate achievement may be opposite to effective parenting. Perfectionism, impatience, and efficiency encouraged at work clash with the tolerance, patience and acceptance of chaos required at home. Executives preoccupied with their own careers sometimes ignore their children, and workaholic executives who were merely average at school try to create children who are everything they weren't.

Relationships with children are thus strongly affected by masculinity and its related emphasis on work. Another aspect of masculinity, the need for power, has particular ramifications for male/female relationships.

The Power-motivated Man and Relationships with Women

A handful of studies conducted during the 1970s examined the impact of men's need for power on their relationships with women. This research is relevant because the need for power is typically pursued and satisfied at work, while relationships with the opposite sex occur outside work. McClelland and his colleagues have been engaged for several decades in research on the need for power (n Power) (McClelland, 1979; Winter, 1973). Men in n Power tend more often to be officers in organizations, to participate more in contact sports, and to accumulate more prestige possessions than do men low in n Power.

Studies of men have shown that n Power is associated with distorted views of women, exploitation of women, and difficulties in sustaining intimate relationships with them. Slavin (1972) found that college men who scored high in n Power viewed women as harming men by their very contact, exploiting and rejecting men, being unfaithful to men, or triumphing over them. In a study of dating couples, Stewart and Rubin (1976) found that hope of power (the approach element of the motive) was associated with dissatisfaction and anticipation of relatively more problems in the relationship on the part of both partners. Power-oriented men scored lower on scales assessing both their love and their liking of their partners. Couples where the man scored higher on hope for power were more likely to break up, and less likely to marry during the following 2-year period.

Studies of married men have confirmed that n Power continues to affect the marriage relationship in the same sorts of ways. In a study of middle-class and working-class men, McClelland, Davis, Kalin and Warner (1972) found that n Power was associated with divorce. In a study of married couples, McClelland, Coleman, Finn and Winter (1976) found that what they termed the 'conquistador' pattern of high n Power, low n affiliation, and low activity inhibition was associated with low ratings of marital satisfaction by both partners and low pair performance in an interpersonal game. Having power over women is therefore an expression of the power-motivated male's generalized tendency to seek impact on another person, even at the cost of intimate and enduring sexual relationships. Or, fearing intimacy with a woman because of feelings of inadequacy, the man high in n Power compensates by pseudo-aggression in the form of dominance over the woman.

Winter, Stewart, and McClelland (1977) examined the relationship of n Power of 51 male college graduates (measured in 1960) and the level of their wives' careers in 1973. The hypothesis they proposed was that n Power in men should be negatively associated with their wives' career level. Power-oriented men should be less likely to tolerate the sharing of power implied by their wives' careers. They might resent the diminished availability of their wives to provide personal service and attention. They would be less flexible and understanding, and less likely to make accommodations. As predicted, husbands' n Power as measured in 1960 was significantly negatively associated with wives' career level in 1973. In addition, wives' career level was significantly negatively associated with husbands' being business executives and husbands' conservative political views. It may be that men high in power in the first place select and marry women with lower career aspirations, perceiving as threatening women with high career aspirations of their own.

In summary, masculinity ideology has implication for men, women, children, and organizations. Some of these are positive, while some are destructive. In the next section, we turn our attention to conceptions of success that arise from the adoption of the traditional masculine ideal.

MEN AND SUCCESS

Weiss (1990) studied successful men—men who keep going, effectively developing their careers and managing their organizations, supporting their families, and meeting their commitments despite the ups and downs of normal living. Weiss and his research team conducted extensive in-depth interviews with 80 successful men. These men had achieved a place in society most would consider satisfactory. They held middle-class occupations, or better. They owned homes in good suburbs or upper-income metropolitan areas. They were between 35 and 55 years of age. They were respected by others around them (work colleagues, neighbors, friends) and they were responsible both to their organizations and to their families.

The men in Weiss' study devoted most of their time and energy to two sectors, work and family. Work provided many things to men: a succession of challenges, the maintenance of self-confidence, a sense of achievement, a position in the community of work, reputation and standing at work, and recognition and emblems of worth. In addition to work, men require a partner to share their lives and establish a home if they are to feel that their lives are complete. Although men stated that family was the most important thing in their lives, they devoted considerably more time and energy to work than to other sectors.

It was inevitable that men experienced stress at work. There was always a possibility of failure since the jobs were challenging. The stakes were high because men wanted their success to be recognized. Weiss found common sources of stress to be the threat of failure, threats to their place in the community of work from hostile or uncooperative co-workers, frustration from workplace impediments to getting the job done, and self-imposed behaviors and attitudes (e.g. anger, impatience, work overload). Stress was experienced when men mobilized their energies to deal with challenges but failed. They continued to struggle and remained mobilized. This mobilization expressed itself through preoccupation with the stress-inducing problem, irritability, restlessness, tension, and sleep disorders.

The men in Weiss's study went to great lengths *not* to discuss work stress at home with their spouses. Discussing work stressors at home broke down an important form of compartmentalization. Home was a haven, a refuge men went to when they left work. It would not be a refuge if men brought work home. Dealing with work problems was his job, not hers. Men also did not want to upset their wives. In addition, the admission and discussion of work stress at home could be seen as a sign of incompetence. But men could discuss *positive* work events and experiences at home. It was also permissible for men to be tired—but not stressed—at home. Being tired at home also indicated to other family members how hard men were working as providers. But when men were stressed at work, though they did not discuss it at home, they were troubled, preoccupied and unacceptable to their family. And family members sensed what was going on.

Let us now consider marriage, the second important sector in men's lives. Marriage provided several critical elements for men including structure, stability, status in their neighborhood and places in their communities. Marriage gave meaning to men's lives and filled needs for attachment—another person truly shares one's life. Weiss found a fairly traditional division of labor in their men's marriages. In addition, the arrival of children increased the division of labor according to men's and women's roles. Men and women were committed to helping out as needed. Men were also committed to notions of equity, and many believed that their current division of labor was fair.

All marriages have points of friction. Weiss found the three most common sources of friction to be disagreements over the way children were being raised, complaints about partner's availability, and difficulties in communication. Men were willing (and able) to tolerate marriages that their wives saw as unsatisfactory. For men, a marriage marked by conflict still provided logistic support and a place in the community of friends and family. Marriage provided a stable and reliable base for their lives, an emotional base and partnership in creating a home and raising children. Men stayed in troubled marriages by staying in charge as best they could, by compartmentalizing, and by accepting the reality that theirs was not a good marriage.

Fatherhood was an important event in men's lives. It helped men make sense of their lives. It provided more meaning to their marriages. It provided a reason for their marriages to continue. But fatherhood also was a burden to marriage. It added new responsibilities. It conveyed a loss of freedom. It was also associated with a sharper division of labor. Children provide a reason for working hard. Children are also a source of pride when they 'do well', and a source of dismay when they 'fail'. Children represented a commitment, an investment, an obligation and a hope. Children that do well afford still another opportunity for a man to respect himself.

The successful men that Weiss studied had membership in a wide array of communities. These included friends, kin, neighbors and fellow members of voluntary associations. These relationships occurred in networks of people who knew each other, where the men had a place, where the men belonged. These relationships, unlike those at work or in the family, were optional. Men typically relied on their wives to manage relationships with kin. Men's friendships were mainly companionships joined by common interests. These friendships were not characterized by frequent contact or close confiding in. Men appeared to be able to 'lose' friends with some, but manageable, discomfort. For men, loss of work or loss of a family member was much more difficult.

The men in Weiss's study wanted to have a good life and to be good men—men they could respect. Being a good man means holding a respected place among men, serving as head to a family and as a model for one's children, and raising one's children properly. Being a good man does not mean being virtuous in every respect, however. Sexual dalliances and affairs were common among the men. The best estimates suggest that about half of white middle-class men have extra-marital experiences.

Let us conclude our summary of Weiss's work by considering issues of change. Weiss saw his men as having limited capacity for change. Work emerged as a critical source of meaning and functioning in the lives of these men, yet men's ways of living overloaded and stressed their marriages (work–family conflict, lack of equity in the household division of labor). Though men had few intimate friends, this did not appear to limit their work effectiveness. Weiss does not anticipate much change in the underlying structure of the lives of men who do well at work. He does not see men reducing their commitment to work. Nor will men reduce their commitment to their families. Weiss also expects little change in the division of labor within marriages and households. Thus, according to Weiss, men who make society work will look pretty much the way he found them to be.

Weiss also found no reason to advocate that these men change their lives, despite some costs. These men have obtained a reasonable standard of living, made productive use of their talents, found some time for family and spouse, and obtained self-respect and the respect of their communities. Most of Weiss' managerial and professional men were relatively satisfied with both their career and personal lives, though all had experienced periods of stress and disquiet. But others paint a less rosy picture.

Career Success and Personal Failure

For all intents and purposes I'm a success! People think I've got it made. I don't know how many times this past year someone has told me I look and sound 'just terrific'. But how can someone who looks so good feel so bad? On the inside, I often waver between depression, feeling totally out of control, and feeling like I'm going to explode because I'm so full of pent-up emotions—confusion, anger, betrayal. I'm not productive at work. I don't feel particularly close to my wife. (Korman & Korman, 1980, p. 133)

The career success and personal failure phenomenon was highlighted and elaborated on by Korman and Korman (1980). A diverse body of literature prior to this work identified aspects of the same phenomenon or contributed relevant information to our understanding of it (Henry, 1961; Ogilvie & Porter, 1974; Bartolome, 1972; Fasteau, 1974; Maccoby, 1976; Steiner, 1972; Walker, 1976).

Career success and personal failure is a syndrome that afflicts some managerial and professional men in mid-life and mid-career. Career success and personal failure refers to experiences reported among men who have attained an unquestionable level of success according to society's criteria (high occupational status, prestige, power and responsibility, substantial income, relative material worth, status in the community). However, simultaneous with this experience of oneself as a career success there is a growing disaffection with one's life as a whole. The individual feels victim to feelings of frustration, grief, loneliness, alienation and despair, and to pressing questions about the meaning and direction of his life. The discrepancy between the individual's career identity with its external trappings and rewards, and the individual's more personal sense of self, forces itself into the individual's consciousness, creating varying degrees of psychological distress which demand resolution.

Why should an individual so obviously successful in his career develop feelings of personal failure? One set of antecedents proposed by Korman and Korman results from new appreciations of life realities resulting from particular work experiences individuals encounter. These include: the realization that life demands are contradictory—one cannot necessarily have it all, the realization that one's view of cause–effect relationships was wrong, the realization that many of one's choices or decisions were made to please others, and the realization that one has few close friends and is basically alone. A second set of antecedents results from the male mid-life stage itself. These include an awareness of decline, advancing age, and goals which will never be achieved, changes in family and personal relationships among self and others, and increased feelings of obsolescence. These antecedents combine, resulting in career-successful men feeling personally and socially alienated. With these feelings come a loss of work interest and job/career/life dissatisfaction. In turn, this leads to psychological distress and a desire to rearticulate a sense of purpose and meaning in one's life (see Figure 7.1).

Antecedents of Career Success and Personal Failure

What type of individuals are likely to fall victim of the career success and personal failure phenomenon? Are some people more likely than others to experience these feelings? The answer to these questions is a 'qualified' yes. Individuals who experience particular kinds of early childhood and adolescent experiences and who encounter particular environmental and situational characteristics at these stages are more likely to develop feelings of career success and personal failure in their later lives.

As children, the executives came from upper-lower or lower-middle-class families and carried memories of financial insecurity from these times. The

239

Proximate influences

Cognitive realization of:

A. Contradictory life demands

B. Disconfirmed expectancies

C. Sense of external control

D. The loss of affiliative satisfactions

The characteristics of the male mid-life stage. These include:

A. Awareness of decline, advancing age, and goals which will never be achieved

B. Changes in family and personal relationships among self-and-others

C. Increasing feelings of obsolescence

Feelings of

Personal and social alienation

Loss of work interest, career, life and job dissatisfaction

Psychological distress

Desire for rearticulation of life, perspective and purpose

Environmental influences and interventions

A. Intervention programs available in work organization

B. Societal programs for facilitating life and career change

C. Quality of relationship with wife and family

D. Environmental (and personal) flexibility and acceptance of change

Possible resolutions

A. Decision for new career and/or new family life

B. Rededication to old career with new perspectives and acceptance of inevitable imperfections of life

C. Acceptance of old career with little interest or enthusiasm; dedication to avocational goals

D. Continuing distress with no resolution

Figure 7.1   Tentative longitudinal model of career success and personal failure

father was the significant authority-figure wielding considerable power and influence, yet his participation in the family life was sporadic or marginal. He was emotionally absent from the family, leaving the responsibilities for home life to his wife. But, mostly due to his influence, parenting of children was authoritarian and controlling, with unspoken norms or sanctions against being emotionally close, expressive, or supportive of one another. There was a strong role differentiation along masculine/feminine sex role lines, and the relationship between the two people appeared to be a function of formalized roles rather than an expression of any genuine emotional intimacy.

Each respondent (all male) reported having been socialized according to an extreme masculine model. Their perception of childhood contained vivid memories of feeling very alone a great deal of the time, of tolerating considerable criticism and of being subject to considerable parental control. They rarely felt good about themselves, felt of little value or consequence to the family, learned not to trust their parents with personal thoughts and feelings and did not see the family as a source of personal happiness or comfort.

Executives who suffered career success and personal failure had entered adolescence with low self-esteem and self-worth. They maintained an emotional distance from their parents and increased the physical distance as much as possible by involvement in pursuits outside the range of parental influence. However, some striking changes did take place during adolescence. They discovered avenues through which they could attain significant feelings of success, satisfaction and happiness. These positive outcomes came from varied sources: intellectual achievements, part-time jobs, music, mechanics, or athletics. These activities provided opportunities to establish feelings of self-respect and self-worth, and to feel a part of the mainstream to some extent. Their sense of self and value of self became firmly anchored to activities, accomplishments and the degree to which they measured up to socially desirable norms or standards. That is, the emphasis is not on *who* the person is, but on *what* he has that will equip him for success in the marketplace.

They bought the success ethic in its entirety and learned to value goals of achievement, material wealth, status and power which then came to direct the course of their later lives. In order to increase the probability of achieving these goals, all reported becoming skilful in developing a fairly uniform set of behavioral responses—high task orientation, a rational, analytic, objective approach to the world, maintaining high activity level and obsessive attention to their career goals. They developed a strong belief in controlling things to their advantage in the external environment without having their felt personal inadequacies or limitations intruding and interfering with their abilities to achieve.

These behaviors and values established in adolescence continued into adulthood. The result was a prolonged intense pursuit of success and its prizes. This demanded a heavy work commitment; a highly competitive, aggressive, and achievement-motivated approach to desired goals; a denial or repression of aspects of the self not directly related to the work and career; and minimal interpersonal commitment and involvements. With regard to the latter, friendships tended to be superficial or 'contacts', and marriages for the most part served status, support and social acceptability functions. The picture that emerges from our respondents' descriptions is rather similar to Friedman and Rosenman's (1974) description of the Type A personality, and to the characteristics of the traditional masculine ideal. Burke and Deszca (1982) reported that Type A men were also more likely to report personal failure experiences. They are all men devoted to their headlong drive towards success. Their work and careers virtually constitute the total sum of their preoccupations and activities. Their career identity, their accomplishments and achievements ultimately define their sense of self, their value and worth. They live denying the need of human connection—an intimacy with a significant few—and remain isolated from an awareness of inner-directed needs, feelings and values.

However, as middle age crept upon them a number of forces combined to change their individual perceptions and feelings about themselves and their past, present and future lives. They began to view their successes and possessions as hollow and their life as empty and meaningless. They were often overwhelmed by a sense of despair which did not fully understand and could not seem to control, and a sense of desperation because they had no guideposts to lead them out of their dilemma. They were not given to introspection and self-analysis. It is at this point that the total experience culminated in a profound sense of personal failure. How intense this experience was for any individual male seemed from our initial observations to depend on how much of the self (e.g. feelings, needs) had been cordoned off or compromised for the sake of attaining career success.

Individual and Organizational Solutions

As the Kormans indicate, there are several ways individuals can resolve feelings of career success and personal failure. These resolutions are not uniformly positive. One resolution involves the individual continuing to work for his organization but dedicating most of his energy and interest to activities outside his work life. He may make his marriage high priority and devote himself to rebuilding the relationship. A commitment might be made to social service activities in the community or to a particular avocation. The individual's need for achievement and success shifts from the job or career to other areas of life. Another resolution involves the individual leaving his organization in favor of constructing a career more responsive to mid-life needs and values. Another resolution involves ending the marital relationship and searching for new emotional ties. Other individuals may rededicate themselves to their career after taking time to develop a new perspective of job demands and roles in relation to their total personality and life space. They may strike a better balance between their work and personal life and enrich their lives in the process. Another resolution involves no change at all, but continuing along in old patterns, ignoring messages from one's body and mind that all is not well. In some cases, the prolonged psychological distress yields to depression and apathy and individuals live out the rest of their lives as alienated, unproductive and devitalized human beings. Others carry on, unhappily struggling and striving until illness or suicide seem to be the only escape (Ogilvie & Porter, 1974).

Kofodimos defines balance as 'a satisfying, healthy and productive life that includes work, play and love; that integrates a range of life activities with attention to self and to personal and spiritual development; and that expresses a person's unique wishes, interests and values' (1993, p. xiii). Several factors have made the striving for balance a higher priority among some managers. These include the presence of more women in the workforce, increasing pressures for harder work and longer hours, the movement of baby-boomers into mid-life and management, and the realization by some that the simple minded pursuit of career success has fallen short in providing happiness.

Achieving balance requires changes in both individuals and organizations. Kofodimos (1993) advocates, at the broadest level, that individuals change their approach to living, and organizations review and change their norms, values and practices. Individuals need to identify the allocation of time and energy that fits their values and needs. Organizations that support balanced need to examine and redefine effective performance at work (more than hours worked per week) as well as to redefine the notions of a career and career success.

Kofodimos provides conceptual frameworks and diagnostic questionnaires to help individuals consider three levels of change; (a) balancing their time, energy and commitment; (b) integrating mastery and intimacy in their approach to living; and (c) developing their real self, values and aspirations. She provides self-assessment questionnaires for organizational discrepancies in three areas: (a) cultural norms encouraging an imbalanced commitment to work; (b) patterns of mastery and intimacy skills valued for leadership; and (c) a vision for organizational balance accompanied by specific change strategies.

Korman and Korman (1980) offer some suggestions for societal and organizational interventions that can be considered. Firstly, with greater recognition of the existence of the problem, professionals in our society can develop programs explicitly designed to help individuals anticipate or resolve the problem of career success and personal failure. This may involve developing personal growth and life planning workshops, assessment centers, career and personal counselling facilities, and self-help materials all specifically designed to aid individuals in alleviating the severity of this experience or coping with it.

Another intervention at the societal level might involve the educational system. Students in high schools and universities could be exposed to the different meanings of the word success; to viable lifestyle options; to stages of

adult development and their relevant tasks, issues and problems; to the interactive effects of work and family life (Burke & Bradshaw, 1981); to goal-
setting and career and life planning activities. Ogilvie and Porter (1974) have
commented on the need to portray the reality of success more accurately. The
societal model pushed so enthusiastically by schools of business and corporate
management development programs (i.e. hard work will bring success, and
success automatically creates the good life, the healthy life) grossly distorts the
reality. Unrealistic expectations as individuals begin their careers result in
eventual disillusionment in mid-life, followed by psychosomatic symptoms,
physical illness, alcoholism and heart attacks. The cost side of the success
ledger must be presented if a balanced view is to be had (Feinberg, 1980;
Greiff & Munter, 1980; Machlowitz, 1980; Bartolme & Evans, 1981).

Perhaps more important and more difficult to accomplish are the shifts in
values in our society and those which would support and endorse (a) definitions of success broader than those linked to career, position and money; (b)
mid-career reassessment and career or job changes; (c) continuing adult education and personal growth.

Interventions at the organizational level are crucially important yet at the
present time are virtually non-existent. Organizations are in a position to
provide assessment and career planning programs for their employees and
many do. Fortunately, there is a growing recognition that these kinds of
programs make little sense without giving consideration to personal life needs
and goals. In addition, it is impossible to ignore the fact that the work life and
personal life of individuals influence each other to a significant degree (Burke
& Greenglass, 1987). it is not unreasonable to expect organizations to consider the impact they are having on the families of their job incumbents, to
understand the extent of that impact by surveys of both employees and their
spouses, to provide adequate counselling facilities for the job incumbents and
their families, and to do a more responsible job of involving and preparing
families for the job and career changes that might affect them.

Organizations can at an early stage in an individual's career identify individuals who are prone to career success and personal failure. Every top management group knows who their workaholics and Type As are and can begin
thinking about a development package which makes these individuals more
aware of what the outcome of their behavioral styles may be on their own and
their families' welfare. Another interesting possibility for organizations is to
make provisions for individual to take sabbaticals, to be assigned to special
assignments which significantly change their day-to-day work and life patterns
and free them to re-examine their life situation and gain new perspective.

Personal growth workshops which fell out of favor with many organizations
because the high expectations of the early T-groups were not met, still have an
important contribution to make. In providing their people with experiences in
such groups, organizations can assist individuals in becoming more conscious
of their breadth and depth and help them to avoid constricting themselves into

a unidimensional mold which will give rise to later, serious personal consequences.

There is increasing evidence that educational and counselling initiative can prove useful in reducing the most lethal aspects of the male role. Friedman and his colleagues (Friedman & Rosenman, 1974; Friedman & Ulmer, 1984) indicate clearly that Type A behavior can be modified with the corresponding reduction in incidence of CHD. Their program (Friedman & Ulmer, 1984) provides detailed information on ways to alleviate time urgency, free-floating hostility and self-destructive tendencies. The program involves cognitive restructuring, behavior modification, self-monitoring, social support, and reinforcement.

On the first day of their program group participants are given a list of ten freedoms, these freedoms representing liberation from behavior patterns which are putting their lives at risk. These are (Friedman & Ulmer, 1984, p. 165):

1. The freedom to overcome your insecurity and regain your self-esteem.
2. The freedom to give and receive love.
3. The freedom to mature.
4. The freedom to restore and enrich your personality.
5. The freedom to overcome and replace old hurtful habits with new life-enhancing ones.
6. The freedom to take pleasure in the experiences of your friends and family members.
7. The freedom to recall your past life frequently and with satisfaction.
8. The freedom to listen.
9. The freedom to play.
10. The freedom to enjoy tranquility.

Williams and Williams (1993) describe a program for controlling hostility, one of the key components of coronary-prone behavior (Williams, 1989). The major strategies involve learning how to deflect anger, to improve relationships, and to adopt positive attitudes.

Feinberg (1980) offers both family and corporate guidelines for corporate bigamists. Kofodimos (1993) provides a variety of self-, family-, and organizational-assessment exercises to facilitate diagnosis priority-setting, and the identification of change strategies coupled with action steps and goals.

There are also a number of workshops available to both men and women to grapple with the discontents of masculinity. Silverstein and Rashbaum (1994) offer one such workshop, entitled 'The courage to raise good men'. The workshop questions traditional motives of manhood and encourages both mothers and fathers to refuse to sanction the emotional shutdown traditionally demanded of boys. Silverstein and Rashbaum also encourage a new way of vaulting traditional 'feminine' behaviors such as empathy, nurturing and compassion. As Kaufman (1993) writes, it is time to start 'cracking the armor'.

CONCLUSIONS

Career success and personal failure is a pattern stemming from the adoption of the traditional masculine ideology in society. It is, however, subject to change, as perceptions of masculinity are socially constructed. And some would say that change has begun to occur.

You've Come a Long Way, Babies!

An examination of the ways men's roles have changed over the past several years reveals that subtle changes are underway in some areas, while others have remained the same. Kimmel (1993) presents a brief sketch of men covering the past 50 years. The 1950s were characterized by conformist organizational men whose primary loyalty was to the powerful, patriarchal organization. The 1970s saw the advent of new organizational men: on the fast track, careerist, success-oriented, using the company as an arena for advancement. Men's liberation emerged in the mid-1970s as a combination social movement and self-help initiative. It began as a response to feminist critiques of masculinity. As its core was the question of why so many men were in despair (boring and unfulfilling jobs, in unhappy marriages, distant from their children, few friends) if they were dominating and powerful. Men's liberation, according to Sawyer (1970) 'calls for men to free themselves of the sex-role stereotypes that limit their ability to be human.' More men came to see traditional masculinity as a burden, a form of oppression. Traditional masculinity was seen, by men's liberation, as a failure. The male sex role was a prescription for despair. Few men could live up to these expectations; thus most men would feel like failures as men.

The 'decade of greed' of the 1980s saw an emphasis on materialism and self-focus. In the 1990s, men have begun rebelling against careerism because of family interests. Attaching one's sense of manhood/masculinity to fulfilling the provided breadwinner role was realistic during the 40 years following the Second World War. This investment created difficulties for blue-collar men in the 1980s and for white-collar men in the 1990s (Gaylin, 1992).

Men who desire both a challenging career and involved fatherhood will have to make choices and compromises. Working women have had to make such choices in the past. Is it possible for men to have it all? There may be some emotional and financial costs for some men in considering these choices—costs of redefining the male role. De-emphasizing the provider/breadwinner role poses such costs as the potential loss of income, loss of male companionship and loss of manhood. There are also real benefits in supporting this redefinition. Kimmel (1993) identifies the following: a more meaningful life for men who want to spend more time with their families; developing a self-concept including non-work activities; and pursuing careers affording greater intrinsic satisfaction.

Gerson (1993) likewise observed men's reassessment of their commitments to work and family. This shows up in increasing varieties of men's patterns of integrating work and family, unlike the historically more common separation of work and family, with work being predominant. In her interview study of 138 men, Gerson examined how they coped with the forces affecting their lives. She identified three categories of men on the basis of two dimensions of commitment: economic contributions to a family and participation in domestic work (child rearing). *Breadwinners* were high on the first and low on the second; *autonomous men* were low on both; *involved men* were high on the second, regardless of their standing on the first.

In the 1950s, breadwinning husbands and homemaking wives represented two-thirds of North American households. Men who were not economically successful or good providers for wives and children were failures. Since then, women have entered the workplace in increasing numbers with a corresponding decline of men as primary breadwinners and social support for the superiority of men has also fallen. Despite this, men's domestic participation has changed very little. Married women have two to three fewer hours of leisure per day than married men do.

Gerson found 36% of her sample were breadwinners, 30% were autonomous and 33% were involved fathers. Her 'involved fathers' most closely fits the characteristics of contemporary men, trying to integrate several aspects of their lives. Men of the 1990s, according to Gerson (1993) are choosing between: freedom and sharing, independence and interdependence, and privilege and equality.

Brod (1987) identifies several factors as undermining the breadwinner role: increasing numbers of working women, changes in work from manual to mental labor, women's and gay liberation which reduced the importance of heterosexual sexual conquest as one indicator of masculinity; changes from a work/efficiency ethic to a consumer/need fulfilment ethic; and changes in the nature of the workforce from heroic leadership to technological expertise. He advocates strengthening men to distance themselves from traditional male socialization (macho, gangs, sports, teams, military training, media images, older males) and more successfully become individuals. This would help to speed the changes in redefining the male role.

Some attitudes, however, have not changed. Norris and Wylie (1995) found that male students stereotyped the successful managers in 'male' terms while women students did not. This replicates a lot of previous work. Women's attitudes have changed while men's have not. Mothers' work experience and education were found to have no effect on men's attitudes.

There are thus subtle changes underway. Fewer men in the 1990s are willing to sacrifice family lives. The preceding studies show signs that the definition of masculinity is changing too—but slowly.

We Still Have a Long Way to Go

Reconstructing or redefining masculinity requires social change. It must occur in early childhood, in schools, in the media—especially television—in universities, in organizations, and through government policies and initiatives. The current trend toward corporate and government restructuring has resulted in massive downsizing and job losses. Might these serve as stimuli for change? Some men may be forced out of the traditional breadwinner role, and some may adopt new definitions of masculinity as a result. Others, however, may respond with fear and a rigid adherence to traditional masculine ideology.

Brod and Kaufman (1994) suggest that contemporary men need to: be open to women's presence and suppressed knowledge; consider men's lives and experiences as those of men and not of humans in general; appreciate how men assume the privileges of a patriarchal society; become aware of how the masculine role oppresses women; and understand why it is so difficult for men to change. Theoretical understanding of men's experiences necessarily becomes personal understanding since it is men's lives that are being examined. It is men's responsibility to challenge an oppressive status quo through changes in men's personal lives as well as changing ideas, structures, processes and organizations.

Freeman (1979) proposes the linking of an *egalitarian ethic* (women and men as equals) with a broader *liberation ethic* (men and women both liberated from sex roles and the masculine values that underlie our culture). An emphasis on equality rests on the assumption that women 'want to be like men or that men are worth emulating; . . . to demand that women be allowed to participate in society as we know it without questioning whether that society is worth participating in' (Freeman, 1979, p. 572). She joins a number of researchers who conclude that both women and men stand to gain from being less like men and challenging the male model equating career with life success.

It is important to move away from thinking that views men as essentially alike, but fundamentally different from women, to consider the variety of orientations among men (Easthope, 1990). The variety of circumstances and pressures faced by men lays the foundation for a variety of options, the range of men's alternative creates a range of choices of male roles into the future. As stated earlier in this chapter, there are multiple forms of masculinity, and all require investigation to increase understanding.

Orton (1993) defines social change as a process of *unlearning* gender- and power-based behaviors that have proved harmful and then *relearning* respectful empowering behaviors that have no reference to gender. This process will take considerable time and practice to realize benefits from it. Orton believes that it is the job of men to point out to other men the dysfunctional aspects of traditional masculinity and support and model new behaviors.

Kimmel (1987) raises the question of how we can change those components of masculinity that limit 'men's development as healthy and fully responsive people'. He identifies three approaches: personal change by men; the creation of political organizations that communicate and lobby for change; and the emergence of broadly based social movements. He further suggests that men are changing, but few do so because they have identified the downside and limitations of masculinity for themselves, but rather from pressures of external forces (e.g. the women's movement).

Maier (1994) indicates why males should change the system that confers unearned advantage to them. Men state they have complaints now which include: why blame individual men for a system they did not create? Women now have the advantage. On the other hand, why should men gain advantages for the suppression of women, regardless of whether or not they created the system?

Brannon's four basic rules of manhood highlight the dilemma for men. These rules have limited men and channelled them away from whatever their real potential might have been. But how would men free themselves from their prison? Suggestions included getting out of the corporate rat race; rejecting competition and aggression; and regaining emotional spontaneity. What was missing in all this was a new model of manhood.

Kimmel (1996) offers 'democratic manhood' as the manhood of the future. Democratic manhood involves inclusion and fighting injustice based on difference. Democratic manhood calls for private and public commitments. Men need to change themselves, foster relationships and nurture their families. In addition, men need to challenge and remake social systems so they, and women, will prosper.

Hearn (1989, 1992) identifies a fundamental catch-22: without changing men, it will be difficult to change management. Without changing management, it will be difficult to change men. One way to attack the problem is to use the power granted to men by the system to change the system. Individuals are always part of the system, but they can be parts that challenge or strengthen the status quo.

In all of these efforts for change, knowledge can serve as the basis for activism. We believe it is possible to be both compassionate towards men and critical of hegemonic masculinity.

Future Research

It is important to move away from thinking that views men as essentially alike, but fundamentally different from women, to consider the variety of orientations among men (Easthope, 1990). The variety of circumstances and pressures faced by men lays the foundation for a variety of options, the range of men's alternatives creates a range of choices of male roles into the future (Kimmel, 1987).

We know very little about the emotional and social lives of managerial and professional men. The following issues warrant attention.

1. Work–family conflict among corporate men.
2. Work–family, and family–work stress spillover.
3. Is there a daddy track? Who is on it? Are there costs?

4. Corporate men as fathers.
5. Corporate men as husbands.
6. Successful marital and family relationships.
7. What is changing about the definition of masculinity? How? and Why?
8. What is really going on in the hearts and minds of corporate men?
9. What do corporate women find rewarding or problematic in their relationships with corporate men?
10. What do corporate men find rewarding or problematic in their relationships with corporate women?
11. Do corporate men have different relationships with other corporate men versus corporate women?
12. How does heterosexuality affect a man's view of masculinity?
13. In what ways are organizations addictive (i.e. promotive of career success and personal failure)? What can be done about this?
14. Can corporate men have feelings of self-worth independent of their organizational roles.
15. What can we learn about men's role as sons, friends, and extended family?

Pursuing this research agenda with both qualitative and quantitative approaches would help portray men as whole people. All too often men seem narrowly focused on work. Although corporate men are generally positive about their lives, this satisfaction is thin, and many seem to lack inner contentment. It is crucial to break the link between job and career success and individual positive regard. Corporate men may even participate in their organizations at levels of optimum performance once a healthy work and family balance is achieved. Moving away from norms of corporate masculinity may have several benefits for both corporate men and women. Men may become more effective managers, more available partners and fathers, and less achievement addicted.

ACKNOWLEDGEMENTS

Preparation of this manuscript was supported in part by the Faculty of Administrative Studies, York University, and the College of Business Administration, Oklahoma State University. Graeme MacDermid assisted in collecting material for the chapter; Louise Coutu prepared the manuscript.

REFERENCES

Acker, J. (1990). Hierarchies, jobs, bodies: A theory of gendered organizations. *Gender and Society*, **4**, 139–158.
Alvesson, M. & Billing, Y. D. (1992). Gender and organization: Towards a differentiated understanding. *Organization Studies*, **13**, 73–103.

American Heart Association Heart Facts (1979). Dallas, TX: American Heart Association.

Bardwick, J. (1984). When ambition is no asset. *New Management,* **1**, 22–28.

Barnett, R. C., Davidson, H. & Marshall, N. (1991). Physical symptoms and the interplay of work and family roles. *Health Psychology,* **10**, 94–101.

Bartolome, F. (1972). Executives as human beings. *Harvard Business Review,* **50**, 62–69.

Bartolome, F. & Evans, P. L. (1981) Must success cost so much? *Harvard Business Review,* **59**, 101–112.

Bem, S. (1974). The measurement of psychological androgyny. *Journal of Personality and Social Psychology,* **42**, 155–162.

Bem, S. L. & Lenney, E. (1976). Sex typing and the avoidance of cross-sex behavior. *Journal of Personality and Social Psychology,* **33**, 48–54.

Betz, N. E. & Fitzgerald, L. F. (1987). The career psychology of women. Orlando, Fl: Academic Press.

Bird, S. R. (1996). Welcome to the men's club: Homosociality and the maintenance of hegemonic masculinity. *Gender and Society,* **10**, 120–132.

Bly, R. (1990). *Iron John.* Reading MA: Addison-Wesley.

Brannon, R. (1976). The male sex role: Our culture's blueprint for manhood and what it's done for us lately. In D. David & R. Brannon (Eds), *The Forty-Nine Percent Majority: The Male Sex Role* (pp. 1–48). Reading, MA: Addison-Wesley.

Brod, H. (1987). *The Making of the masculinities: The New Men's Studies.* Boston: Unwin Hyman.

Brod, H. & Kaufman, M. (1994). *Theorizing Masculinities.* Thousand Oaks, CA: Sage.

Brooks, G. R. & Silverstein, L. S. (1995). Understanding the dark side of masculinity: An interactive systems model. In R. F. Levant & W. S. Pollack (Eds), *A New Psychology of Men* (pp. 280–333). New York: Basic Books.

Brooks, P. (1977). Whatever happened to following in Dad's footsteps? *TWA Ambassador.* May.

Burke, R. J. & Black, S. (1997). Save the males: Backlash in organizations. *Journal of Business Ethics,* **16**, 933–942.

Burke, R. J. & Bradshaw, P. (1981). Occupational and life stress and the family. *Small Group Behavior,* **12**, 329–375.

Burke, R. J. & Deszca, E. (1982). Type A behaviour and career success and personal failure. *Journal of Occupational Behavior,* **3**, 161–170.

Burke, R. J. & Greenglass, e. R. (1987). Work and family. In C. L. Cooper & I. T. Robertson (eds), *International Review of Industrial and Organizational Psychology* (Vol. 2, pp. 273–320). New York: Wiley.

Burke, R. J. & Weir, T. (1977). Working men as fathers of adolescents. *School Guidance Worker,* **33**, 4–9.

Burke, R. J. & Weir, T. (1980). The Type A experience. Occupational and life demands, satisfaction and well-being. *Journal of Human Stress,* **6**, 28–38.

Burke, R. J., Weir, T. & DuWors, R. E. (1979). Type A behavior of administrators and wives' reports of marital satisfaction and well-being. *Journal of Applied Psychology,* **64**, 57–65.

Burrell, G. (1984). Sex and organizational analysis. *Organization Studies,* **5**, 97–118.

Burton, C. (1992). Merit and gender: Organizations and the mobilization of masculine bias. In A. J. Mills & P. Tancred (Eds) *Gendering Organizational Analysis* (pp. 185–196). Newbury Park, CA: Sage.

Butts, D. & Whitty, M. (1993). Why do men work? Money, power, success and deeper values. *Masculinities,* **1**, 35–33.

Cheng, C. (1996). *Masculinities in Organizations.* Thousand Oaks, CA: Sage.

Chesney, M. & Rosenman, R. H. (1980). Type A behavior in the work setting. In C. L. Cooper & R. Payne (Eds), *Current Concerns in Occupational Stress* (pp. 187–212). New York: Wiley.

Cohen, T. F. (1993). What do fathers provide? Reconsidering the economic and nurturant dimensions of men as parents. In J. Hood (Ed.), *Men, Work and Family* (pp. 1–22). Newbury Park, CA: Sage.

Collinson, D. & Hearn, J. (1994). Naming men as men: Implications for work organization and management. *Gender, Work and Organization,* **1**, 2–22.

Collinson, D. L. & Hearn, J. (1995). Men managing leadership? Men and women of the corporation revisited. *International Review of Women and Leadership,* **1**, 1–24.

Collinson, D. L. & Hearn, J. (1996). *Men as Managers, Managers as Men: Critical Perspectives on Men, Masculinities and Managements.* London: Sage.

Crowley, T. (1993). The lie of entitlement. In E. Buckwald, P. R. Fletcher & M. Roth (Eds), *Transforming a Rape Culture* (pp. 341–354). Minneapolis, MN: Milkweed Editions.

Cunningham, A. (1986). In P. Frost, V. Mitchell & W. Nord (Eds), *Organizational Reality: Reports from the Firing Line* (3rd edn, pp. 250–260). Glenview, IL: Scott, Foresman.

Daly, K. (1993). Reshaping fatherhood: Finding the models. *Journal of Family Issues,* **14**, 510–530.

David, D. & Brannon, R. (Eds) (1976). *The Forty-Nine Percent Majority: The Male Sex Role,* Reading, MA: Addison-Wesley.

Easthope, A. (1990). *What a Man Gotta do? The Masculine Myth in Popular Culture.* Cambridge, MA: Unwin, Hyman.

Ehrenreich, B. (1983). *The Hearts of Men: American Dreams and the Flight from Commitment.* New York: Anchor Press.

Ehrenreich, B. (1989). A feminist's view of the new man. In M. Kimmel & M. A. Messner (Eds), *Men's Lives* (pp. 34–43). New York: Macmillan.

Eisler, R. M. (1995). The relationship between masculine gender role stress and men's health risk: The validation of a construct. In R. F. Levant & W. S. Pollack (Eds), *A New Psychology of Men* (pp. 207–225). New York: Basic Books.

Fagenson, E. A. (1989). The mentor advantage: Perceived career/job experiences of protégés vs non-protégés. *Journal of Organizational Behavior,* **10**, 309–320.

Fagenson, E. A. (1990) Perceived masculine and feminine attributes examined as a function of individual's sex and level in the organizational power hierarchy. *Journal of Applied Psychology,* **72**, 204–211.

Falbo, T., Hagen, M. D. & Linimon, D. (1982). The cost of selecting power bases or messages with the opposite sex. *Sex Roles,* **8**, 147–151.

Fasteau, M. F. (1974). *The Male Machine.* New York: McGraw-Hill.

Feinberg, M. R. (1980). *Corporate Bigamy: How to Resolve the Conflict Between Work and Family.* New York: Morrow.

Ferguson, K. (1984). *The Feminist Case Against Bureaucracy.* Philadelphia: Temple University Press.

Freeman, J. (1979). *Women: A Feminist Perspective* (2nd edn) Palo Alto, CA: Maryfield.

Friedman, M. & Rosenman, R. (1974). *Type A Behaviour and Your Heart.* New York: Knopf.

Friedman, M. & Ulmer, D. (1984). *Treating Type A Behavior and Your Heart.* New York: Knopf.

Fromm, E. (1974) *Man for Himself.* New York: Rinehart.

Fromm, E. (1976). *To Have or To Be?* New York: Harper & Row.

Frost, P., Mitchell, V. & Nord, W. (Eds) (1986). *Organizational Reality: Reports from the Firing Line* (3rd Edn) Glenview, IL: Scott, Foresman.

Gaylin, W. (1992). *The Male Ego.* New York: Viking.

Gayton, W. F., Havo, G., Baird, J. G. & Ozman, K. (1983). Psychological androgyny and assertiveness in females. *Psychological Reports,* **52**, 283–285.

Gerson, K. (1993). *No Man's Land: Men's Changing Commitments to Family and Work.* New York: Basic Books.

Gould, R. E. (1974). Measuring masculinity by the size of a paycheque. In J. Pleck & J. Sawyer (Eds), *Men and Masculinity* (pp. 96–100). Englewood Cliffs, NJ: Prentice-Hall.

Greiff, B. X. & Munter, P. K. (1980). *Trade-offs: Executive Family and Organizational Life.* New York: New American Library.

Harrison, J. C. (1978). Warning: The male role may be hazardous to your health. *Journal of Social Issues, 34,* 65–86.

Harrison, J., Chin, J. & Ficarrotto, T. (1989). Warning: Masculinity may be dangerous to your health. In M. S. Kimmel & M. A. Messner (Eds), *Men's Lives* (pp. 296–309). New York: Macmillan.

Hearn, J. C. (1992). Changing men and changing management: A review of issues and actions. *Women in Management Review, 7,* 3–8.

Hearn, J. (1994). Changing men and changing managements: Social change, social research and social action. In M. Davidson & R. J. Burke (Eds), *Women in Management: Current Research Issues* (pp. 192–209). London: Paul Chapman.

Hearn, T. (1989). Men, masculinities and leadership: Changing patterns and new initiatives. *Equal Opportunities International, 8,* 3–11.

Henry, W. L. (1961). Conflict, age and the executive. *Business Topics, 9,* 15–25.

Hochschild, A. (1989). *The Second Shift.* New York: Viking.

Hood, J. C. (1992). *Men, Work and Family.* Newbury Park, CA: Sage.

Howard, J. M., Cunningham, d. A. & Rechnitzer, P. A. (1977). Work patterns associated with Type A behavior: A managerial population. *Human Relations, 36,* 825–836.

Jagaciniski, L. M. (1987). Androgyny in a male-dominated field: The relationship of sex-typed traits to performance and satisfaction in engineering. *Sex Roles, 17,* 529–547.

Johnson, N. B. & Scandura, T. A. (1994). The effect of membership and sex-role style on male–female earnings. *Industrial Relations, 33,* 263–274.

Jourard, S. M. (1964). Some lethal aspects of the male role. In S. M. Jourand, *The Transparent Self* (pp. 46–55). Princeton, NJ: Van Nostrand.

Kanter, R. M. (1977). *Men and Women of the Corporation.* New York: Basic Books.

Kaufman, M. (1993). *Cracking the Armor.* Toronto: Viking.

Keen, S. (1991). *Fire in the Belly.* New York: Bantam Books.

Keillor, G. (1993). *The Book of Guys.* New York: Penguin.

Kiechel, W. III (1989). The workaholic generation. *Fortune, 119* (April), 50–62.

Kimmel, M. S. (1987). *Changing Men: New Directions in Research on Men and Masculinity.* Newbury Park, CA: Sage.

Kimmel, M. S. (1993). What do men want? *Harvard Business Review, 71,* 50–63.

Kimmel, M. S. (1996). *Manhood in America.* New York: Free Press.

Kimmel, M. S. & Messner, M. A. (1989). *Men's Lives.* New York: Macmillan.

Kofodimos, J. (1993). *Balancing Act.* San Francisco, CA: Jossey-Bass.

Korabik, K. (1990). Androgyny and leadership style. *Journal of Business Ethics, 9,* 283–292.

Korabik, K. & Ayman, R. (1989). Should women managers have to act like men? *Journal of Management Development, 8,* 23–32.

Korman, A. & Korman, R. (1980). *Career Success and Personal Failure.* New York: Prentice-Hall.

Lagace, R. R. & Twible, J. L. (1990). The androgyny level of salespeople: Gooses and ganders, or all geese? *Journal of Social Behavior and Personality, 5,* 641–650.

Levant, R. F. (1995). Toward the reconstruction of masculinity. In R. F. Levant & W. S. Pollack (Eds), *A New Psychology of Men* (pp. 229–251). New York: Basic Books.

Levant, R. F. (1996). The new psychology of men. *Professional Psychology: Research and Practice, 27,* 259–265.

Levant, R. F., Hirsch, L., Celentano, E., Cozza, T., Hill, S., MacEachern, M., Marty, N. & Schnedeker, J. (1992). The male role: An investigation of norms and stereotypes. *Journal of Mental Health Counseling*, **14**, 325–337.

Levinson, D. J., Darrow, C., Klein, E., Levinson, M. & McKee, B. (1978). *The Seasons of a Man's Life*. New York: Knopf.

Luthans, F. (1988). Successful vs effective real managers. *Academy of Management Executive*, **2**, 127–132.

Macoby, M. (1976). *The Gamesman*. New York: Simon & Schuster.

Machlowitz, M. (1985). *Workaholics: Living with Them, Working with Them*. Reading, MA: Addison-Wesley.

Maier, M. (1991). The dysfunctions of 'corporate masculinity': Gender and diversity issues in organizational development. *Journal of Management in Practice*, **8**, 49–63.

Maier, M. (1993). 'Am I the only one who wants to launch?' Corporate masculinity and the Space Shuttle 'Challenger' disaster. *Masculinities*, **1**, 34–45.

Maier, M. (1992). Evolving the paradigms of management in organizations: A gender analysis. *Journal of Management Systems*, **4**, 29–45.

Maier, M. (1994). Save the males: Reflections on white male privileges in organizations. Paper presented at the New York State Political Science Association 48th Annual Meeting. Albany, NY, April.

Maier, M. (1996). Confronting the (f)laws of the pyramid: The enduring legacy of the space shuttle Challenger disaster. *Academy of Management Best Paper Proceedings*, 403–407.

Maier, M. (1997). Gender equity, organizational transformation and Challenger. *Journal of Business Ethics*, **16**, 943–962.

Marshall, S. J. & Wijting, J. P. (1980). Relationships of achievement motivation and sex role identity to college women's career orientation. *Journal of Vocational Behavior*, **16**, 299–311.

Maupin, R. J. (1986). The impact of sex-role characteristics on the job satisfaction and success of women CPAs. *The Women CPA*, **48**, 35–39.

Maupin, R. J. & Lehman, C. R. (1994). Talking heads: Stereotypes, status, sex-roles and satisfaction of female and male auditors. *Accounting, Organizations and Society*, **19**, 427–437.

McClelland, R. J. (1979). *Power: The Inner Experience*. New York: Irvington.

McClelland, D. C., Coleman, C., Finn, K. & Winter, D. G. (1976). Motivation and maturity patterns in marital success. Cambridge, MA: Harvard University Laboratory for Social Relations.

McClelland, D. C., Davis, W. N., Kalin, R. & Warner, E. (1972). *The Drinking Man*. New York: Free Press.

McIntosh, P. (1989). White privilege: Unpacking the invisible knapsack. *Peace and Freedom, July–August*, 10–12.

Mettlin, C. (1976). Occupational careers and the prevention of coronary-prone behavior. *Social Science and Medicine*, **10**, 367–372.

Mills, A. J. & Tancred, P. S. (1992). *Gendering Organizational Analysis*. Newbury Park, CA: Sage.

Motowidlo, S. J. (1982). Sex-role orientation and behaviour in a work setting. *Journal of Personality and Social Psychology*, **42**, 935–945.

Newsweek (1991). Drums, sweat and tears, 24 June, 46–51.

Norris, J. M. & Wylie, A. M. (1995). Gender stereotyping of the managerial role among students in Canada and the United States. *Group and Organization Management*, **20**, 167–182.

O'Neill, J. M., Good, G. E. & Holmes, S. (1995). Fifteen years of theory and research on men's gender role conflict: New paradigms for empirical research. In R. F. Levant & W. S. Pollack (Eds), *A New Psychology of Men* (pp. 164–206). New York: Basic Books.

O'Reilly, B. (1990). Why grade 'A' Execs get an 'F' as parents. *Fortune*, 1 January, 36–39, 42, 43, 46.

Ogilvie, B. L. & Porter, A. I. (1974). Business career as treadmill to oblivion: The allure of cardiovascular death. *Human Resources Management*, 7, 14–18.

Orlofsky, J. L. & Stake, J. E. (1981). Psychological masculinity and femininity: Relationship to striving and self concept in the achievement and interpersonal domains. *Psychology of Women Quarterly*, 6, 218–233.

Orton, R. S. (1993). Outside in: A man in the movement: In E. Buckwald, P. R. Fletchedr & M. Rother (Eds), *Transforming a Rape Culture* (pp. 237–246). Minneapolis, MN: Milkweed Editions.

Paley, V. G. (1984). *Boys and Girls: Superheroes in the Doll Corner*. Chicago: University of Chicago Press.

Piotrkowski, C. S. (1978). *Work and the Family System*. New York: Free Press.

Pleck, J. H. (1981). *The Myth of Masculinity*. Cambridge, MA: MIT Press.

Pleck, J. H. (1995). The gender role strain paradigm: An update. In R. F. Levant & W. S. Pollack (Eds), *A New Psychology of Men* (pp. 11–32). New York: Basic Books.

Pollack, W. S. (1995). No man is an island: Toward a new psychoanalytic psychology of men. In R. F. Levant & W. S Pollack (Eds), *A New Psychology Of Men* (pp. 33–67). New York: Basic Books.

Porter, G. (1996). Organizational impact of workaholism: Suggestions for researching the negative outcomes of excessive work: *Journal of Occupational Health Psychology*, 1, 70–84.

Powell, G. N. & Butterfield, D. A. (1979). The 'good manager': Masculine or androgynous? *Academy of Management Journal*, 22, 395–403.

Powell, G. N. & Butterfield, D. A. (1984). The 'good manager': Sex-typed, androgynous, or likeable? *Sex Roles*, 14, 1187–1198.

Powell, G. N. & Butterfield, D. A. (1989). The 'Good Manager': Did adrogyny fare better in the 1980s? *Groups and Organization Studies*, 14, 216–233.

Price, V. A. (1982). The Type A behavior pattern: A cognitive social learning model. *Journal of Occupational Behavior*, 3, 119–130.

Rifkin, J. (1987). *Time Wars: The Primary Conflict in Human History*. New York: Touchstone.

Rosenkrantz, P., Vogel, S., Bee, H., Broverman, I. & Broverman, D. (1968). Sex-role stereotypes and self-concepts in college students. *Journal of Consulting and Clinical Psychology*, 32, 287–295.

Rosenman, R. H., Brand, R. J., Jenkins, C. D., Friedman, M., Strauss, R. & Wurm, M. (1975). Coronary heart disease in the Western Collaborative Group Study: Final follow-up experience of eight and one-half years. *Journal of the American Medical Association*, 233, 872–877.

Rosenman, R. H., Friedman, M., Strauss, R., Jenkins, C. D., Zysanski, S. J. & Wurm, M. (1966). Coronary disease in the Western Collaborative Group Study: A follow-up experience of two years. *Journal of the American Medical Association*, 195, 86–92.

Rosenman, R. H., Friedman, M., Strauss, R., Jenkins, C. D., Zysanski, S. J. & Wurm, M. (1970). Coronary disease in the Western Collaborative Group Study: A follow-up experience of four and one-half years. *Journal of Chronic Disease*, 23, 170–175.

Sawyer, J. (1970). On male liberation. *Liberation*, 15, 32–33.

Scandura, T. A. & Ragins, B. R. (1993). The effects of sex and gender role orientation on mentorships in male-dominated occupations. *Journal of Vocational Behavior*, 43, 251–265.

Schaef, A. W. & Fassel, D. (1988). *The Addictive Organizaiton*. San Francisco: Harper.

Schor, J. (1991). *The Overworked American: The Unexpected Decline of Leisure*. New York: Basic Books.

Silverstein, O. & Rashbaum, B. (1994). *The Courage to Raise Good Men*. New York: Viking.

Slavin, W. (1972). The theme of feminine evil: The image of women in male fantasy and its effect on attitudes and behavior. Unpublished Ph.D. dissertation, Harvard University.

Sostek, A. & Sherman, S. (1977). Report on children of executives. *Behavioral Science*, **8**, August.

Spence, J. T. & Helmreich, R. L. (1978). *Masculinity and Femininity: Psychological Dimensions, Correlates, and Antecedents*, Austin, TX: University of Texas Press.

Spence, J. T. & Robbins, A. S. (1992). Workaholism definition, measurement and preliminary results. *Journal of Personality Assessment*, **58**, 160–178.

Steiner, J. S. (1972). What price success? *Harvard Business Review*, **50**, 69–74.

Stewart, A. J. & Rubin, Z. (1976). Power motivation in the dating couple. *Journal of Personality and Social Psychology*, **34**, 305–309.

Tannen, D. (1990). *You Just Don's Understand*. New York: Morrow.

Thompson, E. H. & Pleck, J. H. (1987). Reformulating the male role. In M. S. Kimmel (ed.), *Changing Men* (pp. 25–36). Newbury Park, CA: Sage.

Thompson, E. H. & Pleck, J. H. (1995). Masculine ideology: A review of research instrumentation on men and masculinities. In R. F. Levant & W. S. Pollack (Eds), *A New Psychology of Men* (pp. 129–163). New York: Basic Books.

Valliant, G. (1977). *Adaptation to Life*. Boston: Little, Brown.

Walker, E. J. (1976). Till business us do part. *Harvard Business Review*, **54**, 94–101.

Weiss, R. S. (1990). *Staying the Course: The Emotional and Social Lives of Men who Do Well at Work*. New York: Free Press.

West, C. & Zimmerman, D. H. (1991). Doing gender. In J. Lorber & S. A. Farrell (Eds), *The Social Construction of Gender* (pp. 13–37). Newbury Park, CA: Sage.

Williams, R. (1989). *The Trusting Heart: Great news about Type A behavior*. New York: Random House.

Williams, R. & Williams, V. (1993). *Anger Kills*. New York: Random House.

Winter, D. G. (1973). *The Power Motive*. New York: Free Press.

Winter, D. G., Stewart, A. J. & McClelland, D. C. (1977). Husband's motives and wife's career level. *Journal of Personality and Social Psychology*, **35**, 159–166.

Woititz, J. G. (1987). *Home Away from Home*. Pompano Beach, FL: Health Communications.

Wong, P. T. P., Kettlewell, G. & Sproule, C. F. (1985). On the importance of being masculine: Sex role, attribution and women's career achievement. *Sex Roles*, **12**, 757–769.

Part III

INDIVIDUAL/ORGANIZATIONAL
ADJUSTMENT

Chapter 8

DRUG AND ALCOHOL PROGRAMS IN THE WORKPLACE: A REVIEW OF RECENT LITERATURE

Michael M. Harris
University of Missouri
and
Michael L. Trusty
Anheuser–Busch Companies

INTRODUCTION

Although workplace drug and alcohol programs have become quite common in the USA, Industrial/Organizational (I/O) psychologists have played a relatively minor role in this area. The purpose of this chapter is to acquaint and update I/O psychologists on issues and problems in this area. The present chapter focuses on research published towards the end of 1991 through 1995. Readers interested in a review covering an earlier period of time should examine Harris and Heft (1992).

The chapter is divided into three major sections. First, research on workplace drug testing programs will be discussed. Second, literature on Employee Assistance Programs (EAPs) will be summarized. Following each of these sections, suggestions for future research will be provided. Finally, we conclude with a review of research on drug and alcohol programs in parts of the world besides North America, and offer a brief overview of legal issues affecting workplace drug and alcohol programs.

We turn now to workplace drug testing. Following a brief introduction to this topic, we review research on different types of drug tests, and summarize findings regarding the relationship between drug use and job outcomes. We then proceed to describe literature on applicant/employee reactions to drug screening programs. We conclude with a discussion of criticisms of drug tests, and offer suggestions for needed research on this topic.

Drug and Alcohol Programs in the Workplace: A Review of Recent Literature by Michael M. Harris and Michael L. Trusty taken from IRIOP 1997 v12, Edited by Cary L. Cooper and Ivan T. Robertson: © 1997 John Wiley & Sons, Ltd

WORKPLACE DRUG TESTING

Introduction

Harris and Heft (1992) found that a large number of companies in the US used drug testing, and that researchers had considered several different types of tests, the validity and cost-effectiveness of drug screening, and applicant/employee reactions to these tests. A review of recent literature indicates that despite some controversies regarding such tests (e.g. see below), drug testing has not waned. Murphy and Thornton (1992), for example, surveyed 324 companies that recruited students from Colorado State University (of which 57% responded) and found that 41% tested candidates and/or employees for drug use. Interestingly, nearly a third of the companies with a drug testing program did random testing; almost 70% reported that a positive test result was confirmed by a second test. Murphy and Thornton reported results on a number of other interesting issues, such as the policies followed if an employee fails the test, test administration and program management, and general policies regarding drug screening. Readers interested in establishing drug testing programs and policies will find this paper of value in understanding what other organizations are doing.

Types of Tests

Harris and Heft (1992) categorized drug tests into three types: physiological, paper-and-pencil, and impairment-based measures. They noted that the first category was by far the most popular, and included procedures such as urinalysis, blood, and hair tests, as well as other less well-known measures (e.g. saliva tests). Use of paper-and-pencil measures appeared to be far less common; impairment tests, which generally relied on hand–eye coordination tasks, were recommended by some drug testing critics, but relatively little seemed to be known about them. Following Harris and Heft, we begin with a review of the physiological tests, followed by discussion of paper-and-pencil measures and impairment tests.

Physiological

Harris and Heft (1992, 1993) observed that urinalysis was, despite some problems, the most popular procedure for drug screening. Simmering and Ones (1994) reviewed numerous other physiological screening procedures, including hair analysis, plasma or blood analysis, fingernail tests and saliva analysis. Each procedure had advantages and disadvantages. Perhaps because urinalysis testing is the most popular, and many of the initial problems with this technique (e.g. poor reliability) have been reduced (Harris & Heft, 1993), no new research on urinalysis was located. However, a number of studies and reports on hair testing were found. These are summarized next.

Hair testing

Hair testing has a number of potential advantages over urinalysis. One major advantage is that the collection of the specimen is much less invasive than urinalysis. Hair also requires no special storage, while urine samples do. Hair samples last considerably longer than do urine samples. Finally, hair samples can determine use of drugs several months prior to the test and can indicate the amount and patterns of drugs used (Mieczkowski, 1992; Simmering & Ones, 1994). On the other hand, hair tests do have some shortcomings. Hair tests will not indicate very recent drug use (e.g. within five to seven days). When head hair is not available, axillary and pubic hair must be used, which may absorb drug traces differently. Third, questions have been raised as to whether passive exposure can affect the hair test, the impact of various approaches to try to 'beat' the test (e.g. washing of one's hair), and whether different types of hair (e.g. fine versus coarse) will affect the analysis (Mieczkowski, 1992). Major groups, such as the National Institute for Drug Abuse, have concluded that insufficient evidence exists to date for hair testing to be accepted as an appropriate method for drug screening (Normand, Lempert, & O'Brien, 1994). The chief concern raised by these groups is that there are no generally accepted analytic procedures or standards for hair tests.

Although we found no studies in the workplace setting, some studies conducted in the penal system have compared hair tests to urinalysis. For example, Feucht, Stephens, and Walker (1994) found that hair analysis identified many more cocaine users (50) than did urinalysis (8), as did Mieczkowski and Newell (1993). However, equal numbers of marijuana users were identified by both procedures. The authors concluded that hair analysis may be more effective in identifying cocaine users than marijuana users. Because there was no way to determine actual drug use in these populations, an alternative explanation is that the hair test leads to more false positives than the urinalysis test.

In sum, despite increased interest in the hair test, it remains to be seen whether this procedure really is an improvement over urinalysis. Anecdotally, we know of at least one large organization that is using hair tests. Whether such tests become as commonly used as the urinalysis test remains to be seen.

Paper-and-pencil tests

Harris and Heft (1992) summarized a few papers addressing paper-and-pencil tests of alcohol and drug use. They concluded that 'results across studies are inconsistent, few validity studies have been published or even reported' (p.247) and many issues remained as to their use in the workplace. An examination of recent literature showed this state of affairs has changed little. Schmidt, Viswesvaran, and Ones (1993) reported a meta-analysis of the validity of integrity tests for predicting drug and alcohol use. Based on 50 studies ($N = 25\ 594$), they found corrected validities to range between 0.23 to 0.48 depending on the nature of the sample (e.g. employee versus student) and the specific criterion (i.e. alcohol versus illegal drug). In all cases, the lower 90% credibility value was greater than zero. They concluded that the operational validity is probably 0.30, and that the tests were of value in reducing substance abuse among employees. The studies used for the meta-analysis, however, suffered from at least two shortcomings. First, all of the studies were based on concurrent validation strategies, although predictive studies are more relevant (Schmidt, Vis- wesvaran, & Ones, 1993). Second, almost all of the studies used self- admissions as criteria. Studies using external criteria may reveal different results (Sackett & Harris, 1984).

Marcoulides, Mills, and Unterbrink (1993) examined the Drug Avoidance Scale (DAS), a paper-and-pencil test, and its relationship with a urinalysis test, for 246 job applicants for a security service company. Marcoulides, Mills and Unterbrink indicated that there was a strong relationship between the DAS and the urinalysis test, but did not provide an effect size.

In sum, despite some interest in paper-and-pencil measures of drug and alcohol use, there appears to be very little new here. Issues such as faking would need to be carefully considered with such measures. It seems likely that at least for the time being, companies will continue to rely on measures other than self-reported attitudes towards drugs or self-reported use.

Impairment-based tests

Harris and Heft (1992) noted that some critics of drug testing advocated an impairment-based test, which would seem to provide the most direct assessment of performance problems. However, like Harris and Heft, we were unable to locate any scientific studies examining such a test. Comer (1993) described a number of potential advantages of one impairment-based test, which required employees to use a joy stick to maintain a cursor in the center of a video screen (readers may note that this seems quite similar to certain video games!). The advantages of this device included minimum testing time (about one minute), reasonable costs (about $100–$200 per employee per year), immediate results, and sensitivity to a wide variety of work impairments (Comer, 1993). Problems with the technique clearly remain, however. The general manager of a transportation company that used this impairment-based test found that the difficulty of the test varied from day to day, which would probably cause frequent false positives and false negatives. The general manager even reported that he passed the test after he had, in his opinion, become too intoxicated to drive a vehicle (Comer, 1994). Hence, anecdotal evidence indicates that impairment-based tests also have shortcomings.

Is Drug Use Related to Job Outcomes?

Although there have been numerous studies addressing the relationship between drug use and job outcomes, the literature is inconsistent. One reason for the inconsistency is that a number of different criteria have been examined, and as described below, the relationships appear to differ from criterion to criterion. Second, some studies have controlled for various factors (e.g. age) in assessing the relationship between drug use and job outcomes, while others have not. Third, even if a statistical relationship is located between drug use and job outcomes, the *size* of the relationship may be small (Harris & Heft, 1993). What follows next is an overview of research on drug use with different criteria, including absenteeism/turnover, accidents, other job behavior, and wages.

Drug use and absenteeism/turnover

A number of studies, including McDaniel (1988), Kandel and Yamaguchi (1987), and Zwerling, Ryan, and Orav (1990), have examined the relationship between drug use and turnover. Although these studies have used a variety of different measures of drug use (e.g. self-report, urinalysis), they consistently report significant relationships with turnover (Normand, Lempert, & O'Brien, 1994). However, examination of the magnitude of this relationship indicates that it is relatively small; for example, McDaniel reported a correlation of 0.08 between self-reported drug use and turnover. Harris and Heft (1993) estimated a correlation of 0.04 between urinalysis tests and involuntary turnover in Normand, Salyards, and Mahoney's (1990) study.

Accidents

While many people assume that drug and alcohol use is a frequent cause of workplace accidents, research shows mixed findings regarding the relationship between drug use and accidents. For example, in similar studies of US Postal workers, Normand, Salyards, and Mahoney (1990) did not find a relationship between drug use and accidents, while Zwerling, Ryan, and Orav (1990) reported a significant relationship between them. Normand, Lempert, and O'Brien (1994) provided a comprehensive review of this literature, and reported mixed results as to the relationship between drug use and accidents. They offered several reasons for this. For example, workplace accidents are relatively rare; as discussed below, the number of employees working while intoxicated is reasonably small, though it probably differs from industry to industry. Moreover, workers who are impaired may simply miss work or avoid performing dangerous tasks. Yet another possibility is that the emphasis on drug and alcohol prevention and testing and extensive publicity to various workplace accidents (e.g. the *Exxon Valdez* oil tanker incident in 1989) has greatly reduced the number of workers who are intoxicated on the job. Finally, Normand, Lempert, and O'Brien (1994) suggested that alcohol and drug use was related to accident rate in the transportation industry; however there was less evidence of this relationship in other industries. Thus, while there is some evidence for a relationship between drug and alcohol use and accidents, the magnitude appears to be smaller than people have assumed.

Other job behavior

Some recent research has examined the relationship between drug use and employees' job attitudes. Lehman and Simpson (1992) found that self-reported drug use was significantly related to a variety of self-reported behavior on the job, including antagonistic work behavior (e.g. arguing with coworkers), even after controlling for factors such as job satisfaction and pay level. However, all of the data were based on self-reports.

Wages

While drug and alcohol use has been found either to be significantly related or not at all related to higher turnover and other problems at the workplace, some research has found greater drug use to be related to higher wages earned by employees. Gill and Michaels (1992) found that after controlling for self-selection effects as well as various demographic factors, users of illegal drugs on average earned higher wages than non-users. Further, users of 'hard' drugs were more likely to be employed than workers who did not use such drugs. Register and Williams (1992) found that when on-the-job and long-term marijuana use was controlled for, general marijuana use was related to higher wages. However, both on-the-job and long-term marijuana use were associated with lower wages. Register and Williams interpreted their results as suggesting that 'after-hours use [of marijuana] might actually increase the worker's productivity on the following day if such use tends to reduce stress and anxiety' (p. 445).

In sum, different studies have come to different conclusions about the relationship between drug use and job outcomes. Harris and Heft (1993) raised a number of questions about this relationship relative to other tests. They pointed out that if the purpose of the drug test is for preemployment screening, there may be other methods (e.g. cognitive ability tests) that are just as valid, if not more valid. They also asked whether drug testing would provide *incremental* validity over other tests; for example, if an organization already uses a cognitive ability test, the drug test may provide little or no additional validity. In defense of the use of drug testing, however, Harris and Heft (1993) pointed to certain advantages of this approach over other traditional tests, such as greater acceptability to unions and less concern over adverse impact problems. Third, they questioned whether there is a linear relationship between drug use and job outcomes. That is, they suggested that low drug use may not negatively affect performance, such as suggested by Register and Williams (1992). In response to this criticism, Harris and Heft (1993) cited a study by Blank and Fenton (1989) that supported a linear relationship such that even low levels of drug use were associated with higher rates of turnover compared with non-drug users.

Why is Drug Use Associated with Workplace Problems?

Assuming that drug use is in fact associated with workplace problems, such as turnover, accidents, and other behavior, some have asked *why* this relationship exists. Harris and Heft (1992) offered two possible explanations. One, use of drugs may create physiological and behavioral changes. Secnd, drug use and job behavior may be related because they are both caused by a third variable, such as a propensity for deviant behavior. Or, both explanations may be right (Normand, Lempert, & O'Brien, 1994, p.132). One recent study addressed these possibilities. Holcom and Lehman (1995) obtained self-reports of substance use, job performance, and general deviance (e.g. attitudes toward risk-taking and non-conformity). Although substance use was highly correlated with job performance, a structural equations model revealed that substance use was not related to job performance once general deviance was taken into account. This study, then, supports the second explanation for a link between drug use and job behavior, namely, that they have a spurious relationship.

Applicant/Employee Reactions

Harris and Heft (1993) reviewed a number of studies addressing applicant and employee reactions to drug testing programs, and highlighted conflicting results. Specifically, Crant and Bateman (1990) found that applicants were less favorably predisposed to an organization with a drug testing program; Rosse and Ringer (1991) found that the presence of such a program had little or no effect on subjects. Harris and Heft offered two methodological reasons to explain the differences. Harris and Heft also reviewed literature suggesting that the nature of the job affects perceptions of the drug screening, and concluded that perceived danger of the job, particularly to the public, was a major determinant of its acceptability. Finally, Harris and Heft noted two studies that had been done in an actual setting. One of these studies compared the importance of procedural justice issues to perceptions of outcome fairness, and found that the former was more critical. A second study, which involved college students' drug testing, revealed that despite many concerns on the part of participants, they felt that the program offered some advantages (e.g. existence of the drug test provided a socially acceptable reason for not using drugs). Harris and Heft (1993) offered several suggestions for future research, including application of research on recruitment, continued investigation of the specific components that affect employee perceptions, and greater use of field rather than laboratory studies.

Recent research on employee and applicant reactions to drug testing has produced some interesting results. First, Mastrangelo (1995) examined undergraduate students' reactions to companies with and without preemployment and random drug screening. Contrary to earlier studies, he found that subjects generally *preferred* an organization that had random drug screening. He also reported a significant interaction with attitudes towards drug testing, such that subjects who favored drug testing were far more favorable towards a company that did such screening. Subjects who were extremely opposed to drug testing were more favorable towards companies that did not have such programs. Kravitz, Stinson, and Chavez (1994) compared college students' ratings of the overall appropriateness and invasiveness of a variety of employment procedures, including interviews, references, personality tests, and cognitive ability tests. They found that averaged across different target jobs (e.g. production worker, manager), a drug test was seen as only slightly less appropriate than a job skills test and accomplishment record, and more appropriate than many other devices including references, cognitive ability tests, and personality measures. In terms of invasiveness, a drug test was about average compared to other procedures: it was viewed as more invasive than references or a cognitive ability test, but less invasive than an honesty test, personality measure, or criminal record check.

Based on these results, it would appear that the use of drug testing has become more acceptable to employees and job applicants. Indeed, contrary to earlier studies, the results from Kravitz, Stinson, and Chavez (1994) suggested that the drug test appears to be at least as well regarded as tools commonly recommended by I/O psychologists, such as personality and cognitive ability tests. Whether this indicates that people have come to see the advantages of drug testing, have become resigned to such procedures, or some traditional tests are held in much lower regard than I/O psychologists realize, is unclear. In support of the first explanation, Verespej (1992) reported a significant decrease in the number of respondents (who were predominantly professional employees and middle- and top-level managers) who regarded drug testing as an invasion of privacy in 1991 compared to a survey done in 1987. Specifically, while 30% viewed drug testing as an invasion of privacy in 1987, fewer than 20% perceived drug testing as an invasion of privacy in 1991. Respondents provided a number of reasons for their support of such screening, including concern over safety, negative impact of drug use on quality and productivity, and perceived financial costs of drug use to the company.

Several recent studies were found that addressed Harris and Heft's (1993) call for further research on the effects of drug testing program features. Crant and Bateman (1993) manipulated the consequence of the testing program (i.e. rehabilitation or termination) and the type of testing (for cause or random). They found that neither factor affected college students' attitudes toward, intention to apply, or willingness to accept a job offer. Raciot and Williams (1993) examined the effect of presence or absence of prior warning of test, testing program consequence (i.e. rehabilitation versus termination), and relevance of safty to the job (i.e. job could lead to serious accidents versus job unlikely to lead to harm) in an experimental design using college students. Raciot and Williams found significant effects of the latter two factors on such variables as the perceived invasiveness and fairness of the testing program; warning did not have a significant effect. Kravitz and Brock (in press) conducted a series of laboratory studies with college students that tested five independent variables: consequences of the testing program (i.e. termination versus rehabilitation), relevance of safety to the job, false positive rate, false negative rate, and the ability of the test to distinguish between current drug impairment and previous drug use. Kravitz and Brock found at least some evidence to support the effect of all five factors on attitudes toward the testing program. Another variable considered by Kravitz and Brock was belief in a just world; as hypothesized, subjects who believed in a just world were more likely to support a drug testing program.

While all of the above studies were performed in a laboratory setting with college students responding to descriptions of hypothetical organizations, Tepper and Braun (1995) examined actual employee reactions to their organizations' random drug testing program. Because the drug testing was required by Federal law, and the respondents worked in jobs where safety issues were of concern, one might expect that reactions would be relatively positive. Mean responses to the three variables which formed the criterion (all of which addressed perceived invasiveness; e.g. 'The drug testing policy in my company is an invasion of privacy'), were roughly neutral. A hierarchical regression analysis indicated that four predictors accounted for 35% of the variance in the criterion: number of times tested (the more often tested, the more negative the reactions), managerial status (managers had more positive attitudes), perceived accuracy (the more accurate the test was perceived to be, the more positive attitudes were), and perceived severity (the more severe the consequences of being drug positive, the more negative the attitudes).

Although the above studies suggest a great deal of congruence between laboratory and field research, Tepper (1994) demonstrated that employees may respond quite differently to a drug screening program, depending on whether or not they have been subjected to the test. In a series of three independent studies, Tepper found that while safety and drug test consequences interacted together to affect perceptions of the program in a laboratory study, a completely different effect was found with employees responding to an actual drug screen. A third study revealed that the dimensions considered by the respondents differ, depending on whether or not they had actually been tested. While employees who had not been tested were most concerned about *distributive* justice aspects, employees who had been tested were more concerned about *procedural* justice aspects.

Drug Testing: An Ongoing Debate

Despite the popularity of workplace drug testing, debate among academics regarding the use of such screening tools has appeared. The arguments against drug testing, and responses to them, are reviewed next.

Drug tests are not valid predictors

Critics of drug testing have argued that evidence for the validity of drug tests is minimal at best (Comer, 1994; Crow & Hartman, 1992; MacDonald, Wells & Fry, 1993). Although the studies reviewed above indicated at least some relationship does exist, the magnitude appears small. In response to this criticism, one might respond that although the relationship is small, there are studies indicating that drug tests are at least somewhat predictive of some job outcomes, including accidents. If we do find that drug tests are predictive of an outcome such as accidents, wouldn't it be unfair to *not* use them? At the same time, as discussed below, several reasons for use of drug testing besides prediction, such as deterrence, have been suggested. Thus, it is possible that drug tests serve some important purposes besides prediction, even though empirical research has not yet been conducted on these issues.

Drug tests are not cost-effective

Even assuming that drug tests are valid predictors of various job outcomes, they may not be cost-effective (Hartman & Crow, 1993; MacDonald, Wells, & Fry, 1993). As summarized by Harris and Heft (1993), the cost-effectiveness or utility of drug testing is a source of much disagreement. Part of the reason for the disagreement is that the two major studies which estimated the cost-effectiveness of drug testing (Normand, Salyards, & Mahoney, 1990 and Zwerling, Ryan, & Orav, 1992) used quite different formulas. Based on their formula, Zwerling, Ryan, and Orav even argued that drug testing was not really cost-effective in Normand, Salyards, and Mahoney's (1990) study. Hartman and Crow (1993) pointed to additional problems with utility analyses, and argued that utility analysis may not provide accurate estimates.

A proponent of drug testing might counter that while utility analysis may not be completely accurate, it is a widely accepted procedure for determining cost-effectiveness (Boudreau, 1991). Moreover, Normand, Salyards, and Mahoney (1990) used standard formulas that have been carefully developed and tested elsewhere (e.g. Cascio, 1987). While certain gains may be slightly overestimated, Normand, Salyards, and Mahoney probably underestimated other gains. From a different perspective, Cavanaugh and Prasad (1994) offered a variety of reasons, besides increased productivity and fewer accidents, as to why companies use drug and alcohol testing. Among the reasons offered are the need to reinforce rationality, uphold moral authority, retain an image of control, and signal corporate responsibility and concern for societal problems. Of course, some might argue that these purposes themselves are misguided or wrong. However, it has been suggested that a preemployment drug testing program may serve as a deterrent, as job candidates who use drugs decide to withdraw from the selection process or simply never apply for the job (Harris & Heft, 1993). Similarly, a random or 'for cause' drug testing program may serve as a deterrent to drug use and serve as a signal to employees that safety is important. Such effects may be difficult to study, but could represent an important organizational benefit.

Drug use is not a prevalent problem

Some have argued that the prevalency of substance use in the workplace is much lower than people think (Crow & Hartman, 1992). The implication is that low prevalence reduces the need for drug testing. This is certainly the case from a predictive viewpoint. Relatedly, some criticize drug testing on the grounds that it ignores other forms of substance abuse, particularly alcohol consumption, that are far more problematic (Comer, 1994).

Normand, Lempert, and O'Brien (1994) provided an excellent summary of research examining the prevalence of substance abuse, including unpublished surveys. Results from a major study, the National Household Survey (conducted in 1990), indicated that for full-time employed workers 18 and older, 7% had used an illicit drug during the past month, while 6.8% indicated heavy alcohol consumption. Workers in some industries reported higher rates of drug and alcohol consumption than others. For example, full-time male workers between the ages of 18 and 34 in the construction industry were the most likely group to take illegal drugs in the past month (20%) and to engage in heavy alcohol use (26%). Professionals were least likely to use illegal drugs (only 9% reported usage); the least likely workers to engage in heavy drinking were in the repair services (9%). Based on these findings, as well as results from other sources, Normand, Lempert, and O'Brien suggested that overall 'approximately 7 percent of workers reported having used an illicit drug and approximately 6 percent reported having drunk heavily in the last month' (p.99). Do these results suggest that drug use is too rare to make a testing program cost effective? Not necessarily. Utility analysis indicates that the cost-effectiveness of a test depends on several factors, only one of which is the base rate (Boudreau, 1991). These data also suggest that certain industries may find greater benefits from a drug testing program than others. It is also interesting that heavy drinking rates were quite comparable to rates of illegal drug use. The assumption, then, that alcohol use is much more of a problem than illicit subtance use may be incorrect.

Drug testing is unfair to applicants and employees

While there are various laws that restrict or even ban the use of drug testing in certain cases, some industries require drug testing (Harris & Heft, 1992).

Several researchers have argued, however, that drug testing is unfair to applicants and employees. There are a number of different points to this objection. First, some argue that applicants and employees should not be required to disclose information about or be subjected to tests for matters not relevant to the company (Comer, 1994). Since drug use after work hours may not have an effect on on-the-job behavior (and even if it does, so do many other activities, such as staying up late at night), this argument suggests that drug testing (other than perhaps 'for cause' reasons) would be unfair, much as asking about a person's age, race, or religion would be deemed irrelevant and unfair. A proponent of drug testing might respond that this issue gets at where one draws the limit between privacy and the company's right to know. While age, race, and religion are personal matters, the fact that one might have committed a crime at some point, for example, is something the company has a right to know. Similarly, illicit drug use, which is a crime in the USA, is something the organization has the right to know about because it may affect work.

Second, some argue that the drug validity evidence that does exist is merely due to a spurious relationship between race, job outcomes, and drug test (Comer, 1994; Horgan, 1990). In response to this claim, Harris and Heft (1993) pointed to research indicating that race neither moderates (e.g. McDaniel, 1988) nor mediates (e.g. Normand, Salyards, & Mahoney, 1990; Zwerling, Ryan, & Orav, 1990) the relationship between drug test and job outcomes. Moreover, critics have not offered empirical data to support the notion of a spurious relationship.

A third point critics raise is that drug testing is disliked by applicants and employees (Comer, 1994). In response to this argument, as reviewed above, recent research indicates that many respondents actually prefer organizations that do drug testing. In addition, research summarized above indicates that employees may feel either positively or negatively about a drug screening program, depending on how it is designed and implemented.

In sum, we agree that drug testing is a debatable issue. Our hope is that the debate serves as an impetus for further empirical research in the area, and as a stimulus for more careful thinking about the advantages and disadvantages of drug testing.

Workplace Drug Testing: Suggestions for Future Research

Based on our review, we have several suggestions for future research on workplace drug testing programs. One area of research that requires further investigation concerns the relationship between drug use and job outcomes. Although this same recommendation was offered by Harris and Heft (1992), more work is still needed on this issue, using a variety of different criteria. It will also be important to continue to examine different demographic, attitudinal, and situational factors that may mediate or moderate this relationship.

Although a relatively large data base has been gathered for some criteria (e.g. accidents), there is a noticeable lack of research for other criteria (e.g. general job performance).

A second important area for research is to compare different tests in terms of reliability, validity, and cost-effectiveness. Far too little is known about how procedures such as urinalysis, hair tests, and paper-and-pencil measures compare along these dimensions. It is possible that the best test to use will depend on the particular purpose. For example, a hair test may be most useful for random tests, while urinalysis might be most appropriate for preemployment screening. Perhaps most importantly, research is needed to examine all possible effects of a drug testing program. For example, do such programs really have a deterrence effect? Do certain types of programs have a negative effect on employee attitudes and behavior (e.g. turnover)?

Third, more research is needed to examine *why* drug use is related to job outcomes. While two possibilities were described here, research on wage advantages of drug users suggests that the linkage may be much more complex. For example, it is possible that while drug use has detrimental effects on certain types of performance (e.g. eye–hand coordination), its relaxant effect faciliates other types of performance.

Fourth, more studies are needed, particularly in actual settings, to understand applicant and employee reactions to drug testing programs. Research on applicant reactions to various tests (e.g., Macan, Avedon, Paese, & Smith, 1994; Smither, Reilly, Millsap, Pearlman, & Stoffey, 1993) has suggested a variety of factors, such as perceived face validity, that affect perceptions. Research comparing different types of drug screening programs (e.g. preemployment testing, random testing, 'for cause' testing) might find that different factors affect perceptions of the tests. Further, research by Tepper (1994) points to the need to separately examine employees who have been tested and those who have not been tested.

Finally, practically all of the published research has examined applicant or employee reactions to *urinalysis tests*. While some researchers have assumed that employees and applicants will react more favorably to alternative tests (e.g. the hair test; an impairment test), there is no empirical research to support those assertions. Field studies regarding this issue are sorely needed.

EMPLOYEE ASSISTANCE PROGRAMS

Harris and Heft (1992) divided research on EAPs into four basic areas: supervisor reactions to EAPs, employee reactions to EAPs, EAP adoption/implementation, and evaluation of EAPs. We first discuss some descriptive information regarding EAPs, followed by a review of recent literature in each of these four areas.

EAPs: Descriptive Information

As reported by Harris and Heft (1992), EAPs have become popular in industry, business, and government in the last few decades; there is no evidence to suggest any change in this state of affairs. According to Blum and Roman (1992), almost half of full-time employees in the USA who are not self-employed have access to an employer-provided EAP. Despite their popularity, research indicates that they are not frequently used. Harley (1991) found that on average, supervisors referred only one subordinate out of 100 over a six year period. Burke (1994) found that fewer than 6% of one company's employees had used the EAP, presumably at any point during their employment with the organization. Park (1992) reported that out of a total employee population of just under 2000, only 621 employees had initiated contact with the EAP staff over the last six years. Assuming the number of employees remained the same over the six years, this represents a usage rate of about 5%, which meshes with the estimate by Blum and Roman (1992). Given that most EAP programs address issues besides drug and alcohol use, such as depression, the percentage of workers using them seems quite low.

In the largest data base of employees using an EAP (Blum & Roman, 1992; 6400 employees who used an EAP from 84 work facilities), there was a nearly even mix of men (45%) and women (55%), most of whom were white (70%) or black (22%). Over half (52%) were married. Employees represented all levels of education, job level, and income. In terms of referral source, employees using the EAP reported a number of agents that were influential in their decision to seek help. The most commonly cited influential agents (in terms of the number of employees reporting) were: self (29%), supervisor (31%), coworker who used the EAP (25%) and coworker who had not used the EAP (25%). The employee's spouse was rated as influential by 19% of the respondents. Interestingly, the company records indicated the following sources for referral agent: self (44%), informal supervisor (16%), formal supervisor (11%), and peer (14%).

Finally, EAP staff diagnosed most clients as having two or more problems. Somewhat surprisingly, the most commonly diagnosed problem was psychological/emotional issues (44% of the clients were diagnosed as such), followed by marital problems (28%) and other family problems (31%). Relatively few clients were diagnosed with either an alcohol or drug problem (16% were diagnosed with an alcohol problem, 3% with a cocaine problem, and 4% with 'other' drug problems). Drug and alcohol use, then, appears to be much less of a factor in EAP use than one would imagine (though a portion of clients came to the EAP because of drug or alcohol use of a family member). One implication is that EAPs are used far more often for problems other than alcohol and drugs. Whether employees are going to other help sources for treatment of alcohol and drug problems, or whether they tend to ignore these problems and avoid seeking help, is unclear.

Supervisor Reactions to EAPs

Harris and Heft (1992) identified a number of studies addressing the role of the supervisor in EAP referrals. Much of this literature was based on a model developed by Gerstein and his colleagues (e.g. Gerstein, 1990), which adapted a bystander intervention theory from social psychology to explain the conditions under which supervisors would be willing to refer a subordinate.

In the last few years, Gerstein and his colleagues continued to examine the role of the supervisor in EAP referrals. Gerstein, Lynn, and Brown (1991) examined the effect of two factors: severity of the employee's problem and type of setting (e.g. school, hospital, or manufacturing business) on subjects' willingness to refer hypothetical employees. Although setting did not affect willingness to refer, the more severe the employee's problem was, the more willing subjects were to refer. Gerstein, Lynn, and Brown (1991) interpreted both results in accord with their theoretical model. Gerstein, Wheeler, and Gaber (1994) found that while a training program on handling troubled employees was not significantly related to number of employees actually referred by the supervisor, span of control was related. That is, in accord with their hypothesis, Gerstein, Wheeler, and Gaber (1994) found that supervisors with a smaller span of control tended to have referred more employees. Gerstein, Moore, Duffey, and Dainas (1993) examined the relationship between the sex of the referring supervisor and the sex of the employee. They found that while there was no main effect of either variable on EAP referrals, the interaction was statistically significant. Thus, female supervisors were more likely to refer women than men to the EAP. However, male supervisors were equally likely to refer men and women. Again, Gerstein et al. (1993) interpreted this result in light of their theoretical model, which suggests that individuals are more likely to help others they feel similar to.

Harley (1991) examined some factors that might precipitate supervisors' referral of an employee to the EAP. He found that job performance and the occurrence of a dramatic event at work involving the subordinate (e.g. arriving at work intoxicated) were significant predictors of supervisors' referral to the EAP. Based on these results, Harley concluded that contrary to EAP philosophy, supervisors use the EAP referral as a last resort, rather than as an early attempt to improve subordinate behavior.

Employee Reactions to EAPs

Harris and Heft (1992) suggested that despite the importance of employee perceptions and attitudes in the decision to use an EAP, there was a dearth of research on this important topic. The little literature that did exist suggested several variables that were important in an employee's decision, such as familiarity with the EAP, confidentiality, and opportunity to attend during work hours.

A number of recent articles were located that addressed employee reactions to an EAP. Two major dependent variables were examined in this line of research: satisfaction with the EAP and willingness to go to the EAP. With regard to the former variable, Burke (1994) found that employees who used the EAP were generally satisfied, with the average response ranging from 3.6 to 4.1 on a 1–5 scale (1 = very dissatisfied; 5 = very satisfied). Park (1992) found that 93% of the employees were either satisfied or very satisfied with the EAP and 91% would ask for additional help from the EAP.

A larger number of studies examined employes' willingness to use an EAP. In perhaps the most sophisticated study of this variable, Milne, Blum, and Roman (1994) tested a structural equation model using five predictors of propensity to use the EAP: confidentiality/trust, familiarity with the EAP, perceived support of top management for the EAP, perceived support of one's supervisor for the EAP, and accessibility of the EAP. Not only did confidentiality/trust have a direct effect on propensity to use the EAP, but it also served as a mediator for all four other predictors. Milne, Blum, and Roman concluded that 'confidence in the EAP is a highly significant contributor to propensity to use the program' (p.140).

Hall, Vacc, and Kissling (1991) examined a plethora of predictors of willingness to use an EAP, including demogrpahic factors (e.g. sex), social support network, attitudes towards the EAP (e.g. perceived efficacy of the EAP), and perceptions of alternative help sources. Although all factors were statistically significant, attitudes towards the EAP comprised the best predictors. Several predicted interactions were also significant.

May (1992) addressed the impact of different referral sources on expectations of the EAP using a laboratory study, in which some subjects were told to imagine that their supervisor had referred them, while the other subjects were told to assume they had self-referred. There was, however, no significant effect of referral source. May offered several possible explanations for the lack of differences, including the artificial nature of the study.

Several studies have examined demographic predictors of employees who use the EAP. Sullivan and Poverny (1992) examined the EAP of a large university located in southern California. They found that in proportion to their numbers, staff tended to utilize the EAP more frequently than faculty. Younger employees tended to use the EAP more frequently than older employees, and professional/supervisory staff were more likely to use the EAP than non-exempt staff. Sullivan and Poverny suggested that some of these patterns may have been due to different health plans, since faculty tended to have a health insurance programs that offered other options (e.g. psychological counseling). Although Gerstein et al. (1993) found that neither employee race nor sex were related to actual EAP use, Gerstein, Wheeler, and Gaber (1994) reported a significant relationship between organizational level and actual EAP use wherein mid-level staff were more likely to use the EAP than were higher-level or lower-level employees.

Evaluation of EAPs

Despite their prevalence, past reviews have noted there is a dearth of rigorous evaluation of EAPs (Harris & Heft, 1992). One of the most widely publicized evaluations was conducted at McDonnell–Douglas. In that study, employees who used the EAP were compared with employees who had received treatment for problems from other sources. The former group was found to have lower absenteeism, fewer terminations, and lower medical costs as compared to the latter group (Author, 1993). Interestingly, the difference between the two groups emerged over several years, rather than immediately. Nevertheless, questions have been raised regarding the methodology used in this study (Normand, Lempert, & O'Brien, 1994). For example, there was no evidence whether these two groups were comparable on variables such as age, sex, and income.

No recent studies were located that provided rigorous evaluations of EAPs. However, several papers were found that examined aspects related to EAP effectiveness. Yu, Chen, Harshman, & McCarthy (1991) compared three groups of employees who sought treatment for substance abuse. Group 1 ($N = 73$) consisted of employees whose treatment costs exceeded $300 the first year of the study and had no additional treatment in the next two years; Group 2 ($N = 18$) consisted of employees whose treatment costs were $300 or more over the three years covered in the study; Group 3 ($N = 32$) consisted of employees who failed to follow through with their treatment or whose treatment costs were less than $300 (e.g. they were unable to obtain much treatment due to scheduling problems). Examination of medical costs for each of the three groups indicated that Group 1 experienced an average decline of 48% in medical expenses, while medical expenses increased for employees in Groups 2 (93%) and 3 (116%). A key implication is that substance abuse treatment may, in the long run, be quite cost-effective. On the other hand, the increase in medical expenses of participants in Group 2 suggests that substance abuse treatment is no automatic panacea. Yu et al. offered several reasons as to why employees in Group 2 showed dramatic increases in medical costs, such as greater reliance on medical treatment and non-random sampling procedures.

Walsh, Hingson, Merrigan et al. (1991) examined alternative treatment programs following entry into the EAP. Subjects ($N = 227$) were randomly assigned into one of three treatments: (i) inpatient hospitalization; (ii) joining an Alcoholics Anonymous (AA) group; or (iii) opportunity to use a program of their choice. A variety of dependent variables were measured over a two-year period, including need for additional treatment, length of sobriety, and job outcomes (e.g. number of terminations). The results showed significant differences between the three groups on a number of measures, including need for additional treatment and length of sobriety. In most cases, Group 1 employees showed significantly fewer problems (e.g. intoxication) than the other two groups. The AA group and the choice group were generally not significantly different from one another. Interestingly, however, because of the cost of hospitalization, the expenses associated with the treatment (including initial treatment) for Group 1 and Group 2 were virtually identical. There were no significant differences on any of the job outcomes. Finally, at the end of the study, amount of alcohol consumed, number of people classified as alcoholic, and number of job problems experienced declined greatly for all three groups. Thus, these results suggested that use of an EAP over a two-year period may dramatically reduce substance abuse problems. Nevertheless, without a control group receiving no treatment, it is difficult to draw rigorous conclusions about the efficacy of an EAP program versus no EAP program.

Foote and Erfurt (1991) compared a strategy wherein some employees using the EAP received a follow-up contact with a counsellor, while other employees received the regular treatment (i.e. no follow-up contact). They found limited support for a difference between these two groups—the major exception was that employees in the follow-up group had significantly lower treatment costs. No information was provided as to whether the additional costs of follow-up contact outweighed the benefits.

By way of summary, Harris and Heft (1992) predicted that 'rigorous evaluation studies [of EAPs] . . . will be slow in coming, if indeed they appear at all' (p.258). Several years later, this prediction appears to have been accurate. On a positive note, however, Harris and Heft urged that additional research be conducted on specific aspects of EAPs; the literature summarized above indicates that there has been some progress in that direction. More informed choices can be now made as to which features (e.g. what sources should be used by the EAP) to incorporate in an EAP.

EAP Adoption/Implementation

Harris and Heft noted several studies examining adoption and implementation of EAPs. Only one new study was located in this area. Bennett, Blum, and Roman (1994) found that controlling for various other variables, companies in low unemployment areas and low turnover rates were most likely to have adopted an EAP. Bennett, Blum, and Roman offered two different explanations for their finding. One, businesses experiencing high turnover might feel that investing in employees who have a high likelihood of leaving is not cost-effective. Second, organizations that have an EAP might foster greater employee commitment, thereby reducing their turnover rate. Obviously, these explanations have very different theoretical and practical implications.

Employee Assistance Programs: Suggestions for Future Research

While research on EAPs has certainly increased in the last few years, and some theoretical models have been developed in this area, a great deal of work remains. One issue that clearly stands out is the need for further work on the referral process. Particularly in light of the small number of employees who make use of an EAP, the need to better understand the dynamics of how employees decide to go remains critical.

As reviewed above, Gerstein and his colleagues have developed a model to understand supervisors' willingness to refer an employee; however, no comprehensive, well-developed model has been developed that addresses the self-referral process and what leads employees to actually go to an EAP. Towards that end, we suggest application of image theory (Beach, 1990) to understand this process. Although a detailed description of image theory and how it might apply to EAP use is beyond the scope of this paper, a brief overview is warranted. Image theory assumes that people use three basic structures of knowledges, or images, in making decisions. One image incorporates one's values (e.g. morals, ethics, or more generally, principles). These values form the core standards for making decisions. The next image, referred to as trajectory, constitutes one's short- and long-term goals or desired outcomes. An example from the work context may be promotion to area manager. The third image, the strategic image, involves plans and methods for attaining these goals. Image theory assumes that people must somehow process constant information and deal with continuous decision. In order to do this, people adopt a very simple method of information processing, referred to as screening. Screening is based on simple heuristics, in which decisions are rejected if they do not meet certain basic criteria. Only if these basic criteria are met will the individual consider the information or decisions in greater detail. Lee and Mitchell (1994) have addressed the notion of 'shocks', or events that force the individual to make much more careful judgments and decisions.

In the present context, an employee with a drinking or drug problem may have certain values or principles that relate to substance use (e.g. 'a little alcohol never hurt anyone'), which in turn lead him or her to reject the need to go to the EAP. It may be that only a shock (e.g. a strong warning from his or her supervisor about poor job performance) will force the employee to consider the need for an EAP more carefully, and thus lead him or her to go to the EAP.

Application of image theory offers some potentially interesting areas for research. First, given that image theory assumes two basic types of decision making processes, depending on the point in process, the factors considered in choosing to use or not use the EAP may differ as a function of the issues facing the employee. Second, image theory would lead one to consider different approaches in addressing employee problems. For example, for certain employees, some types of shocks (e.g. a supervisory reprimand versus a coworker confrontation) may be more helpful than others, depending on their value image. In short, image theory is a relatively new approach to understanding how people make decisions. Although its application to the workplace is even more recent, it has been used to understand turnover (Lee & Mitchell, 1994) and job search and choice (Stevens & Beach, 1994).

Related to all this work is the importance of different sources that appear to serve as encouragement to utilize the EAP. As Blum and Roman (1992) indicated, coworkers appear to play a greater role than heretofore has been recognized.

In terms of EAP effectiveness, given that their presence appears to be so well entrenched in industry, business and government today, we suspect that there is only limited interest among practitioners in demonstrating their utility. However, there is likely to be greater interest in how to best design EAPs, and how to broaden their appeal to employees. It is therefore in these latter two areas that more research is likely to appear. In this regard, we reviewed some research that addressed the effectiveness of different aspects of an EAP. Much more work is needed here.

With regard to why employees choose to use the EAP, most of the research has addressed employees in general, and whether or not they are willing to go. Perhaps it would be more beneficial to study why employees who could have gone to an EAP chose to go to other help sources. Research by Sullivan and Poverny (1992) provides some possible directions for research on this issue; follow-up work is clearly needed.

Finally, in terms of EAP adoption, there is very little research. Anecdotal and testimonial evidence comes from organizations that have adopted EAPs; a study examining organizations that decide not to use an EAP would be quite valuable. For example, are these organizations simply not convinced that an EAP would be cost-effective? Or, do these organizations have a view that employees with a problem should seek help on their own?

WORKPLACE DRUG AND ALCOHOL PROGRAMS AND PRACTICES OUTSIDE NORTH AMERICA

Although the vast majority of research on workplace drug and alcohol programs was conducted in North America, there has been some writing and research on this issue in other countries as well. We located literature on three countries: New Zealand, Sweden, and Germany. A summary of this literature follows next.

New Zealand

Inkson (n.d.) conducted a survey of alcohol programs and practices in companies with 100 or more employees ($N = 305$) located in New Zealand. They found that respondents perceived alcohol to be a relatively unimportant problem, with 53% indicating that alcohol abuse is a 'minor' problem, and almost 20% indicating that alcohol abuse was not a concern. Only 2% felt that alcohol abuse was a major concern. Nevertheless, over half of the respondents agreed that there may be hidden problems created by alcohol in their organization. Almost half (47%) of the respondents indicated that their company did not have a policy for dealing with alcohol problems, while 30% stated that the policy existed but not in written form. Slightly more than 20% had a written policy. In terms of actions that would be taken with an employee having an alcohol problem, few respondents indicated that a rehabilitation program or formal assistance program (e.g. EAP) would be provided. Inkson also queried respondents as to how actual situations involving an alcohol problem had been dealt with. Contrary to the previous statements, disciplinary action was indicated in about one-third of the cases, whereas some type of counseling treatment was mentioned in well over half of the situations.

Pringle (in press) surveyed senior managers from 60 medium and large private-sector companies in New Zealand. These businesses were from a mix of industries, including manufacturing, construction, transportation, and financial services. A large percentage of respondents (87%) indicated that they used alcohol as part of their work activities; whether the alcohol was consumed at the work site, at home, or other locations (e.g. restaurants) was not clear. However, managers of 5 out of 6 companies reported that alcohol was kept on their premises (typically in a senior manager's office or boardroom). Most of the respondents had some contact with a problem drinker at work. The most common action cited for dealing with a problem drinker at work was talk or referral for counseling (28%), termination or warning (25%), or no action if his or her work was acceptable (22%).

In terms of company policies and practices, Pringle (in press) reported that only 25% of the companies had a formal, written policy on alcohol, which is very close to the number reported by Inkson (n.d.). None of these companies had an EAP. Alcohol was reported to have a variety of important uses in the workplace. Specifically, respondents viewed alcohol as a necessary aspect of client interaction (e.g. for entertainment), as a reward to employees (e.g. for celebrating a successful sale), and as a gift to important individuals. As observed by Pringle, alcohol 'is part and parcel of business life' (p.15).

Unlike the USA, then, there appears to be far less emphasis on substance abuse issues in the New Zealand workplace. Moreover, the little attnetion that has been paid focuses on alchol abuse, and not illegal substances. Finally, cultural norms appear to be less disparaging of alcohol use than perhaps is the case in the USA.

Sweden

Karlsson (1990) reviewed drug and alcohol programs in Sweden. In terms of the prevalence of drug and alcohol usage, Karlsson reported that 10% of males and 1–2% of females were estimated to be alcohol abusers in the general population. Less information was available as to the percentage of drug users in the general population. Research examining the prevalence of drug and alcohol problems in the workforce was quite sparse, especially compared to research in the USA, but one study had indicated that 4% of men and 1% of women abused drugs.

With regard to drug and alcohol programs, Karlsson observed that Swedish work laws provide for a myriad of rules regarding the treatment of employees with drug and alcohol problems. For instance, the Work Environment Act affects how the company addresses substance abuse problems; other laws make it difficult for workers to be terminated. Together, these laws have led many companies to adopt alcohol and drug programs. Based on an analysis of seven companies (ranging from manufacturing firms to a state-owned nuclear power plant) with such programs, Karlsson found a number of interesting findings. First, very few employees had made use of the services (less than 1% of the workforce). The supervisors and managers were perceived as a major problem that had to be overcome. None of the companies had conducted a formal evaluation of the program; yet the program was widely believed to be very effective, based on the number of employees who had returned or been able to remain on the job. Finally, four of the seven companies had an alcohol and drug testing program. Only one of them, however, conducted this testing at the preemployment stage; the other three tested 'for cause'. The most commonly used approaches were urinalysis and a breath test. Interestingly, one company, a paper mill, had recently begun testing because two employees were found to be drug-users.

Thus, as in the USA, alcohol and perhaps drug problems are viewed as important workplace problems. EAPs seem quite widespread in Sweden. Some of the issues identified by Karlsson (e.g. low usage rate) are similar to concerns in the USA. Drug testing does not appear to be as prevalent in Sweden as it is in the USA.

Germany

While many companies appear to have adopted alcohol and drug programs and policies in Germany, research on them is scarce (Fuchs & Rummel, 1993). It is estimated that 5% of employees are alcoholics, while another 10% are at risk for becoming alcohol abusers in Germany. Fuchs and Rummel surveyed 377 managers of a company with an alcohol and drug program three years after its inception. They found that most respondents understood that alcohol problems were not due to a lack of the person's willpower, and agreed that alcohol use in the workplace was not permitted. At the same time, about half of the managers indicated that use of alcohol may be necessary when interacting with customers. Fuchs and Rummel asserted that this attitude contradicts the need to refrain from alcohol at the workplace. In terms of other issues related to the alcohol prevention program, Fuchs and Rummel reported relatively positive findings regarding such things as respondents' willingness to refer, attitudes towards the program, and so forth. Given increased attention to drug and alcohol problems, further research is likely to be of interest to German companies.

LEGAL ISSUES IN DRUG AND ALCOHOL PROGRAMS

Alcohol and drug programs in the workplace have resulted in a variety of lawsuits. Segal (1994) provides a well-written practical guide to legal issues surrounding drug and alcohol testing. Among the issues he raises are common law invasion of privacy restrictions, the role of the union in approving a drug testing program, need for reasonable suspicion testing, and civil rights laws (e.g. Americans with Disabilities Act; Civil Rights Act of 1964). Segal describes how use of a drug test based on suspected addiction to support a termination may be cause for legal action by the employee. Harris and Heft (1993) reviewed other laws, such as state regulations, that affect drug and alcohol testing.

Parliman and Edwards (1992) reviewed employer liability issues in connection with an EAP. They described two types of lawsuits that workers have filed in this regard. The first type of lawsuit involves a claim that the company's action involved a violation of right to privacy. For example, in one lawsuit, the company allegedly met with the psychologist who had treated an employee at the EAP, and asked him about the employee's problems. Despite the fact that the employee had not authorized the psychologist to share their conversation, he proceeded to share information about her personal problems with company representatives. After the company terminated the employee, she sued for invasion of privacy and subsequently won. The second type of lawsuit involves charges of infliction of severe emotional distress. In a court case involving this legal concept, an employee who was suffering from depression as well as an alcohol problem met with an EAP counselor for help. During the meeting, which the employee's supervisor also attended, the employee was told that he must go for inpatient alcohol treatment or be fired. Moreover, the employee had to inform the company of his decision by the end of the day. When the employee asked for an extension of the deadline, he was told that a postponement of the deadline would result in his dismissal. At that point, he was told he was fired; the next day, the company reversed its decision, but the employee proceeded to sue. Ultimately, a jury gave him $30 000 in compensatory pay and $100 000 in punitive damages. Clearly, companies that have an EAP must be careful to ensure they do not violate pertinent laws.

CONCLUSION

We have reviewed recent literature on drug and alcohol programs in the workplace. This area remains an important one for organizations, and companies will continue to devote resources to such programs. We suggested a number of issues for future research. While I/O psychologists have so far been involved in a few limited questions regarding workplace drug and alcohol programs, we believe they have an important role to play in terms of research, practice, and public policy recommendations.

ACKNOWLEDGEMENT

The authors would like to thank Leslie Greising for typing the references and reviewing the chapter.

REFERENCES

Author (1993) How McDonnell Douglas cost-justified its EAP. *Personnel Journal*, 72, 48.

Beach, L. R. (1990) *Image Theory: Decision Making in Personal and Organizational Contexts*. Chichester: Wiley.

Bennett, N., Blum, T. C., & Roman, P. M. (1994) Presence of drug screening and employee assistance programs: Exclusive and inclusive human resource management practices. *Journal of Organizational Behavior*, 15, 549–560.

Blank, D. L. & Fenton, J. W. (1989) Early employment testing for marijuana: Demographic and employee retention patterns. In S. W. Gust and J. M. Walsh (eds), *Drugs in the Workplace: Research and Evaluation Data* (pp.139–150), Rockville, MD: National Institute on Drug Abuse.

Blum, T. C. & Roman, P. M. (1992) A description of clients using employee assistance programs. *Alcohol Health and Research World*, 16(2), 120–128.

Boudreau, J. (1991) Utility analysis for decisions in human resource management. In M. Dunnette and L. Hough (eds), *Handbook of Industrial and Organizational Psychology* (pp.621–745). Palo Alto, CA: Consulting Psychologists Press.

Burke, R. J. (1994) Utilization of employees' assistance program in a public accounting firm: Some preliminary data. *Psychological Reports*, 75, 264–266.

Cascio, W. F. (1987) *Costing Human Resources: The Financial Impact of Behavior in Organizations*, Second edition. Boston: Kent.

Cavanaugh, J. M. & Prasad, P. (1994) Drug testing as symbolic managerial action: In response to 'A case against workplace drug testing'. *Organization Science*, 5(2), 267–271.

Comer, D. R. (1993) Workplace drug testing reconsidered. *Journal of Managerial Issues*, 5(4), 517–531.

Comer, D. R. (1994) A case against workplace drug testing. *Organization Science*, 5(2), 259–271.

Crant, J. M. & Bateman, T. S. (1990) An experimental test of the impact of drug-testing programs on potential job applicants' attitudes and intentions. *Journal of Applied Psychology*, 75, 127–131.

Crant, J. M. & Bateman, T. S. (1993) Potential job applicant reactions to employee drug testing: The effect of program characteristics and individual differences. *Journal of Business and Psychology*, 7(3), 279–290.

Crow, S. M. & Hartman, S. J. (1992) Drugs in the workplace: Overstating the problems and the cures. *Journal of Drug Issues*, 22(4), 923–937.

Feucht, T. E. Stephens, R. C., & Walker, M. L. (1994) Drug use among juvenile arrestees: A comparison of self-report, urinalysis and hair assay. *Journal of Drug Issues*, 24(1), 99–116.

Foote, A. & Erfurt, J. C. (1991) Effects of EAP follow-up on prevention of relapse among substance abuse clients. *Journal of Studies on Alcohol*, 52, 241–248.

Fuchs, R. & Rummel, M. (1993) Chemical dependency at work and organisational development: A management training programme aimed at the superiors of an institute for financial services. In J. Bellabarba, R. Fuchs, L. Rainer, & M. Rummel (Chairs), *Chemical Dependency at Work Employees Assistance Programmes (Substance*

Abuse): Our work in the Context of Company Internal Health Promotion Programmes. Symposium presented at the Sixth European Congress on Work and Organizational Psychology in Alicante, Spain.

Gerstein, L. H. (1990) The bystander-equity model of supervisory helping behavior: Past and future research on the prevention of employee problems. In P. M. Roman (ed.) *Alcohol Problem Intervention in the Workplace.* New York: Quorum Books.

Gerstein, L., Lynn, D., & Brown, P. (1991) Type of setting, employee substance abuse, and hypothetical supervisors' EAP referrals. *Journal of Drug Issues, 21*(4), 817–824.

Gerstein, L., Moore, D. T., Duffey, K., & Dainas, C. (1993) The effects of biological sex and ethnicity on EAP utilization and referrals. *Consulting Psychology Journal, 45*(4), 23–27.

Gerstein, L., Wheeler, J. L., & Gaber, T. G. (1994) The relation of the supervisory training and span of control to EAP referrals. *Consulting Psychology Journal, 46*, 19–22.

Gill, A. M. & Michaels, R. J. (1992) Does drug use lower wages? *Industrial and Labor Relations Review, 45*, 419–434.

Hall, L., Vacc, N. A., & Kissling, G. (1991) Likelihood to use employee assistance programs: The effects of sociodemographic, social-psychological, sociocultural, organizational, and community factors. *Journal of Employment Counseling, 28*, 63–73.

Harley, D. A. (1991) Impaired job performance and worksite trigger incidents: Factors influencing supervisory EAP referrals. *Employee Assistance Quarterly, 6*(3), 51–70.

Harris, M. M. & Heft, L. L. (1992) Alcohol and drug use in the workplace: Issues, controversies, and directions for future research. *Journal of Management, 18*, 239–266.

Harris, M. M. & Heft, L. L. (1993). 'Preemployment urinalysis drug testing: A critical review of psychometric and legal issues and effects on applicants', *Human Resource Management Review, 3*(4), 271–291.

Hartman, S. J. & Crow, S. M. (1993) Drugs in the workplace: Setting Harris straight. *Journal of Drug Issues, 23*(4), 733–738.

Holcum, M. L. & Lehman, W. E. K. (1995, May) A Structural Model of Negative Job Performance: Assessing the Causal Roles of Deviance and Substance Use. Paper presented at the annual meeting of the Society for Industrial Organizational Psychology, Orlando, Florida.

Horgan, J. (1990) Test negative: A look at the 'evidence' justifying illicit-drug tests. *Scientific American, 262* (March), 18–19.

Inkson, J. H. K. (n.d.) Employers' Attitudes to Alcohol Abuse Among Employes: A Preliminary Study, Unpublished manuscript.

Kandel, D. B. & Yamaguchi, K. (1987) Job mobility and drug use: An event history analysis. *American Journal of Sociology, 92*, 836–878.

Karlsson, C. (1990) *Programmes on Alcohol and Drugs at Swedish Workplaces.* ALNA Council of Sweden.

Kravitz, D. A. & Brock, P. (in press) Evaluations of drug testing programs. *Employee Responsibilities and Rights Journal.*

Kravitz, D. A., Stinson, V., & Chavez, T. L. (1994, April) Perceived Fairness of Tests Used in Making Selection and Promotion Decisions. Paper presented at the Annual Meeting of the Society for Industrial Organizational Psychology, Nashville, Tennessee.

Lee, T. W. & Mitchell, T. R. (1994) An alternative approach: The unfolding model of voluntary employee turnover. *Academy of Management Review, 19*(1), 51–89.

Lehman, W. E. K. & Simpson, D. D. (1992) Employee substance abuse and on-the-job behaviors. *Journal of Applied Psychology, 77*, 309–321.

MacDonald, S., Wells, S., & Fry, R. (1993) The limitations of drug screening in the workplace. *International Labour Review, 132*(1), 95–113.

Macan, T. H., Avedon, M. J., Paese, M., & Smith, D. E. (1994) The effects of applicants' reactions to cognitive ability tests and an assessment center. *Personnel Psychology*, 47(4), 715–738.

Marcoulides, G. A., Mills, R. B., & Unterbrink, H. (1993) Improving pre-employment screening: Drug testing in the workplace. *Journal of Managerial Issues*, 5(2), 290–300.

Mastrangelo, P. (1995) Do college students still prefer companies without employment drug testing? Paper presented at the tenth annual conference of the Society for Industrial and Organizational Psychology, Orlando, FL.

May, K. M. (1992) Referrals to employee assistance programs: A pilot analogue study of expectations about counseling. *Journal of Mental Health Counseling*, 14(2), 208–224.

McDaniel, M. (1988) Does pre-employment drug predict on-the-job suitability? *Personnel Psychology*, 41, 717–729.

Mieczkowski, T. (1992) New approaches in drug testing: A review of hair analysis. *Annals of the American Academy of Political and Social Science*, 521, 132–150.

Mieczkowski, T. & Newel, R. (1993) Comparing hair and urine assays for cocaine and marijuana. *Federal Probation*, 57(2), 59–67.

Milne, S. H., Blum, T. C., & Roman, P. M. (1994) Factors influencing employees' propensity to use an employee asisstance program. *Personnel Psychology*, 47, 123–145.

Murphy, K. R. & Thornton, G. C. (1992) Characteristics of employee drug testing policies. *Journal of Business and Psychology*, 6(3), 295–309.

Normand, J., Lempert, R. O., & O'Brien, C. P. (1994) *Under the Influence? Drugs and the American Work Force*. Washington DC: National Academy Press.

Normand, J., Salyards, S., & Mahoney, J. (1990) An evaluation of pre-employment drug testing. *Journal of Applied Psychology*, 75, 629–639.

Park, D. A. (1992) Client satisfaction evaluation: University employee assistance program. *Employee Assistance Quarterly*, 8(2), 15–34.

Parliman, G. C. & Edwards, E. L. (1992) Employee assistance programs: An employer's guide to emerging liability issues. *Employee Relations Law Journal*, 17(4), 593–601.

Pringle, J. K. (in press) Managers' alcohol use: Roles and symbolic functions. *Journal of Business and Psychology*, 9(4).

Raciot, B. M. & Williams, K. J. (1993) Perceived invasiveness and fairness of drug-testing procedures for current employees. *Journal of Applied Social Psychology*, 23, 1879–1891.

Register, C. A. & Williams, D. R. (1992) Labor market effects of marijuana and cocaine use among young men. *Industrial and Labor Relations Review*, 45, 435–448.

Rosse, J. G. & Ringer, R. C. (1991, April) Applicant Reactions to Paper-and-Pencil Forms of Drug Testing. Paper presented at the annual meeting of the Society for Industrial and Organizational Psychology, St. Louis, Missouri.

Sackett, P. R. & Harris, M. M. (1984) Honesty testing for personnel selection: A review and critique. *Personnel Psychology*, 37, 221–245.

Schmidt, F. L., Viswevaran, V., & Ones, D. S. (1993, August) Validity of Integrity Tests for Predicting Drug and Alcohol Abuse. Paper presented at the American Psychological Association Convention, Toronto, Canada.

Segal, J. A. (1994) Urine or you're out. *HR Magazine*, 39, 30–38.

Simmering, M. J. & Ones, D. S. (1994, July) Pre-employment Drug Testing Methods in the United States. Paper presented at the 23rd International Congress of Applied Psychology, Madrid, Spain.

Smither, J. W., Reilly, R. R., Millsap, R. E., Perlman, K., & Stoffey, R. W. (1993) Applicant reactions to selection procedures. *Personnel Psychology*, 46, 49–76.

Stevens, C. K. & Beach, L. R. (1994) Application of Image Theory to Job Search and Choice Processes: New Directions for Theory and Research. Unpublished paper.

Sullivan, R. & Poverny, L. (1992) Differential patterns of EAP service utilization among university faculty and staff. *Employee Assistance Quarterly*, 8(1), 1–12.

Tepper, B. J. (1994) Investigation of general and program-specific attitudes toward corporate drug-testing policies. *Journal of Applied Psychology*, 79, 392–401.

Tepper, B. J. & Braun, C. K. (1995) Does the experience of organizational justice mitigate the invasion of privacy engendered by random drug testing? An empirical investigation. *Basic and Applied Social Psychology*, 16(1&2), 211–225.

Verespej, M. A. (1992) Drug users—not testing—anger workers. *Industry Week*, 241(4), 33-34.

Walsh, D. C., Hingson, R. W., Merrigan, D. M., Levenson, S. M., Cupples, L. A., Heeren, T., Coffman, G. A., Becker, C. A., Barker, T. A., Hamilton, S. K., McGuire, T. C., & Kelly, C. A. (1991) A randomized trial of treatment options for alcohol-abusing workers. *New England Journal of Medicine*, 325(11), 775–782.

Yu, J., Chen, P. J., Harshman, E. J., & McCarthy, E. G. (1991) An analysis of substance abuse patterns, medical expenses and effectiveness of treatment in the workplace. *Employee Benefits Journal*, 18, 26–30.

Zwerling, C. Ryan, J., & Orav, E. J. (1990) The efficacy of preemployment drug screening for marijuana and cocaine in predicting employment outcome. *Journal of the American Medical Association*, 264, 2639–2643.

Zwerling, C., Ryan, J., & Orav, E. J. (1992) Costs and benefits of preemployment drug screening. *Journal of the American Medical Association*, 26, 91–93.

Chapter 9

WORK ADJUSTMENT: EXTENSION OF THE THEORETICAL FRAMEWORK

Aharon Tziner
Université de Montréal
and
Elchanan I. Meir
Tel-Aviv University

The concept of person–environment (P–E) fit has received ample attention in the literature in the context of work attitudes and work behavior (Edwards, 1991; Edwards & van Harrison, 1993; Tziner, 1990). This fit is based on the interaction between an individual's work-related characteristics and the attributes of the work environment in which the person functions. The central proposition is that fit enhances manifestations of well adjustment or well-being at work (e.g. high performance, organizational commitment), whereas misfit serves as a major cause of negative outcomes (e.g. absenteeism, dissatisfaction).

A close perusal of the P–E fit literature in the work context reveals that although both subscribing to the same proposition noted above, two major theories have emerged in an attempt to explain how and why various attitudinal and behavioral outcomes result from fit/misfit. These are: (i) The Theory of Work Adjustment (Dawis & Lofquist, 1984), where fit/misfit is referred to as correspondence/discorrespondence; and (ii) Holland's (1973, 1985) Congruence Theory, where fit/misfit is termed congruence/lack of congruence or incongruence.

We shall first offer a review of each of these theories, with suggested amendment judged necessary. Subsequently, we shall attempt to incorporate both into a single theoretical framework.

Work Adjustment: Extension of the Theoretical Framework by Aharon Tziner and Elchanan I. Meir taken from IRIOP 1997 v12, Edited by Cary L. Cooper and Ivan T. Robertson: © 1997 John Wiley & Sons, Ltd

THE THEORY OF WORK ADJUSTMENT (Dawis & Lofquist, 1984)

Correspondence and Work Adjustment

An individual's adjustment to the work milieu has long attracted interest because it is construed as an essential component of effective organization functioning (Cascio, 1991). The theoretical frame that has offered the most compelling explanation of the process leading to this state is the Theory of Work Adjustment (Dawis & Lofquist, 1984).

Central to this theory is the notion of correspondence between the individual and his or her work environment. In the earlier formulation of this theory, correspondence was defined as a 'harmonious relationship between the individual and his environment: suitability of the individual to the environment and of the environment to the individual, and a reciprocal and complementary relationship between the individual and his environment' (Lofquist & Dawis, 1969, p. 45). A basic tenet of this theory is that the individual seeks to achieve, and acts to maintain, such mutual correspondence. Thus, attaining and sustaining work adjustment is a continuous and dynamic process.

Moreover, within the context of work organizations, two types of correspondence must prevail in order for work adjustment to emerge. These are:

Correspondence I: The individual's skills, knowledge, abilities and personality traits must match the requirements of the job, as well as the expectations deriving from the organization's culture and particular structural features (e.g. managerial procedures, communication systems, etc.).

Correspondence II: The job and organizational environment must satisfy the employee's work-related needs. For instance, Bretz, Ash, and Dreher (1989) reported that employees with a high need for achievement tend to be attracted to environments that encourage and reward competitive effort and accomplishments.

Correspondence I has been postulated to lead to satisfactoriness, denoting the degree to which the individual employee meets job requirements and organizational expectations. Correspondence II has been assumed to result in work satisfaction, the extent to which the individual employee experiences fulfillment of his or her work-related needs. Both work satisfaction and satisfactoriness are necessary for the employee to develop work adjustment. Following Dawis & Lofquist (1984), this state is indicated by an employee deliberately choosing to be associated with a particular work organization over alternative employment opportunities (voluntary tenure). However, it should be noted that the decision to maintain a contractual relationship is not the sole prerogative of the employee: the organization also retains those employees whom it considers to possess work qualities appropriate to the task.

This notion has been neatly incorporated into Schneider's (1983, 1987) attraction–selection–attrition conceptual scheme, which clearly demonstrates that forces within the organization operate over time to attract, select and retain those individuals who are the most congruent with the organization's characteristics and expectations. This results in the creation of increasingly homogeneous groups of employees, with respect to background, work abilities and orientation, and work personality.

Several typologies have been presented in the literature to describe the relationship between workers' personality traits and the work conditions conducive to their adjustment to work environment (Correspondence I). For example, Holland (1985) describes individual employees with a realistic type of personality who share certain personality and functional attributes (interests, skills, abilities, traits) and who seek to create a congruent environment (i.e. one that allows them to satisfy their needs and interests).

In the same vein, Friedman & Rosenman (1974) have described the high Type A personality as typically a highly competitive achiever, constantly struggling against time and people, and expressing excessive hostility in response to frustration. Following this paradigm, Burke & Dezca (1982) have posited that a less structured work environment may be perceived by such a person as potentially less coercive, restrictive and frustrating, thus offering better opportunities for personal objectives to be realized. Likewise, Bretz, Ash, & Dreher (1989) have shown that high achievers prefer organizations in which workers are rewarded according to accomplishments, rather than seniority.

While confirming the previous observation, Turban & Keon (1993) have also demonstrated that employees with a high need to achieve are attracted to smaller organizations. They suggest that the relatively small size is perceived as providing more opportunities to be personally responsible for outcomes and to receive personalized feedback and rewards, conditions that are highly compatible to the needs of high achievers.

With respect to the degree of centralization in an organization, Turban & Keon (1993) found that such employees with low self-esteem were more attracted to decentralized structures. In such environments, opportunities for exercising responsibility are likely to be diffused or shared, and the participatory nature of the decision-making process tends to offer increased opportunities for recognition and satisfaction.

Likewise, Tziner & Falbe (1990) have demonstrated that individuals acting in an organizational milieu which they perceived as corresponding to their achievement orientation, exhibited higher levels of performance, work satisfaction and organizational commitment than counterparts, displaying incongruency.

Finally, Bretz & Judge (1994) illustrated empirically that individuals to whom the organizational environment appeared congruent with their organizational preferences reported a higher level of job satisfaction and had a longer tenure with their organizations than individuals experiencing less congruence of this type. Moreover, Bretz and Judge's data confirmed an indirect effect of organizational preferences—organizational environment on certain indicators of career success, such as salary and job level.

At this stage, we can conclude that: (i) Correspondence, in general, is a relationship in which the individual employee and the work organization are mutually responsive; and (ii) work adjustment, the extent to which a worker chooses to stay in his or her present organization (when faced with alternative prospects for employment), is concurrently determined by work satisfaction and satisfactoriness.

It should be noted, however, that both the individual employee and the work organization are constantly changing. Therefore, attainment of work adjustment as a particular point in time does not necessarily ensure its subsequent persistence. Consequently, adjusting to work requires that both the employee and the organization engage in a continuous and active process of mutual readjustment.

Dawis & Lofquist (1984) state that in a search for adjustment, the individual may either attempt to change the organizational environment (i.e. act on the environment) or opt for changing his or her reactions to it. In either case, however, each individual's way of interacting with the organizational environment is determined by his/her personality style. This style denotes a profile, characteristic of each individual, with respect to four distinct dimensions: (i) the degree of quickness in reacting/acting (termed *celerity*); (ii) the level of activity exhibited while reacting/acting (*pace*); (iii) the typical pattern of pace displayed while acting/reacting (*rhythm*); and (iv) the duration of the action/reaction process (*endurance*). If an individual's personality style corresponds to the personality profile required for adequate functioning in a particular organizational environment, then attainment of work adjustment becomes probable. Otherwise, either the individual or the organizational environment must change to avoid strain.

Thus, personality style constitutes an essential component of the personality factor which, along with skills, knowledge and abilities, determines Correspondence I, assuming respective job and organization requirements for these factors are satisfied.

In addition, Dawis & Lofquist (1984) assert that whenever work adjustment is disrupted, for whatever reason, affected individuals do not necessarily undertake the process of readjustment immediately. This is contingent upon a personality trait they term flexibility, meaning the degree of tolerance for discorrespondence with organizational environment before the need to launch some action in order to reduce the discorrespondence and restore work adjustment.

To put it in other words, flexibility denotes the amount of discorrespondence one is able to tolerate before being motivated to do something about it, either by acting on the environment (active adjustment) or by acting on oneself (reactive adjustment). If all attempts to regain adjustment fail, it is predicted that the individual will not remain in the frustrating organizational environment. The extent of persistence in attempting to achieve readjustment before deciding to leave is termed perseverance. This constitutes an additional personality trait conceived as an important factor for forming Correspondence I.

According to Dawis & Lofquist (1984), work adjustment *per se* is unobservable directly; rather it is both the antecedents and the outcomes that are amenable to observation and measurement. Classically, the antecedents are work satisfaction and satisfactoriness, to which we would add, following Saks (1995), organizational commitment and job involvement. The most common behavioral manifestations of the outcomes include absenteeism, voluntary turnover (or voluntary tenure), intentional organizational misbehavior and organizational citizenship behavior.

Antecedents and Outcomes of Work Adjustment

Many definitions of the concept of work satisfaction have been offered over the years (see Locke, 1976). On the whole, work satisfaction is seen as the collection of attitudes held by an individual concerning particular facets of his or her work, including working conditions, organizational policy, recognition, supervision and pay. These attitudes may be more or less favorable, depending on the discrepancy between the individual's work-related needs, desires and expectations and what is actually attainable from a specific job in a particular organizational setting. Stated briefly, work satisfaction is a function of the degree of correspondence between a worker's needs and the need-gratifying capacity of the work setting (Betz, 1969; Porter, 1963).

Reasonably well-established empirical evidence has indicated that work satisfaction with various aspects of work is negatively related to turnover. This trend tends to corroborate the connection between the level of work satisfaction and the voluntary decision to stay in an organization, as predicted by the Theory of Work Adjustment. According to Dawis & Lofquist (1984), this link is mediated by work adjustment.

Several studies have sought to elaborate this link. Hom, Caranikas-Walker, Prussia, & Griffith (1992) contend that work maladjustment is a necessary but insufficient mediating factor to account for work dissatisfaction that results in turnover. They concur with Mobley, Horner, & Hollingsworth (1978) that withdrawal cognitions (thoughts of quitting, the intention to leave the job or seeking another job) would also have to evolve as mediating precursors for turnover to occur.

Gerhart (1990) has stressed the wider contextual framework in which these mediating behaviors manifest themselves. He notes that when slumps in the economy make it hard to find alternative work, dissatisfied employees generally try to hold on to their jobs. Hulin (1991) expressed this notion in more general terms by stating that 'dissatisfaction should lead to organizational turnover only if the dissatisfied individual perceives that there are better alternatives available' (p. 446). Conversely, individuals who very much like their jobs and feel attached to their organizations may still be tempted by prospects of better career advancement elsewhere. Nevertheless, on the whole, the satisfied tend to stay, while the dissatisfied tend to leave (Blau & Boal, 1987).

In addition, workers' commitment to an organization has been found to be an important variable linked to work satisfaction (Cheloha & Farr, 1980; Hom, Katerberg, & Hulin, 1979) and to turnover (Cohern, 1993). Organizational commitment is a psychological state that both characterizes the employee's relationship with the organization and has implications for the decision to continue or discontinue membership in that organization.

Although for some time it has been fashionable for 'organizational commitment' to be treated as a unitary concept, researchers have recently provided increasing empirical evidence of the existence of a three-dimensional structure consisting of: (i) 'affective commitment'; (ii) 'continuance commitment'; and (iii) 'normative/moral commitment' (Allen & Meyer, 1990; Hackett, Bycio, & Hausdorf, 1994; Jaros, Jermier, Koehler, & Sincich, 1993).

Strong affective attachment develops when employees' experiences within an organization are consistent with their goals, values and expectations. A state of continuous commitment develops as employees recognize that they have accumulated investments or benefits that would be lost if they left. Normative/moral commitment emerges as a result of socialization experiences that emphasize the appropriateness of remaining loyal and the receipt of benefits that have created a sense of obligation to reciprocate.

Empirical findings demonstrate that employees with a strong affective commitment voluntarily stay with the organization because they identify with it and therefore *want* to stay; those with a strong continuance commitment stay on because they *need* to; and those with a strong normative/moral commitment because they feel they *ought* to do so.

Sommers (1995) has provided certain empirical evidence in support of the negative links between voluntary turnover and both affective and normative/moral commitment. Given the existing documentation of the relationship between work satisfaction and organizational commitment (Mathieu & Zajac, 1990), we may readily speculate that the relationship between work satisfaction and voluntary stay (tenure) with an organization is also partially accounted for by some of the effective components of organizational commitment.

Another variable repeatedly described as a salient determinant of voluntary turnover, though less so than organizational commitment, is job involvement (Cotton & Tuttle, 1986). Job involvement is defined as the extent to which the individual identifies psychologically with his or her job (Blau, 1985; Kanungo, 1979). This notion has also been causally linked to work satisfaction (Kanungo, 1982), which would lead us to believe that it may also be responsible in part for turnover.

The relationship of both organizational commitment and job involvement to work satisfaction should not come as a surprise. Organizational commitment draws on the belief that the organization can aid individuals in meeting some of their existence needs (Alderfer, 1969), while job involvement draws on the belief that the job has the ability to fulfil growth or psychological needs. In view of this shared frame of reference, it is only natural to assume that work satisfaction is related to both organizational commitment and job involvement. The existence needs underlying continuance commitment correspond to the extrinsic aspects of work satisfaction, while the self-actualization needs gratified by job content correspond to the intrinsic aspects of work satisfaction.

Abundant research has been conducted on the relationships between work satisfaction, absenteeism and turnover (e.g. Mitra, Jenkins, & Gupta, 1992; Mobley, 1982; Price & Mueller, 1986). For example, a meta-analysis performed by Mitra, Jenkins, & Gupta (1992), in which 33 correlations from 17 studies were combined, revealed a corrected mean correlation of 0.33 between absenteeism and turnover. Similarly, it has been demonstrated that work satisfaction affects turnover. Three additional meta-analyses (Hackett & Guion, 1985; McShane, 1985; Scott & Taylor, 1985) provide reasonable support to the employee absenteeism—work satisfaction relationship (i.e. an estimated coefficient of correlation slightly exceeding 0.20).

In his synthesis of previously published studies, Hackett (1989) uncovered a fairly substantial correlation between absenteeism and job involvement ($r = 0.36$) and a much weaker association of absenteeism with organizational commitment ($r = 0.12$). These findings led him to conclude that the intrinsically motivating aspects of the work itself (as reflected by job involvement) appear to have a stronger effect on absenteeism. We suggest this correlation be regarded with caution, since Hackett (1989) used an *overall* measure of organizational commitment, rather than investigating the possible differential patterns of the relationship between absenteeism and each of the three distinct facets of this variable, as described above, namely, affective, continuance and normative/moral commitment.

These findings clearly indicate that, beyond the singular concept of work satisfaction prescribed by the Theory of Work Adjustment, there is an entire gamut of work-related attitudes—work satisfaction, job involvement and organizational commitment—that underlie a spectrum of withdrawal behaviors, most notably, absenteeism and turnover.

So far we have dwelled upon one of the backbones of the Theory of Work Adjustment.

| Correspondence II | → work satisfaction (and additional work-related attitudes, e.g. job involvement, organizational commitment) | → work adjustment/ maladjustment | → voluntary tenure with the organization, absenteeism, or voluntary turnover |

We would now like to turn to its second conceptual component, namely:

Correspondence I → satisfactoriness   → work   → voluntary tenure
                                          adjustment/   with the
                                          maladjustment   organization or
                                                                     voluntary/
                                                                     involuntary
                                                                     turnover

Satisfactoriness, we will recall, concerns the extent to which the organization is satisfied with the performance of the employee. The Theory of Work Adjustment suggests that a high level of satisfactoriness is conducive to work adjustment, the outcome of which will be voluntary tenure with the organization. Conversely, a low level of satisfactoriness engenders work maladjustment and consequent voluntary or involuntary turnover.

Bycio, Hackett, & Alvares (1990) conducted a review of empirical findings that indicated that a very strong relationship exists between performance and involuntary turnover ($r = -0.51$, $r = -0.52$, in two separate studies) and between performance and voluntary turnover ($r = -0.31$, $r = -0.26$, again in two separate studies). Additional data in Bycio, Hackett, & Alvares' (1990) investigation supports the proposition that work satisfaction and satisfactoriness (i.e. performance) interlink with one another (mean coefficient of correlation $r = 0.25$).

Parenthetically, Bycio, Hackett, & Alvares (1990) also supported a strong association of performance with organizational commitment (mean $r = -0.36$). Similar findings emerged from Brett, Cron & Slocum's (1995) investigation, whose unique contribution was to delineate a new variable, the 'extent of economic dependency on work', which was found to moderate the relationship of both performance—work satisfaction and performance–organizational commitment.

A different avenue of investigation was pursued by Williams & Livingstone (1994), who revealed that productive professors were more likely to leave than less productive professors because they could obtain sizable increases in pay by moving on. However, untenured poorly performing professors were also more likely to leave, this time because they realized that they would not be granted tenure.

On the basis of these findings, the following propositions, emanating from the Theory of Work Adjustment, seem to be tenable: (i) the probability that individuals will be forced out of their work environment is inversely related to satisfactoriness; and (ii) the probability that individuals will leave their work environment inversely related to work satisfaction.

Two other possible outcomes, which appear to be located at opposite poles of the same continuum, are organizational intentional misbehavior and organizational citizenship behavior.

Organizational intentional misbehavior is defined as any intentional action by members of the organization which defies and violates shared organizational norms or expectations, and core societal values, mores or standards of proper conduct (Vardi & Wiener, 1992). According to Robinson & Bennett's

(1995) typology, organizational misbehaviors consist of such elements as sabotage, lying about hours worked, verbal abuse, stealing from co-workers or the company, intentionally working slowly and wasting resources. Organizational citizenship behavior designates behavior above and beyond the call of duty, behavior essential for organizational effectiveness that goes beyond role prescriptions (Smith, Organ, & Near, 1983).

Drawing on social exchange theory (Blau, 1964; Gouldner, 1960), we can posit that when employees experience fulfillment of their work-related needs (work satisfaction) they will eventually sense a desire to reciprocate. Organ (1988) suggests that one likely avenue for employee reciprocation is organizational citizenship behavior. As indicated, this syndrome is detectable when employees engage in innovative and spontaneous activities that are discretionary, and consequently unrewarded, in the context of the organization's reward system.

Organizational intentional misbehavior, in contrast, is likely to be instigated when employees perceive their work-related needs as being strained and their values as discordant with those propounded by the organization. What this describes, in effect, is a state of intense work dissatisfaction resulting from a low level or blatant lack of Correspondence I.

Finally, ample evidence has been produced over the years of the negative effects of work maladjustment on the individual. These include psychological manifestations (e.g. burnout, depression), psychological disorders (e.g. elevated blood pressure, high level of cholesterol) and behavioral strains (e.g. excessive drinking, smoking) owing either to discorrespondence between work ability requirement and the employees' actual work-related competence (Discorrespondence I), or to the discorrespondence between work-related interests/needs and organizational/occupational commensurate rewards (Discorrespondence II) (Blau, 1981; French & Caplan, 1972; Meir & Melamed, 1986; Smith & Tziner, 1995; Tziner, 1990). Further discussion of this issue, along with a model of the process involved in linking strains with the two types of discorrespondence, can be found in Tziner & Dawis (1988). Several of this model's predictions were recently investigated and corroborated by Sutherland, Fogarty, & Pithers (1995).

In light of these findings, it seems appropriate to suggest that the Theory of Work Adjustment be amended to incorporate the antecedents and outcomes of work adjustment elaborated upon here. Figure 9.1 depicts the interrelationships of the components in such an extended theory.

HOLLAND'S CONGRUENCE THEORY (1973, 1985)

Congruence and Well-being

An alternative conceptualization of individual–work environment correspondence is offered by Holland (1973, 1985). Using the notion of congruence

294

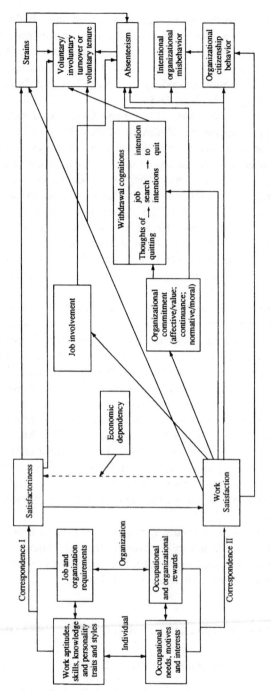

Figure 9.1 The interrelationships of the components of the extended theory of Work Adjustment

rather than correspondence, Holland claims that, in general, congruent person–environment interactions, in contrast to incongruent interactions, are conducive to well-being in the workplace, as indicated by satisfaction, stability and achievements.

Thus, according to Holland (1985), people flourish in an environment which fits their type. In his words: 'Different types require different environments. For instance, Realistic types flourish in Realistic environments because such an environment provided the opportunities and rewards a Realistic type needs' (p. 5). The fit between personality type and environment type is labeled congruence. Conceptually, it is possible to distinguish between two types of congruence, namely: (i) environmental congruence—the fit between personality type and environmental type; and (ii) occupational congruence—the fit between vocational interests and the requirement of an occupation.

It is worth noting that empirical investigations of the veracity of Holland's Congruence Theory have focused largely on satisfaction as an indicator of well-being. Thus, the following review of the findings, as well as the subsequent suggested interpretations, primarily invoke satisfaction as the indicator of well-being.

The overall question that must be addressed is: Why are congruence and work satisfaction related? The answer will have to be compatible with the variance among the established findings on the relationship between these two factors as well as with the fact that the correlations between congruence and either stability or achievements have consistently been found to be very low.

Meta-analyses by Assouline and Meir (1987) and by Tranberg, Slane, & Ekeberg (1993), reviews by Spokane (1985) and Edwards (1991) and the annotated bibliography by Holland and Gottfredson (1990) all cover studies of both environmental and occupational congruences. In the following elaboration of the relationship between congruence and satisfaction, however, a distinction is made between these two types of congruence.

Environmental Congruence

The explanation of the relationship between environmental congruence and satisfaction is based on Holland and Gottfredson (1976), Meir (1989), and Meir and Yaari (1988). In terms of the learning theory, '. . . the individual receives positive reinforcements from his/her environment for congruent behavior, and negative reinforcements for incongruent behavior. The positive reinforcements give rise to satisfaction and further congruent behavior, as well as the desire to remain in the environment. . . . Where the environment is important to the individual, such reinforcements cannot be disregarded' (Meir, 1989, pp. 226–227).

Empirically, in order to examine the level of an individual's environmental congruence, it is necessary to: (i) test the personality type of all the people in the environment; (ii) define the environmental type by finding the specific type with the highest frequency; and (iii) compare the individual's type with that of the environmental. Since the measurement of all people in a given environment is generally an unwieldy task, most studies either make do with experts' judgements as to environmental type (as the comparative basis for assigning individual congruence scores) or rely on the measurement of available respondents.

In the breakdown of correlations in Assouline and Meir's (1987) meta-analysis, it was found that the mean correlation between 'congruence with the others in one's environment' (environment congruence) and satisfaction was 0.29 (20 correlations, total $n = 995$, 95% confidence interval between 0.20 and 0.38). The overall mean correlation between congruence (all kinds) and satisfaction was found to be only 0.21 (53 correlations, total $n = 9041$, 95% confidence interval between -0.09 and 0.51). Thus, environmental congruence seems to correlate more highly with satisfaction than does occupational congruence. In light of these findings, Meir, Hadas, & Noyfeld (in press) suggest that 'a person can more easily disregard the incongruent reinforcements in his or her occupation (e.g. by compensating through avocational activity) than in his or her social environment'.

Occupational Congruence

A review of several definitions may be helpful in understanding the occupational congruence—satisfaction relationship. Within the work context, Shartle (1956) defines 'position' as a set of tasks that a single worker has to fulfill in his or her work, 'job' as the set of similar positions in a given organization, and 'occupation' as the group of similar jobs in different organizations. Thus, every worker has to perform a number of tasks with this number varying from one position to another. Lower level positions usually involve only a few tasks, in some cases only one (e.g. gathering, selecting or packing of fruit or industrial products). Generally, the higher the position, the greater the number of tasks to be performed. For example, a university rector or city mayor may have to carry out as many as 50 tasks.

We may speak of an individual's degree of satisfaction in a particular occupation as the extent to which the tasks involved make demands on the worker's time, unique skills and training. Thus, violinists will probably feel more satisfied if the greater proportion of their time and effort is devoted to playing the violin (on which, among other considerations, their reputation rests), as opposed to spending an inordinate amount of time on the administrative side of handling the orchestra.

The organizational tasks that characterize high-level jobs tend to force the individual either to develop some interest in those specific decision-making and instruction-giving aspects or to face the prospect of burnout and its inevitable negative consequences on satisfaction, stability and achievement. This burden of tasks that deflects from the optimization of professional skills goes a long way in explaining the phenomenon of top managers who are unhappy with their jobs, despite high salaries and status.

In lower level occupations, the character of the tasks is simple: the training is on-the-job, no higher education is required, the work is monotonous and repetitive, and the status and income of the worker are low. Moreover, the abilities and education of the majority of the workers on the lower level are limited, so that promotion is inhibited. However, their abilities and education are generally congruent with task requirements, so that satisfaction may well emerge and few incentives will be necessary to keep them in their jobs. Conversely, workers whose potential abilities and education exceed their task requirements and who find few outlets for self-accomplishment or skill utilization are unlikely to perceive the job as a source of satisfaction. Such people will be more prone to the benefits of extrinsic reinforcements, such as income, security and status, if they are to be retained at work.

Lack of satisfaction does not necessarily result in one's leaving the position. There might be sufficient extrinsic gratifications which justify the decision not to leave. The unsatisfied worker may also remain in a job because of lack of initiative to move to another job, lack of self-confidence, real or assumed loss of fringe benefits, instrumental commitment, lack of alternative job openings, and so on. Yet, as long as the unsatisfied worker stays put, the lack of occupational satisfaction will be reflected in his or her motivation and performance.

The basic conditions of equivalent occupations across different organizations are generally such that shifts between organizations without real change in work conditions are rare. If, however, a job in any other organization is perceived as more compatible to the workers' set of task preferences—e.g. a disliked task is less required; a favored task is more salient—a change of workplace can be expected.

For example, a full professor with tenure might move to a different university because in the new workplace less emphasis is placed on teaching undergraduates. We could thus assert that in the former university there was insufficient organizational or value congruence in teaching undergraduates.

A further illustration may be found in a study on bank tellers (Meir & Navon, 1992), in which a distinction was made between Conventional-Social and Conventional–Enterprising bank branches. Here the degree of congruence between personality type and bank type was found to be related both to the tellers' satisfaction and to their supervisors' evaluations.

The concept of 'satisfaction' is, in fact, a construct combining various aspects of satisfaction. It seems logical to suppose that these are positively interrelated within a person, as well as between people. In other words, a matrix of all positive correlations among many aspects of satisfaction can be assumed to exist. The true satisfaction score of an individual is thus the personal weighted sum of these various aspects, while the same individual's empirical satisfaction score may vary along with the salience of each aspect in particular. For example, the salience of satisfaction with the probability of being promoted is likely to change with the information that one's colleague was promoted.

Occupational (or job) satisfaction is also a more specific term which expresses a variety of feelings. It consists of a momentary good feeling, as well as a general positive estimate of the opportunities to continue to have such a good feeling without expectations of frustrations. One of the empirical measures of occupational satisfaction is the worker's evaluation of the extent of opportunities for the tasks involved in the occupation to fit his or her specific skills and task preferences, in comparison to the estimate of such opportunities in a different occupation. Similarly, job satisfaction can be assessed in part by a comparison of the extent of good feeling the worker would have in the current occupation, but in a different organization. Other measures include satisfaction with work conditions, salary, status, work values and perception of promotion possibilities.

It thus emerges that satisfaction is not constant. It varies along the time dimension because of the alterations in such varied aspects of the job as tasks or technology, perceived promotional options and burnout. This variation in satisfaction across time is true both for the general meaning of the term and for the more specific aspects of occupational satisfaction described above. Considering this degree of variation in the concept of satisfaction, we can see that it is impossible to define a single measure which could predict any specific kind of satisfaction in a correlation beyond the stability of satisfaction itself as a measure (notwithstanding the problem of error effect, as in any measuring process).

In sum, it can be said that occupational satisfaction in the workplace depends on the level of fit between the tasks an individual has to perform in his or her occupation and his or her particular skills and preferences. The level of fit is the plateau for the relation between congruence and satisfaction, and in empirical measurements this plateau is a limen which cannot be reached. This idea was behind Spokane's (1985) reference to the '0.30 magic correlational plateau' (p. 335) between congruence and satisfaction. This may well help us to understand why the mean congruence–satisfaction correlation in the meta-analysis reported by Assouline and Meir (1987) was only 0.21 and why Tranberg, Slane, & Ekeberg (1993) found the mean to be only 0.20.

For some people, occupational choice is virtually accidental (a chance meeting, a personal offer by an employer, the continuation of a temporary position), while for others this choice is the outcome of careful consideration of the options.

What advantage holds for those whose occupational choice follows a thorough survey of options and comparison of alternatives? It goes without saying that such a survey raises the probability of congruence between one's particular skills and preferred activities and the eventual occupational choice. In other words, the mean level of such measures as satisfaction, stability and achievements of those who entered their occupations through a process of reasoned occupational choice can be expected to be higher than that displayed by workers whose choice of job followed a more random or fortuitous process.

As we have noted, the mean correlations found between congruence and satisfaction are low; only about 0.20 (Assouline & Meir, 1987; Tranberg, Slane, & Ekebert, 1993). The variance between the results in the various studies seems to depend on the 'group importance' variable found by Meir, Keinan, & Segal (1986) to correlate 0.77 (rank order) with the correlation between congruence and satisfaction. Their explanation was that if the group is important to the individual, the reinforcements given by the group members for congruent or incongruent behavior produce a meaningful positive or negative impact, respectively, on the worker.

It could be argued that the correlation between congruence and satisfaction is so very low that perhaps it cannot even serve as a worthwhile goal, with or without a counsellor's help. We feel this to be an incorrect conclusion. Besides the high value which we recommend be placed on this critical objective, it is pertinent to note that even if the correlation is low, differences in satisfaction may be significant.

This important finding has been demonstrated by Meir (1995). By transforming the correlation coefficient to Binomial Effect Size Display (BESD), (Rosenthal, 1990), the superficially low 0.21 correlation found in the meta-analysis of Assouline and Meir (1987) actually showed that 'the ratio of satisfied people among those who made congruent occupational choices compared to those whose choices were incongruent was 60.4: 39.6.' (p. 343).

CONCLUSIONS

At this point the reader might well ask: To what extent are the Theory of Work Adjustment and Holland's Congruence Theory similar or different, and are they compatible?

According to the Theory of Work Adjustment (i) employee abilities, knowledge, skills and personality traits *must correspond* (Correspondence I) to work (job and organization) requirements and expectations: and (ii) employee desires (needs, interests) *must correspond* (Correspondence II) to the work (job and organization) gratifications available to fulfill these desires. These two kinds of correspondence are conceived as prerequisites for work adjustment.

The Congruence Theory deems both (i) *occupational congruence* (correspondence between employee work-related interests and work supplies available to meet them) and (ii) *environmental congruence* (correspondence of employee personality and the dominant personality type in the work milieu) as essential preconditions for attaining well-being.

It is thus obvious that *occupational congruence* concords perfectly with Correspondence II, particularly if we extend occupation to incorporate the organizational milieu wherein the work is performed. *Environmental congruence*, however, accounts only partially for the domain subsumed by Correspondence I, namely, personality traits or attributes.

Consequently, if we extend Holland's theory to encompass a variety of congruencies—for example (i) between attitudes, beliefs or values concerning modes of conduct on the one hand, and prevailing organizational norms and values in the relevant organizational milieu on the other; or (ii) between the employee's abilities, skills or knowledge on the one hand and work requirements on the other—we wind up forging a theoretical framework that is coherent with the Theory of Work Adjustment, in so far as the factors of congruence and correspondence are concerned.

It is worth noting also, that Hesketh (1995) compared a model of early career development by Feij, Whitely, Piero, & Taris (1995) with concepts deriving from the Theory of Work Adjustment in order to show that the latter offers a broader theoretical framework than the former approach, whereas the former provides ways for improving conceptualization and measurement of the Theory of Work Adjustment. Similarly, we feel that the incorporation of Holland's Theory into the Theory of Work Adjustment can make a valuable contribution to better conceptualizing and measuring the personality traits and correspondent required traits of organizational personality in the latter theory.

Additionally, as we have noted, the degree of well-being at work may be reflected in outcomes that extend beyond work satisfaction, such as absenteeism, physiological strains, voluntary tenure and organizational citizenship. Thus, the construct of well-being at work may incorporate the same indicators as the outcomes of work adjustment. In this amended form, Holland's Theory of Congruence becomes consistent with, and could in fact be integrated into, the Theory of Work Adjustment.

In conclusion, a conceptual theoretical groundwork has been laid here for a clearer understanding of the nature of work adjustment and for the means to better predict and foster this state. It remains to submit this amended Work Adjustment Theory to a thorough confirmatory empirical investigation.

Moreover, note should also be taken of the most recent findings that have examined the possible effects of non-work factors, such as life satisfaction (Judge & Waternabe, 1993), on well-being in the workplace. These should certainly be incorporated into any future investigations.

Finally, the reader will have noticed the absence herein of any discussion of the issue of correspondence (fit) operationalization. This deliberate exclusion was the result of our decision to devote this chapter to the conceptual and theoretical aspects of congruence, while integrating two dominant theories: the Theory of Work Adjustment and Holland's Congruence Theory. The issue of operationalizing congruence and the associated methodological problems is sufficiently important, and vast in scope, to merit a separate discussion, as is indeed the case in Edwards (1991) and in Hesketh & Gardner (1993). We believe that by reference to these two illuminating papers, along with the current chapter, the reader may be rewarded with a full and exhaustive treatment of both the theoretical and the practical aspects of work adjustment.

AUTHORS' NOTE

We gratefully acknowledge the SSHRC research grant (to the first author) which made it possible to prepare this chapter.

When this chapter was written, the first author was visiting with the School of Business Administration, Bar-Ilan University.

REFERENCES

Alderfer, C. P. (1969) A new theory of human needs. *Organizational Behavior and Human Performance*, **4**, 142–175.

Allen, N. J. & Meyer, J. P. (1990) The measurement and antecedents of affective continuance and normative commitment to the organization. *Journal of Occupational Psychology*, **63**, 1–18.

Assouline, M. & Meir, E. I. (1987) Meta-analysis of the relationship between congruence and well-being measures. *Journal of Vocational Behavior*, **31**, 319–332.

Betz, E. (1969) Need-reinforcer correspondence as a predictor of job satisfaction. *Personnel and Guidance Journal*, **47**, 878–883.

Blau, G. (1981) An empirical investigation of job stress, social support, service length, and job strain. *Organizational Behavior and Human Performance*, **27**, 279–302.

Blau, G. J. (1985) A multiple study investigation of the dimensionality of job involvement. *Journal of Vocational Behavior*, **27**, 19–36.

Blau, G. J. & Boal, K. B. (1987) Conceptualizing how job involvement and organizational commitment affect turnover and absenteeism. *Academy of Management Review*, **38**, 261–271.

Blau, P. (1964) *Exchange and Power in Social Life*. New York: Wiley.

Brett, J. F., Cron, W. L., & Slocum, J. W. (1995) Economic dependency on work: A moderator of the relationship between organizational commitment and performance. *Academy of Management Journal*, **38**, 261–271.

Bretz, R. D. Jr, Ash, R. A., & Dreher, G. F. (1989) Do people make the place? An examination of the attraction – selection – attrition hypothesis. *Personnel Psychology*, **42**, 561–581.

Bretz, R. D. Jr & Judge, T. A. (1994) Person–organization fit and the theory of work adjustment: Implications for satisfaction, tenure and career success. *Journal of Vocational Behavior*, **44**, 32–54.

Burke, R. J. & Dezca, E. (1982) Preferred organizational climates of type A individuals. *Journal of Vocational Behavior*, **21**, 50–59.

Bycio, P., Hackett, R. D., & Alvares, K. M. (1990) Job performance and turnover: A review and meta-analysis. *Applied Psychology: An International Review*, **39**, 47–76.

Cascio, W. F. (1991) *Managing Human Resources: Productivity, Quality of Work Life, Profits* 3rd edn. New York: McGraw-Hill.

Cheloha, R. & Farr, J. (1980) Absenteeism, job involvement, and job satisfaction in an organizational setting. *Journal of Applied Psychology*, **65**, 467–473.

Cohen, A. (1993) Organizational commitment and turnover. *Academy of Management Journal*, **36**, 1140–1157.

Cotton, J. L. & Tuttle, J. M. (1986) Employee turnover: A meta-analysis and review with implications for research. *Academy of Management Review*, **11**, 55–70.

Dawis, R. V. & Lofquist, L. H. (1984) A Psychological Theory of Work Adjustment. Minneapolis: University of Minnesota Press.

Edwards, J. R. (1991) Person–job fit: A conceptual integration, literature review, and methodological critique. In C. L. Cooper and I. T. Robertson (eds), *International Review of Industrial and Organizational Psychology*, Vol. 6 (pp. 283–357). Chichester: Wiley.

Edwards, J. R. & van Harrison, R. (1993) Job demands and worker health: Three-dimensional reexamination of the relationship between person–environment fit and strain. *Journal of Applied Psychology*, **78**, 628–648.

Feij, J. A., Whitely, W. T., Peiro, J. M., & Taris, T. W. (1995) The development of career enhancing strategies and content innovation: A longitudinal study of recruits. *Journal of Vocational Behavior*, **46**, 231–256.

French, J. R. P. Jr & Caplan, R. D. (1972) Organizational stress and individual strain. In A. J. Marrow (ed.), *The Failure of Success* (pp. 30–66). New York: Amacon.

Friedman, M. & Rosenman, R. H. (1974) Job stress and employee behavior. *Organizational Behavior and Human Performance*, **23**, 372–387.

Gerhart, B. (1990) Voluntary turnover and alternative job opportunities. *Journal of Applied Psychology*, **75**, 467–476.

Gouldner, A. W. (1960) The norm of reciprocity. *American Sociological Review*, **25**, 165–167.

Hackett, R. D. (1989) Work attitudes and employee absenteeism: A synthesis of the literature. *Journal of Occupational Psychology*, **62**, 235–248.

Hackett, R. D., Bycio, P. & Hausdorf, P. A. (1994) Further assessments of Meyer and Allen's (1991) three-component model of organizational commitment. *Journal of Applied Psychology*, **79**, 15–23.

Hackett, R. D. & Guion, R. M. (1985) A reevaluation of the absenteeism–job satisfaction relationship. *Organizational Behavior and Human Decision Processes*, **35**, 165–167.

Hesketh, B. (1995) Personality and adjustment styles: A theory of work adjustment approach to career enhancing strategies. *Journal of Vocational Behavior*, **46**, 274–282.

Hesketh, B. & Gardner, D. (1993) Person–environment fit models: A reconceptualization and empirical test. *Journal of Vocational Behavior*, **35**, 315–442.

Holland, J. L. (1973) *Making Vocational Choices: A Theory of Careers*. Englewood Cliffs, NJ: Prentice-Hall.

Holland, J. L. (1985) *Making Vocational Choices: A Theory of Vocational Personalities and Work Environment*. Englewood Cliffs, NJ: Prentice-Hall.

Holland, J. L. & Gottfredson, G. D. (1976) Using a typology of persons and environments to explain careers: Some extensions and clarifications. *The Counseling Psychologist*, **6**, 20–29.

Holland, J. L. & Gottfredson, G. D. (1990, August) *An annotated bibliography for Holland's theory of vocational personalities and work environments*. Paper presented at the annual meeting of the American Psychological Association. Boston, MA.

Hom, P. W., Caranikas-Walker, Prussia, G. E., & Griffith, R. W. (1992) A meta-analytical structural equations analysis of a model of employee turnover. *Journal of Applied Psychology*, **77**, 890–909.

Hom, P. W., Katerberg, R. & Hulin, C. R. (1979) Comparative examination of three approaches to the prediction of turnover. *Journal of Applied Psychology*, **64**, 280–290.

Hulin, C. (1991) Adaptation, persistence and commitment in organizations. In M. D. Dunnette and L. M. Hough (eds), *Handbook of Industrial and Organizational Psychology*, 2nd edn, Vol. 2 (pp. 445–505). Palo Alto, CA: Consulting Psychologists Press.

Jaros, S. J., Jermier, J. M., Koehler, J. W. & Sincich, T. (1993) Effects of continuance, affective and moral commitment on the withdrawal process: An evaluation of eight structural equation models. *Academy of Management Journal*, **36**, 951–995.

Judge, T. A. & Watanabe, S. (1993) Another look at the job satisfaction–life satisfaction relationship. *Journal of Applied Psychology*, **78**, 939–948.

Kanungo, R. N. (1979) The concepts of alienation and involvement revisited. *Psychological Bulletin*, **86**, 119–138.

Kanungo, R. N. (1982) *Work Alienation*. New York: Praeger.

Locke, E. A. (1976) The nature and the causes of job satisfaction. In M. D. Dunnette (ed.), *Handbook of Industrial and Organization Psychology*. Chicago: Rand McNally.

Lofquist, L. H. & Dawis, R. V. (1969) *Adjustment to Work*. Minneapolis: University of Minnesota.

Mathieu, J. E. & Zajac, D. M. (1990) A review and meta-analysis of antecedents, correlates and consequences of organizational commitment. *Psychological Bulletin*, **108**, 171–194.

McShane, S. L. (1985) Job satisfaction and absenteeism: A meta-analytic reexamination. *Canadian Journal of Administrative Sciences*, **2**, 68–77.

Meir, E. I. (1989) Integrative elaboration of the congruence theory. *Journal of Vocational Behavior*, **35**, 219–230.

Meir, E. I. (1995) Elaboration of the relation between interest congruence and satisfaction. *Journal of Career Assessment*, **3**, 341–346.

Meir, E. I., Hadas, C. & Noyfeld, M. (in press) Person–environment fit in small military units. *Journal of Career Assessment*.

Meir, E. I., Keinan, & Segal Z. (1986) Group importance as a mediator between personality–environment congruence and satisfaction. *Journal of Vocational Behavior*, **28**, 60–69.

Meir, E. I. & Melamed, S. (1986) The accumulation of person–environment congruences and well-being. *Journal of Occupational Behavior*, **7**, 315–323.

Meir, E. I. & Navon, M. (1992) A longitudinal examination of congruence hypotheses. *Journal of Vocational Behavior*, **41**, 35–47.

Meir, E. I. & Yaari, Y. (1988) The relation between congruent specialty choice within occupations and satisfaction. *Journal of Vocational Behavior*, **33**, 99–112.

Mitra, A., Jenkins, D. G., & Gupta, N. (1992) A meta-analytic review of the relationship between absence and turnover. *Journal of Applied Psychology*, **77**, 879–889.

Mobley, W. H. (1982) *Employee Turnover: Causes, Consequences, and Control*. Menlo Park, CA: Addison-Wesley.

Mobley, W. H., Horner, S. O., & Hollingsworth, A. T. (1978) An evaluation of precursors of hospital employee turnover. *Journal of Applied Psychology*, **63**, 408–414.

Organ, D. W. (1988) *Organizational Citizenship Behavior*. Lexington, MA: Lexington.

Porter, L. W. (1963) Job attitudes in management: Perceived importance of needs as a function of job level. *Journal of Applied Psychology*, **47**, 144–148.

Price, J. & Mueller, G. (1986) *Absenteeism and Turnover of Hospital Employees*. Greenwich, CT: JAI Press.

Robinson, S. L. & Bennett, R. J. (1995) A typology of deviant workplace behaviors: A multidimensional scaling study. *Academy of Management Journal*, **38**, 555–572.

Rosenthal, R. (1990) How are we doing in soft psychology? *American Psychologist*, **45**, 775–776.

Saks, M. A. (1995) Longitudinal field investigation of the moderating and mediating effects of self-efficacy on the relationship between training and newcomer adjustment. *Journal of Applied Psychology*, **80**, 211–225.

Schneider, B. (1983) Interactional psychology and organizational behavior. In B. M. Staw and L.L. Cummings (eds), *Research in Organizational Behavior*, Vol. 5 (pp. 1–31). Greenwich, CT: JAI Press.

Schneider, B. (1987) E = F (P, B). The road to a radical approach to person–environment fit. *Journal of Vocational Behavior*, **31**, 353–361.

Scott, K. D. & Taylor, G. S. (1985) An examination of conflicting findings on the relationship between job satisfaction and absenteeism: A meta-analysis. *Academy of Management Journal*, **28**, 588–612.

Shartle, C. L. (1956) *Occupational Information*. New York: Prentice-Hall.

Smith, C. A., Organ, D. W., & Near, J. P. (1983) Organizational citizenship behavior: Its nature and antecedents. *Journal of Applied Psychology*, **68**, 653–663.

Smith, D. & Tziner, A. (1995) The moderating effects of affective disposition and social support on the relationship between person–environment fit and strains: An empirical investigation on nurses. Unpublished manuscript. Université de Montréal.

Sommers, M. J. (1995) Organizational commitment, turnover and absenteeism: An examination of direct and indirect effects. *Journal of Organizational Behavior*, **16**, 49–58.

Spokane, A. R. (1985) A review of research on person–environment congruence in Holland's theory of careers. *Journal of Vocational Behavior*, **26**, 306–343.

Sutherland, L. F., Fogarty, G. J. & Pithers, R. T. (1995) Congruence as a predictor of occupational stress. *Journal of Vocational Behavior*, **46**, 292–309.

Tranberg, M., Slane, S., & Ekeberg, S. E. (1993) The relation between interest congruence and satisfaction: A meta-analysis. *Journal of Vocational Behavior*, **42**, 253–264.

Turban, D. B. & Keon, T. L. (1993) Organizational attractiveness: An interactionist perspective. *Journal of Applied Psychology*, **78**, 184–193.

Tziner, A. (1990) *Organizational Staffing and Work Adjustment*. New York: Praeger.

Tziner, A., & Dawis, R. (1988) Occupational stress: A theoretical look from the perspective of work adjustment theory. *International Journal of Management*, **5**, 423–430.

Tziner, A. & Falbe, C. M. (1990) Actual and preferred climates of achievement orientation and their relationships to work attitudes and performance in two occupational strata. *Journal of Organizational Behavior*, **11**, 159–167.

Vardi, Y. & Wiener, Y. (1992) *Organizational misbehavior (OMB): A calculative-normative model*. Paper presented at the annual meeting of the Academy of Management, Las Vegas.

Williams, C. R. & Livingstone, L. P. (1994) Another look at the relationship between performance and voluntary turnover. *Academy of Management Journal*, **37**, 269–298.

Chapter 10

VACATIONS AND OTHER RESPITES: STUDYING STRESS ON AND OFF THE JOB

Dov Eden

Faculty of Management, Tel Aviv University, Israel

VACATIONS AND OTHER RESPITES: STUDYING STRESS ON AND OFF THE JOB

Respite research began as a search for a way to examine the impact of job stress on strain using a more rigorous method than most previous job stress research. Respites were used as control occasions when stress was 'off' to detect the causal effects of acutely stressful events on strain in a repeated-measures, on-again–off-again design. Over time, studying stress during such interevent respites, especially vacations, began to emerge as a topic of study in its own right. This chapter traces this development. First, the strength of the respite research paradigm is described, and a link to existing stress theory to enrich this largely atheoretical line of research is proposed. After reviewing the respite research conducted to date, the chapter concludes with an agenda for future directions in which respite research may evolve.

The Respite Design and its Advantages

Respite research offers a way of testing the stressor–strain hypothesis by comparing levels of strain while individuals are alternately on and off their jobs. Being on and off the job serves as an objective proxy for varying exposure to objective job stressors. In respite research, we repeatedly measure the same workers' perceptions of stressors and experiences of strain before, during, and after the respite. A respite from work may be a day off, a weekend, a vacation, or some other form of absence from the work setting when the everyday pressures of the job are presumed to be absent. Our initial aim in respite research was not to study the respite; rather, it was to study the effects of job stressors and their absence. Objectively speaking, workers are exposed to job stressors on their jobs and are generally not exposed to those stressors while away on a respite from their jobs. The respite serves as a 'control' occasion during which the individual is removed from the job and its stresses. Detecting a decline in perceived job stressors during the respite validates this objective definition (Eden, 1990a). Thus, in respite research we study the impact of job stressors using repeated-measures designs, when job stressors are intermittently 'on' and 'off.' Data gathered this way can be analyzed as a 'partially interrupted time series' (Cook & Campbell, 1979; Eden, 1982, 1990a), a statistically powerful design in which repeated measures accrue abundant degrees of freedom even in small samples. It is a natural quasi-experiment that rules out the major threats to internal validity posed by measuring both stressors and strain just once, using questionnaires completed by the same individuals. Because a time-series design is relatively free of causal ambiguity, Cook and Campbell (1979) stated that 'This design is obviously a very powerful one for inferring causal effects' (p. 222) and rated it very high on internal validity. The rival explanation that a decline in stress and strain caused a respite such as vacation, or that an increase in job stress and strain caused a return to work, are ruled out. Short of experimentally subjecting participants to job stressors, respite research may be the closest one can get to internal validity in ethically acceptable stress research.

The most rigorous experimental methods, both in the laboratory and in the field, in which the experimenter raises stress to examine its impact on strain, are largely unavailable to the job stress researcher. Laboratory settings are so far removed from everyday work situations that their external validity is extremely limited; any stress effects produced in the laboratory would arouse serious doubts concerning the extent to which similar effects could be produced in actual work circumstances, where the threat to well-being is real. Field experimentation has a different limitation. Because arousing stress is hypothesized to have deleterious effects on psychological well-being and performance, few researchers would be willing to conduct such research. Furthermore, management as well as academic Human Subjects Review Boards (i.e., 'Helsinki committees') would likely squelch such potentially harmful research before it got started. For these reasons, almost all job stress research has been done using nonexperimental correlational or cross-sectional designs. The result is a huge literature comprised mostly of causally ambiguous findings. Causal interpretation of such findings is based on theory and common sense, but not on rigorous scientific method.

It is easy to fall into the stereotyped thinking behind statements such as 'Of course stress causes strain!' and 'Some things are obvious and do not require proof'. However, this is poor science. There have been numerous examples of fascinating research in which the validity of accumulated findings concerning the effects of X on Y has been beclouded by showing that Y causes X. For example, Adler, Skov, and Salvimini (1985) have shown that job satisfaction influences ratings of job characteristics rather than the other way around as hypothesized by Hackman and Oldham's (1980) job design model, and Lowen and Craig (1968) showed that subordinates' performance influences their managers' leadership style as much as, or more than, leadership influences performance. Given that such 'obvious' causes have been shown to be affected by their putative effects, it is unreasonably risky to assume that stress causes strain and to interpret stressor–strain correlations as evidence for the causal impact of stress on strain. Furthermore, it is perfectly reasonable to hypothesize that strain influences perceived stress. Dissatisfied, anxious, depressed, and harassed individuals perceive the world differently from those not afflicted by such strains. Therefore, it is as tenable that observed stress–strain relationships result from the effects of strain on stress as from the effects of stress on strain.

Causal ambiguity is compounded by the widespread practice of job-stress researchers in computing stress–strain correlations on observations obtained using the same individuals' responses to the same kind of measures. That is, the same workers complete questionnaire measures of both stress and strain, creating single-source bias. Even if stress and strain were not related, such single-source, single-method measurement would be expected to yield correlations between the variables so measured. Therefore, such correlations are weak evidence of a relationship, not to speak of causal effects. It is disconcerting that so much correlational and cross-sectional research showing static relationships between single-source, single-method measures of stress and strain—and interpreting the results causally—gets published. Respite research is free of most of these pitfalls.

Vacation

The most prevalent respite from work is the weekend. The Mosaic Sabbath day of rest from work and toil, which revolutionized the world of work in ancient times, evolved into its present largely standard 2-day format only a generation ago. Although the typical employee accumulates about 100 days of weekend time off work each year, there has been almost no study of the restorative value of this respite nor any research devoted to increasing its contribution to on-the-job productivity.

The next most prevalent respite from work is vacation. Aron (1999) has traced the emergence of vacation as an integral part of the employment experience in the United States. The dominant Puritan values were inimical to time off work as idle time squandered on frivolous recreation. Sundays were best used for 'listening to sermons on the virtues of work and the potential dangers of play' (p. 34). In early nineteenth-century usage, 'vacation' meant time away from school for students and teachers. Only in the 1850s did the word vacation begin to take on its modern meaning of respite time away from work for the enjoyment of leisure. Prevailing attitudes had shifted toward viewing the pleasures derived from recreation and amusement as restorative, ultimately contributing to the productivity of a worker returning with renewed mental and spiritual strength to face the stressful daily tribulations of work. Within a few more generations, taking vacation spread from the wealthy leisurely class to the working masses and paid annual leave became an institutionalized part of American worklife. In Europe the struggle for the legitimization of respites from work apparently was easier in coming. There, vacations are still called 'holidays' (derived from 'holy days,' hinting at their origin in time off work for religious devotion) and, at least until recently, they were more plentiful there than in the United States (Cooper, 1999).

How Does Respite Relieve Stress and Strain?

Most observers would agree that a respite from work can ease the aversive consequences of stress on well-being by punctuating the otherwise constant aggravation caused by incessant job demands. However, most treatises on vacation have been published in popular and practitioner oriented outlets. We all 'know' that our coveted vacation respites are important for our health and well-being, so nobody thought of studying them systematically—until recently. Most treatment of vacation has been rather shallow, and the psychological mechanisms through which respite contributes to well-being have gone largely ignored. Most authors appear simply to have assumed that a respite fulfills a spontaneous restorative function and have provided no theoretical explanation of the phenomenon. For example, Quick and Quick (1984) discussed vacation and leisure as methods for managing stress. Noting that the impact of vacations has rarely been studied, they stated there is evidence that individuals have greater tolerance for adversity after a vacation. They neither presented nor cited the evidence.

Leisure and pychological well-being

Rubenstein (1980), who surveyed retrospective accounts of vacation experiences, reported that the most popular motive respondents expressed for a vacation was relaxation. The Random House Thesaurus lists as antonyms for relaxation 'work, toil, labor, strain' (p. 593). Thus, 'relaxation' really means nothing more than the absence of job strain; in the present context, relaxation as a theoretical construct explains nothing. The literature on leisure extols its beneficial consequences for well-being (e.g., Iso-Ahola, 1988). Caldwell and Smith (1988) reasoned that the essence of leisure is freedom, intrinsic satisfaction, and self-determined experiences that result in psychological gains. Hull (1990) concluded from his review that leisure promotes positive mood, in turn influencing cognition and behavior long after the person has left the leisure setting. This implies respite after-effects. However, no evidence for this was presented. Ragheb and McKinney (1993) found that greater satisfaction with leisure was inversely associated with academic stress among students. This converges with Kaufman's (1988) generalization that the lower the leisure satisfaction, the higher the anxiety among retired persons.

The theoretical basis of the leisure and relaxation approach is very lean. Moreover, given the research methods used, causality in the leisure studies is indeterminate; perhaps those who experience less academic stress enjoy their leisure time more, and anxious individuals enjoy leisure, and everything else in life, less than persons free of anxiety. The respite phenomenon deserves a richer theoretical base and stronger empirical support.

Life-events theory

According to Holmes and Rahe (1967), both positive and negative life events require readjustment and are therefore stressful. Their Social Readjustment Rating Scale includes vacation as a stressful event. However, evidence shows that positive events can have positive impact on well-being. Cohen and Hoberman (1983) found that positive changes buffered the effects of negative ones; positive events had what they called a 'stress-sheltering effect.' Furthermore, Vinokur and Caplan (1986) found that pleasant events promote health. To the extent that vacation is pleasant, it should reduce strain. Thus, the restorative function of respite from work is consistent with the life-events approach. However, it still does not explain much. Why do pleasant events promote health and well-being?

Conservation of resources (COR) theory

Hobfoll's (1989) conservation of resources (COR) approach appears uniquely appropriate as a theoretical basis for explaining the respite effect (see also Hobfoll & Freedy, 1993). Whereas most stress theories focus on how people react to stressors, COR theory makes novel predictions about what happens in *the absence of stress*. According to COR theory, stress occurs when individuals either are threatened with resource loss, actually lose resources, or fail to gain resources after resource investment. Those who possess strong pools of resources often experience spirals of resource gain because initial gain begets further gain. The cycle of gain generates its own positive energy because resource accretion means that more resources can be invested in obtaining still further gains. Consistent with COR theory's primacy-of-resource-loss argument, Lee and Ashforth (1996) found in a meta-analysis of the correlates of burnout that emotional exhaustion was more strongly related to work demands that may have resulted in resource loss than resource gain. This implies that a respite may alleviate burnout by halting the resource loss cycle. During vacation or other time off work, rest, reflection, and reconnecting with such sources of social support as family and friends replenish depleted physical and emotional resources, enabling further resource gains.

According to COR theory, interrupting loss spirals and creating gain spirals is the best course for stress resistance because it is preventative. Hobfoll and Shirom (1993) suggested that a relaxation period between stress episodes allows regrouping of resources such as social support and sense of mastery, replenishing resource reservoirs. A vacation of a couple of weeks or so may be the best way to facilitate such regrouping. Thus, adopting COR theory, one may conceive of respite as a time to replenish depleted personal resources. This implies the need to measure resource levels before and after respites as a test of COR theory and as a way of increasing our understanding of how respites work to relieve stress and strain. Unfortunately, such measurement has not been part of respite research to date. Confirmation of COR theory in future respite research would also imply practical applications for increasing the utility of time off work.

Review of Respite Research

Below, the respite research is reviewed and summarized. Table 10.1 lists the major studies reviewed chronologically from earliest to latest conducted.[1] This review is followed by an agenda for future respite research.

Physiological respite research

Numerous studies of physiological strain have used repeated-measures designs that included respites from work (or studies for student samples). These

Table 10.1 Major respite studies

Authors	Respite	Sample
Caplan & Jones (1975)	Computer shutdown	Students
Eden (1982)	Respites between critical events	Student nurses
Lounsbury & Hoopes (1986)	Vacation	Sundry blue-collar
Eden (1990a)	Computer shutdown and vacation	Computer users
Westman & Eden (1997)	Vacation	Clerks
Etzion, Eden, & Lapidot (1998)	Reserve military service	Engineers, technicians
Etzion & Sapir (1997)	Vacation	Production workers
Westman & Aharon-Madar (1998)	Vacation	Manufacturing
Westman, Etzion, & Yoffe (1999)	Business trips	High-tech employees
Etzion & Westman (1999)	Vacation and semester break	Duel-career couples
Eden & Westman (in progress)	Sabbatical leave	Academic faculty

studies were always undertaken with the objective of gauging the effects of stress on strain, not to study the respite for its own sake. For example, Halberg, Engeli, and Hamburger (1965) measured the epinephrine 17-ketosteroid excretion of one worker daily for 4 years. They found a crest at midweek and a decline during weekends. Similarly, Frankenhaeuser, Lundberg, Fredrikson et al. (1989) found support for the healthful effects of a single day off. They found that blood pressure, heart rate, and epinephrine excretions were reduced on the day at home compared to on the job. They also found that subjective tiredness increased during the day at work and peaked after work; during the day at home, workers felt more relaxed and in a good mood. Thus, though meager, the evidence shows that respites of only a day or two can bring relief from job stress. These findings highlight the stressfulness of the job and were so interpreted by the authors. Little if any thought was given to the respite *per se*.

Some stress research has involved respites of more than a day or two. For example, Glaser, Kiecolt-Glaser, Speicher, and Holliday (1985) measured changes in students' resistance to viruses at three points in time: the day before a final exam, the day of the exam, and upon returning from a semester break. They found differences in resistance on these three occasions. After the semester break resistance was highest, indicating low strain. The Glaser et al. research program was focused on psychoneuroimmunology (PNI). PNI researchers take it as axiomatic that stress is lower during the summer vacation than during exams, and time their collection of immunological data accordingly to assess the effects of stress on the immune function. Again, although the NI focus is on stress rather than on respite effects, the findings support the respite hypothesis.

The first respite study

The first published research using the term 'respite' was Eden's (1982) study of critical job events (CJEs), undertaken with the aim of studying the impact of the acute stress engendered by such events on strain using a more internally valid method. Though not the first repeated-measures study of stress, it was the first job stress study with five repeated measures of job stress and psychological and physiological strains. It enabled the author to draw causal conclusions that were not based on correlations between questionnaire measures of stress and strain completed by the same individuals. Indeed, there were no correlations at all in the report. Thus, it was free of the same-source–same-method bias that has plagued so much stress research. The participants were 39 first-year student nurses. Participants gave questionnaire responses and blood samples on the morning of two critical events, which were the first time reporting for work in uniform in a hospital ward and the day of the final examination in nursing. Both events had been identified by previous first-year students as particularly stressful, if not harrowing, experiences. These CJEs were sandwiched in between three routine measurement occasions during which objective stress was at its relatively low chronic, not acute, level. These were the respite occasions. Analysis showed that both subjective stress and psychological and physiological strain waxed on the objectively acutely stressful CJEs and waned on the routine, respite occasions, supporting the stress–strain hypothesis. The data were more consistent for the second CJE than for the first, indicating that not every CJE arouses the same amount of stress and that not every respite can be expected to provide equal relief. What was entirely consistent across the five occasions was that anxiety, systolic and diastolic blood pressure, pulse rate, and serum uric acid rose and fell by statistically significant amounts in the predicted pattern, confirming the hypothesis that job stress causes strain. The rival hypothesis that rising and falling levels of strain had caused acute stress by determining the timing of the CJEs was untenable.

The first vacation study

Rubenstein (1980) concluded from her survey of retrospective accounts of vacation experiences that most workers feel a vacation relieves tension, enabling personal growth and satisfaction. Rubenstein was perhaps the first in the social science literature to consider vacation as a valued feature of worklife in its own right, rather than as an 'off-again' phenomenon that is of interest because of what it is *not*. However, the retrospective method poses a serious threat to the validity of Rubenstein's findings.

In what appears to have been the first empirical, pretest-posttest study undertaken with the express purpose of studying vacation for its own sake, Lounsbury and Hoopes (1986) compared job and life satisfaction before and after vacation. They found that satisfaction with vacation was related to subsequent satisfaction with life and work. They interpreted before-after differences in work and nonwork variables as evidence that vacation had an impact. However, their single-group, two-occasion, pretest-posttest design was vulnerable to many threats to internal validity (Cook & Campbell, 1979). Moreover, the uniformly positive correlations may be a result of positive and negative affectivity (see Brief, Burke, George, Robinson, & Webster, 1988; Schaubroeck, Ganster, & Fox, 1992). The addition of more occasions or of a control group, or both, would be needed to render the results more convincing. Nevertheless, Lounsbury and Hoopes (1986) did break new ground in publishing the first empirical evaluation of vacation as a work phenomenon of interest in its own right.

Computer shutdown studies: finding vacation while seeking stress-free occasions

The opportunity to do more respite research presented itself when the staff at Tel Aviv University was notified that the computer center was to be shut down for refurbishment during the upcoming Passover holiday. This was a golden opportunity to replicate and expand upon Caplan and Jones's (1975) pioneering study of the stressfulness of a computer shutdown at the University of Michigan. Although Caplan and Jones had conceived of their study as stress research based on measuring reactions to a naturally imposed stressful event, it can be reinterpreted as a respite study. They found that anxiety, depression, and heart rate were lower after the summer vacation respite than they had been 5 months earlier when their participants were experiencing the stress of heavy workload in anticipation of the shutdown. Though they conducted observations on only two occasions, Caplan and Jones had provided the first empirical evidence that may indicate the ameliorative effects of a vacation respite from role stress.

Eden (1990a) extended Caplan and Jones's (1975) two-occasion design to four occasions, one of which was while the participants were at home for the holiday during the shutdown. He found that during the holiday stress and physiological strain declined and later returned to prevacation levels after returning to work. However, during the vacation, psychological strain remained at the chronic levels measured during the normal course of work. Eden explained this failure of the respite to relieve psychological strain in terms of the lingering effects of the acute stressfulness of the rush to get work completed before the shutdown and of the users' anticipation of an exceptionally demanding workload awaiting them upon return from their forced vacation. He also speculated about the potential stressfulness of the off-work 'respite' experience itself. This sparked further thinking about the possibility of vacations being a mixed blessing. They may provide relief from job stress for some workers, but also add new kinds of stresses. Eden cited evidence suggesting that wife-beating increases during weekends and holidays at home. He also discussed the fade-out effect that was evident in the return of stress and strain to their prevacation levels by the time of the posttest a month after returning to work. Finally, he suggested that vacation stress may evolve into an area of study in itself. Thus, studying work and respite with repeated-measures designs was launched as a method of revealing patterns of job stress and its relief.

Measuring stress and strain during vacation to study job stress

Westman and Eden (1997) measured stress and burnout before, during, and after vacation. They had a high degree of internal validity due to the relatively large number (i.e., five) of occasions. They had 76 clerical employees complete measures of perceived job stressors and experienced burnout twice before a 2-week company-wide vacation, once during vacation, and twice after the vacation. They detected substantial declines in burnout during the vacation and a return to prevacation levels of burnout by the time of the second postvacation measure, 3 weeks after returning to work. Comparison of the two prevacation measures, taken 6 weeks and 3 days before vacation, indicated no anticipation effects. However, the return to work showed gradual fade-out, as burnout returned part way toward its prevacation level by 3 days after the vacation, and all the way by 3 weeks after the vacation. Women and those who were satisfied with their vacations experienced the greatest relief; however, both of these subsamples also experienced the quickest fade-out. Westman and Eden detected the respite effect and its complete fade-out among all subgroups analyzed; the subgroups differed only in degree of relief experienced and rate of fade-out. Westman and Eden discussed burnout and its relief in terms of 'burnout climate' at work and in terms of interpersonal stress crossover (see Westman, in press; Westman & Etzion, 1995; Westman & Vinokur, 1998). This study initiated the search for moderators in stress and respite effects, and showed that moderators were indeed there to be detected. Moreover, Westman and Eden were the first to invoke COR theory as a post hoc explanation of their respite results.

Reserve military service as a respite from job stress

Etzion, Eden, and Lapidot (1998) extended the scope of respite research by studying a novel respite from job stress. Arguing that active reserve service in the Israel Defense Forces serves as a release mechanism for 'letting off steam' among Israeli men, they predicted that being away from job stressors would have an ameliorative impact on burnout. Furthermore, relying on repeated measures for quasi-experimental control, previous respite research had lacked a comparison group of similar others not simultaneously experiencing a respite. The lack of a comparison group threatens internal validity because the confounding effects of that large cluster of influential variables called 'history' (Campbell & Stanley, 1966) cannot be entirely ruled out. Etzion, Eden, and Lapidot rectified this by comparing 81 men who were called up for active reserve service to 81 matched controls in the same company who were not called to service during the same period. Each reservist and his control completed questionnaires shortly before the first left work for a stint of reserve service and immediately upon his return. Job stress and burnout declined among those who were mobilized. There was no change among the control respondents. Furthermore, both the quality of reserve service and the degree of detachment from work moderated these respite effects; the greater the detachment, the stronger the effect that positive reserve service experience had in relieving reservists of stress and burnout. Those who failed to achieve psychological detachment during their reserve service respite failed to reap its benefits. Etzion, Eden, and Lapidot concluded that reserve service is a special case of stress-relieving get-away from work that may be experienced as an ameliorative respite akin to vacation. However, the strength of the respite effect depends on the degree to which the individual is psychologically detached from the job back home. Etzion, Eden, and Lapidot further proposed focusing future research on psychological detachment, on the job as well as during respites from work.

Although Etzion, Eden, and Lapidot emphasized that they studied reserve service as a respite to highlight the effects of job stress, their study expanded the realm of respite research beyond a stray day or two off or annual vacation with an expanded conceptualization of respite to include *any* off-job experience. This opened up an entire area of inquiry concerning the nature of the off-job experience itself. Is it compulsory or voluntary? Long or short? Positive or negative? Does the respite have its own built-in stressors that might offset the relief gained from the absence of the chronic job stressors? Would spending a period of paid time off-site, say, for prolonged training or an extended business trip, also provide respite relief from chronic job stress?

Etzion, Eden, and Lapidot discussed the implications of the recent spread of mobile telephones, portable laptop computers, and email hookups while traveling as potential threats to relief-giving detachment while away from the workplace. The computerized telecommunications revolution has been so rapid that it now appears that Etzion, Eden, and Lapidot underestimated its impact. Unless workers disconnect when they go on leave, their jobs will continue to consume their personal resources and they will be denied the restorative benefits of respite. The lightening diffusion of these means of getting connected indicates that the world of work is oblivious to this danger.

Vacation for vacation's sake

Next, Etzion and Sapir (1997) measured perceived job stressors and burnout among industrial workers before members of one group went on vacation, after they returned to work, and 3 weeks later. A matched comparison group of workers who remained on their jobs throughout the study completed questionnaires on all three occasions. The combination of three repeated measures and a matched comparison group makes this an especially highly internally valid study. Etzion and Sapir detected a respite effect; both job stress and burnout were rated lower after vacation than before. Three weeks later job stress reverted to its initial level; however, burnout remained low. Job stress and burnout remained constant across all three occasions in the control group, which had no respite. By title and emphasis, Etzion and Sapir's study was perhaps the first to put the focus on vacation as the topic of research, rather than as a 'control' event useful for studying job stress.

Impact of respite on performance

Westman and Aharon-Madar (1998) expanded vacation research into attendance and performance measures not previously examined in respite research. They had 87 employees in a food manufacturing company complete self-report measures of job stress, burnout, and performance on three occasions, 10 days before a 10-day company-wide vacation, immediately after the vacation, and a month after returning to work. They also obtained data on absenteeism both for health reasons and other reasons from personnel files. They found substantial declines in stress and burnout immediately after vacation and a return to prevacation levels 4 weeks after returning to work. Furthermore, self-reported performance was significantly higher immediately after vacation than before vacation; however, it, also, returned to its prevacation level a month after returning to work. Moreover, the health-related absentee rate immediately after vacation did not differ significantly from the rate before vacation; however, the rate dropped significantly 4 weeks after vacation. Absenteeism for other reasons was lower 2 weeks after vacation than before vacation; 4 weeks after vacation absenteeism was significantly lower than prior to vacation but higher than immediately after the vacation. Finally, moderator analysis did not replicate the previous findings of Westman and Eden; there were no differences between men and women or between those who enjoyed their vacations and those who did not. The respite effect and its complete fade-out were detected among all subgroups analyzed. The innovation in Westman and Aharon-Madar's study was in demonstrating respite effects on performance and absenteeism. Replication using objective performance measures and absentee rates among comparable workers not on vacation at the same time would establish respites as a potential source of renewed human energy to fuel organizational effectiveness.

Business trips as respites

Westman, Etzion, and Yoffe (1999) studied the impact of overseas business trips on job stress and burnout among 57 employees of Israeli high-tech companies who travel abroad as part of their job. This was a sample accustomed to overseas travel; their average annual number of trips abroad was four, and the average stay was 6 days. Participants completed questionnaires thrice, 10 days prior to going abroad, once during their stay abroad, and 1 week after returning home to their regular jobs. A substantial decline in stress was detected immediately after the trip. Job stress was higher before the trip and during the stay abroad than after returning to the permanent worksite. Burnout was significantly lower after returning from the trip than before leaving for the trip. Burnout was also lower upon returning from the trip than during the stay abroad, but the difference was not significant. Finally, respondents who were satisfied with their trip reported less job stress and burnout than did those who were less satisfied with their trip.

Westman, Etzion, and Yoffe interpreted their findings as showing that an overseas business trip does not have the same impact as a vacation even though the employee is absent from his regular work environment. They attributed the high level of burnout prior to the trip to excessive overload, ambiguity, and threatening job demands, and described the period abroad as also characterized by ambiguity and overload. Both the anticipation of the overseas trip and the work abroad itself may have had a negative impact on employees. Only when the employee returns to his or her routine job does the burnout level decrease. This may be evidence for a delayed respite effect, which should be pursued in follow-up research.

Westman, Etzion, and Yoffe have shown that a working respite is not the same as a vacation respite. Still, their participants reported less stress and strain after return, indicating a postrespite effect. This may be different from a vacation respite effect that is experienced *during* the respite. Westman, Etzion, and Yoffe's results thus highlight the importance of distinguishing between different types of respites. One future development may be a typology of respites, each type with its distinguishing characteristics and the degree of relief from stress and strain that it affords. We need research on other types of working respites, such as when absenting the routine workplace for training.

Studies of respite as a moderator

A novel tack is to use the respite not as the independent variable that occasions stress and strain, but instead as a high-stress–low-stress moderator. In two studies, Etzion and Westman (1999) analyzed the relationships between stress and burnout among dual-career couples on two occasions, one stressful and the other a less stressful respite. They were seeking evidence for crossover of strain between partners and interpreted their results as showing that crossover of burnout occurred on the stressful occasion but not during the respite. An intriguing implication of these findings is that contact between spouses may or may not occasion contagion, depending on when the contact occurs. If Etzion and Westman's findings can be replicated, then salutogenic interventions geared toward facilitating cross-partner relief (e.g., reducing a wife's strain in order to facilitate a reduction in the husband's strain) may be worthwhile during stressful times but would be of no value during a respite, when such a reduction would not cross over to him anyway. Of course, a simple explanation of Etzion and Westman's findings is that there was no stress crossover during the low-stress respite because there was no stress to cross over. At any rate, comparing stress–strain crossover relationships during high and low stress periods is an innovation that might spur further use of respite occasions in moderator analyses to help clarify the high-stress–low-stress conditions under which other variables relate to each other.

An Agenda for Future Respite Research

Respite research will undoubtedly expand. It has evolved from respite as a no-stress or low-stress occasion to vacation, reserve military service, and business trips as respites in their own right. Below are some of the directions future respite research is likely to take. The main points are listed in Table 10.2.

Table 10.2   An agenda for future respite research

Type and length of respite
Preventing or delaying fade-out to prolong respite relief
Psychological moderators (e.g., expectations, self-efficacy, affectivity, work addiction)
Respite performance
Vacation stress (e.g., unmet expectations, lost baggage, flight delays)
Psychological detachment versus high-tech tethers
Demographic moderators (e.g., gender, age, number of children)
Postrespite performance effects
Respite effect versus the 'rosy view effect'
Sabbatical leave as a respite

Type and length of respite

We already know that business trips differ from vacations. We need more knowledge about how different types and lengths of respites provide different amounts of relief. Considering COR theory, respites evidently differ in the extent to which they provide opportunity for replenishing exhausted psychological resources. Any further respite research should take this into account and measure repletion opportunity as a potential moderator.

Maximizing respite relief

Most of the research has shown that respite relief is short-lived. However, that does not mean that the relief obtained cannot be prolonged. Eden (1990a) and Westman and Eden (1997) called for research to pinpoint the ideal length and frequency of vacations to provide maximal respite relief. Such knowledge would serve as a guide to optimization of vacation timing. The same total respite time may be cut up in different ways; some ways may offer greater relief than others. Etzion and Sapir (1997) found that a vacation of over 2 weeks had the same ameliorative effects as a shorter one (10–14 days). They suggested that several short vacations may be more beneficial over time than one annual vacation of the same total duration. Quick and Quick (1984) suggested that five 3-day weekends may be better than a 1-week vacation. The 3-day weekend respite enjoyed by persons working a 4 × 10 weekly work schedule (4 days, 10 hours each) could be compared to the 2-day weekend respite afforded by the standard 5-day work week.

Multiplicity of reasons for enjoying a respite[2]

When returning employees say they enjoyed their vacation, what makes them say that? There are numerous answers to this question. This multiplicity of reasons for answering in a particular way is a potential threat to the validity of respite research. The variables that can determine whether a vacation provides relief or misery can be classified as either characteristics of the individual such as personality traits, attitudes, and expectations, or as external features of the respite itself, such as its length, whether or not it is job-related, whether voluntary or involuntary, the type of activity involved, harrowing extraneous incidents that may occur during the respite, and the degree of detachment from the back-home job that it provides. The individual's expectations prior to the respite, self-efficacy, and positive or negative affectivity, are posited to moderate whether the situational factors that characterize a respite promote or inhibit respite relief.

Respite relief as a self-fulfilling prophecy: expectation effects

We speak of a self-fulfilling prophecy when the expectation that an event will occur makes its occurrence more likely (Merton, 1948). Self-fulfilling prophecies are endemic to our lives, including our worklives (Eden, 1990b). Expectations have been shown to influence whether or not an event occurs, the extent to which it occurs, and how individuals react to its occurrence. One rather dramatic example that is relevant to respite research involves seasickness and performance at sea as a self-fulfilling prophecy. Eden and Zuk (1995) increased naval cadets' seasickness self-efficacy experimentally by informing them that, once at sea, they had little risk of experiencing serious seasickness and that they would be able to perform well despite any seasickness they may experience on rough seas. Cadets so informed reported less seasickness and obtained higher objective performance ratings than did randomly assigned control cadets. The effectiveness of the expectancy treatment was greater than that of the various pharmacological means used to prevent or relieve seasickness. This shows that one experiences an event as one expects to experience it. Expecting less seasickness and good performance, the experimental cadets fulfilled their prophecy and underwent the experience as they expected. Similar self-fulfilling prophecy experiments in organizations have shown that expectations can influence such varied outcomes as the likelihood of finding a job, of volunteering for special forces, and the rehabilitation of disadvantaged youths in a remedial program (for reviews see Eden 1992, 1993; Eden et al., 2000). One can only wonder how many expensive vacation voyages have been spoiled due to similarly preventable seasickness!

The present hypothesis is that a self-fulfilling prophecy process is at work when one goes on vacation or takes any other kind of a break from everyday work routine. We go on vacation, take business trips, participate in off-site training programs, and travel to professional conferences and scientific meetings with expectations. These expectations may be for the level of scientific presentations, the accommodations, the travel itself, the ambiance at the meeting, reuniting with friends, and any other features that may be important to the individual. The expectancy hypothesis is that these expectations increase the likelihood that whatever is expected will occur. For example, the traveler who expects to miss his or her flight doesn't try as hard to make it to the airport on time and ends up missing it; the diner who expects bad food at a restaurant enjoys the food less; the scholar who expects boring presentations at the meeting is more bored than one who expected exciting presentations; the conventioneer who expects to have a good time with his or her colleagues enjoys the social aspects of the conference more than the one who arrives expecting not to enjoy the experience socially. The expectancy hypothesis holds for any aspect of a respite that arouses expectations.

The expectancy hypothesis can be tested simply by measuring the respondent's expectations prior to the beginning of the respite. For example, studying reserve military service as a respite, Etzion, Lapidot, and Eden (1998) found that the respite afforded the reservists relief from job stressors and burnout. However, there was variance in the amount of relief experienced. The expectancy hypothesis would be that those who expected more relief got more relief. Similarly, Westman and Eden (1997) found variance in the amount of relief experienced by employees during an annual vacation from work and Westman, Etzion, and Yoffe (1999) found variance in the reactions of various employees returning from a business trip. The self-fulfilling prophecy prediction would be that employees who expect greater reduction in stress and strain while on vacation or away for business will experience a greater reduction. Thus, the expectancy hypothesis can be tested simply by adding a measure of expectations to the questionnaire completed on the prerespite occasion.

A bolder approach to testing the respite expectancy hypothesis would entail an experimental treatment designed to raise participants' expectations for relief prior to their respite. The experimenter would inform employees about to depart for off-site training that they are about to experience a highly favorable program that has won raves from previous trainees, or implant positive expectations in the minds of employees about to embark on a business trip that the experience should be a favorable one. The expectancy prediction is that such a treatment will render the period away from the job a more favorable experience. The addition of an experimental treatment to the repeated-measures field study methods used to date would add a greater degree of experimental rigor to respite research and increase its internal validity. Testing experimental treatments would also point the way to practical application of the knowledge that has been accumulating with regard to respite effects.

Raising expectations to increase participants' enjoyment of an upcoming event is not a novel idea. Countless travel agents 'sell' clients on the enjoyment they are about to reap from the expensive tour package they are purchasing. This is not unlike the color insert we find upon unwrapping the new gadget that we have just purchased, informing us that we can expect many years of trouble-free satisfaction from the product. The world of marketing knows that, irrespective of the product or service, customers end up being more satisfied if they expect to be satisfied. What would be novel in the expectancy research proposed is that it would be done under controlled conditions and would be intended to increase participants' respite relief, not to maximize marketers' profits.

Respite research has consistently found that the respite effect produced by being off the job for a while fades soon after returning to work. This is unfortunate, because it means that the benefits the individual reaps from the respite in terms of 'recharged batteries,' reduced strain, and a general boost to well-being are short-lived. Though there have been several calls for research to seek ways of extending the length of respite relief to prolong its benefits, no specific ideas as to how to do so have been proposed. An experimental expectancy treatment might be able to meet this need. Inasmuch as expectations influence how individuals experience the future, a treatment could be administered to employees upon their return. The treatment would be focused on expectations for continued savoring of their vacation joy and benefiting from reduced burnout. This would require some convincing information from a credible source to be conveyed to the employees, either before their departure for the respite or immediately upon their return, that would get them to expect prolonged relief. The prediction would be that those led to expect longer relief will benefit from slower fade-out of respite relief.

Self-efficacy and respite 'performance'

Somewhat related to expectancy effects, yet still distinct from them, are self-efficacy effects. Self-efficacy is defined as one's belief in one's ability to mobilize the mental, motivational, and emotional resources needed to execute the courses of action required to meet situational demands (Bandura, 1997). There is strong meta-analytic evidence that self-efficacy and performance are related (Stajkovic & Luthans, 1998). There is also experimental evidence that boosting self-efficacy improves performance (e.g., Eden & Aviram, 1993; Eden & Kinnar, 1991; Eden & Zuk, 1995). Generalizing to respite research, let us assume that a respite from work is a life event to be undertaken. Indeed, many persons purposely choose grueling vacations that are quite stressful and stretch their coping resources. For many others, a vacation planned to be a restful and tranquil time-out turns out to be nerve-wracking. Holmes and Rahe's (1967) Social Readjustment Rating Scale includes vacation as a stressful life event because, whether positive or negative, a vacation is an experience that requires readjustment and is therefore potentially stressful. Thus, we can look at any respite as requiring some adaptation or coping on the part of the individual. A reasonable prediction, based on self-efficacy theory and existing evidence for the relationship between self-efficacy and performance, is that persons high in self efficacy will 'perform' better on their respite. The interesting aspect of this prediction is the meaning of 'performance' off the job.

We can define performance as meeting the demands of the situation. 'Performance' usually refers to job performance. On the job, when output is readily quantifiable, defining and measuring performance is relatively simple. An out-of-town or overseas business trip or training course is midway between on- and off-the-job, and measuring performance is still relatively easy. However, off the job, it is not so simple. We need a definition of off-the-job performance. If job performance is the extent to which the employee meets the demands of the job, performance during the respite is the extent to which the individual meets the demands of the respite. For a leisurely vacation, good performance may entail having fun or achieving relaxation. However, even planned sightseeing tour vacations and holiday hotel vacations can be demanding. There are the potential hazards of missing the flight, forgetting to pack essential items not easily obtained on tour, losing luggage, cameras, binoculars, and other expensive personal items, being robbed or burglarized, running out of money, rental car breakdown, quarrels with others on the tour, getting detached from the group in a foreign country and having difficulty finding one's way back to the hotel, squabbling with spouse, whining children, getting sick, inclement weather, and disliking the food. The list is endless. The self-efficacy prediction is that the individual high in self-efficacy undertakes these challenges more vigorously, copes more actively, and withstands better any temporary setbacks that may occur. Vacationers with low vacation self-efficacy fret, engage in negative self-talk ('I'll be stranded without my suitcases!') and even sit out some of the planned activities, preferring to let other, hardier souls undertake the 'zany' outings to exotic high spots on the tour. By so doing, they relinquish their claim to some of the fun and enjoyment they could have had. The specific relevant variable is 'fun self-efficacy,' defined as the individual's belief in his or her capacity to derive pleasure from a situation. Some people know that they can manage to have fun even under highly demanding job requirements, whereas others believe they cannot have fun even while on vacation. Respite self-efficacy, or belief in capacity to enjoy the respite, is thus predicted to be a determinant of fun, enjoyment, and relief from stress and strain while on the respite.

Respite researchers can include respite self-efficacy in their studies in two ways. First, they can measure it and analyze it as a moderator, predicting that those high in respite self-efficacy enjoy their respites more than do those who are low, and that their levels of stress and strain rise and fall more than do those of the lows. Experimentally, we could attempt to develop a treatment designed to raise respite self-efficacy, similar to the treatments used successfully to raise self-efficacy in order to improve performance in other domains. Such treatment already exists, though it is not called self-efficacy training. Some airlines conduct programs in helping travelers with flight phobias overcome their trepidation so that they will purchase tickets and fly. The present proposal is to extend this to raising participants' belief in their capacity to enjoy the whole package, not just the flight.

Positive and negative affectivity

Positive and negative affectivity influence the level of respondents' answers to questionnaire items in general, and in stress research in particular (Brief et al., 1988; Schaubroeck, Ganster, & Fox, 1992). We can generalize this to respite research and predict that some of the individual differences in how employees report their respite experience will be determined by affectivity. However, the repeated-measures method used in respite research controls the potential confounding of evidence for respite effects by affectivity. An individual high in positive affectivity would be expected to respond consistently favorably relative to other respondents, but still to respond more favorably during the respite than before it or after it. Similarly, an individual high in negative affectivity would be expected to respond consistently unfavorably relative to other respondents, but also to respond less unfavorably during the respite than before it or after it. Thus, affectivity is another potential moderator. To the extent that affectivity is a reflection of a personality trait, not merely a response style, it is predicted that individuals characterized by high negative affectivity enjoy (or at least report enjoying) their respites less, and that the respite effect is either nil or smaller for them. Conversely, individuals characterized by high positive affectivity enjoy their respites more, and the respite effect is larger for them. Testing this would require simply measuring positive and negative affectivity and analyzing it as a moderator. The moderation effect is not to be detected in terms of greater mean relief among those with positive affectivity compared to the negatives; rather, it is predicted to be evident in greater change across time in mean relief among the positives than among the negatives.

Work addiction

Workaholics are an interesting group for respite research. Their response to imposed absence from the workplace, as for annual vacation, may be opposite to that of workers who are not addicted to their jobs. Westman and Eden (1997) analyzed their data separately for those designated workaholic and found that they were less burned out than the others, and that they experienced less variation in stress and strain across the various occasions. The results seemed to be indicating that the workaholics were less influenced by the respite. However, Westman and Eden's measure of workaholism was deficient, and these results were not reported. Future respite research should include a good measure of work addiction and test it as a moderator.

Psychological detachment versus high-tech tethers

The emergence of psychological detachment as a moderator of respite relief (Etzion, Eden, & Lapidot, 1998) promises to be a major factor in future respite research. In particular, the growing dissemination of portable means of communication from anywhere to anywhere threatens the very benefit of getting away, just now when we have begun to document the salutogenic effects of being away. It is doubtful that one can be in constant contact with the sources of stress while away and still derive the restorative benefits of being away. If Etzion, Eden, and Lapidot's results are replicated, the implication for human resource management may be that these electronic tethers should be confiscated before one departs for vacation, and that employees should be ordered not to attempt making contact with vacationing colleagues.

Respite effect versus the 'rosy view effect'

Mitchell, Thompson, Peterson, and Cronk (1997; see also Mitchell & Thompson, 1994) conducted three studies among students on respites, including a Thanksgiving vacation at home, a tour of Europe, and a bicycle trip in California. Mitchell et al. defined three time perspectives and measured participants' feelings and cognitions at least once during each time perspective. They measured prospective expectations prior to the respite, current perceptions during the respite, and how the participants remembered the respite experience retrospectively some time after it was over. The authors reported evidence for the 'rosy view effect' inasmuch as participants expected and recalled the experience as more positive than they described it while experiencing it. The authors concluded that people have a more positive view of the event prior to its occurrence (i.e., rosy prospection) and afterwards (i.e., rosy retrospection) than while it is happening. The prospective rosy view effect was stronger than the retrospective version. When tested separately, the preevent–during-the-event differences were mostly significant, whereas the during-the-event–postevent differences were not. The general finding, replicated in the three studies of quite different respite events, was that expectations and memories were more positive than were concurrent evaluations of the experience. Mitchell et al. proposed several psychological mediators to explain the rosy view phenomenon.

An interesting divergence between the respite research and the rosy view research is that the former typically finds individuals in a more positive state during the respite than before it and after it, whereas the latter has shown that respondents are more negative about the experience during the respite than before it and after it. This apparent contradiction can be explained in terms of what is measured, how it is measured, and when it is measured in both types of research. Mitchell et al. altered the wording of their items for each time perspective. This renders their method different from that used in respite research, in which the same variables (e.g., stress and burnout) are measured repeatedly with the same measures, always concurrently, and patterns of rising and falling mean values are tracked. The respite researcher always asks the respondent how he or she feels 'right now' while completing the questionnaire. This is different from altering item wording for the different occasions and asking respondents to indicate on different occasions what they expect in the future, how they feel right now, and how they presently recall the experience from the past. Actually, the respite method prevents the potential confounding of the results by the rosy view effect because in respite studies we do not ask participants to indicate their expectations or memories of the respite; there is no prospection or retrospection. Therefore, all the psychological processes that Mitchell et al. invoked to explain the rosy view effect are not relevant to respite research and do not confound it. The rosy view effect and the respite effect are different, though related, phenomena. Indeed, Mitchell et al.'s rosy view research highlights the importance of using current measures in respite research, and not relying on participants' recall for what they were experiencing; such recall is tainted by rosy retrospect.

It may be worth pursuing the integration of these two effects. For example, an experimental treatment designed to prolong postrespite relief may be elaborated to include also harnessing the retrospective rosy view effect as a booster. Returning employees subjected to the anti-fade-out treatment could be given questionnaires sometime after their return to work in which they would be asked to recall how pleasurable the respite was. Properly utilized, the retrospective rosy view may be an auxiliary means of stoking pleasurable memories and deferring fade-out of respite relief.

A caveat implied by the rosy view findings is that it is risky to infer the effects of a respite from measurements made before and after but not *during* the respite. Because obtaining data while people are away can be difficult or impossible, some researchers have sufficed with before and after measures only. For example, Lounsbury and Hoopes (1986) compared job and life satisfaction among their participants before and after vacation. They interpreted before-after differences in work and nonwork variables as evidence that vacation had an impact on these variables. However, they measured nothing during vacation. Lounsbury and Hoopes' measures may have been contaminated by rosy view bias, and may have overestimated the size of the respite effect. In light of the rosy view phenomenon, measurement during the respite is indispensable to valid inference.

Another thought sparked by considering the differences between the rosy view research and respite research is that retrospection may be more important than current experience. After all, life's respites are ephemeral, and most of what we experience during the respite vanishes, only to be replaced by our memory of it. The experience comes and goes fast, but the memory lives on in our minds, sometimes for quite extended periods of time. If it can be shown that positive retrospective memories of respite experiences have salutary effects, then individuals may continue reaping the benefits of their positive respites long after the experience itself has ended. Therefore, it may be more efficient to enhance the memory of a positive experience than to try to make the experience itself more positive. This line of thinking again points to the potential importance of well-designed postrespite debriefing.

Sabbatical leave as a respite

Another direction is a study by Eden and Westman[3] (in progress) of academic staff on Sabbatical leave. Despite the fact that we spend as much as one-seventh of our own careers on Sabbatical, researchers have almost totally neglected Sabbatical leave as a phenomenon worthy of investigation. Like vacation, the treatment of Sabbatical in the literature has been mostly nonempirical and descriptive. According to Toomey and Connor (1988) Sabbaticals historically have been viewed as a way to deal with stress and job burnout, to broaden professional skills, and to provide an opportunity for personal growth. Jarecky and Sandifer (1986) reported that 80% of the medical school faculty members whom they interviewed rated their general satisfaction from their Sabbatical experience as 8 or higher on a 10-point scale. Interviewees reported using the Sabbatical as an opportunity to think about their careers, redefine objectives, and reconsider family roles. The Sabbatical enabled them to 'reestablish a sense of intellectual liveliness,' including the development of new research interests, and it gave them time to think through problems in depth. According to Neidle (1984), Sabbaticals provide rest, recreation, new ideas, and otherwise alleviate burnout. He furthermore suggested that leaves of about 3 months would provide 'an ideal device' for preventing occupational stress. The basis for this suggestion was not made clear. Sorcinelli (1986) focused on the benefits of Sabbaticals. Respondents were 112 college faculty members who, by means of interviews and questionnaires, pointed to several advantages of a Sabbatical. These included opportunity to initiate research, open up fresh scholarly interests, catch up with new developments, and a chance for respite from teaching and administrative responsibilities. Taking time off permitted them to renew their intellectual and emotional resources. Similarly, Hendel and Solberg (1983) found that the most frequently mentioned benefits of a quarter leave program were 'gave me insight into my research' and 'gave me a break from teaching and/or administration.' Most of these findings describing the benefits of a Sabbatical exemplify resource repletion and suggest the appropriateness of COR as a nomological net to guide the Sabbatical research. Accordingly, we are measuring sense of control, freedom from obligations, self-esteem, social support, and satisfaction repeatedly to determine whether indeed the Sabbatical functions as a respite that affords the individual a chance to replenish these resources and gain new ones.

We and our colleagues in several countries are collecting data from samples of university faculty members before, during, and after their Sabbatical leave in the attempt to replicate previous findings obtained studying short respites in semester- or year-long Sabbatical respites. Does a longer respite afford greater relief? Is fade-out slower after a longer respite? What role does having a family along with one on Sabbatical play in enhancing or muffling respite relief? Does detachment from one's permanent university post moderate the effect? Has modern communication ruined it forever, or can one still achieve psychological detachment despite being in constant touch electronically with one's home department? These are some of the questions we expect to answer based on this longitudinal, repeated-measures, cross-cultural study.

Conclusions

Respite research is not an alternative to longitudinal tracking of large samples. However, its more clear-cut causal interpretation should serve to reassure the larger community of stress researchers who must rely on theory and causal modeling to anchor their causal interpretations, but can never rule out as convincingly the alternative hypothesis that something else caused the observed relationships. Thus, respite research provides a methodologically rigorous way to test causal stress theories.

Practically speaking, exhausted employees will take their respite in an effort to replenish their coping resources and to restore their sense of mental health. Recent research by Wright and Cropanzano (1998) shows that taking the respite may be in the form of costly turnover. The sooner we learn how to use our accumulating knowledge of respite effects, the sooner we will be able to help management and human resources officers to utilize well-planned and properly timed vacations and other forms of leave to improve individual health, increase productivity on the job, and reduce costly turnover. Individual employees will be better off, and the organizations that employ them will be more effective.

REFERENCES

Adler, S., Skov, R. B., & Salvimini, N. J. (1985). Job characteristics and job satisfaction: When cause becomes consequence. *Organizational Behavior and Human Decision Processes*, **35**, 123–139.

Aron, C. S. (1999). *Working at Play: A History of Vacations in the United States*. New York: Oxford University Press.

Bandura, A. (1997). *Self-efficacy: The Exercise of Control*. New York, NY: Freeman.

Brief, A., Burke, M., George, J., Robinson, B., & Webster, J. (1988). Should negative affectivity remain an unmeasured variable in the study of job stress? *Journal of Applied Psychology*, **73**, 193–198.

Caldwell, L. L. & Smith, E. A. (1988). Leisure: An overlooked component of health promotion. *Canadian Journal of Public Health*, **79**, S44–S48.

Campbell, D. & Stanley, J. (1966). *Experimental and Quasi-experimental Designs for Research*. Chicago: Rand McNally.

Caplan, R. D. & Jones, K. W. (1975). Effects of work load, role ambiguity, and Type-A personality on anxiety, depression and heart rate. *Journal of Applied Psychology*, **60**, 71–719.

Cohen, S. & Hoberman, H. (1983). Positive events and social supports as buffers of life change stress. *Journal of Applied Social Psychology*, **13**, 99–125.

Cook, D. & Campbell, D. T. (1979). *Quasi-experimentation: Design and Analysis Issues for Field Settings*. Chicago: Rand McNally.

Cooper, C. (1999). The changing psychological contract at work. *European Business Journal*, 11(3), 114–118.

Eden, D. (1982). Critical job events, acute stress, and strain: A multiple interrupted time series. *Organizational Behavior and Human Performance*, **30**, 312–329.

Eden, D. (1990a). Acute and chronic job stress, strain, and vacation relief. *Organizational Behavior and Human Decision Processes*, **45**, 175–193.

Eden, D. (1990b). *Pygmalion in Management: Productiviiy as a Self-fulfilling Prophecy*. Lexington, MA: Lexington Books.

Eden, D. (1992). Leadership and expectations: Pygmalion effects and other self-fulfilling prophecies in organizations. *Leadership Quarterly*, **3**, 271–305.

Eden, D. (1993). Interpersonal expectations in organizations. In P. D. Blanck (Ed.), *Interpersonal Expectations: Theory, Research, and Applications* (pp. 154–178). Cambridge: Cambridge University Press.

Eden, D. (1998b, May). *Respite research: Studying stress on and off the job*. Presented at the Seventh International Conference on Social Stress Research, Budapest.

Eden, D. & Aviram, A. (1993). Self-efficacy training to speed reemployment: Helping people to help themselves. *Journal of Applied Psychology*, **78**, 352–360.

Eden, D., Geller, D., Gewirtz, A., Gordon-Terner, R., Inbar, I., Liberman, M., Pass, Y., Salomon-Segev, I., & Shallit, M. (2000). Implanting Pygmalion Leadership Style through workshop training: Seven field experiments. *Leadership Quarterly*, 11, 171–210.

Eden, D. & Kinnar, J. (1991). Modeling Galatea: Boosting self-efficacy to increase volunteering. *Journal of Applied Psychology*, **76**, 770–780.

Eden, D. & Westman, M. (1998). *Sabbatical leave as a respite from Job stress: Proposal for a longitudinal study among academic staff*. Faculty of Management, Tel Aviv University.

Eden, D. & Zuk, Y. (1995). Seasickness as a self-fulfilling prophecy: Raising self-efficacy to boost performance at sea. *Journal of Applied Psychology*, **80**, 628–635.

Etzion, D. & Sapir, O. (1997, April). *Annual vacation: Duration and relief from job stress and burnout*. Paper presented at the 12th Annual Conference of the Society for Industrial and Organizational Psychology, St Louis.

Etzion, D., Eden, D., & Lapidot, Y. (1998). Relief from job stressors and burnout: Reserve service as a respite. *Journal of Applied Psychology*, **83**, 377–585.

Etzion, D. & Westman, M. (1999, August). *Vacation and the crossover of strain between spouses: Stopping the vicious cycle*. Presented at the Meeting of the Academy of Management, Chicago.

Frankenhaeuser, M., Lundberg, U., Fredrikson, M., Melin, B., Tuomisto, M., Myrstern, A., Hedman, M., Bergman-Losman, B., & Willin, L. (1989). Stress on and off the job as related to sex and occupational status in white-collar workers. *Journal of Organizational Behavior*, **10**, 321–346.

Glaser, R., Kiecolt-Glaser, J. K., Speicher, C. E., & Holliday, J. E. (1985). Stress, loneliness, and changes in herpes virus latency. *Journal of Behavioral Medicine*, **8**, 249–250.

Hackman, J. R. & Oldham, G. R. (1980). *Work Redesign*. Reading, MA: Addison-Wesley.

Halberg, R, Engeli, M., & Hamburger, C. (1965). The 17 ketosteroid excretion of healthy men on weekdays and weekends. *Experimental Medicine and Surgery*, **23**, 61–64.

Hendel, D. D. & Solberg, J. (1983, April). *Sabbatical and leave experiences of female and male faculty at a large research university*. Paper presented at the Annual Meeting of the American Educational Research Association, Montreal, Canada.

Hobfoll, S. E. (1989). Conservation of resources: A new attempt at conceptualizing stress. *American Psychologist*, **44**, 513–524.

Hobfoll, S. E. & Freedy, J. (1993). Conservation of resources: A general stress theory applied to burnout. In W. B. Schaufeli, C. Maslach, & T. Mark (Eds), *Professional Burnout: Recent Developments in Theory and Research* (pp. 115–129). Washington, DC: Taylor & Francis.

Hobfoll, S. E. & Shirom, A. (1993). Stress and burnout in the workplace: Conservation of resources. In T. Golombiewski (Ed.), *Handbook of Organizational Behavior* (pp. 41–61). New York: Marcel Dekker.

Holmes, R. M. & Rahe, R. H. (1967). The social readjustment rating scale. *Journal of Psychosomatic Research*, **11**, 213–218.

Hull, R. B. (1990). Mood as a product of leisure: Causes and consequences. *Journal of Leisure Research*, **22**, 99–111.

Iso-Ahola, S. E. (1988). The social psychology of leisure: Past, present, and future research. In L. A. Barnett (Ed.), *Research about Leisure: Past, Present and Future* (pp. 75–93). Champaign, IL: Sagamore.

Jarecky, R. K. & Sandifer, M. G. (1986). Faculty members' evaluations of sabbaticals. *Journal of Medical Education*, **61**, 803–807.

Kaufman, J. E. (1988). Leisure and anxiety: A study of retirees. *Activities, Adaptation and Aging*, **11**, 1–10.

Lee, R. T. & Ashforth, B. E. (1996). A meta-analytic examination of the correlates of the three dimensions of burnout. *Journal of Applied Psychology*, **81**, 123–133.

Lounsbury, J. W. & Hoopes, L. L. (1986). A vacation from work: Changes in work and nonwork outcomes. *Journal of Applied Psychology*, **71**, 392–401.

Lowen, A. & Craig, J. R. (1968). The influence of level of performance on managerial style: An experimental object-lesson in the ambiguity of correlational data. *Organizational Behavior and Human Performance*, **3**, 440–458.

Merton, R. K. (1948). The self-fulfilling prophecy. *Antioch Review*, **8**, 193–210.

Mitchell, T. R. & Thompson, L. (1994). A theory of temporal adjustments of evaluation of events: Rosy prospection and rosy retrospection. In *Advances in Managerial Cognition and Organizational Information Processing*. Vol. 1 (pp. 85–114). Greenwich, CT: JAI Press.

Mitchell, T. R., Thompson, L. , Peterson, E., & Cronk, R. (1997). Temporal adjustments in the evaluation of events: The 'rosy view.' *Journal of Experimental Social Psychology*, **33**, 421–448.

Neidle, E. A. (1984). Faculty approaches to combating professional burnout. *Journal of Dental Education*, **48**, 86–90.

Quick, J. C. & Quick, J. D. (1984). *Organizational Stress and Preventive Management*. New York: McGraw-Hill.

Ragheb, M. G. & McKinney, J. (1993). Campus recreation and perceived academic stress. *Journal of College Student Development*, **34**, 5–10.

Random House Thesaurus (college edition). (1984). New York: Random House.

Rubenstein, C. (1980). Vacations, expectations, satisfactions, frustrations, fantasies. *Psychology Today*, **14**, 62–76.

Schaubroeck, J., Ganster, D., & Fox, M. (1992). Dispositional affect and work-related stress. *Journal of Applied Psychology*, **77**, 322–335.

Sorcinelli, M. D. (1986, April). *Sabbaticals and leaves: Critical events in the career of faculty*. Paper presented at the Annual Meeting of the American Educational Research Association, San Francisco, California.

Stajkovic, A. D. & Luthans, F. (1998). Self-efficacy and work-related performance: A meta-analysis. *Psychological Bulletin*, **124**, 240–261.

Toomey, E. L. & Connor, J. M. (1988). Employee sabbaticals: Who benefits and why. *Personnel*, **65**, 81–84.

Vinokur, A. & Caplan, R. (1986). Cognitive and affective components of life events: Their relations and effects of well-being. *American Journal of Community Psychology*, **14**, 351–370.

Westman, M. (1997). Crossover of stress and strain in the workplace. *Human Relations*, in press.

Westman, M. & Aharon-Madar, M. (1998, May). *The impact of a vacation on stress, burnout, and performance*. Paper Presented at the Seventh International Conference on Social Stress Research, Budapest.

Westman, M. & Eden, D. (1997). Effects of vacation on job stress and burnout: Relief and fadeout. *Journal of Applied Psychology*, **82**, 516–527.

Westman, M. & Etzion, D. (1995). Crossover of stress, strain and resources from one spouse to another. *Journal of Organizational Behavior*, **16**, 169–181.

Westman, M., Etzion, D., & Yoffe, Y. (1999, April). *The Impact of Short Overseas Business Trips on Job Stress and Burnout*. Presented at the Fourteenth Annual Conference of the Society for Industrial and Organizational Psychology, Atlanta.

Westman, M. & Vinokur, A. (1998 in press). Unraveling the relationship of distress levels within couples: Common stressors, emphatic reactions, or crossover via social interactions? *Human Relations*, **51**, 137–156.

Wright, T. A. & Cropanzano, R. (1998). Emotional exhaustion as a predictor of job performance and voluntary turnover. *Journal of Applied Psychology*, **83**, 486–493.

NOTES

1. The studies are reviewed in chronological order. The dates in the published references do not reflect the order in which the various studies were conducted.
2. Some of the ideas discussed below were aired in a paper entitled 'Respite Research: Studying Stress On and Off the Job" presented at the Seventh International Conference on Social Stress Research in Budapest, May, 1998, and in a presentation entitled 'Expectations, Affectivity, and Respite Effects: Do We Experience the Relief We Expect?' at the meeting of the Academy of Management in Chicago, August, 1999.
3. A copy of the research proposal is available from the author on request.

INDEX